BEYOND THE BEACHHEAD

The 29th Infantry Division in Normandy

Joseph Balkoski

**with a foreword by
Stephen E. Ambrose**

STACKPOLE
BOOKS

0 11557 02682 5

Copyright © 1989, 1999 by Stackpole Books

Published by
STACKPOLE BOOKS
5067 Ritter Road
Mechanicsburg PA 17055
www.stackpolebooks.com

Cover design by Wendy A. Reynolds

Cover image of 29 Let's Go! *used by permission of artist James Dietz, 29th National Guard Association and American Arts & Antiques, Seattle, Washington.*

Printed in the United States of America

10 9 8 7 6 5 4

SECOND EDITION

Library of Congress Cataloging-in-Publication Data

Balkoski, Joseph
    Beyond the beachhead: the 29th infantry division in Normandy / Joseph
Balkoski; with a foreword by Stephen E. Ambrose.—[2nd ed.]
        p. cm.
        Bibliography: p.
        Includes index.
        ISBN: 0-8117-2682-7
        1. World War, 1939–1945—Campaigns—France-Normandy. 2. United States.
Army. Infantry Division, 29th—History. 3. Normandy (France)—History. I. Title.
    D756.5.N6B34   1999
    940.54'2142—dc21   98-53788
                                                                              CIP

This book is dedicated to
the memory of
John Purley Cooper, Jr.,
Commanding Officer, 110th Field Artillery Battalion,
29th Infantry Division, United States Army, 1942–1945
and
to all members
of the 29th Infantry Division,
1941–1945

CONTENTS

LIST OF ILLUSTRATIONS

LIST OF MAPS

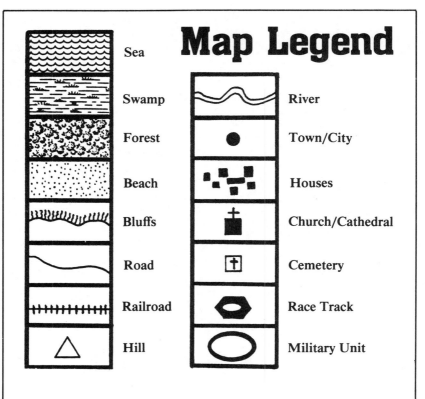

Map Legend

Symbol	Label	Symbol	Label
	Sea		River
	Swamp		Town/City
	Forest		Houses
	Beach		Church/Cathedral
	Bluffs		Cemetery
	Road		Race Track
	Railroad		Military Unit
	Hill		

Abbreviations

Arty	artillery	Fus	fusillier
AA	anti-aircraft	HQ	headquarters
AT	antitank	Inf	infantry
Bn	battalion	Med	medical
Co	company	MP	military police
E	engineering	Rgt	regiment

FOREWORD
by Stephen E. Ambrose

They were the first American troops on the British Isles in World War II. They didn't want to be there. They would have much preferred to be back home in Virginia, Delaware, Maryland, getting on with their educations, getting started on their careers, courting, marrying, having kids of their own. But there was an evil force loose in the world, and it fell to these guys from the 29th Division— the Blue and Gray—along with their compatriots in the U.S. Army, to destroy that force.

They were the first ashore on D-Day. The 116th Regiment of the 29th Division took the heaviest casualties of any regiment in the war, many of them in the first few minutes of the assault on Omaha Beach, which is why the National D-Day Memorial is in Bedford, Virginia, today. Once again, they didn't want to be there. They would have much preferred to be throwing softballs, not hand grenades; shooting .22s at rabbits, not M-1s at other young men. But they did their duty and at the end of the day they were on top of the bluff.

From D-Day through the Battle of Normandy, the 29th Division was locked in a death embrace with the German 352d Division. By late July, when the 29th took St. Lô, there was scarcely an unwounded man in either division from the D-Day roster. By then, in fact, the 352d no longer existed, while the 29th's rifle companies had taken close to 100 percent casualties. Medics in the 29th measured gains in the hedgerow fighting by grains of morphine administered. One of them figured that it took thirty-two grains per hedgerow.

Still the 29th stayed in the line, committed to combat. It was in combat for 242 days. Total casualties were 28,776. The percent of turnover for the division as a whole—including staff, support elements, artillery units—was 204. The figures fail to speak to us of the pain, the misery, the terror of combat, or the triumph of the men of the 29th, those citizen soldiers who endured and prevailed in the most extreme experience anyone could ever go through. But Joseph Balkoski fills in those human gaps in this magnificent account.

PREFACE

When *Beyond the Beachhead* was first published, I had naively assumed that my interest in the 29th Infantry Division and the Normandy campaign had come to a happy conclusion. I would, presumably, go on to research and write about other, completely different, subjects.

It did not work out that way. Ten years later, I am still drawn to the annual 29th Infantry Division reunion; still making pilgrimages to Normandy to visit sites related to the division; still corresponding with division veterans, their children, even their grandchildren; still visiting the National Archives to unearth obscure material that someday will, with some luck, solve some of the persistent historical mysteries of D-Day and St. Lô. If anything, my devotion to the 29th Division's history has increased markedly over the past decade.

Writing a history book is a little like building one's own house. One not only creates something, but uses it every day, takes pride in its construction, corrects its mistakes, and lives with it and inside of it for the rest of one's life. The end product will always exist. But unlike a house builder, the history writer strives to create a product for the enjoyment and edification of others. Indeed, while writing *Beyond the Beachhead*, I considered it an inestimable blessing that I was given an opportunity to speak for a group of men, both living and dead, who have had virtually no historical voice over the past half century, men who endured terrible ordeals for the sake of a noble but seemingly unachievable goal of "a better world," men whose actions are still little understood.

History cannot exist without curiosity. Historians, therefore, have a responsibility to stimulate interest in past events, if only to prevent those events from evaporating from a society's consciousness and being lost forever. History lives in people's psyches; it thrives upon the innate inquisitiveness humans demonstrate about their own remote experiences or those of their ancestors. That is how I came to write *Beyond the Beachhead*, how many people came to read it, how I and others continue to learn from the momentous events it describes.

Any historian would be proud to see his book still in print a decade after its publication. I suspect, however, that good historians are, for the most part, humble people. When a historian writes about an era during which he was not even alive, he is struck by how elusive the truth can be and how often he has to guess at it. It is only natural to wonder: Did I get it right? For a military historian, this concern is acute. War is chaos. And when writing about war, the historian must concede that mere words are inadequate tools to convey the products of chaos: death, pain, fear, elation, despair, pride.

Beyond the Beachhead is a compilation of a thousand stories, pieced together like a jigsaw puzzle into a larger whole. Every one of those stories could be elaborated: What I dispose of in a paragraph or two in truth deserves ten, twenty, even one hundred times more space to get to the heart of that particular tale. To provide such elaboration would of course yield a book too heavy to even lift. Nevertheless, I consider myself fortunate that the stories of *Beyond the Beachhead*, subjects whose proverbial surfaces have only been scratched, have aroused in me and others a desire to learn more, to dig deeper into the historical puzzle.

On page 218, I describe the story of Captain Elmer Norval "Doc" Carter, the surgeon of the 1st Battalion, 115th Infantry, 29th Division, who was killed in the Bois de Bretel, north of St. Lô, on June 17, 1944. I present the story of Dr. Carter in only four sentences, using it as an example of the brutality of the Normandy fighting. The account was based on two secondary sources and a single interview with a 29th Division veteran at a reunion.

More than eight years after the publication of *Beyond the Beachhead*, I received a phone call from a man identifying himself as Walter Carter, the son of a soldier whose death I related in my book. For a few moments I did not even recall the incident, but after a little prodding from Walter it came back to me: Walter was in fact Dr. Carter's son. Walter had been only two years old when his father was deployed overseas and four years when his mother, Fernie, informed him of his father's death. Much later, upon Fernie's death in May 1995, Walter discovered in her attic a large collection of letters written by his father during World War II. The discovery encouraged him to learn more about his father, the 29th Division, D-Day, and the Normandy campaign. Walter then decided to write a book about his father's life, focusing on Dr. Carter's wartime experiences as described in his letters to Fernie and others. Walter had read *Beyond the Beachhead* and its four-sentence description of his father's death; hence his phone call to its author.

When I read a draft of Walter's book, entitled *Elmer Norval Carter: A Portrait —Husband, Father, Doctor, Soldier*, I was deeply moved. Throughout my own research, I had been used to interviewing veterans, all elderly men, but Dr. Carter's words were a powerful reminder that the battles related in my book were fought by men in the prime of their youth. Those lucky enough to have survived I would interview later on. But those who died in Normandy, like Carter, never got the chance to grow old, to swap stories with other veterans at reunions, to sit down with me forty or fifty years later by a comfortable fire and talk of D-Day and St. Lô. When I read Carter's letters, I could not help but think that if the German who killed him had flown just a few inches off line, I would be talking to him on the phone rather than to his son. Instead, more than fifty years after Carter's death, I had the heartbreaking but highly complimentary honor of walking the little country lane in the Bois de Bretel with Walter and his family, tracing the last hours of his father's life.

Every soldier killed in Normandy had a life story, family and friends who mourned his death, and perhaps, like Dr. Carter, those who miss him even after more than a half century. In *Beyond the Beachhead*, one of my primary purposes was to remind the modern reader that the 29th Infantry Division contained thousands of such soldiers, all of whom were asked to do a dirty but essential job, which they sacrificed their lives to accomplish. I consider it important that later generations of Americans understand exactly how this job was accomplished, and that its fulfillment was achieved with great cost.

I wish now that I could have used Dr. Carter's words to demonstrate the profound emotions experienced by 29th Division soldiers as they prepared to enter the battle for the first time. In one of his last letters to his wife, penned on board his assault ship two days before D-Day, Carter wrote:

> Fernie, my sweetheart, I feel that I shall see you again. You and the boys. But if I don't, I want you all to remember that my love for you cannot be said or put on paper. It can only be felt. You have meant everything to me that is good and happy. Since tomorrow is D-Day (and we weigh anchor tonight), I won't be able to write for a few days. May God help us in our mission. I hope to return to you all. God bless you Fernie, you Tom, and you Walter Ford.

I also wrote *Beyond the Beachhead* to correct some of the common misconceptions about the American army that have been perpetuated in recent years. It has become fashionable for historians, particularly British historians, to categorize the U.S. Army in World War II as a homogeneous force of nearly identical and interchangeable units manned by a vast melting pot of faceless conscripts. This highly inaccurate description does the army a historical disservice. In his study of the Normandy campaign, *Overlord*, British author Max Hastings consumes eleven pages listing British and Canadian army units that participated in the battle, down to 800-man battalions. Conversely, he disposes of the U.S. Army in half a page, listing no unit below a 14,000-man division. Hastings also makes the astonishing statement, "Few American infantry units arrived in Normandy with a grasp of basic tactics."

The implication is clear: Even small British and Canadian units nurtured a special élan based on their unique histories and regional affiliations. The U.S. Army, on the other hand, was a collection of nameless outfits, devoid of tradition, manned by inexperienced civilians disguised as soldiers, clumsily, even incompetently, focused on nothing more than their immediate military mission. How could, for example, the 29th Division's seemingly undistinctive 116th Infantry Regiment possess the esprit de corps of the British army's historic King's Own Scottish Borderers or the Grenadier Guards?

I attempted to settle that question a decade ago in *Beyond the Beachhead*, and I will summarize the answer again in this preface. On the eve of D-Day, the 29th Infantry Division had been training actively for almost three and a half years. It had a solid core of officers and senior noncommissioned officers who had experienced military training for an even longer period. The units within the division, such as Virginia's "Stonewall Brigade" and the "Dandy Fifth of Maryland," had a special cohesion based on history and their soldiers' common regional backgrounds. And, as for the American army's supposed lack of experience and inferior grasp of tactics, one need only point to the 1st Infantry Division, the 29th's landing partner on Omaha Beach, which had already participated in three campaigns, including two major amphibious landings, prior to D-Day.

Dr. Carter's resolute but somber words, written to his wife Fernie just before the 29th Infantry Division landed on Omaha Beach, expressed the near-universal confidence of American soldiers on the eve of D-Day:

> Everyone is deadly serious. We realize that we are to hit soon and on D-Day (early). We have been chosen very carefully and found to be the best troops in the army today. This is no idle boast; it is fact. Another division goes in with us who are equally well trained and their advantage is they have seen combat. To bed with minds too heavy for thinking. Everyone sleeps, but restlessly.

The U.S. Army of World War II has never been credited by historians as being very literary. While researching *Beyond the Beachhead*, I did not expect to encounter any Hemingways or Sassoons. Nevertheless, during the writing of the book, I was consistently surprised, and continue to be surprised by the extraordinary expressiveness of 29th Division soldiers in their letters, diaries, and postwar memoirs. They speak for themselves in *Beyond the Beachhead*, but I will add another eloquent witness in this new preface, one who, sadly, I never met.

PFC Ugo Giannini, a native of New Jersey, was a member of the 29th Division's Military Police Platoon. He landed on the Dog Green sector of Omaha Beach as 7:40 A.M. on D-Day, only seventy minutes after the disastrous first wave. He returned to the beach the next day, sat down on top of the bluffs, and later composed the following essay:

> I retraced my way from the battered remains of Vierville-sur-Mer. I walked slowly, dragging my unwilling soul with me and forcing it to inhale the death odor. I was alone searching for my comrades, 37 men who were hurled ashore yesterday morning (or was it years ago?). I walked, stopped, resumed again, always against the visible signs of war. Which way did it go? I reached the first enemy machine gun emplacement, leaned heavily against its hard sand bags. They were vomiting their white dusty guts. It was still, very still, but I heard the war crashing, exploding in my ears, my nose, and mouth. I drew from a smashed, wet pack of cigarettes. The nicotine tasted sweet. I inhaled thick quantities of smoke like vaporous balls of opaque cotton. I wanted to forget, to stop thinking or feeling. I wanted to rest or die. A thin plaster of white mud, darker brown where it was still wet, painted my legs, my boots, my hands. And yes, it must have been inside of me too.

I cannot help but think that, for Americans, Omaha Beach was the Gettysburg of World War II. Gettysburg was just one of hundreds of major battles in the American Civil War, but its particular significance was recognized by all almost immediately. It was not for twenty or twenty-five years, however, that Americans came to view Gettysburg as more than simple military history. The battle eventually came to symbolize the entire Civil War, even the whole troubled experiment of American democracy. The Gettysburg battlefield has since been memorialized, probably more than any other battlefield in history. More than 135 years later, its monuments still speak powerfully, reminding Americans of the immense sacrifices endured by a distant and tragic generation.

Surely historical perspectives change as an event passes further into the past. Like Gettysburg, Omaha Beach no longer can be viewed as a mere military operation. Instead, more than a half century after its occurrence, American has begun to perceive it as a symbol of an entire generation's sacrifice, a microcosm of the supreme but costly triumph of America's World War II ordeal. If readers will capture some sense of that sacrifice in *Beyond the Beachhead*, I consider my task in writing the book well worth it.

For many years after publication of *Beyond the Beachhead*, I resided on the fringe of the Gettysburg battlefield and was a frequent visitor to Cemetery Hill, the site of Lincoln's Gettysburg Address and the final resting place of thousands of Union soldiers killed in the battle. In Normandy, on the bluffs overlooking Omaha Beach, there is another American military cemetery, strikingly similar to Gettysburg's in its powerful emotional effect on the visitor. At the annual Gettysburg "Remembrance Day" celebration, commemorating the November 19, 1863, anniversary of Lincoln's Address, I used to watch an actor deliver Lincoln's simple speech to a somber and absorbed crowd, and I could not help but think of how appropriate Lincoln's words would have been to the widows, descendants, and friends of those who, four score and one year after Gettysburg, lost their lives in Normandy and now lie buried in the cemetery at Omaha Beach. In part, Lincoln said:

> We cannot dedicate, we cannot consecrate, we cannot hallow this ground. The brave men, living and dead, who struggled here have consecrated it far above our poor power to add or detract. The world will little note nor long remember what we say here, but it cannot forget what they did here. It is for us the living, rather, to be dedicated here to the unfinished work which they who fought here have thus far so nobly advanced.

One of the most obvious conclusions I reached during my research for *Beyond the Beachhead* was that a great deal remains to be learned about Omaha Beach and the subsequent battle of Normandy. In the decade since the publication of the book, I have continued to learn, and I hope to prolong the learning process in the years ahead, both from my own and from others' research. And with some good luck and decent health, I hope to live to at least age ninety, for then I will witness the 100th anniversary remembrance of the Omaha Beach landing on D-Day, at which I will proudly state, "I knew those guys." But that is a long way off. In the meantime I must reaffirm the sentiments expressed on the dedication page of *Beyond the Beachhead* and declare for posterity, as I should have in the preface to the first edition, that any lapses of fact in the book are my own, for which I take full responsibility.

Joseph Balkoski
Baltimore, Maryland
October 1998

ONE

INTRODUCTION
Twenty-Nine, Let's Go
June 1944

1. GO AHEAD, TWENTY-NINE

The veterans of the 1st Infantry Division could hardly believe it. On maneuvers, these National Guardsmen of the 29th Division actually wore their helmet straps hooked underneath their chins. In fact, the 1st Division G.I.'s noticed that these green 29ers did *everything* by the book. They were always clean-shaven, their uniforms were just right, and—most amazing of all—their jeeps were always spotless. The 1st Division men knew from experience that the ubiquitous mud of the English moors dried on a jeep like plaster. Were the 29ers washing their jeeps every day? The old hands from the 1st Division shook their heads in amazement. Only green troops could carry on like this.

It was bad enough that the 29ers looked like picture-book soldiers. But these guardsmen actually seemed enthusiastic about fighting, even though they had not yet heard a shot fired in anger. So when the 1st and the 29th Divisions joined forces to practice amphibious landings on the south coast of England in the spring of 1944, the 1st Division men snickered among themselves as they watched the 29ers, with their strange little blue and gray patches on their left shoulders, marching up and down the dunes, chanting their divisional battle-cry, ''Twenty-nine, let's go!'' One of the more sarcastic 1st Division old-timers put his hands to his mouth and yelled over, ''Go ahead, twenty-nine, we'll be right behind you!'' The combat veterans of North Africa and Sicily roared with laughter.

The men of the 1st Division had a special pride in their outfit. The "Big Red One" was the oldest division in the US Army and had seen continuous service since 1917. By 1943, the division had fought a bitter nine-month campaign in the Mediterranean, and the men were grumbling that someone else should do some fighting for a change—particularly a division like the 29th, which had not yet been in combat. The old regulars joked, half seriously, that the US Army consisted of the 1st Division and eight million replacements.

The 29th had been training in Great Britain for so long that it had picked up the derisive nickname, "England's Own." The division was a National Guard outfit, primarily from Maryland and Virginia. The guardsmen were sensitive to criticism, for they had been under close scrutiny by their Regular Army cousins since before Pearl Harbor. The guard officers who had survived the army's weeding out process were eager to show that they were good soldiers. So when the 29th was coupled with the 1st Division for training exercises, the 29ers viewed the combat veterans with a tinge of envy and a touch of awe—but also with a fierce competitive spirit.

It didn't take long for the 29ers to lose their feelings of inferiority. Lt. Col. John P. Cooper, the Commanding Officer (CO) of the 29th Division's 110th Field Artillery Battalion, was shocked when he saw a lieutenant colonel from the 1st Division sitting in a jeep during a firing exercise, reading a book under the protection of the jeep's cloth rain hood during a light drizzle. A 29er was never—but never—to ride in a jeep using that hood, no matter what the weather. "We came away from those exercises knowing that the appearance of the 1st Division was not up to the standards of the 29th, and we felt proud because we knew we could do as well as they could," Cooper recalled. "We had very high spirit and morale . . . but we also had sense enough not to brag too damn much."

The 1st and the 29th Divisions were not just training partners. On Sunday, May 28, 1944, the men of both divisions learned that they would be going into action together in the first wave of the long-expected invasion of Europe, scheduled for June 5. Their destination was a four-mile stretch of sand known as Omaha Beach in the French province of Normandy. The 29th Division was assigned the western half of the beach, the 1st Division the eastern.

The two outfits made an odd pair. Although their missions appeared identical, the divisions themselves could not have been more different. One division had Regular Army origins and still had a core of crusty old professionals; the other was a division of citizen-soldiers. One division possessed plenty of combat veterans who were hardened realists about war; the other was filled with inexperienced troops who had a tinge of idealism. One division had twenty-seven years of continuous history; the other had only three years of active service and something to prove. But both divisions had one thing in common: they were entirely confident of success.

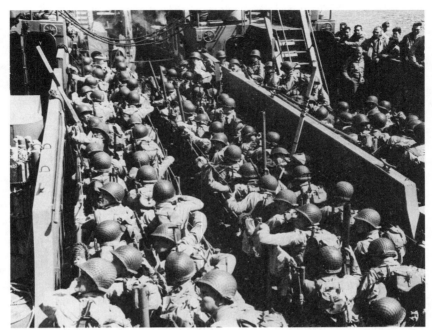

American troops in England embarking for the invasion of Europe, May 1944. *Courtesy Military History Institute.*

At the end of May, most 29ers boarded their transports in historic Plymouth harbor, where Sir Francis Drake had watched the approach of the Spanish Armada in 1588 and the Pilgrims had set sail for America in the *Mayflower* in 1620. One of the 29th's three regiments, however, boarded its ships in the Cornish resort town of Falmouth. The embarkation went without a hitch, a fact which was not surprising since the division had been practicing this procedure for the last six months. The 29ers lined up at their designated loading sectors, and an embarkation officer made a last-minute roll call; then, with a few shouts of "Twenty-nine, let's go!" the men struggled up the gangplanks with their heavy load of equipment. The ports were so crowded that several assault ships could not be loaded at dockside. Instead, the 29ers waited on the "hards"—beaches that had been covered with wire mesh so that vehicles could drive on the sand—for ferries that would take them out to their transports.

On May 31, after the 29th Division assault transports had been loaded, vessels scheduled to bring their troops ashore on D-Day waited for darkness to avoid snooping German aircraft and then sailed east for the Dorsetshire ports of Weymouth, Portland, and Poole, where all the transports and warships destined for Omaha Beach (code-named "Force O") were to assemble before setting out for Normandy. It was only an overnight trip to the Force O marshalling ports, but the ships sailed in massive convoys for self-protection, hugging the southern English coast, on constant alert against German submarines and E-boats. When the ships arrived the next morning, the 29ers looked over the rails with disbelief: they had never seen so many ships in one place before. It was a heartening sight.

But then came the waiting.

For several days, as the transports gently bobbed up and down at their moorings, the 29ers had little to do but think. But this was no place for meditation; the 29ers were crammed so tightly into their ships that it was impossible to take a step without bumping into somebody.

The G.I.'s occupied themselves in different ways. The most common pastimes were poker and shooting craps, which, in the best army tradition, were loud and boisterous entertainments. In Company F, 175th Infantry Regiment, the men formed an impromptu hillbilly band to entertain the troops. When the company CO angrily demanded to know how the men had managed to smuggle two guitars, an accordian, a ukulele, and mouth organs on board, the men apologized profusely and blamed a packing mistake. The music, with the CO's approval, went on.

Here was a good chance to sample navy life, and the 29ers, for the most part, were favorably impressed. The G.I.'s were amazed to discover that the navy was serving white bread, chicken, ice cream, steak, and limitless hot coffee. "Some of us thought this to be the last meals for the condemned," noted 1st Lt. Edward G. Jones, Jr., of the 29th Division Cavalry Recon Troop. A few 29ers on board British transports inquired coyly about the "tot of rum" that Royal Navy sailors were supposed to receive, but much to the Yanks' disappointment, there was not a drop of alcohol to be had.

Several 29ers, contemplating their impending task, undoubtedly harbored a secret wish that they had joined the navy. Most of them, however, were resigned to their fate. Someone had to do the fighting, they figured. Besides, the navy was not so safe; for after all, one couldn't dig a foxhole in the water.

The word finally came on Sunday, June 4. Force O set out at last for Normandy. The departure was an emotional moment, and even self-confident men became quietly contemplative about their fate. Sgt. Roy Stevens, a platoon sergeant in Company A, 116th Infantry, leaned on the rail of his transport and stared at the green fields of England, wondering aloud whether he would ever see them again. A buddy of his by the name of Parker, occupying an adjacent place on the rail, joined in the sentimental meditation. After Parker had left the United States in 1942, his wife had given birth to a baby girl. He remarked to Stevens that as long as he got to see his daughter at least once, he wouldn't mind dying in this war.

At 4:30 A.M. on June 4, General Eisenhower met at Southwick House, outside of Portsmouth, with senior leaders of the Supreme Headquarters, Allied Expeditionary Force (SHAEF) to discuss the prospects for the invasion. The weather for June 5, Eisenhower learned, would be awful. Because the impending amphibious assault was heavily dependent on moderate seas and decent visibility, Eisenhower reluctantly ordered the invasion convoys recalled at 5:00 A.M. Some 29th Division transports had already come within sight of the French coast when the recall signal was issued; others had not even left port.

Eisenhower met again with his subordinates at Southwick House on the evening of June 4. A more favorable weather report was presented, and it took the supreme commander only fifteen minutes to declare June 6 as D-Day. At 2:00 A.M. on June 5, the order putting the convoys in motion for Normandy was reissued. The 29ers who had just returned to port hardly had time for a hot meal and a decent cup of coffee before they were heading out to sea again.

This time there was no recall order. The convoys followed the southern coast of England until they reached "Area Z," a circular assembly sector near the Isle of Wight. Area Z was dubbed "Piccadilly Circus" by the planners because on the situation maps all the invasion routes came together at this one circle, only ten miles in diameter. From Area Z across to the Norman coast the ships followed one of five lanes that had been painstakingly swept by minesweepers. Each lane corresponded to an invasion beach: Utah, Omaha, Gold, Juno, Sword.

The crossing was not easy. The wind was high, and the seas were choppy; the ungainly assault ships were difficult to handle. As the ships pitched and rolled in the swell, the incessant wind whistled shrilly through the cables and rigging. This was an eerie noise to the landlubbers; it sounded as if a giant flute was providing an unearthly musical accompaniment to the parade of the vast armada.

Seasickness was almost more than the 29ers could stand. They had been warned about this peril for months, and seasickness pills were issued to all troops. The 29ers discovered, however, that the pills made them drowsy; so some division members stopped taking them for fear of coming ashore on Omaha Beach half-asleep.

Even with the pills, many men got sick during the voyage across the Channel. A training booklet called *Army Talks* advised the troops; "If you do get sick, remember that there are others who are trying to fight off the same feeling." The 29ers were advised to use one of the bags provided by the navy, or to "get it to the rail—to leeward, pal, leeward." One sarcastic G.I. wisecracked that he had been trained to come ashore spewing *lead*, not just spewing.

Most of the 29ers stayed below. "There was really nowhere to go and no [desire] to get away from the companionship of our buddies," said one sergeant in the 116th Infantry. Halfway through the voyage, the bosuns whistled and the loudspeakers blared, "Now hear this!" Everyone fell silent. Inspirational speeches by Prime Minister Winston Churchill and President Franklin D. Roosevelt were then broadcast over the ships' loudspeakers. But the 29ers were not in the mood for this kind of patriotic talk; several hooted in derision. "We all thought, isn't that nice? If you had a couple of violins, you could put it to music," recalled one staff officer.

Most 29ers talked with their buddies, seeking reassurance that everything was going to be all right. The enemy, they figured, would be obliterated on the beach by the air corps and the navy. All G.I.'s in the company would automatically get the Bronze Star after the invasion, joked the first sergeant of Company A, 116th Infantry. The men roared with laughter. The optimists declared that the 29th Division had been overseas now for a year-and-a-half; as soon as the invasion was over, the whole outfit would go home to help train new recruits. The pessimists declared that the army was going to foul up this operation somehow, and it was not going to be easy, no matter what anybody said.

The voyage was long, but few 29ers got any sleep. Some of the men, who had been aboard their transports now for almost a week, struck up friendships with navy or Coast Guard sailors. On one ship, Capt. Robert M. Miller, a Baltimorean who was CO of Company F, 175th Infantry, discovered that the ship's captain, Commander Bryan Quirk, was also a Baltimore native. As the two men reminisced about their home town, Miller pointed out that his company, a Maryland National Guard outfit, had dozens of Baltimoreans, since its home armory was in that city. The quartermaster, another Baltimorean named Griffen, inquired if Miller knew his older brother, Guy, who was serving in the 175th. Guy was the adjutant of the 1st Battalion, and Miller knew him well. Miller pointed to another ship, just off the port quarter, in which Guy's company was embarked. The two brothers hadn't seen each other for three years, so communication was hastily arranged between the two ships. A lively conversation ensued with flickering signal lamps instead of spoken words.

At 2:50 A.M. on June 6, Force O ships began to drop anchor eleven miles off Omaha Beach, safely out of range of German coastal artillery. The 29th Division's 116th Infantry, which was to lead the division ashore on D-Day, was concentrated in three transports: 1st Battalion in *Empire Javelin*, a Royal Navy ship; 2nd Battalion in *Thomas Jefferson*; and 3rd Battalion in *Charles Carroll*. Many of the G.I.'s in the 116th were National Guardsmen from little towns in rural Virginia. They spoke with a Southern drawl that was distinctively Virginian: the word "out" was pronounced "oot" and "about" as "aboot." The 116th was thoroughly infused with the spirit of the Confederacy, and the men referred to their outfit as the "Stonewall Brigade," after Stonewall Jackson's famous Virginia unit, which had fought for the South from First Manassas to Appomattox Court House.

Sunrise, which came at 5:58 A.M. that day, was still three hours away. It was so dark on the tossing sea that for all the 29ers knew, they might have been in the middle of the Atlantic. The G.I.'s realized, however, that the invasion was proceeding as planned, for as the transports anchored, the men could see German anti-aircraft fire bursting over the western horizon. Somewhere in that direction, behind Utah Beach, American paratroopers were already fighting for their lives. Meanwhile, the 29ers downed a hot meal courtesy of their navy brethren.

On *Thomas Jefferson*, Maj. Sidney Bingham, CO of the 2nd Battalion of the 116th, scrutinized the navy coxswains who had the critical task of transporting his men safely to the beach. He was shocked, for they all looked like eighteen-year-old kids.

The 29ers could not see a single star when they looked upward; the sky was completely overcast. The ships were quiet except for the slapping waves and the whistling eighteen-knot wind. To the west, the 29ers could make out the big black silhouette of the battleship *Texas*, leading a column of cruisers and destroyers inshore; to the east was another dark hulk, the battleship *Arkansas*. The quiet would obviously not last much longer.

The bosuns' whistles suddenly sounded. Then a message over the loudspeakers: "Now hear this! All navy hands man your battle stations." The 29ers, who realized their turn was next, watched the scurrying sailors impassively. The bosuns' whistles sounded again. The loudspeakers crackled: "Now hear this! All assault troops report to your debarkation areas."

2. INVASION

The Stonewallers kept looking for the bombers. They had been told that hundreds of B-24 Liberators from the 8th Air Force would blast the German defenses sometime before the first wave hit the beach. This cheery prospect delighted the infantrymen, and they looked forward to a close-up view of the spectacular show. If any Germans survived the inferno, the infantrymen still weren't worried. There would be so many bomb craters in the sand, they figured, that every G.I. would have his own ready-made foxhole, courtesy of the Army Air Force. The 29ers, however, did not realize that the invasion planners were so confident of quick success on the beach that they had ordered the air force to use bombs with quick fuses, which did not form craters upon impact. According to the "top brass," craters on the beach would obstruct the movement of vehicles across the tidal flat.

At 3:15 A.M. on June 6, the men of the 116th Infantry stood silently at their debarkation stations, waiting to board the ungainly landing boats that would carry them eleven miles to the beach. The G.I.'s were organized into thirty-one-man sections—one section per landing craft. Every section was commanded by a single officer; six (sometimes seven) sections comprised a company. Four Stonewall Brigade rifle companies had the unenviable task of landing in the first wave on the 29th Division's half of the beach.

A section was, in theory, a self-sufficient fighting force. Each section was divided into several combat teams, all of which were trained to deal with different contingencies. The teams would occupy a precise position in the landing craft so that when the boat hit the beach, the G.I.'s would storm ashore in some semblance of combat order. The officer would be in the bow, followed by a five-man rifle team, a four-man barbed wire cutting team, two two-man Browning Automatic Rifle teams, two two-man bazooka teams, a four-man mortar team (with a 60mm mortar), a two-man flamethrower team, and a five-man demolition team carrying bangalore torpedoes and satchel charges. A medic and the assistant team leader would sit in the stern with the three-man navy crew. The G.I.'s were so laden with ammunition and equipment that every step was a strain. It was difficult to imagine how they would get through chest-deep water. The poor man with the flamethrower could hardly move at all.

The Stonewallers were warned that they would probably not be resupplied until June 8, so everything they carried, except ammunition, would have to last for two days. Rations, extra clothing, and first aid pouches were stuffed into the men's haversacks; ammunition was carried on belts and in boxes. A special assault jacket, worn over the standard uniform, had six huge pockets for miscellaneous loose equipment, ammunition, and food. Grenades were hitched onto metal rings on the shoulder harnesses. Around their chests the men wore life belts, which they kept one-third inflated. In an emergency, they could be fully inflated in an instant by breaking a compressed air capsule on the front of the belt. When the belt filled with air, it squeezed the chest like a vise. The Stonewallers, however, were wary of these life belts. If the wearer wasn't careful and the belt inflated around the stomach rather than the chest, his center of gravity would turn him upside down, and he would drown.

In anticipation of German use of chemical warfare, the Stonewallers' uniforms were specially treated so that they could not be penetrated by gas. The 29ers hated this sticky and clammy material, which had a vile smell when it got wet. Every 29er, of course, also carried a gas mask.

Finally it was time to board the landing craft. The *Empire Javelin*, the *Thomas Jefferson*, and the *Charles Carroll* each carried about thirty assault boats, which were securely hung over the deck by the ships' davits. In military parlance, one variety of these eight-ton boats was known as "Landing Craft, Vehicle, Personnel"—LCVP for short. An almost identical boat used by the 116th was the "Landing Craft, Assault," or LCA, a British version of the LCVP. Loading was a simple task: the men of the 116th would simply climb aboard the LCVPs or LCAs from their debarkation stations on deck, a procedure the navy called "rail-loading." But some unlucky members of the first wave—and all men in later waves—did not have this luxury. Instead, to board their landing craft, which pitched and rolled crazily beneath them on the water's surface, they had to descend flimsy cargo nets strung over the sides of the transports. This procedure was one of the most frightening aspects of an amphibious assault, especially when the men were carrying sixty or more pounds of equipment. In England, the 29ers had practiced going up and down cargo nets, but practice did not bring confidence.

Over the navy loudspeakers came the command, "Away all boats!" The davits, straining under the weight of the landing craft and the tightly packed 29ers, swung the LCVPs over the side and slowly lowered them into the water. Over the creaks and groans of the davits the Stonewallers called out to their friends in nearby boats with a few final words of encouragement. It was still too dark to see, but the voice of a friend through the inky blackness was as reassuring as a pat on the back.

On *Empire Javelin*, a British transport, an LCA carrying a command party of 29ers from the 1st Battalion, 116th Infantry, was stuck for thirty minutes in its davits halfway down the ship's side—directly beneath the scupper for *Empire Javelin*'s "head" (latrine). "During this half-hour, the bowels of the ship's company made the most of an opportunity that Englishmen have sought since 1776," recalled Maj. Tom Dallas, the battalion executive officer. "Yells from the boat were unavailing. Streams, colored everything from canary yellow to sienna brown and olive green, continued to flush into the command group, decorating every man aboard. We cursed, we cried, and we laughed, but it kept coming. When we started for shore, we were all covered with shit."

It took about an hour to load the first-wave boats and lower them into the sea. This was the moment when the 29ers most needed their seasickness pills; for in the rough seas off Normandy, the little assault boats bobbed up and down on the waves like bathtub toys. The LCVPs were only thirty-six feet long and eleven feet across, so there wasn't room enough for everyone to sit down. Most men preferred to stand anyway, since their heavy backpacks made it difficult to get up from a sitting or kneeling position. The lucky ones were assigned places along the sides of the LCVP, where they could peer over the edge of the boat and watch the panoply of war. The men in the center of the boat—especially short men—could see nothing but the backs of their friends. The waves smacked into the sides of the boats every few seconds, and it was only a matter of minutes before everyone was soaked to the skin with frigid sea water. Many of the LCVPs took on so much water that the men had to bail with their helmets. The Stonewallers' worst fear was that a great wave would swamp their LCVPs and send them pitching into the ocean, where they would be swept away by a current, unseen in the darkness, and drown.

A laconic message painted on the raised bow ramps of the LCVPs said ''No Smoking.'' This prohibition provoked laughter, for only a magician could have lit a cigarette under such conditions.

The whole invasion depended on perfect timing. Every G.I. was supposed to know the precise moment when his assault boat's ramp would drop, the exact spot on the beach where he was to land, and the job facing him after he crossed the tidal flat. According to the plan, the first wave of the 116th Infantry would hit the beach at exactly 6:31 A.M. The 116th's three transports were anchored eleven miles offshore, so plenty of time had to be allowed for the nine-knot landing craft to reach the beach at their appointed times. Most of the Stonewallers were in their LCVPs shortly after 4:00 A.M., so, much to the men's disgust, they had to stand like toy soldiers in the packed boats for two-and-a-half hours. Then, of course, they had to fight the Germans.

The first wave LCVPs formed up in proper order and circled their mother ships, waiting for word to head toward the beach. The young coxswains, who had to pilot their boats in almost total darkness, were just as scared as the infantrymen. The circling continued for thirty minutes; then, at about 4:30 A.M., bullhorns sounded the order to head for shore. The 29ers knew they were on their way the moment the landing craft engines revved to full power. The Stonewallers clutched their weapons more tightly and fiddled nervously with their accouterments, vainly trying to make their burdensome loads more comfortable. When the order came, the circles of landing craft uncoiled into columns and headed for the beach.

But the beach was still over an hour away, and there was plenty of time for more seasickness and misery. As the boats rode up and down the wave crests and troughs, the wind and spray whipped from the southwest straight into the men's faces. Now and then, a wall of water smashed into the boats' ungainly square bows with a loud crack.

The Stonewallers wondered how much more of this they could take. Some figured that whatever the beach had in store, it was probably no worse than these awful boats. This operation had been practiced several times, but rehearsals meant nothing anymore. In the practice runs the men had felt little fear, of course, but now they were filled with trepidation. The darkness exacerbated a terrible sense of loneliness. They looked up plaintively into the night sky, hoping to catch a comforting glimpse of the B-24s. Still no bombers.

Pitching and rolling crazily, the boats plowed through the waves toward the beach for more than half an hour before the first hint of the coming dawn appeared about 5:00 A.M. In the misty pre-dawn light, which grew in intensity by the minute, the 29ers looked around; what they saw was reassuring. Everyone, it seemed, was where he was supposed to be. Off to the right was the battleship *Texas* and her supporting flock of cruisers and destroyers; on the left was the *Arkansas* and a similar batch of escorts. The 116th's three transports were now nothing more than small gray silhouettes on the northern horizon.

At 5:35 A.M., a German battery to the east opened up. Several shells splashed near the *Arkansas*, and giant fountains of water erupted from the sea like geysers. The shelling reminded the Stonewallers that the sea was not the only enemy they would have to fight that day. At 5:50 A.M.—eight minutes before sunrise—it was light enough for the 29ers to look over the sides of their landing craft and make out the prominent features of the Normandy coast they had studied so intently on maps and models. The sky was overcast, and in the subdued morning light the coast looked drab and gray.

All hell suddenly broke loose. The 29ers watched in amazement as all around them Allied warships opened fire at last. The German battery that had fired earlier on the fleet seemed puny in comparison. It was as if a little boy had provoked a great bull with a peashooter.

The Stonewallers looked over their right shoulders to watch the *Texas*. When the old battlewagon fired her 14-inch guns, she rocked backward from her own blast. Lighting up the sky as if an artificial sun had broken through the clouds for a moment, great orange-black flashes burst out of the gun muzzles, and fiery red threads appeared and disappeared in an instant, disclosing the path of the shells toward their targets. Then, a few seconds later, the 29ers felt the rumbling concussion and the thunderous report of the guns.

The Stonewallers were fascinated by the spectacle. In England, General Bradley had promised "ringside seats for the greatest show on earth." And soon the Stonewallers would be participants.

The coxswains piloting the 29th Division LCVPs seemed oblivious to the crashing bombardment. Their eyes were riveted on several "control" vessels anchored between the landing craft and the beach. At 6:00 A.M., the long columns of LCVPs reached the "line of departure" (LOD), about two-and-a-half miles offshore. The LOD, which was the point at which the landing craft were to form for the final run-in for the beach, was marked by a ragged line of patrol craft ("PCs" in Navy parlance). The unsightly little PCs had a role far out of proportion to their size, for their job was to show the landing craft the way to their beach sectors. If the PCs failed in their mission, the invasion could go awry.

It was still too early to leave for the beach—departure was scheduled for 6:13 A.M.—so the columns of landing craft coiled up again, each company of six boats forming a circle opposite its beach sector. The coxswains waited. As the boats went round and round like floating carousels, the Stonewallers had an opportunity to take a good look at Omaha Beach.

The 29ers continued to glance upward, searching the sky for the promised bombers. The men could see nothing but RAF Spitfires providing low air cover over the assault area in case the Luftwaffe made an appearance. The

Stonewallers couldn't see the bombers through the cloud layer, nor could they hear the roar of the B-24 engines over the din of the ships' guns. The G.I.'s couldn't hear the bombs falling several miles beyond Omaha Beach, couldn't know the planes had delayed the release of their bombs by seconds to avoid an accidental bombing of the densely packed landing craft. The bombardiers, unable to see through the clouds, had to reckon by instruments alone. As a result, not a single B-24's bomb fell on its Omaha Beach target.

At 6:13 A.M., the coxswains brought the boats out of their circles and deployed into a line abreast, parallel to the beach, 4,000 yards offshore. When the twenty-four boats in the 116th's four first-wave companies lined up opposite their beach sectors, they formed a ragged line one-and-a-half miles long. Somewhere to the east, the 1st Division LCVPs were doing exactly the same.

Actually, the first American units scheduled to come ashore on Omaha Beach did not belong to either the 1st or the 29th Division. That distinction belonged to the 741st and 743rd Tank Battalions, which were to land their Sherman tanks a minute or two ahead of H-Hour. The Stonewallers could see several big 126-ton "Landing Craft, Tank" ("LCT," for short) 300 yards in front of them, churning clumsily towards the beach. Each LCT carried three or four Sherman tanks, and the 29ers were happy to have them in front.

It was full daylight as the LCVPs began their run-in to the beach. The morning mist was slowly dissipating, and as the Stonewallers neared the shore, they could make out the colorful hues of the shore, particularly the white sand and the dark green grass of the bluffs beyond the tidal flats.

But something was wrong.

The navy was still blasting away at the German defenses, and thick black smoke billowed from the bluffs where the shells had set beach grass afire. Some of the young coxswains became disoriented because the smoke had obscured the landmarks by which they were navigating. Even worse, an exceptionally strong flood current of over two knots swept the boats to the east, toward the 1st Division sector. The coxswains tried to watch adjacent LCVPs, but station-keeping was almost impossible under the influence of the current.

The 29ers could see the sands clearly now, and what they saw shocked them. The beach was a few hundred yards wide and as flat as a billiard table. There were no craters; the 29ers could see that a bomb hadn't landed anywhere near the beach. The men realized that if the Germans on the bluffs had survived the Allied naval fire, they were going to make life very unpleasant for the first wave. And on a beach with no bomb craters, there would be no places to hide.

The closer the boats got to the beach, the more frenzied and deafening the naval bombardment became. Every ship with a gun joined the fray. Out in front of the 116th's boats, the Stonewallers could see the Sherman tanks firing their 75mm guns over the bow ramps of their bobbing LCTs. The tankers gave little thought to accuracy. Their wild fire was probably more helpful to the Stonewallers' morale than harmful to the Germans.

Incredibly, the din got louder. When the 29th Division boats were a half-mile offshore, nine special LCTs, which had been configured to fire thousands of rockets into the German defenses on the bluffs, let loose with their salvos. The whooshing rockets arched directly over the boats in the first wave, and their roar was like the final crescendo of a great symphony. One member of Company A recalled that the noise of the rockets gave him his first real fright during the passage to the beach. But with all their noise, the rockets were encouraging. With such fantastic weapons on the Allied side, the Stonewallers wondered how the Germans could survive this final onslaught. Like the fireworks they resembled, however, the rockets did little damage. Most of them missed their targets by a wide margin.

The 116th Infantry lost one boat before the Germans even fired a shot. Company A's LCA 5, the next-to-last boat on the 29th Division's right flank, was swamped 1,000 yards offshore and went down like a stone. One Company A man recalled that something—perhaps a rock or an obstacle—staved in the bottom of the boat, which flooded almost immediately. The Stonewallers jumped overboard and popped air capsules to inflate their life belts. Shedding their equipment as fast as they could to avoid being dragged underwater, the men floated up and down on the waves, teeth chattering from fear as well as from cold, wondering whether they would be picked up before they drowned.

The boats were only 500 yards out now. Still no German fire. Some men dared hope that the invasion would be as easy as a landing exercise on England's Slapton Sands.

But the Germans had not been driven from the bluffs. In Company A's sector, enemy mortar and artillery shells suddenly exploded near the boats, sending up tall columns of water which slowly cascaded back into the sea. When the company was less than 100 yards from shore, one of its LCAs was hit by a shell—some said it was a mine—and the boat disintegrated. The survivors scrambled over the sides, discarded their equipment, and swam for shore.

In other sectors, the boats fought the flood current but were forced eastward, and they approached the beach opposite raging grass fires. The Stonewallers could scarcely see the bluffs through the heavy pall of black smoke. Luckily for the G.I.'s, the Germans could see even less.

The thunderous naval bombardment was coming to an end. In front of the 116th's boats, several Shermans, their guns blazing, roared down the lowered LCT bow ramps onto the sand.

Now it was the 29th Division's turn. The men in Company A had it worst. German artillery was falling near their boats with alarming frequency, but the enemy's fireworks had only just begun.

A few bullets pinged sharply off the landing craft. At that moment, the

Stonewallers knew that the beach would be hell. The Germans seemed to be taunting the Yanks, zeroing their machine guns on the boats as if they were test-firing on a range. Their deadly work would begin in earnest when the men of Company A disembarked and raced across the wide tidal flat. The last fifteen seconds in the boats were the worst fifteen seconds of the men's lives.

Only thirty more yards to the beach. Three-and-a-half years of training had come to this. The men pondered glumly the irony of practicing for the invasion for so long only to be killed during their first seconds on Omaha Beach.

Some men shut their eyes and prayed; others cursed. A few joked half-heartedly about army life insurance. But most were too frightened and miserable to do or say anything at all. Anyway, there was no more time for words. With a jolt, the boats hit bottom and crunched forward on the sand. Then the ramps went down.

TWO

STATESIDE
The Blue and the Gray Division
1917–1942

1. MOBILIZATION

The 29th Division had come a long way in a short time. When the German army conquered France in June 1940, four years before the invasion of Normandy, the 29th Division as such existed only two weeks per year, when National Guardsmen from Maryland, Virginia, and Pennsylvania gathered for annual training at military encampments throughout their respective states. In the twenty-two years since the end of World War I, the division had assembled in its entirety only three times.

A guardsman felt a sense of institutional loyalty to his company first and his regiment second; the division was a distant third. Each company had its own recruitment area, except for the city of Baltimore, which was the domain of the entire 5th Maryland Regiment. The men within each outfit usually knew one another intimately. They had gone to the same schools, they worked for the same companies, and they spoke the same regional dialect. Weekend and evening training was a gathering of friends more than a military exercise.

The 29th Division was hardly a well-practiced military unit in 1940. As the Germans smashed through Belgium and Holland, many National Guard officers were riding to the hounds over the Maryland and Virginia countryside. Occasional polo matches were arranged with Regular Army officers. Col. George Patton frequently attended National Guard horse shows.

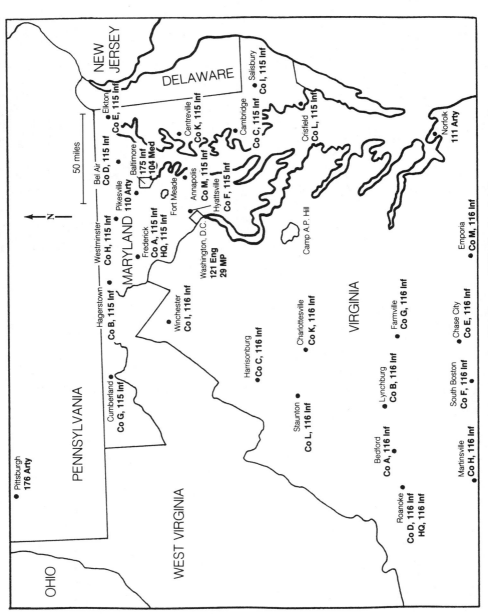

29th Division Armories, 1941. See page 288 for further details.

Troops from the 110th Field Artillery during pre-war annual training. *Courtesy Cooper Armory.*

Guardsmen still marched in fancy full dress uniforms with white cross-belts, gleaming buttons, and tall black shakos topped with white plumes. Officers were referred to as "dandies" and "silk stocking boys," and no one took offense because everyone knew that was exactly what they were. The men trained with materiel left over from World War I and didn't complain. The equipment had worked before, the guardsmen figured, and it would work again.

And then the Germans rolled into Paris.

The 29ers knew then that their training routine would inevitably assume a more serious tone. What they failed to realize was how rapidly change would occur. The first sign was the extension of the annual training period from two weeks to three weeks. Furthermore, the exercises planned for the summer of 1940 were to be the grandest ever attempted in the United States in peacetime. For their three weeks of training, the guardsmen of the 29th Division were deployed to upstate New York to participate in First Army maneuvers involving over 100,000 men.

Gossips declared that the 29th would soon be called to Federal service for an entire year. Some guardsmen, however, found this rumor hard to believe. The war in Europe was England's problem, they figured, and it appeared unlikely that the United States would get involved in another European conflict. To many 29ers, Hitler was only the latest in a long line of tinhorned

European dictators with dreams of conquest; he would never dare challenge the United States. For these guardsmen, the thought of leaving their civilian jobs and families for a godforsaken army post was unthinkable. After all, the country was at peace.

The rumors suddenly became believable when Maj. Percy Black, a former American military attaché in Berlin, came to Maryland and Virginia armories to speak on German weapons and tactics. The guardsmen were curious about the famous German panzers and the new word that had recently entered the lexicon: "blitzkrieg."

Black gave them that and more. He told the 29ers bluntly that the Germans were the toughest and best soldiers in Europe. He emphasized the German doctrine of *Schwerpunkt*, which demanded the concentration of all possible firepower and men on a narrow front. He remarked that the morale of the German army was sky-high. He had never seen a drunken or undisciplined German soldier. Lt. Robert Miller of the 175th Infantry recalled, "It was a shock to learn what we would be up against."

In the summer of 1940, President Franklin D. Roosevelt was hinting about a conscription law, which, if passed by Congress, would be the first peacetime draft in the history of the United States. The 29ers guessed that if the national emergency were serious enough to require Selective Service, mobilization of the National Guard could not be far behind. They were right.

The Selective Service bill passed Congress in September. Shortly thereafter, older guardsmen and those with vital civilian jobs were retired from the guard. High-ranking officers visited the guardsmen's civilian employers: mobilization was imminent, the officers said, and employers would have to be prepared to accept the departure of their workers who were guard members. It was just a question of time.

Official orders arrived in October. The 29th Division would be mobilized early in 1941. The guardsmen spent the last three months of 1940 putting their civilian affairs in order. Then they were given physical exams and issued new uniforms. Mobilization day was set for Monday, February 3. The men reported to their local armories that day with mixed feelings. Most had never figured that joining the guard would lead to full-time military duty. For many, the call-up was an unwanted diversion from their civilian lives; others considered mobilization an adventure.

The guardsmen lolled around in their civilian clothes for a few hours on spartan army cots, which were tightly packed onto the armories' gymnasium floors. The surprised citizen-soldiers discovered that the weeding-out process of the previous four months had cut each company's manpower almost in half. Eventually, everyone put on his uniform and was issued a weapon. They were in the army now.

Each outfit soon departed its home armory for Fort George G. Meade, located halfway between Baltimore and Washington, D.C. Meade would be the 29th Division's home for more than a year. The post had been built almost overnight in 1917 to house part of the multitude of recruits preparing to go "Over There."

By 1941, Meade was no longer a collection of dilapidated wooden barracks in a rural backwater. It was, in fact, the fourth largest "city" in Maryland. New construction was proceeding at a furious pace when the 29th Division arrived, and the place was a mess. One officer described it as a "sea of mud." Most of the barracks were unfinished, and the men housed inside were perpetually cold. The "streets" existed only in someone's imagination.

For a while, the men loved it. The novelty of the soldier's life was exciting. The men had the chance to fire their weapons with regularity, and they played with their stylish new two-and-a-half-ton GMC trucks and ultra-modern radios. They met 29ers from other outfits and argued good-naturedly about who was best. On the march or in the local pubs, they sang. The men of the 175th, formerly the 5th Maryland Infantry, rewrote the words to an old British army tune:

> Now Old King Cole was a merry old soul,
> And a merry old soul was he;
> He called for his pipe and he called for his bowl,
> And he called for his generals three.
> "The Army's shot to hell," said the generals,
> "What's my next command?" said the colonels,
> "Where's my boots and spurs?" said the majors,
> "We want ten days leave," said the captains,
> "We do all the work," said the shavetails,
> "Right by squads, squads, right," said the sergeants,
> "Hut two, hut two, hut," said the corporals,
> "Beer, beer, beer," said the privates,
> Merry men are we!
> There's none so fair,
> As can compare,
> To the old Fifth Infantry!

But army life soured quickly. The worst part about it was boredom. Between drills, the 29ers had little to do. The movies in the post theaters were dull—and they never changed anyway. Aside from films, entertainment opportunities were few, except for the ubiquitous prostitutes that stalked the fringes of the post. A Washington newspaper editor described Meade as a "whorehouse." The troops complained bitterly that not enough weekend passes were issued. They declared that there was so little that had to be done on the weekends that eighty percent of a company could leave Meade and not be missed. Sometimes, even when a pass was issued, the men were furious because it was granted on such short notice that travel arrangements to nearby cities could not possibly be made.

The worst part of life at Meade was the mindless Army discipline. The citizen-soldiers tired quickly of cleaning guns that were already clean and polishing buttons and boots that already shined. Several officers and NCOs, the men felt, were bullies. The troops complained that they never knew the purpose of their training exercises. Recalled one 29er, "Frequently we were told to get our packs together to go out on ROOP [Reconnaissance, Observation, Operation, and Position]. We were marched away. We set up guns. The communications men put down their lines. No one knew what was going on or why. At the end we were simply marched back again. We hadn't any idea what had been done. Was this training?"

In April 1941, the first draftees arrived. Fort Meade had not been prepared to receive a large influx of Selective Service men. Not enough uniforms were available to clothe everyone, so some of the new troops were issued old World War I woolen uniforms or Civilian Conservation Corps outfits. When rifles weren't available, the new men used wooden substitutes. At first, the guardsmen laughed at the strangely accoutered draftees, but by summer everyone had been properly fitted out and looked like a real soldier.

Many of the conscripts were Marylanders or Virginians, and they had little difficulty acclimating to the weather or gaining acceptance from the guardsmen. The newcomers, in fact, usually outnumbered the old hands in each outfit. In the 175th Infantry, which had an authorized strength of about 3,500 men, 2,000 of the troops were draftees.

The tedium of training was sometimes broken when units pulled out of Meade for exercises at nearby encampments. The artillery went to Indiantown Gap, Pennsylvania, for live fire training. Infantry and artillery units in regiment-sized teams visited Camp A. P. Hill, near Bowling Green, Virginia, for two weeks of maneuvers.

On one occasion a 29th Division truck convoy traveling between Meade and A. P. Hill attempted to cross a new Potomac River bridge twenty-five miles south of Washington without paying the required tolls. A bridge official stopped the convoy and insisted that the men pay full tolls for each truck—which they did. The commander of the 29th Division was outraged. He ordered all troops traveling between the two posts to move by way of Washington, which was a longer and more difficult trip. When the story reached the newspapers, the Governor of Maryland hastily announced that tolls would no longer be charged for military vehicles.

Several lucky officers—and, more rarely, enlisted men—got a break from Meade when they received orders to attend branch schools, such as the Infantry School at Fort Benning, Georgia (nicknamed the "Benning School for Boys"), the Gunnery School at Fort Sill, Oklahoma, or the Engineer School at nearby Fort Belvoir, Virginia. When the men returned to the division after their eight-week courses, they told their friends wondrous stories of new weapons and equipment on army drawing boards. The division, however, would not receive this new materiel for at least another year.

By mid-summer, the 29ers wondered what more they needed to learn about military tactics. They felt ready to fight should the United States enter the war, but some men still did not think of Germany or Japan as a real threat, and a few said so openly.

Morale was dropping fast. The men's spirits were particularly bad in July, when FDR, claiming a national emergency, asked Congress to extend the draftees' one-year enlistment by another six months. This Service Extension Act, as it was called, passed the House by only one vote. Afterward, Secretary of War Henry Stimson spoke on radio extolling the sacrifices of the American soldier and emphasizing the grave nature of the global situation. Many 29ers listening, especially the draftees, responded with Bronx cheers and raucous laughter.

Then a bombshell dropped. The August 18, 1941, issue of *Life* magazine featured an article by an anonymous author who described the shocking emotional deterioration of the 27th Division, a New York National Guard outfit then stationed at Fort McClellan, Alabama. The author claimed that fifty percent of the division was threatening to desert in October. The writer noted the word "OHIO" scribbled all over latrine walls and division vehicles; it stood for "Over the Hill In October."

Most of the New Yorkers, the article declared, were openly rebellious and showed no signs of common military courtesy. They deeply resented being trapped in a rural backwater hundreds of miles from their homes, and above all they were angry about the Service Extension Act, which condemned them to another six months of a dreary, pointless existence.

The *Life* attack was so scathing that the *New York Times* decided to undertake its own investigation, using a distinguished World War I veteran named Hilton Howell Raily. With War Department approval and support, Raily traveled the country from coast to coast in August and September. Keeping a low profile, he visited army posts to discover if the *Life* article had accurately portrayed army morale. The first camp visited by Raily—only three days after publication of the *Life* article—was Fort Meade.

One of Raily's friends, a newspaperman in Washington, warned him that the *Life* article could just as easily have been written about the 29th Division. Raily visited the headquarters of Maj. Gen. Milton A. Reckord, the 29th's commanding general, who had served in the Maryland National Guard since 1901. Reckord was a crusty character, and Raily described their conversation as "brief and unsatisfactory." The general condemned the *Life* article and firmly declared that his 29th Division was a first-rate outfit with top-notch morale. Reckord charged that "Even if it [the *Life* story] were true of one division, its publication was a subversive act and served only a destructive purpose."

Raily got nowhere. Reckord rasped that he didn't care what his men thought as long as they were prepared to fight—and that was that.

"Accordingly, with another plan in mind, I retired," wrote Raily. He hired a twenty-eight-year-old investigator who was instructed to wander around Meade and its nearby bars and then report on the men's morale. Although he conversed with only about fifty 29ers, the investigator reported disturbing news. He wrote to Raily, "Maj. Gen. Milton Reckord, Commanding Officer, is rarely referred to except when someone says, 'Shit on him.' He may think morale is OK because all his subordinates have to tell him it is. If his powers of observation are any good at all, though, he should know better. The head chaplain is respected more than any other officer. The men feel that if they have a champion at all, it is he."

Actually, the 29ers' spirits were low merely because they were bored. Raily, in fact, eventually concluded that life was relatively good at Meade, especially compared to what he discovered later that summer on his country-wide tour. At other army camps in the South, Raily witnessed drunken melees in town squares, enlisted men openly ridiculing their officers, widespread threats of desertion, and total apathy about the international situation. Once, Raily came across some National Guard officers in Alexandria, Louisiana, who behaved so disgracefully that he attempted to photograph the scene for his report. He was, however, prevented from doing so.

The most important issue for the men was their forced retention in the army when they felt the country was not immediately in danger of war. "Morale took a nose dive after the vote in the House on extension of the service period," one soldier told Raily. Said another man, "The government isn't fooling us. We know there is no possibility of Hitler coming over here. We are being jockeyed into a war that we ought to damn well keep out of."

Although 29ers were not fond of the Service Extension Act, they were relatively happy because they were close to home—especially the many Baltimoreans in the division. If a 29er had an upcoming furlough, he could make travel arrangements and visit his family or girlfriend, or even see the tourist sights in nearby Washington. On the other hand, New York City boys stationed in an army camp in rural Georgia had none of these amenities; their rock-bottom morale was hardly surprising. In Raily's final report for the *Times*, in fact, one of his strongest recommendations was that National Guard divisions be stationed close to their home region.

Lt. Gen. Lesley J. McNair was furious when he read the Raily report. McNair, who was Chief of Staff of US Army General Headquarters in Washington, D. C., was never an admirer of the National Guard. Raily's scathing comments on flagging army morale only fueled his scorn for the army's citizen-soldiers. In an October 14 letter to Gen. George C. Marshall, the Army Chief of Staff, McNair recommended the immediate demobilization of the guard. "The National Guard is built on an unsound foundation in that its officers have had little or no training as such," McNair wrote. "The Guard now is or soon will be occupying space and facilities which could be used to better advantage for new units, organized soundly and led adequately. It would be better to ease Guard units out of the picture as fast as others can be created in their places." Marshall, however, was a man with a cooler temperament, and he decided to take no action except to allow McNair to instigate a campaign to purge the army of incompetent officers.

Guard and reserve officers were appalled by McNair's attitude. Several remarked that they had no hope for future promotion because of the discrimination imposed by the so-called "WPPA" (West Point Protective Association). "Regular Army officers undermine the morale of the Reserve officers, against whom they are prejudiced," said one reserve officer. "They start out asking us if we are from West Point. We hit upon a pat answer that stops them dead: 'No, we paid for our education.' "

General Marshall himself, however, was not a West Pointer and, having served a stint earlier in his career as an instructor of National Guard troops, he understood their strengths and foibles. He knew the guard was not as bad as McNair believed.

Several 29th Division officers, however, were emotionally scarred by McNair's scrutiny. They lived in fear of being forced to leave the army in disgrace or of spending the next few years behind a desk in South Dakota. They devoted themselves utterly to perfecting their military skills so that McNair's spies would find no deficiencies. As a result, a few 29th Division officers turned into martinets and were despised by their men—a feeling that persisted as late as the Normandy campaign.

Throughout the controversy triggered by the *Life* article, the 29ers remained busy. On September 13, the division set out for A. P. Hill for two weeks of intensive training. The division then headed straight for Fort Bragg, North Carolina, to join several other divisions in an elaborate two-month series of wargames and maneuvers. As the Red (enemy) army stalked the Blue (friendly) force in mock combat in the Carolina woods, local farmers gaped at the sight of army trucks, bearing giant white signs painted with the word "TANK" rumbling down the dusty country roads. The army, it seemed, was short of real tanks. Meanwhile, the soldiers argued good-naturedly among themselves about who was "killed" and "captured" in the sham fights. The 29ers had little time for carping and no audience to listen to them anyway.

The 29th, along with several other outfits including two of the army's new armored divisions, played at war in the Carolinas until late November. Eventually, the weather became uncomfortably cold, the maneuvers ended, and the 29ers packed up their trucks and prepared to return home to Meade. A rumor spread through the camps that the National Guard divisions would be demobilized within the next month since they were now fully trained. Most 29ers found this gossip plausible and looked forward to spending the Christmas holiday as civilians again.

The 29th Division truck convoys headed north. They reached A. P. Hill in early December. Then, on December 7, the men flipped on their radios and heard the news.

2. HERITAGE

One of the first things a recruit did upon joining the Maryland or Virginia guard in the inter-war period was to learn the history of his regiment. Since all three infantry regiments in the division traced their lineages back to the pre-Revolutionary War period, the history lessons were not easy. In the 5th Maryland—nicknamed the "Dandy 5th" because of its fancy gray full-dress uniforms—the men learned how their forebears had suicidally charged the British lines and saved Washington's army at the Battle of Long Island on August 27, 1776. Supposedly, Washington watched the Marylanders in action and lamented, "My God, what brave men I must lose today!" When their spirited new regimental march, "The Dandy Fifth of Maryland," was composed in 1935, the guardsmen paraded down the streets of Baltimore singing the words:

> Brooklyn Heights we stormed for Washington,
> Monmouth, too, our valiant efforts won,
> Scott Key saw our colors flying,
> We took Monterey, half-trying,
> "Over there," another call to fame,
> Found us smashing through,
> Bearing in battle's flame,
> The old Red, White, and Blue!

The 116th Infantry was the old 2nd Virginia, which dated back to 1760. But to the men of this outfit, the regiment's crowning glory came 100 years later during its service in the army of the Confederate States. The 2nd Virginia was the senior regiment among those that served with Stonewall Jackson in the legendary Stonewall Brigade in the Army of Northern Virginia. Most members of the 116th could proudly recite the story of the Battle of First Manassas (or First Bull Run), when Confederate Gen. Barnard Bee uttered the words that gave the regiment its nickname: "There stands Jackson like a stone wall! Rally behind the Virginians!'' Thus, the men came to call themselves ''Stonewallers,'' and they treasured their Confederate traditions.

The 115th Infantry was derived from the 1st Maryland, which had been raised in the hills of western Maryland during colonial days. During the Civil War, divided loyalties in the western counties of the state led to the formation of two 1st Maryland regiments—one in the Confederate States army and the other in the United States Army. These two outfits met each other in battle in May 1862 at Front Royal in the Shenandoah Valley. After the Civil War, the 1st Maryland became more than just a western Maryland outfit, recruiting men from all parts of the state—even from the distant Eastern Shore—except Baltimore.

The 29th Division also included several artillery outfits with their own rich histories and traditions. During the inter-war years, National Guard artillery regiments attracted a large number of blue-blooded young aristocrats from the Maryland and Virginia horse country. Artillery pieces were still horse-drawn, and excellent opportunities and facilities for horseback riding were available at National Guard armories. The War Department finally took the horses away from guard artillery units in 1935, but a handful of mounts were retained for ceremonial occasions and for the regimental polo teams.

The 110th Field Artillery Regiment was recruited in Pikesville, a Baltimore suburb that, in those days, was far enough outside the city to attract several members of the prestigious Green Spring Valley Hunt Club. The 111th Field Artillery was a Virginia unit based in Norfolk, and the 176th Field Artillery was from Pittsburgh.

In 1917, many people thought it a terrible idea to assign Southern boys and Yankees to the same military unit. But when the 29th Division was first organized in July of that year, three months after the American declaration of war against Germany, the army did exactly that. It assembled National Guard units from Virginia, Maryland, New Jersey, and Delaware at the Jersey shore and called them the 29th Division. Those who were still refighting the Civil War worried that the 29ers would fight each other more than they would the Germans. But the army didn't think so. In fact, it purposefully emphasized the historic lineage of the division's National Guard units. The 29ers wore a circular blue and gray patch on their left shoulders, symbolizing Northern and Southern solidarity in the current national crisis, and the outfit became known as the ''Blue and Gray Division.''

In France, the 29th participated in the Meuse-Argonne offensive and remained in continuous combat for three weeks. Gen. Milton Reckord, who was then a regimental commander in the division, recalled that when his outfit went overseas, every one of his men was a Marylander. After the Meuse-Argonne, all but three states in the United States were represented in the regiment.

After World War I, the New Jersey and Delaware troops were transferred

This patch, worn on the left shoulder, is the 29th Division symbol.

from the division and were replaced by a second Virginia regiment. The 29th did not assemble in its entirety again until 1935.

Relations between guardsmen from different outfits were not always smooth. In 1922, the 1st and 5th Maryland Regiments (known as the 115th and 175th Infantry Regiments, respectively, during periods of Federal service) gathered for a summer encampment on the banks of the Gunpowder River, north of Baltimore. The 1st was a rural outfit, mostly from western Maryland; the 5th was a city unit, overwhelmingly from Baltimore. Insults flew from the moment camp opened, and tempers quickly flared. The situation soon deteriorated, and wild brawls between the men of the 1st and the 5th broke out all over camp. The guard officers could do nothing to stop it, and Regular Army troops had to be called in to restore order.

It was quite a division.

3. WARGAMES

The sign over the front door of the Elkton Armory had a simple message:

WHY BE DRAFTED? ENLIST NOW
    Co. E, 1st Inf
    Maryland National Guard
    Distinct Advantage Over Conscription
    Apply at Office

It was difficult to inveigle men into the military between the wars. Those who joined the National Guard had their own diverse motives for signing up. In truth, the 29th Division was a microcosm of American society—except that the division had no blacks and no women. Some men joined the guard for fun; a few signed up because they were patriots; some enlisted because they needed the money.

In his appraisal of the non-commissioned officers of the 29th Division, Hilton Raily's anonymous young assistant unconsciously echoed the Duke of Wellington's scathing evaluation of his British redcoats. "Our army is composed of the mere scum of the earth," Wellington noted. Based on his surreptitious interviews with 29ers around Fort Meade in 1941, Raily's assistant noted that "the non-commissioned officers [of the 29th Division] appear, in general, to have been recruited from the sewers of Baltimore."

This was a harsh judgment. The 29ers were ragged in appearance and rough in manners because times were hard in the United States. The country was still in the midst of a deep economic depression, and a large percentage of the population—especially in large cities like Baltimore—was desperately poor. Many of those who joined the army were tough characters who had not had easy lives. They never knew where their next meal—or their next drink—would come from.

Yet some said they would have joined the guard even if they hadn't been paid. A few were hardened realists who saw another European war as inevitable and wished to get a taste of army life. But most of all, those who eagerly sought out the guard did so out of a spirit of adventure. They loved the outdoor life and sought soldierly camaraderie.

In 1935, Robert M. Miller joined Company E, 175th Infantry, as a private. He recalled; "My father observed to me that war in Europe was coming, that the United States would eventually be drawn into it, and that it was advisable for me to experience military training. He was emphatic that to be a soldier was not just to learn to take care of yourself, but to be prepared to lead others. I was somewhat surprised, but his advice had always been good, and I acted upon it." In 1940, Miller was commissioned from the ranks as a second lieutenant.

According to Hilton Raily, the soldiers' biggest problem before Pearl Harbor was a lack of purpose. He compared the army to a football team undergoing intensive training with no opponents to play. Pearl Harbor, of course, changed everything. The United States suddenly found itself with three evil antagonists, and the army's spirit was aroused overnight. By early 1942, the Raily Report, with all its dire evaluations of army morale, seemed an archaic document, though it had been written only eight weeks before Pearl Harbor. Now, the grumblers within the army kept their petty grievances to themselves. Insubordination would no longer be taken lightly.

Everyone in the 29th Division knew they would eventually fight; it was just a question of when and where. In truth, the 29th Division's transition from peace to war was remarkably smooth. An observer might not have noticed much change.

But army life was still boring. Anyone who expected the division to be shipped to a glamorous South Sea island, where they would train to fight the Japanese, was sorely disappointed. Instead, the division adhered to the same old training schedule, broken only by weeks of tedious guard duty all over the east coast.

In late December and early January, the 115th and 116th found themselves patrolling beaches from the Outer Banks of North Carolina to Atlantic City, New Jersey. This assignment was taxing, for the coastal sectors for which each battalion was responsible were vast. The sentries paced up and down desolate dunes while icy winter winds blew sand in their faces. The 29ers stared out to sea hour after hour with their binoculars, but no one really expected to see any Germans. Inexplicably, the troops had almost no ammunition. Some men went on patrol with only one clip for their M1s. The artillerymen had only a few shells for each gun. If a German U-boat had landed commandos on the beach, the 29ers could have done little but yell for help.

The division was eventually relieved of its beach patrol duties by coast artillerymen and local home guards, but this did not mean an end to tiresome guard details. Both the 115th and 175th spent most of January and February guarding warehouses, railroad junctions, and docks throughout Pennsylvania, Maryland, and Virginia.

The 29ers on distant sentry duty eventually made their way back to Fort Meade, where the division assembled in its entirety once again. But life at Meade had changed drastically since Christmas. For one thing, the spirit and discipline of the troops had surged. The 29ers were hardly enthusiastic about going into combat; rather, they were acclimated to army life at last and were willing to do their fair share until the war was won. Now the 29ers wore their uniforms even when they were off-duty.

Even the newspapers noticed the change. A headline in the Baltimore *Sun* on January 29 proclaimed,

FORT MEADE SOLDIERS BECOME A GRIM, BUSINESS-LIKE LOT
Advent of War Changes Their Bearing—
They're Determined To Be Ready When Call Comes

The surprised 29ers also discovered that now they could have a good time at Meade without getting drunk or visiting a prostitute. Four post movie theaters provided an early and a late show nightly, and the 29ers could see a first-run film for fourteen cents. Fort Meade, which had offered little to interest the G.I.'s prior to Pearl Harbor, was now a regular stop for USO shows,

Hollywood movie stars, and famous Big Bands. Several 29ers even wanted to stay in camp during their furloughs.

The 29ers' favorite pastime was the weekly dance at Meade's service club. Before the war, this mixer was avoided by the men since they had no hopes of meeting any interesting members of the opposite sex. Now, however, the army was bringing in hundreds of attractive young women from Baltimore and Washington for dances, and the 29ers eagerly awaited the night when they could jitterbug, foxtrot, and waltz all over the dance floor. The story of one lucky private in the 116th Infantry who was asked for a dance by a beautiful redhead quickly spread throughout the division. The woman was Ann Rutherford, Mickey Rooney's co-star in the famous "Andy Hardy" movies.

The 29ers were starting to look and act like hardened soldiers. They marched smartly, their shiny brown shoes smacking in perfect unison on the freshly laid pavement at Fort Meade. As their fork-tailed company guidons fluttered at the heads of long columns of four, the men, dressed in long woolen overcoats and World War I tin hats, strutted with as much soldierly bearing as they could muster.

Sometimes, they sang old army songs.

> There are smiles for second looies,
> There are smiles for sergeants too,
> There are smiles when you're reprimanded,

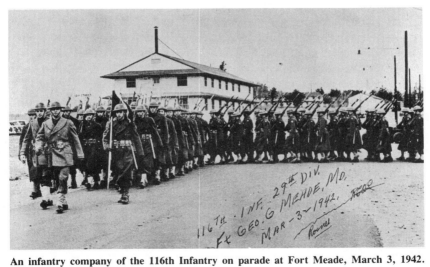

An infantry company of the 116th Infantry on parade at Fort Meade, March 3, 1942. *Courtesy Fort Meade Museum.*

There are smiles for each wrong thing you do,
There are smiles when feet are worn and weary,
There are smiles when you're told to do KP,
But the smiles I get down in the guardhouse,
Are the damndest smiles I ever wish to see.

The army bugle regulated their lives. "The first favor they can do soldiers is to amputate the lungs of all buglers," declared one 29er. Reveille,
mess call, assembly, fatigue call, taps—the 29ers learned them all, and even
knew the traditional words to the calls. Mess Call was their favorite:

Soupy, soupy, soupy,
Without a single bean.
Porky, porky, porky,
Without a piece that's lean.
Coffee, coffee, coffee,
Without a drop of creeeeeam.

And Fatigue Call:

With a pick and with a shovel and with a hoe
With a sentry at your back you want to say no;
With a pick and with a shovel and with a hoe
Down in the ditch you go.

Meanwhile, major changes were brewing in the 29th Division. The army
believed that sixty-one-year-old General Reckord was too old to lead a modern division in the field. In early January, the general, who had led the 29th
since 1934, was placed in command of the Third Corps Area, an administrative rather than a combat command.

The new commanding general was Maj. Gen. Leonard T. Gerow, who
arrived at Meade on March 2. Gerow, a Virginian and a graduate of the
Virginia Military Institute, was a good choice for the command. So many
other VMI alumni were in the division that Gerow joked that his first few days
at Meade felt like a class reunion. Furthermore, veteran National Guard officers who were sensitive about the "West Point Protective Association" were
pleased by Gerow's selection.

One of the general's aides recalled, "Gerow was a man of the old school.
He was not the type to be familiar even with his contemporaries." Gerow was
not, however, a martinet. He did not care for fawning staff officers, and he
frequently called for honest discussion in the decision-making process.

Gerow's new command was essentially a mini-army. The 29th Division

Maj. Gen. Leonard Gerow, Commanding General, 29th Infantry Division, February 1942–July 1943. *Courtesy Cooper Armory.*

was 22,000 men strong and included enough support units to make it self-reliant in combat. In static conditions, the division could fight independently and deal with virtually any exigency with little help from corps or army except for the provision of food and ammunition. The 29th, like most other US Army divisions at that time, was referred to as a "square" division since it consisted of four regiments, divided into two brigades. With 5,000 more men than a German infantry division, the 29th was a powerful fighting force.

But the army no longer believed in the square division concept. Square divisions had worked well enough during World War I, when units remained in the same trenches for weeks at a time and supply services were not strained. After the Germans blitzed Europe in 1939 and 1940, however, World War II seemed destined to be anything but static. The US Army's highest-ranking officers were deeply troubled when they contemplated how square divisions would perform in mobile warfare. The divisions were heavy in support services and would be difficult to move rapidly in battle. Even General Pershing, the commander of the American Expeditionary Force (AEF) in World War I, was in favor of scrapping the square divisions.

Armies have never considered it unsportsmanlike to imitate other armies. The US Army in 1941 was no exception. General McNair, the driving force behind a major organizational change, felt that the "triangular" divisions used by most European armies were more suitable for mobile warfare than were square divisions. Triangular divisions were smaller, leaner outfits. They had only three infantry regiments (hence the name), and all support regiments were pared to battalion size. The chain of command was significantly simplified, as the division commander now dealt directly with his regimental COs rather than indirectly through brigades. The divisions were reduced to 15,500 men. Any special units that might be required in combat, such as tanks, tank destroyers, or anti-aircraft artillery, could quickly be provided by corps or army.

Regular Army divisions converted to the triangular format in the summer and fall of 1941. In November of that year, the 29th Division received word that it, too, would convert, and the change was implemented on March 11, 1942.

The transformation was something of a shock to the 29ers. A large number of men woke up one morning to discover that their outfits had been redesignated and transferred to another camp, or even disbanded altogether. The entire 176th Infantry Regiment (the "Richmond Blues") departed for guard duty in Washington, D.C. An engineer battalion was transferred to the 37th Division, which was about to be shipped to the South Pacific. These and other developments, such as the transfer of an entire battalion of the 175th Infantry to the Army War Show (which was touring the country, stirring up patriotic fervor), left the 29ers wondering whether there would be any 29th Division at all in a few more months.

When spring came, it was time to show off. Half a million Baltimoreans turned out on an unseasonably hot Monday, April 6, to watch the 116th Infantry form up at the 5th Regiment Armory and march down Howard and Baltimore Streets past the reviewing stand at City Hall, where the old enemy of the National Guard, General McNair, took their "eyes left" salute. The bands played "Way Down Upon the Suwanee River"—one of the 116th's favorite tunes—and "Over There," as the crowd cheered and waved tiny American flags.

The 29th left Fort Meade for good in mid-April to make room for a new division, the 76th. For the next two months, the division encamped at A. P. Hill, where the 29ers resumed their training and wargames amid the Virginia pine forests. The weather got warmer, and the men watched open-air movies at night. Just outside the boundaries of the camp was the tiny village of Bowling Green, which offered little in the way of recreation. The G.I.'s usually took a crowded bus into nearby Fredericksburg, the only decent-sized town in the vicinity.

On July 6, the 29th Division departed A. P. Hill for a second series of Carolina maneuvers. The participants took these wargames seriously, since everyone realized that they could be shipped overseas at any time.

On August 17, the 29th was pulled out of the Carolina maneuvers and ordered south to Camp Blanding, Florida, halfway between Jacksonville and Gainesville. Blanding was designated as the division's new home station, and the 29ers were delighted by the change. The men promptly took advantage of Florida's famous sunshine by thronging the beaches of Jacksonville and old St. Augustine.

In early September, the army announced that all four of the 29th Division's artillery battalions would be transferred to the Artillery School at Fort Sill, Oklahoma, to act as demonstration troops. With no artillery, the 29ers were convinced that the division wasn't going anywhere soon, and they happily settled into camp life at sunny Blanding. It appeared that the division would spend another winter in camp, and the men believed that there was no better post in which to spend it than Blanding. The army, at last, had given the 29ers a break.

But things had a way of changing fast in the army. Even as the division artillery was entraining for the long trip to Oklahoma, orders arrived on September 6 that the 29th was to prepare for immediate overseas deployment.

The long-awaited moment had come. But was the division headed to Europe or to the Pacific? The destination was confidential, but the 29ers soon learned that the trains from Blanding would take them north. If they were going to the Pacific, the 29ers figured, the trains would head west; so it must be Europe.

The sudden orders to move north caught the 29th Division by surprise. It proved extraordinarily difficult to recall the 29ers on weekend leaves and extended furloughs. Throughout north Florida, army trucks with blaring loudspeakers combed the streets of every town and city, calling for 29ers to report to Blanding immediately. Twenty-niners who had gone out of state were contacted by telephone. Once everyone returned, the 29ers spent a week waterproofing weapons with Cosmoline grease and packing them into enormous wooden crates.

The train ride north from Blanding was lonely. When the trains stopped to take on water and food, the officers posted armed guards around the cars so that civilians could not approach and ask probing questions of the soldiers. The trains never stopped for more than a few minutes at a time, anyway.

They passed through Petersburg, Richmond, Ashland, Fredericksburg, Washington, D.C., the old training ground at Fort Meade, and Baltimore. The Maryland and Virginia guardsmen stared out the windows, transfixed. When, if ever, would they see their home towns again?

The trains finally disgorged the 29ers at Camp Kilmer, New Jersey, on September 18. Maj. John Cooper ushered his artillerymen of the 110th Field Artillery Battalion off the cars at 1:00 A.M. in the middle of a blinding rainstorm. As the men formed up on the platform, Cooper noticed a scowling colonel with a pencil-thin moustache and G.I. eyeglasses observing the proceedings. Cooper approached him and saluted.

"Well, we got 'em off the trains pretty fast, didn't we, Colonel?" asked Cooper.

"It could've been a lot faster if you'd poked 'em in the ass," growled the colonel.

The mysterious colonel was Charles D. Canham, a West Pointer who had been transferred to the division to instill some Regular Army discipline in the 29ers. Cooper sighed. The West Pointers would no doubt make life difficult for the guardsmen in the upcoming months.

Camp Kilmer was not a typical US Army post. It existed only to house the hundreds of thousands of G.I.'s preparing to ship from New York to Britain. The 29th was one of the first division-sized outfits to undergo the embarkation rigamarole, and the 29ers could see that the kinks in the procedure had not yet been worked out. The men were infuriated by a steady stream of contradictory orders that had them packing, unpacking, and repacking their cloth barracks bags. The 29ers were also annoyed by the strict secrecy requirements. No one was even permitted to utter the words "29th Division" for fear of Nazi spies.

But the whereabouts of the division were hardly secret. The 29ers saw to that. They desperately wanted to see their families before going overseas, and hasty rendezvous—strictly against orders—were arranged by telephone. When the division settled down at Kilmer, hundreds of wives, sweethearts, parents, and siblings eagerly waited in nearby towns to see their soldier-boys. If German spies really were on the prowl, they would have had no trouble locating the 29th Division.

In the next ten days, every 29er received at least one twenty-four-hour pass. Kilmer was situated outside New Brunswick, only thirty miles southwest of New York City, and several men used their passes to enjoy a night out in the big city. Others simply spent the time with their families in a hotel near Kilmer. A few got in cars or trains and traveled back to Maryland or Virginia for a quick meal, a hasty conversation, one last night at home.

On September 26, the 116th Infantry, plus artillery and support units, left Kilmer by train for Hoboken, where they were to board ferries for the passage across the Hudson River to New York. The tracks and train station platforms were lined with thousands of people, who waved, cheered, even cried. The 29ers were touched. The war was still young enough so that civilians got very emotional when watching the troops depart.

It was dark when the 29ers crossed the river, but the men could make out the huge black bulk of the 81,000-ton Cunard ocean-liner *Queen Mary* tied up alongside the dock. Near the *Queen Mary* was the even larger *Queen Elizabeth*, another Cunard liner which would take the rest of the division across the Atlantic the following week.

The 29ers disembarked from the ferries in long, scraggly lines and slowly inched their way across the pier and up the gangplank of the giant ship. On the morning of September 27, aided by tugs, the *Queen Mary* backed out of its berth and slowly made its way down the Hudson, past the Statue of Liberty, through the Narrows, and out to sea.

THREE

ENGLAND
"Us and the Home Guard"
October 1942–June 1944

1. TRANSATLANTIC

"Lizzie" and "Mary" sailed so fast that they didn't have to cross the Atlantic in a convoy. The *Queens* cruised at a steady twenty-eight knots. At that speed it was almost impossible for a German U-boat, which moved at only twelve knots—seven knots submerged—to intercept them. If by some stroke of luck a German U-boat captain found himself directly in the path of an oncoming *Queen*, he still had little likelihood of launching an accurate torpedo salvo, since the ocean liners changed course at least once every eight minutes. The *Queens* turned so frequently that it looked as if they were negotiating an invisible obstacle course.

At first, the zigzagging drove the 29ers mad. Sharp course changes at twenty-eight knots heeled the ships over, slid dishes off tables, and tumbled men out of their cots. But the men soon stopped complaining. The reason for caution was clear: they carried 15,000 soldiers apiece—so many more than the *Queens*' usual passenger capacity, in fact, that meals had to be served in three shifts.

If someone fell overboard, he would be out of luck. The 29ers were told to wear their life preservers at all times, but the risk was too great to have allowed a stop in the middle of U-boat-infested waters to mount a rescue operation. A single torpedo from one of these predators could send the ships—and most of the 29th Division—to the bottom in a matter of minutes. Furthermore, everyone was warned not to throw anything overboard, since the crafty U-boat captains might be able to determine the *Queen*s' route by a mere scrap of a 29er's garbage. At night, the ships maintained strict blackouts. The men were not even permitted to light cigarettes on deck.

The 29ers got their first tastes of British life on the *Queen*s. The 29ers hated English food, and even aboard the *Queen*s, no one expected the trip overseas to be luxurious. The Yanks examined the strange British currency with interest. The differences among pence, shillings, crowns, and pounds were difficult for the Yanks to understand. Difficult, that is, until a few impromptu poker games and craps shoots broke out.

Once, on the *Queen Elizabeth*, a first sergeant in the 175th Infantry grabbed his captain's arm and urged him to come and look at something on the bridge. When the two men got there, the captain's mouth dropped open. There, standing at the wheel, steering this great ocean liner, was a twelve-year-old boy. Too short to see out the window, he stood on a crate. Some Cunard officers, seeing the consternation in the Americans' faces, came over to calm them down. It was common practice in the British merchant service, they said, for young apprentice seamen to learn their profession by actual practice. The captain and his sergeant, only partly mollified, departed the bridge shaking their heads.

On October 2, when *Queen Mary* was some 160 miles from her destination, she was met off the northern Irish coast by a Royal Navy flotilla. The flotilla consisted of six destroyers and a single cruiser, HMS *Curacao*. Each of the destroyers took up station two or three miles distant from *Mary*, forming an anti-submarine screen around the liner. *Curacao* was supposed to provide protection against enemy air attacks, so she assumed a position as close as possible to *Mary*. It was a beautiful autumn day with calm seas and perfect visibility. The 29ers watched the British warships with interest, for they were the first signs of life beyond *Mary* the men had seen for six days. They took particular interest in the sleek *Curacao*, which dashed from one side of *Mary* to another like an undisciplined puppy hovering around its new master.

Maneuvers in close proximity to a giant ocean-liner were tricky even under the best conditions. When both the liner and its escorts were zigzagging violently, these maneuvers were downright dangerous. Around noon, *Curacao* unexpectedly crossed *Mary*'s bow and the two ships missed each other by only a few hundred yards. Some 29ers even began to take bets on whether the two ships would collide.

They didn't have to wait very long. At 2:10 P.M., the senior officer on the bridge of *Queen Mary* noticed that *Curacao*, only 400 yards off the *Mary*'s starboard bow, was converging on the liner's course. He turned *Mary* slightly to port, but he noticed to his horror that the cruiser was also turning to port, seemingly intending to cross the liner's path. Immediately, *Mary* turned to port as sharply as she could, but it was too late. *Mary* slammed directly into the port side of *Curacao* and cut her into two pieces. In a matter of minutes, both sections of the cruiser went down amid a giant pall of dense black smoke. The *Queen Mary*, under strict orders not to stop for any reason, sailed on. Ultimately, only ninety-seven sailors were rescued by the destroyers, while over 300 were lost. Disaster had struck in spite of, and partly because of, *Mary*'s precautions.

The witnesses were shaken. The worst part was simply sailing away and watching the cruiser go down. Several 29ers flung life preservers overboard, but the effort was futile. Ironically, most 29ers, who were below decks at the time, had no idea that anything unusual had happened. It was a strange way to be introduced to the realities of war. Although the 29ers had not even seen a German, they had already learned a lesson: their lives would be cheap in the next several years.

The *Queen Mary*'s captain called all 29th Division officers to the main lounge and came right to the point. The officers and their men were not to mention a word of this incident to anyone for the rest of the war. The *Queen*s were so important to the Allied war effort that the Germans could not be permitted to learn even the most trivial details of their operations.

The *Queen*s headed for Greenock, a small port twenty miles down the River Clyde from the Scottish city of Glasgow. *Mary*, showing some slight bow damage from the collision the previous day, arrived on October 3; *Elizabeth* anchored on October 11. The 29ers came ashore carrying full equipment, including enormous cylindrical barracks bags that were packed so tightly they looked as if they would burst. Expecting cold and damp weather, the 29ers wore their long woolen overcoats. Their new "coal scuttle" helmets had a slight resemblance to the German model and surprised the civilians, making some of them think the Nazis had arrived.

The men formed up on the quay. Then, to the strains of "Over There," they marched off to the railroad station, bags perched on their shoulders, looking like battalions of humpbacks. No one below the rank of colonel knew where the division was going.

2. CULTURE SHOCK

The 29ers spent most of their first day in Britain on trains. On the long ride south to their new cantonments, the 29ers gazed out the windows at the lush countryside, the immaculate train stations, the neat British homes. The 29th Division would take over Tidworth Barracks, an old cavalry camp in Wiltshire, only ten miles from the ancient monoliths of Stonehenge on Salisbury Plain. Tidworth had permanent, albeit spartan barracks, but it lacked enough room for the whole division, since troops from the 1st Infantry Division still occupied parts of the post. The 1st Division, however, was soon to depart for the invasion of North Africa, scheduled for November 8. The 29th Division units that could not fit into Tidworth were quartered in cities and towns throughout Oxfordshire.

By early November, enough space had opened at Tidworth to squeeze the entire 29th Division into camp. Finally, an intense training schedule began. For a while, tactics and weapons practice took second place to physical conditioning. One reporter who followed the 29th Division for the Baltimore *News-Post* watched the 29ers at Tidworth. "Everyone seems to be in a furious hurry," he wrote. "A group of men will start walking, for instance, from a howitzer to the mess hall, and suddenly, when about halfway, they all break into a trot. Almost everywhere they go, they walk part of the way and then start running. It isn't youthful enthusiasm or haste to finish—it's orders." The 29ers also made weekly route marches over the beautiful English countryside.

Sometimes units pulled out of Tidworth for a week or two of special exercises. The artillery frequently traveled to the Okehampton firing range in Devon where the cannoneers practiced with their new 105mm howitzers. Some units also went down to the southern English coast to participate in coastal defense exercises. With the heavy fighting on the Eastern Front and in North Africa, everyone realized that there was little chance of a Nazi invasion of Britain. Nevertheless, the coast still had to be defended. But there were so few troops stationed in England in 1942 that the 29ers joked that Britain's defense consisted of "us and the Home Guard."

Despite food shortages in Britain, the 29ers ate well. US Army rations, which the British found wildly extravagant, were supplemented by fresh vegetables from British gardens. After a while, the 29ers joked that if they saw any more Brussels sprouts, they'd go on a hunger strike. Sometimes a soldier would trade his cigarettes, chocolate, or soap to a local farmer for an egg—a very rare item. After proudly showing the egg to his buddies, the 29er would go off by himself to soft-boil it in his mess tin.

Occasionally the 29ers did double-duty as farmhands. The previous spring, a British regiment stationed at Tidworth had planted thousands of potatoes, but the unit was called away to North Africa before the crop could be harvested. Before it got too cold, the 29ers got down on their hands and knees in the fields and dug the potatoes out. For a while, at least, French fries took the place of Brussels sprouts.

Getting used to the new surroundings took a long time. At first the British seemed cold, perhaps frightened of the Yanks. Then, as incidental contacts at pubs and markets became more frequent, the British and Americans slowly warmed to each other. The local people were surprised to discover that most 29ers were not uncouth men who spat tobacco juice in public. The Yanks were equally surprised to learn that most of the English were not arrogant snobs.

The American soldiers and the local residents laughed about their wildly different pronunciations of the same words. The British were always amused at the American way of saying the word "lieutenant:" The Yanks said "lootenant" whereas the British said "lef-tenant." The British were baffled by differences among the Virginians' drawl, the harsh urban accent of the Baltimoreans, and the Yankee twang of the New Englanders.

British beer was warm and flat. One Baltimorean said that drinking it was "like talking to yourself." Driving on the left-hand side of the road—the "wrong" side, as the Yanks would say—was baffling enough. But rural road signs had been removed by government order to hinder German invaders, and the 29ers were forever getting lost on the labyrinthine country lanes. To make matters worse, when the Yanks asked for directions, several farmers thought they might be German spies and volunteered no information.

At Christmas, the 29th Division won the hearts of the local children. All the divisional units sponsored parties in nearby villages for the school kids, and the Yanks contributed extra rations, candy, and gifts. American musicians entertained the children with sing-alongs to Christmas carols and popular folk songs. At the 110th Field Artillery's party in the village of Adderbury, the kids laughed and cheered when a sergeant dressed up as Father Christmas, the British version of Santa Claus, distributed presents to all of the children, calling them by name as he did so.

Then there was the weather, which was much worse than the 29ers had expected. After a few weeks of English autumn, the 29ers were depressed by the daily gray overcast and continual drizzle. "England's language cannot adequately portray England's weather," one 29er lamented. "It must be lived in to be appreciated. Not that I mean to advocate such a course, God forbid. . . . Week in, week out, it was all the same. Clouds, fog, rain, perhaps a few minutes of sunshine in a few days."

On their weekly marches, the men cursed the sodden ground that kept their boots interminably wet. Most men promptly got footsores from wet shoes. Fortunately, the old-timers in the division had a cure: always use two pairs of socks and plenty of foot powder, they said, and after the march, soak the feet in hot water.

Whole outfits of 29ers would sometimes receive thirty-six-hour passes. Most men set out for London, where they spent the day sightseeing, then bedded down for the night at the American Red Cross. Others decided to spend their off-duty time near camp, traveling to Stonehenge and local castles and manor houses. A few men passed the time visiting their new English girlfriends.

But the novelty of England was quickly wearing off. By February 1943, after four months of dreary weather and rigorous training, the 29ers were homesick. A Baltimore newspaper, the *News-Post*, had prepared for just such an eventuality. After the 29th Division had gone overseas, the paper sponsored a film to be shipped over to Britain for the amusement of the 175th Infantry, a Baltimore outfit. The newsreel showed clips of Baltimore sights, such as the Battle Monument, Lexington Market, Pimlico horseraces, Mount Vernon Square.

When the "Dandy Fifth" saw the film at Tidworth, the men went wild. After four months in a strange place, it felt good to see familiar sights again. The G.I.'s chatted excitedly during the film and roared with laughter at some of the strange things the Baltimoreans were doing in the name of patriotism—like the "Miss Victory" beauty pageant.

But the audience suddenly fell silent. There on the screen were the troops' families, smiling and waving enthusiastically at the camera. The 29ers stared intently, looking for familiar faces. It was a home movie for a family of thousands. Dozens of pretty young women held up gurgling babies, who looked bored by the goings-on. Elderly gentlemen and ladies stared self-consciously at the camera, smiling sheepishly. The 29ers who could recognize their families—and some who couldn't—came away from the film with tears in their eyes.

The 29ers cheered up when spring came. The men were finally getting used to training. Furthermore, the hikes and tactical exercises were less of a strain as the weather improved. The troops had also become fond of the little English villages near Tidworth.

The 29ers wondered whether the division would soon be shipped to North Africa. By the spring of 1943, the Tunisian campaign had swallowed up several American divisions, and many more—including some National Guard outfits—were on the way to that theater directly from the United States. The 29th was still the only American infantry division in England, and it did not appear likely that it would see any action in northwest Europe in the near future.

The 29ers were puzzled about their role in World War II. The army, however, had big plans for the Blue and Gray Division and wanted it to stay exactly where it was. Since the entry of the United States into the war, high-ranking American generals had been vigorously demanding a massive Allied military build-up in Britain—code-named Operation "Bolero"—and a subsequent cross-channel assault against German-occupied France. The British had agreed to Bolero in principle in 1942, but Churchill's insistence upon an aggressive Mediterranean strategy consumed the bulk of American forces that were originally slated for shipment to Britain. Moreover, the US Navy's attention was firmly fixed on the Pacific. American admirals argued against any plan that would rob the fleet of the landing craft and warships needed in a Pacific offensive against the Japanese.

Bolero was postponed from 1942 to 1943, and then, when it appeared that the Allies had a good chance of knocking Italy out of the war, from 1943 to 1944. To the British, fighting the Germans in France was not a cheery prospect. The Americans, however, who based their blunt philosophy of war on the experiences of Grant and Sherman in the Civil War, insisted that a direct attack upon the enemy's strongest forces was the only way the war could be brought to a speedy conclusion.

By 1944 the Yanks were no longer swayed by Churchill's eloquent arguments about the "soft underbelly" of Europe. To rekindle Bolero, the Americans prepared to ship nine US Army divisions to Britain between August 1943 and the end of the year, and an additional nine between the beginning of 1944 and the invasion of France. The 29th Division would no longer be alone.

To make more room for the influx of American troops, the division moved out of Tidworth in May 1943 and was assigned to scattered cantonments in Cornwall and Devon, England's two westernmost counties. The 29ers were intrigued by their new homes. The weather, especially along the southern coast, was the most moderate in Britain, a vast improvement over the abominable weather the 29ers had experienced at Tidworth. The troops were amazed to find palm trees and sub-tropical plants in the coastal villages.

Unfortunately, the 29ers had to earn the respect of the local people all over again. Having been in England for seven months already, however, the Yanks were at least no longer suffering from culture shock. After a few weeks, the men became as fond of the Cornishmen and Devonians as they had been of the Wiltshire natives.

Several kinks had to be worked out between the US and British armies. When the 110th Field Artillery arrived in Cornwall, it took over the Duke of Cornwall's Light Infantry Barracks, an old British army post in the quaint town of Bodmin, twenty-five miles west of Plymouth. No British troops remained in the barracks except the regimental bandsmen, who kindly offered to play for the 110th's parades. Several days later, the 110th formed up for a battalion review, and the cannoneers stepped off smartly as the band enthusiastically broke into a lively march. But something was wrong. The G.I.'s were completely out of step. Puzzled, Lieutenant Colonel Cooper later went to see the elderly bandmaster, who quickly identified the problem. His musicians were playing at the proper British army cadence, but this cadence was several steps per minute faster than the official American beat. The bandmaster apologized profusely and said it would never happen again. From that moment on, the band played at the American cadence and the cannoneers marched in perfect step.

The 29ers hated maneuvers on the moors. There was not a sign of human life in the ghostly hills of Dartmoor or Bodmin Moor, and the wind blew so incessantly that trees could not survive. It rained almost 100 inches a year on Dartmoor, as opposed to only about thirty inches in the nearby city of Plymouth. Had it not been for maneuvers, the 29ers would have remembered only

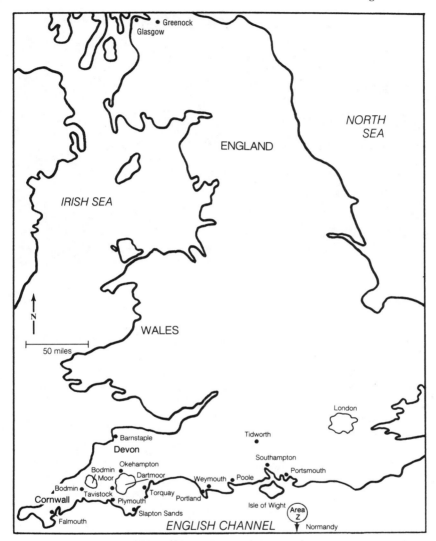

29th Division in Britain, 1942–44.

the moors' rugged beauty: the grotesque granite rock formations, the stubby wild ponies, the pink foxglove wildflowers. But whenever the Yanks went into the moors on an exercise, they came back soaked, muddy, and miserable. Said one artilleryman, "One thing we could be sure of: it was good training for combat, for if a man could come through these spells on the moors, nothing nature could devise could have any effect on his health or morale."

The 115th Infantry on Dartmoor, sometime in 1943. *Courtesy Cooper Armory.*

3. GERHARDT

The 29th Division was getting a new commanding general, and the 29ers were apprehensive. Their old commander, General Gerow, was well liked by the 29ers, but he had been promoted to the command of V Corps. The new man, Maj. Gen. Charles Hunter Gerhardt, was scheduled to arrive by airplane directly from the United States in late July 1943.

The rumors about Gerhardt were not good. When the 29ers learned that he was a West Pointer, an old cavalryman and avid polo player, and—worst of all—a disciplinarian of the old school, they expected trouble. The new man would likely be an old-fashioned army traditionalist who held the National Guard in contempt. The whole division braced itself for his arrival.

Gerhardt was commanding the newly raised 91st Division at Camp White, Oregon—6,000 miles from Cornwall—when he received his new orders from the War Department. He had not been overseas during the war and knew little of his new command, but a high-ranking staff officer familiar with the 29th gave him three hints about his new job: first, he would have to conduct vigorous amphibious training since the 29th Division would likely be involved in the upcoming invasion of Europe; second, he must be tactful with the influential Lady Astor, a Virginia woman who had married an English aristocrat, moved to Plymouth, and become the first female member of Parliament; third, the 29th was a National Guard division, and discipline would be lax. Gerhardt certainly knew what to do about that.

The 29ers were prepared for a flamboyant character, and they were not disappointed. In their first encounters with the new general, who took over the division on July 22, the men could tell that Gerhardt took his soldierly appearance very seriously. With his shiny cavalry boots, polished leather holster and belts, and decorative neckerchief, he was every inch a general.

Gerhardt was a short man with a slight build—the perfect cavalryman. He didn't like people to get too close to him. "That's far enough! That's far enough!" he would sputter, raising his hand in warning as an aide approached. He was nearly bald, but the men rarely saw him without his helmet. The chin strap, of course, was always properly hooked underneath his lower lip, as per official regulations.

Gerhardt found it difficult to sit still. Paperwork was not to his liking; he wanted to be out in the field by 10:00 A.M. to watch his units train. When in command of the 91st Division, he rode by himself around camp on horseback, shirtless, watching every move his men made. He was not talkative, but when he had something to say, the words came out rapidly, in short bursts, like sputtering machine gun fire. "He was full of the devil and pranced about," an observer noted.

Gerhardt had been destined to be a soldier. His father was a career officer who served in both the Spanish-American War and World War I. One of young Charlie's earliest memories was of his father's happy return from military service in Cuba to the family's Virginia Beach home in 1902. As the Gerhardt family moved from post to post, the youngster was captivated by army traditions and strove to follow in his father's footsteps. In June 1913, just after his eighteenth birthday, he obtained an appointment to the US Military Academy at West Point as a member of the class of 1917. Graduating only two months after the American entry into World War I, the fresh second lieutenant was promptly shipped overseas, where he served as an aide to the commanding general of the 89th Division.

The army was a dead-end career in the inter-war years. Young officers like Gerhardt realized that they might serve fifteen years at one rank before promotion. Gerhardt shifted from one remote army post to another in the 1920s and 30s, serving stints as a staff officer, instructor, and cavalry squadron commander. Such a career was typical between the wars, and many officers were convinced that it would lead nowhere. To get to the top, an officer had to be utterly dedicated to his military career—and that is precisely what Gerhardt was. He realized that an army officer could leap from anonymity to fame almost overnight. That was what happened after the Japanese attacked Pearl Harbor when Gerhardt found himself in command of a 15,000-man infantry division.

Gerhardt was an astute observer of his soldiers' morale. When he took over the 29th Division, he deduced that the men were well trained and in good

Maj. Gen. Charles H. Gerhardt in 1943, when he commanded the 91st Infantry Division in Oregon. *Courtesy National Archives.*

physical condition, but that they were not as high-spirited as he wished. The reason for this was clear. "When Gerhardt arrived, he learned of the old seven-day training week, the tiny percentage of men who had been granted furloughs, and all the old 'drive, drive, drive, criticize forever, squeeze every minute out of a man's day' attitude that had driven many men to a 'hell with it all' attitude," Lieutenant Colonel Cooper recalled. "But one of the first things Gerhardt did was order a three-day rest for the whole Division. This was a wonderful boost to the troops' morale."

The general had a simple philosophy: a division's combat efficiency reflected the skills of its senior officers. Soon after assuming command of the division, Gerhardt traveled from camp to camp asking lieutenants and captains how they felt about their senior officers. This was an extraordinarily unusual approach for a general. According to Gerhardt, however, training troops thoroughly was simple enough; the real difficulty lay in finding good battalion and regimental COs to lead the men in battle. "This war is won at battalion level," he insisted.

He drove home his point one day at a special assembly of senior officers at division headquarters in Tavistock, a small town ten miles north of Plymouth. The meeting convened in a courtroom of the Tavistock Court House.

Fifteen battalion COs, all lieutenant colonels and majors, filed into the jury dock and took their seats with expressions of misgiving. The three regimental COs, all full colonels, and the divisional artillery chief, a brigadier general, sat at a nearby table, looking equally apprehensive. Meanwhle, Gerhardt, carrying an M1 rifle, paced in front of the judge's bench.

Suddenly he banged the rifle on a table. Turning to the nervous officers, he screamed, "A year from today, one out of every three of you will be dead, and the toll will be higher if senior commanders don't know their stuff and don't get out of their chairs and don't stop harassing their people over the phone!"

Gerhardt ordered each of the three regimental COs and the artillery chief to take a turn on the witness stand for some "cross-examination." As soon as each officer reached the stand, the general fired a steady stream of questions: "Tell me how you would give an infantry squad the order to deploy and commence firing." "Give me the basics of the M1 rifle." "How many yards between each man in a march column?" "How many machine guns in the weapons platoon?"

The officers knew who was boss when the meeting was over. At the same time, Gerhardt knew whom he could trust and whom he would have to keep an eye on. Of the four men who took the stand, only General Sands—the artillery chief—emerged untarnished. His answers to Gerhardt's questions were all perfect. The others, according to a witness, "turned purple and stammered a lot." When the cross-examination was over, Gerhardt shouted, "How in hell can you lead your men if you don't know what a private should know—and I don't want to ever hear you jumping on battalion COs for not being in their offices. They should be out training people. Meeting dismissed!"

Several battalion COs present at the meeting tried to hide their shock, and they wondered whether Gerhardt was crazy. Others thought they had a friend in the new general. Said one battalion CO, "I knew in my heart that if we tried our damndest, he would be our friend—and he always was in many, many ways."

Gerhardt wanted every man in the division to fear him. Only two weeks after his arrival, he had already succeeded. He had a habit of sneaking up on the troops when they least expected it, and if he found something amiss in their dress or demeanor, there was hell to pay. The buckled helmet chin strap was Gerhardt's cause célèbre; almost every 29er got a dressing-down from the general at one time or another for leaving his chin strap dangling. And these were no casual scoldings. Like an angry drill sergeant, Gerhardt would strut up close to the offender and bark in his face, "Get that goddamned chin strap hooked *now*, soldier!"

He was a stickler for neatness. The men had to shave every day, their uniforms had to be perfect, barracks rooms had to be spotless, and above all, jeeps had to be clean. When Gerhardt spotted a dirty jeep—it didn't matter whose—there would be big trouble. Once Cooper had his outfit on an invasion exercise on the north coast of Devon. The colonel's jeep, which had been driven up and down the dunes all day, was coated with wet sand and mud. Out of nowhere came General Gerhardt.

"Colonel, that jeep is a goddamned disgrace!" screamed the General.

"Yes, sir," replied Cooper.

"Well, clean it up now!"

"General, how am I going to clean it up here on the beach with no fresh water?"

"I don't care how you do it, Colonel, just get it done and report back to me in an hour."

Gerhardt had his own jeep, of course, which he named *Vixen Tor* after a hill on Dartmoor. The general told his driver, Sgt. Bob Cuff, that the jeep had better be kept clean because it was the model for all other jeeps in the division. This was a difficult task, and poor Cuff recalled that he sometimes washed *Vixen Tor* five times a day.

Major generals in command of divisions were allowed to be dictators, and no one could do anything about it. Gerhardt took pleasure in his absolute power. "Gerhardt was a powerful personality, and he stamped it on the division and made it a highly individualistic outfit," recalled Cooper. "He placed his mark upon it so strongly that to understand the division and its spirit, one has to understand Gerhardt."

When Gerhardt wanted a job done, he expected it to be completed, no questions asked. And if the task were difficult—or even impossible—so much the better, because the general liked to test his men's ingenuity to see how they would perform in an emergency.

One night, Gerhardt announced to his aide, Lt. Bob Wallis, that waffles would be nice for breakfast the next morning. Then he turned on his heels and left. Waffles were unheard of in England, and where was Wallis going to get a waffle iron? Wallis and the cooks feverishly put their minds to the problem and came up with an idea. While the cooks prepared the batter, Wallis searched for a piece of wire gauze that could mimic the checker-board mold of a waffle iron. The final product, although not perfect, at least resembled a waffle. The general was delighted with his breakfast. "Mighty fine, Wallis, mighty fine," he declared. The 29ers always knew he was pleased when he said, "mighty fine."

Discipline was part of the general's master-plan. Good morale was another. Gerhardt was obviously a firm believer in Napoleon's famous dictum that in war morale is three times more important than strength. He wanted his men to think not only that they were better than the Germans, but also that

Sgt. Robert Cuff, General Gerhardt's driver. *Courtesy Robert Cuff.*

they were superior to any other troops in the entire US Army. With these objectives in mind, the general gave the division its battle-cry: "Twenty-nine, Let's Go!" He demanded that the troops use the slogan in battle drill, on all official correspondence, and on all divisional signposts. The 29ers were somewhat skeptical at first, but, as always, General Gerhardt didn't seem to care.

The general was proud of his men, or at least what he had turned his men into. Sometimes, however, the 29ers' discipline lapsed in public. One day, Gerhardt was playing golf with a retired British army officer. As the Englishman stepped forward to tee off, he complimented the general on the impressive appearance and soldierly behavior of the 29ers. Gerhardt beamed. But just as Gerhardt's partner began his backswing, several truckloads of 29ers passed on a nearby road. Everyone in the trucks screamed "Fore!" at the top of their lungs and roared with laughter as the Englishman almost toppled from surprise. Even Gerhardt chuckled.

During Gerhardt's obligatory visits to Lord and Lady Astor's home in Plymouth, he charmed Lady Astor by bringing her vegetables and fresh meat, which were extremely hard to come by in English homes. During dinner, Lady Astor chatted about her younger days in Virginia, and the general filled her in on how things had changed since she had left. In the lilting tones of an authentic Cornish dialect, Lady Astor sometimes entertained the guests with local jokes, much to Gerhardt's amusement. The general even rewarded Lady

Astor for her participation in a division talent show by presenting her with a white pig—an allusion to one of her jokes—painted on both sides with the divisional blue and gray symbol. Gerhardt appointed Lady Astor an honorary private and later promoted her to sergeant and eventually to second lieutenant.

After a few months of Gerhardt—whom the men now called "Uncle Charlie"—the men were hardened to their upcoming tasks in the war. But the toughening process was not easy, and some men who could not adapt to the new general found themselves in different outfits. The general's driver, Sergeant Cuff, secretly considered asking for a transfer at first. But, thinking better of it, he decided to do things Gerhardt's way. Later, Cuff was glad he did. The things he experienced in combat, he said, would have driven him mad if he hadn't come around to Gerhardt's way of thinking.

Many 29ers agreed with Cuff, and most even came to admire Gerhardt for the pride the general had instilled in the division. The enlisted men also realized that Uncle Charlie was far tougher on his majors and colonels than he was on the privates.

The general visited the men frequently, even in combat. Almost every 29er came to have a Gerhardt story, and most of these anecdotes cast the general in a favorable light. A sergeant at division headquarters recalled picking up a snowball and hurling it at one of his friends who was standing nearby. Unfortunately, Generals Gerhardt and Sands were directly in the line of fire. The snowball missed its intended target and smacked Uncle Charlie squarely in the chest. The sergeant expected his career in the 29th Division to be over, but Gerhardt simply stared at the G.I. for a moment, then said, "That's a helluva pitching arm you've got there, soldier."

A man was either a close friend or an untrusted enemy to Gerhardt; there were no feelings in between. He watched over his friends, but he made his enemies' lives hell. Many 29ers, particularly officers, despised him for it. Maj. Glover Johns, who began his career in the 29th Division as a liaison officer on the division staff, held Gerhardt in high esteem, but he admitted that the general was "a gutty, pushy, arrogant little bastard . . . with a Napoleonic complex" who was "admired and respected by many (including myself); hated by probably a greater number."

Among enlisted men, there was no such thing, in Gerhardt's view, as a guardsman or a draftee. If a man was in the 29th Division, he was simply an American soldier, and Gerhardt didn't care how he got there. The essence of the war to Gerhardt was to instill the spirit and traditions of the old Regular Army in citizen-soldiers. Only in this way, Gerhardt believed, would America win the war. There was no better person for this job than Gerhardt, the very model of an Old Army soldier. When the war was over, the men could go back to their jobs and families, and the general could go back to playing polo. But until that time came, the general was . . . well, the general.

4. TRAINING

The Cornishmen must have thought the 29ers were barmy. Sometimes, when a 29th Division jeep was winding along a lonely road through the moors, its passengers suddenly drew their Colt .45's and blazed away at a boulder or a fence-post. The Yanks especially liked to show off their marksmanship when a British automobile approached from the opposite direction. Recalled Cooper, "Probably many Cornishmen and Devonians thought that real American cowboys had arrived at last."

Once in a while the 29ers let fly with a hand grenade at a rabbit or some other wild animal. Some locals even said the Yanks were dropping grenades onto the moors from their Piper Cub airplanes as if they were practicing to be air force bombardiers.

Actually, this bizarre behavior was all part of the new spirit of aggressiveness that General Gerhardt had infused into the division. The general had a simple military tenet about tactics. "Shoot like the mischief," he liked to say. "Stir 'em up. Let 'em hear you coming. Scare the living hell out of them."

Gerhardt was appalled by army rules that restricted his men to weapons practice only on carefully supervised firing ranges. He wanted the 29ers to get used to using their guns boldly. So when the men were out on their own on the lonely moors, Gerhardt encouraged them to practice free shooting with pistols and carbines. When he was out in the countryside in *Vixen Tor*, the general was one of the most enthusiastic practitioners of this habit. In fact, it was Uncle Charlie himself who flew over the moors in a Piper Cub, dropping hand grenades out of the window onto the bogs, howling with delight.

The 29ers found it difficult to maintain their spirits at a fever-pitch when they knew they wouldn't see action for a long time. But Gerhardt didn't care; there was always something new to learn, he figured, and there was always a way of getting better at what the men already knew. Soon after Uncle Charlie's arrival, the training routine began to change.

The 29ers learned to climb up cargo nets hung from thirty-foot walls; they embarked onto Royal Navy barges and stormed ashore on a Cornish beach; they were taught how to waterproof their vehicles; they received thousands of "Mae West" life preservers; and they learned how to swim.

Mandatory swimming instruction began for all members of the division shortly after Gerhardt's arrival. The men, however, did not enjoy jumping into freezing Cornish streams and ponds, and the frequent rains made the lessons even more uncomfortable.

Gerhardt was adamant about the swimming lessons. One brisk and rainy autumn day, the general came across Lt. Col. Cooper's 110th Field Artillery Battalion splashing across a local mill pond near Bodmin. Uncle Charlie beamed as he leaped out of *Vixen Tor*.

"Goddammit, Cooper, I want to tell you, it's wonderful! Wonderful!" the general said, reaching out to shake Cooper's hand.

"What's so wonderful, General?" said Cooper, shivering.

"Well, the training schedule said you were supposed to swim today, and you're swimming! That infantry battalion you're bivouacked with is back there in the mess hall having a map reading exercise because it's drizzling! I gave them hell. Mighty fine, Cooper, mighty fine!"

An officer in the 110th eventually found a heated indoor pool in the beautiful resort town of Torquay, twenty-five miles east of Plymouth. Instead of swimming in the local ponds near Bodmin, detachments from the battalion shuttled back and forth to the luxurious pool, and overnight, swimming instruction was transformed from the most despised training exercise in the division to the most desirable.

In July 1943, there was a new rumor that the division would start amphibious assault exercises soon. Some of the division's new training regimens made it obvious to the men that this rumor was true. In April 1943, the British government had provided the US Army with a short stretch of beach along the north coast of Devon near the villages of Braunton and Barnstaple. This beach soon became the United States Army Assault Training Center. American techniques of amphibious warfare, which would be put into practice on the beaches of Normandy the following summer, were established here.

In September 1943, the 29th Division was selected as the first outfit to undergo amphibious training at the assault center. The practice site could accommodate only one regiment, however. Therefore, Gerhardt rotated his three regiments: first, the 116th; then the 175th; and finally, the 115th. The 116th returned in 1944 for a refresher course. Each infantry regiment was accompanied to the assault center by an artillery battalion as well as by engineers and medical personnel. The course lasted three weeks, during which the men rehearsed landings from the navy's new assault boats, such as the LCT (Landing Craft, Tank) and the LCI (Landing Craft, Infantry). The 29ers also perfected their small unit tactics and practiced on new weapons such as flamethrowers, bazookas, and bangalore torpedoes.

The invasion exercises were a welcome respite from the daily training drudgery. But as soon as each regimental team returned from the assault center to its permanent encampments, the men trudged once again to the desolate moors for more wargames. Gerhardt was a firm believer in realistic training. He wanted his 29ers to get used to the sights and sounds of battle so they could learn to overcome panic when they were under fire.

In the summer of 1943, a new man had been assigned to the 29th Division who would prove to be the perfect supervisor of such training. He was Brig. Gen. Norman Cota, and he was the 29th Division's new assistant commander. This position, only recently established in the army, stemmed from the need for a high-ranking officer who could be the division's unofficial chief of infantry. Previously, the second-in-command had been the artillery chief who, of course, did not specialize in infantry tactics.

Cota was the former chief of staff of the 1st Infantry Division during the North African campaign, but it was difficult to imagine a more unlikely staff officer. A man who liked to lead troops in the field, Cota was a natural for the new assistant commander post. His interpretation of this job, in fact, was to spend as much time away from division headquarters as possible. For most of a typical training day, he was on the moors with the 29ers, giving personal instruction in tactics to units as small as twelve-man squads. The 29th Division was an appropriate home for Cota, for he was also an expert in amphibious assault techniques. Prior to his arrival at the 29th, Cota had served a stint in Lord Louis Mountbatten's Combined Operations Headquarters, a command whose primary function was to study the principles of seaborne invasion.

Cota's fearlessness inspired confidence. With an unlit cigar clenched between his teeth and an old-fashioned walking stick in his hand, Cota led the men in practice charges across the soggy heaths, only fifty yards behind a crashing artillery barrage. This was the best way, Cota thought, to get the men used to the deafening sounds of battle and to give them faith in their artillery. The 29ers were apprehensive about this exercise at first, but they figured if the old man with the walking stick could do it, they would be all right.

The 29ers were inspired by Cota's sangfroid and intrigued by his odd habits. The men would watch in amazement as "Dutch"—a nickname of unknown origin—wandered through the training camps, seemingly lost in another world, singing nonsensical ditties to himself. One of his favorites went, "If I knew the answer to this, what a hell of a smart guy I'd be."

In private, Cota was quiet and affable, but when he led the men in training—and later in battle—he acted the crusty old squad leader, and the 29ers loved it. He patted the troops on the back when they did well, but he rarely lost his temper when they didn't. When Gerhardt and Cota conferred, they made an odd pair: the short and dapper Uncle Charlie paced back and forth nervously, crisply barking out orders, while Cota—tall, stocky, and carelessly dressed—stood and listened impassively. Gerhardt and Cota got along famously. Cota was the only man in the division allowed to leave his chin strap unhooked.

Both Cota and Gerhardt were slowly turning the 29ers into better soldiers, Cota through inspiration and Gerhardt through fear. The men were taught to take initiative in battle and to expect the unexpected. Several high-spirited 29ers, however, got carried away. One night a patrol on a practice mission from Battery A, 110th Field Artillery, sneaked into division head-quarters in a manor house just outside of Tavistock. The raiders got into Uncle Charlie's office, made off with all his desk paraphernalia and the division safe, and drove away in a stolen truck. Gerhardt loved this kind of spirit, although he wished the men had directed it against someone else.

Anyone who couldn't meet the rigorous training standards was trans-ferred unceremoniously out of the division. Some companies in fact lost al-most fifty percent of their men during the division's training period in Eng-land. Those who were transferred had mixed emotions. Some were happy to be free of the harsh life on the moors and were relieved to end up in a rear-echelon supply unit. Others who felt a strong bond with the men in their outfits were humiliated by the transfer and felt they had let their friends down. Generally, the men who survived training were those who had a strong incen-tive to make a strenuous effort to stay where they felt at home. Gerhardt wanted all 29ers to feel precisely this way.

Gerhardt may not have cared that most of his enlisted men were guards-men or draftees, but he made a sharp distinction between Regular Army and National Guard or Reserve officers. Senior National Guard officers, in partic-ular, were fearful of being humiliated by Uncle Charlie. The old antagonisms between professional and amateur soldiers, which had been so pronounced before Pearl Harbor, were not quite dead. Many 29th Division guard and Reserve officers knew they were being carefully scrutinized by their com-manding general, and they felt they would have to work twice as hard as a West Pointer to prosper. Several officers believed that the only way to gain Gerhardt's respect was to become a tougher soldier than Uncle Charlie him-self.

Brig. Gen. William Sands, the gruff old artillery chief and third-in-command of the division, was one of these men. Sands, who had been a lawyer in civilian life, was the senior guard officer in the 29th Division. Fiercely self-confident, he was determined not to end up behind a desk in the States. In response to Gerhardt's harsh standards, Sands turned into a marti-net. "Sands was afraid of being busted and wanted absolute perfection from his troops," a subordinate recalled. Many of his artillerymen hated him for it.

The 110th Field Artillery once threw an elaborate party at a manor house outside Bodmin. The party was a great success. A divisional artillery staff officer who attended the festivities enthusiastically described the merriment to Sands the next morning. The staff officer chuckled when he related the grand entrance of the battalion's five battery commanders. Announced by a butler who rapped his staff loudly on the floor, each man was decked out in full-dress uniform with a bright red scarf—the artillery's traditional color—around his neck.

Sands exploded when he heard about the scarves. He got in his jeep and drove to the 110th's headquarters in Bodmin. He confronted the battalion CO, Lieutenant Colonel Cooper, and rebuked him harshly. Those scarves were not prescribed dress, he growled, and he never wanted the men to wear them. Cooper replied meekly that it wouldn't happen again.

Meanwhile, the men were still training on the moors every day, and they still hated every minute of it. One day, after another dreary trek into the Cornish hills, Capt. Maurice Clift, a company CO in the 115th Infantry, put his feelings into verse, mimicking the meter of John Masefield's famous poem ''Sea Fever.'' Clift called his poem ''To the Moors.''

> I want to go out to the moors again,
> To the fog and the rocks and rain,
> To the gorse and the marsh and muddy pools,
> Wherein the boys have lain.
>
> I want to go out to the moors again,
> To retrace each painful stride,
> To look again at the hills wherein,
> The sheep and rabbits hide.
>
> I want to go again to the moors,
> To follow their winding trails,
> To stand again on their lonely slopes,
> In the cold and the rain and the gales.
>
> Oh, I'll go out to the moors again,
> But mind you and mark me well:
> I'll carry enough explosives,
> To blow the place to hell.

As unpleasant as training was, the prevailing question in everyone's mind was how they would stand up to combat, both mentally and physically. By early 1944, the division had been in active service for three years, and almost none of the men had seen a shot fired in anger. Despite the realistic training, the 29ers knew that the real thing would be vastly different, and they wondered about their chances of survival.

Gloomy rumors about what the fighting would be like, gleaned from sketchy reports from the North African and Italian Fronts, spread among some troops. One particularly melancholy rumor got the attention of the 29th Division's junior officers. Platoon and company level leaders, the gossips said, wouldn't last long in combat.

When word got around that the division was beset by depressing chatter of this sort, the generals worried about the men's morale. Lt. Gen. Omar Bradley, the chief of United States ground forces in Britain, came to Cornwall and Devon in early 1944 to address the issue of these demoralizing rumors as frankly as possible. The laconic general traveled from town to town, speaking frankly to groups of 29th Division officers. Well, some lieutenants and captains *would* die, Bradley declared, but the best insurance against getting killed was for the officers to learn their jobs to the best of their abilities. The first platoon and company COs to be killed, Bradley warned, would be those who paid little attention to training.

During one set of maneuvers on Bodmin Moor, as a battalion of the 115th Infantry advanced close behind a friendly artillery barrage, a private was nicked in the throat by a tiny piece of shrapnel. When the boy touched his neck and then looked at the blood on his fingers, he fainted. Several weeks later, when the same men were in real combat, they looked back and chuckled over their innocence. Little scratches from flying metal proved to be common wounds in Normandy, and riflemen considered themselves lucky if these were the extent of their injuries.

The 29ers no longer felt that the division was a distant outpost of American civilization. By January 1944, almost one million American soldiers were in Britain—four times the number present when General Gerhardt had arrived in July 1943. Eleven American divisions in addition to the 29th were now deployed in English cantonments.

The 29th Division, of course, had been in England longer than any other American outfit, and by now, the 29ers felt right at home in Devon and Cornwall. Many men, in fact, romanced the local girls and ended up getting married, although an enlisted man first had to get his CO's permission to do so.

The 29ers had a favorite new song called "Roll Me Over." It was bawdy and easy to memorize, two characteristics that contributed to its vast popularity in the division. In part, it went:

> Roll me over,
> Yankee soldier.
> Roll me over,
> Lay me down,
> And do it again.
>
> Oh, this is number one
> And the fun has just begun.
> Roll me over,
> Lay me down,
> And do it again.

The verses went from "number one" to "number ten," and concluded:

Oh, this is number ten;
Let's start all over again.

The 29ers knew that they would not have to wait much longer for combat. So many Allied troops were crammed into Britain, the men figured, that the generals would have to use them soon. Actually, planning for the invasion of France, finally code-named "Overlord," had begun in June 1943, one year before the actual assault. General Gerow, commander of the American V Corps and former commander of the 29th, was informed of the plan in September, and Gerhardt was let in on the secret shortly thereafter. The first tentative Overlord plans were for an invasion of the Normandy coast in May 1944 by one American infantry division—presumably the 29th—and two British divisions. For the next eight months, however, most 29ers were ignorant of their role in the invasion.

Of course, the 29ers had strong hints about what they would do. The men continued to practice amphibious assaults on a far larger scale than those first experimental landings on the north coast of Devon in the fall of 1943. The largest amphibious maneuver, labeled "Operation Duck," took place in December 1943 and January 1944. The 1st Division, which had returned to England from the Mediterranean in November 1943, joined the 29th for this exercise, and both divisions stormed ashore on the south coast of Devon along a stretch of tidal flats called Slapton Sands. While destroyers and cruisers hammered simulated German pillboxes with live shells, the men slithered and crawled along the sands, blowing gaps in barbed wire and firing their rifles into the coastal dunes.

In April 1944, the division practiced again on Slapton Sands in an amphibious exercise called "Operation Fox." Later that month, Slapton Sands was the scene of an identical exercise for VII Corps troops. This time, however, nine German E-boats penetrated the assault convoys and sank two huge transports. Over 700 men from the 4th Division were killed, far more than that outfit would lose two months later on Utah Beach.

When high-ranking generals came calling, the 29ers got their strongest hint yet that a major operation was afoot. The 29ers were used to training in anonymity; for over a year after the division's arrival in Britain, few three or four-star generals paid attention to the Blue and Gray division. While the division trained endlessly, the men read in the newspapers about the exploits of Generals Eisenhower and Montgomery in North Africa and Sicily. For a while, the 29ers figured that they, too, would soon find themselves in the Mediterranean. But when those big-name generals were transferred to Britain and eventually came to Devon and Cornwall to scrutinize the 29ers on the moors, it was easy to figure out that the 29th Division would enter combat soon, probably in France.

In January 1944, General Montgomery traveled throughout Cornwall and Devon to visit all three 29th Division regiments. Although he was nervous at first, he quickly learned that American soldiers liked informality. Monty once caught up with a battalion of the 115th Infantry on a training exercise on Bodmin Moor. Wearing his famous black beret, Monty jumped up on the hood of his jeep and called for the Yanks to gather around him in an enormous semi-circle. In his high-pitched, nasal voice, he remarked that the 29ers looked ferocious in their full battle gear, but for this talk he wanted the men to take off their helmets. Monty joked that, with their helmets removed, the men didn't look quite so fierce anymore; he even noticed a few bald heads in the crowd. The 29ers laughed, but Monty got more serious when he lectured the troops on the importance of learning their jobs. The German soldier was good, he warned. But a well-trained Briton or American could be better.

"You couldn't help liking the man," said one 29th Division officer of Monty. Best of all, Monty was a proven winner. The 29ers found it comforting to be associated with a general who had thrashed Rommel in the North African desert. Monty liked the 29ers, too. He wrote a personal note to Gerhardt, complimenting him on the discipline and appearance of the men.

Gen. Dwight D. Eisenhower, Maj. Gen. Charles H. Gerhardt, and Air Marshal Sir Arthur W. Tedder observe a 29th Division review in England, early 1944. *Courtesy National Archives.*

General Eisenhower, who had been appointed the supreme commander of Overlord in December 1943, came to inspect the 29th Division in April 1944. During a visit to the 121st Engineer Battalion, Ike encountered a 29er manning a .50 caliber machine gun mounted in the back of a truck. The general questioned the soldier about the gun, and the G.I., to Ike's shock, professed complete ignorance about how it worked. After Eisenhower questioned the man further, the 29er finally had to admit, "I don't know how to shoot this gun, sir. I'm a medic. They just told me to get up here and stand behind this thing. So I'm doing it." Eisenhower beat a hasty retreat, trying not to laugh.

5. OPERATION OVERLORD

In early May 1944, some G.I.'s in the 115th Infantry noticed a little brick building in Bodmin. Though no bigger than a backyard shed, it was surrounded by a double row of barbed wire and guarded twenty-four hours a day by several heavily armed sentries. Only a handful of officers who displayed a mysterious identification card were permitted entry. This was altogether too much security for a nondescript building.

Only the "Bigots" knew, and they weren't saying anything. "Bigot" was the code-name for an officer who had been informed of the secret Allied plans for the invasion of France. Senior American generals and admirals had been let in on the secret as early as autumn of 1943, but 29th Division regimental and battalion COs were not told of the plan until the spring of 1944. When they received a copy of the Top Secret Overlord orders, each 29th Division regimental CO set up a secret headquarters, like the little brick building in Bodmin. Under no circumstances were the plans to leave the headquarters, and only those with Bigot identification cards would be permitted entry.

The 29th Division Bigots were hardly surprised to discover that their division was to be in the first wave of the invasion of France. Their target landing beach, code-named "Omaha," was on the Normandy coast ten miles east of the mouth of the Vire River. The 1st and the 29th Divisions, which together comprised the V Corps, would assault Omaha on D-Day, then scheduled for June 5. The 29th's 116th Infantry was to be attached temporarily to the 1st Division and would comprise half the first wave. The 16th Infantry of the 1st Division comprised the other half. The rest of the 1st and the 29th Divisions would land in later waves. At the same time, the 3rd Canadian and the 3rd and the 50th British Infantry Divisions would land to the east on Juno, Sword, and Gold Beaches, while the American 4th Infantry Division assaulted Utah Beach, fifteen miles northwest of Omaha.

The complexity of the invasion scheme encouraged the 29th Division Bigots, for it was obvious that the planners had put great effort into this operation. But the scheme would be worthless if the Germans found out about it, so the Overlord planners kept the number of Bigots to a minimum. Only one month before the invasion, in fact, only about 200 29ers knew where the division was headed. The vast majority of 29ers remained ignorant of their fate, even when the entire division was pulled out of its encampments without warning in mid-May and moved to special assembly areas on the coast near Plymouth and Falmouth.

Several G.I.'s wondered whether this was just another in a series of embarkation and landing exercises on Slapton Sands. This time, however, the 29ers noticed the "exercise" was being conducted differently than in the past. For one thing, there was an unusually strong emphasis on camouflage against air detection. Furthermore, the men were under strict orders not to leave their new marshalling areas, which were, in fact, sealed by thick coils of barbed wire and guarded by sentries twenty-four hours a day. Some stern-faced strangers, who were eventually found to be from the Counter Intelligence Corps, even patrolled the 29th Division enclosures and listened to what the men were saying to make sure no one was speaking indiscreetly. The 29ers didn't take long to figure out that this was no rehearsal.

The trip from the 29th Division cantonments to the coastal marshalling areas was unforgettable. It was the height of spring, and nature was resplendent. "Hedges that lined the narrow, winding roads were green and fragrant," wrote Lou Azrael, a reporter for the Baltimore *News-Post*. "Gorse splotched the broad and rolling moors with gold. From the tops of hills, irregular patches of farms spread in kin-folk shades of brown and green."

But hidden behind nature's beauty was an armed camp. MPs in sparkling white helmets gestured like robots at every crossroads, giving directions to the incessant stream of rumbling truck convoys and snapping smart salutes to passing officers. The 29ers peered out of their trucks in amazement at stockpiles of military equipment lined up on the roadsides, mile after mile. On each giant pile of shells, a simple sign bore a single word, "Explosives," painted in red letters. Ironically, the olive drab army trucks, rather than blending into the surroundings, contrasted sharply with nature's bright spring colors.

The men called the new marshalling areas "sausages" because of their elongated appearance on operations maps. Most of the 29th Division's enlisted men would remain in the sausages for almost two weeks. Boredom was their worst enemy. For the first week, the 29ers—most of whom were still uninformed about when and where the invasion would take place—had little to do except clean and waterproof their weapons and vehicles. A few daredevils, including two privates in the 116th Infantry, sneaked out of camp at night, tunneled under the barbed wire, and lit out for a nearby village looking for fun. There was little more to do outside the marshalling areas than inside, however, and with the multitude of MPs roaming the camps, unsanctioned forays beyond the wire were rare.

The generals took steps to keep the men entertained. The gray light of movies glowed every night through enormous tents in the woods. Loud-speakers blared American Forces Network radio from dawn to dusk. Even Glenn Miller's famous Army Air Force band traveled from camp to camp giving concerts of its famous swing music. For a few moments, the 29ers forgot the war as they listened to the bouncy strains of "In the Mood" and "Pennsylvania 6-5000."

Several officers at division headquarters reasoned that there would be no chance for festivities in the near future, so they threw a party at a local golf club. A 29er corporal from New York who once played the accordion in vaudeville led a sing-along for the guests, who included a few American nurses. No one talked of war. When it came time to leave, the men sang "God Save the King"—they knew the words by now—and "The Star Spangled Banner." An elderly ex-Royal Navy officer who ran the club wept openly at the sight of American soldiers, about to go into battle, singing the British national anthem.

At the end of May, the Bigots let all the 29ers in on the secret. First company COs and platoon leaders were told, and they then informed their enlisted men. The 29ers were not surprised at their role in Overlord, but they were amazed at the meticulous planning that had gone into the scheme. Officers showed their men rubber models of Omaha Beach that simulated the coastal terrain with remarkable accuracy. The 29ers were told the exact time and place their outfits would land and what they had to do to get off the beach. They studied aerial photos and 1:7,000 maps of their sectors, which indicated enemy positions as small as individual machine gun pits. They were assured that the Germans on the beach would be blasted with bombs and naval gunfire prior to the landing. Every man in the division was even issued 200 French francs. The army thought of everything.

Sometimes the plans went too far. Once, a colonel from SHAEF head-quarters came to a Plymouth theater to speak to 29th Division senior officers. The colonel took the stage and proceeded to outline an elaborate plan, to which all 29th Division units were supposed to adhere rigidly. The colonel insisted that as soon as each outfit came ashore, its vehicles must head straight for special de-waterproofing stations, which would be set up at regular inter-vals along Omaha Beach. There would be experts at each station, the colonel said, who would remove the waterproof Cosmoline grease from the vehicles. If not removed, the Cosmoline would eventually cause the vehicles to break down. The COs of units scheduled to land in the first few waves listened in amazement.

"Question!" called out Lieutenant Colonel Cooper. "We're supposed to be the first troops ashore. How are you going to get there with your experts before we do?"

"Well, you can de-waterproof on your own if necessary," replied the SHAEF colonel.

"But suppose we're fighting the Germans. Are we supposed to de-waterproof or fire at the Germans?"

"Now don't be ridiculous, Colonel."

"I don't mean to be ridiculous," said Cooper. "But you're presenting this as an order in General Eisenhower's name."

General Gerhardt saved the day. He was sitting next to Cooper and he reached over, grabbed him by the arm and sat him down. "Shut up, you goddamn fool," Gerhardt whispered. "You know you'll do as you see fit on D-Day, so to hell with these guys! But keep quiet or you'll get busted right here and now."

The spirits of the 29ers were good. Humor, however, sometimes turned grisly. A soldier pointed to his buddy's wrist. "That's a nice watch you've got. That's the first thing I'm going to take off you." This kind of fanciful joking helped several men deny the finality of death. A lieutenant in an administrative unit, not scheduled to come ashore until three days after the invasion, joked, "The only danger I'm likely to have is from the air raids or land mines. I'll be mad as hell if one of them bumps me off. If I'm on the front line and get killed, I'll be sorry but not mad." Someone made up a song called "Happy D-Day to You," based on the birthday tune, and the 29ers quickly picked it up and sang it in the marshalling areas.

The 29ers were outwardly confident. A staff officer at division headquarters let it be known that he was willing to make a bet of ten pounds—a considerable sum in those days—that the Germans would surrender within three months of D-Day. He had difficulty finding any takers. Capt. John K. Slingluff, commander of Company G, 175th Infantry, recalled, "We were just about as cocky as any outfit can get. . . . We could think to ourselves, well, there are 140 million people in the United States. About twelve million of those [actually eight million] are in the Army. About 75,000 are going to make that initial invasion, and we are it. We were damn proud of it." But for most 29ers, the jokes and the talk only temporarily allayed the fear. When the men had a quiet moment to themselves, they lay down and reflected, wondering apprehensively whether they would survive the next month. It was not a cheery prospect.

The 29ers didn't care about the historical significance of their task or their patriotic duty. The army recognized and accepted these feelings, and its training circulars avoided gushing jingoism. Instead, the army dealt matter-of-factly with the task facing its men and wrote in language the citizen-soldiers would understand. The *Army Talks* pamphlet, issued in May 1944, devoted only a single page, at the end of the booklet, to the rationale for America's entry into the war. "In liberating Nazi-ridden Europe, you are removing a threat to your own homeland,'' it declared. ''As you move onward and look at the destruction and misery around you, thank God that your own land has been spared the agony of German occupation.'' Maj. Sidney Bingham, the CO of the 2nd Battalion of the 116th Infantry, summed up the feelings of most 29ers when he stated, ''I must, with candor and honesty, point out that what I, and I suspect most of my superiors, associates and subordinates were fighting for was not ideals but rather an overwhelming desire to kill Germans, to avoid being killed oneself, and to achieve the terrain objectives we had trained so hard and long to reach.''

The big-name generals paid return visits to the 29th Division. At a theater in Plymouth, General Montgomery spoke to battalion and regimental COs from both the 1st and 29th Divisions. Monty paced melodramatically back and forth on the stage with his hands clasped behind his back, urging all commanders to push their outfits ahead relentlessly without concern about their flanks; the flanks were his responsibility, he said. The Germans under Rommel would do their best to ''Dunkirk'' them, he warned. Therefore, rapid exploitation from the beach during the first several days, when the Germans would not yet have positioned their mobile panzer divisions to counterattack, would be of vital importance. Montgomery's confidence was infectious. But some officers were so exhausted from poring over Overlord plans that they couldn't help dozing off during Monty's talk.

General Bradley returned to the 29th Division to speak to the 116th Infantry, the 29th Division's spearhead on Omaha Beach. On a hillside outside Plymouth, the entire Stonewall Brigade, consisting of 3,500 men, gathered around a tiny wooden platform wired with a single microphone. Bradley stood there impassively. The ''G.I. General'' gave a simple speech, during which he invoked the historic lineage of the 116th and stressed its vital role in the upcoming invasion. Bradley emphasized that the 116th was not alone; the navy and the Army Air Force, he said, would prepare the way. He concluded with a prediction the men would remember: ''You men should consider yourselves lucky. You are going to have ringside seats for the greatest show on earth.''

The 29ers also heard inspirational talks from their regimental and battalion COs. Col. Paul ''Pop'' Goode, CO of the 175th Infantry, held up the regiment's invasion orders, which were as thick as a big-city telephone directory, and snapped, ''Here it is, gentlemen. Study it. Learn it.'' Then, melodramatically, Goode dropped the orders to the floor with a resounding crash and growled that all these complicated plans boiled down to one thing: get off the boats and keep moving, no matter what happened, no matter how confused the situation. It was as simple as that.

The CO of the 116th Infantry, Col. Charles Canham—''Stoneface'' to his men—ordered all officers to read a memo to their outfits prior to embarkation.

It said, "There is one certain way to get the enemy out of action and that is to kill him. War is not child's play and requires hatred for the enemy. At this time we don't have it. I hope you get it when you see your friends wounded and killed. Learn to take care of yourself from the start. Remember the Hun is a crafty, intelligent fighter and will not have any mercy on you. Don't have it on him."

General Cota, who was slated to play a vital role in the invasion, addressed his staff bluntly. "This is different from any of the other exercises that you've had so far," he said. "The little discrepancies that we tried to correct on Slapton Sands are going to be magnified and are going to give way to incidents that you might first view as chaotic. The air and naval bombardment and the artillery support are reassuring. But you're going to find confusion. The landing craft aren't going in on schedule and people are going to be landed in the wrong place. Some won't be landed at all. The enemy will try, and will have some success, in preventing our gaining a lodgement. But we must improvise, carry on, not lose our heads. Nor must we add to the confusion."

Finally, at the end of May, it was time to board the transports. The 29ers, at last, were going to war.

FOUR

THE ENEMY
Festung Europa
1940–1944

1. GRENADIER MÜLLER

Army Talks featured a cartoon character by the name of Grenadier Fritz Müller. Fritz was the American interpretation of the typical German soldier— a Teutonic version of "G.I. Joe" or "Tommy Atkins." The *Army Talks* cartoon portrayed Fritz as a lunkheaded oaf, but the pamphlet warned the G.I.'s that Grenadier Müller was a first-rate soldier. "If you think he is a goose-stepping, mechanical automaton," said the pamphlet, "you are in for a rude awakening—that is, if you wake up in time. He has been in the army longer than you; he is by nature an eager beaver and extremely anxious to be a good soldier; his officers have carefully instilled into him a spirit of independent action; his school days have left a deep imprint on him of his own great superiority and the power of the German war machine."

Unfortunately for Fritz Müller, the German war machine in France was in poor shape at the beginning of 1944. Ever since the conquest of France in 1940, and especially since the attack on the Soviet Union in June 1941, western Europe was something of a backwater for the German army. The Russian Front consumed men faster than they could be shipped east. In 1943 alone, the Germans lost over two million "Fritz Müllers" on the Russian steppes.

Until the fall of 1943, the German army in France and the Low Countries had little to fear from Anglo-American action. There were simply not enough Allied troops in Britain to mount a serious amphibious assult. The Germans were content with quiet garrison duty. "The hard-pressed Eastern Front, always short of forces, looked with envy at the apparently sleeping army in the west," recalled a German general from *Oberkommando der Wehrmacht* ("OKW," or Armed Forces High Command). When the situation in the east became critical, many of the "sleeping" troops in France were promptly shipped to Russia. Between the fall of 1942 and the summer of 1943, in fact, twenty-eight divisions were transferred from west to east.

By the end of 1943, the best German divisions had departed France. Those that remained were filled with physically impaired men, many of whom had been wounded on the Eastern Front. Furthermore, Grenadier Fritz Müller was appalled to discover that he could not understand some of his fellow soldiers. Almost 10 percent of a typical German division in France consisted of troops from Poland, Czechoslovakia, Alsace, and several other European regions currently under German domination. Several battalions were comprised entirely of ex-Soviet prisoners of war (*Osttruppen*), whose loyalty varied from day-to-day depending on the situation on the Eastern Front.

German veterans of the Russian Front, known as *Russland-Kämpfer*, scorned the occupation troops in France and sarcastically referred to the quiet western theater as a "soldier's rest camp" (*eine Art Truppen-Erholungsheim*). Field Marshal von Rundstedt, the Commander-in-Chief in the west, eventually had to issue an order warning the *Russland-Kämpfer* to refrain from insulting the garrison troops.

Because most of the German divisions in France had little to do except guard the coast, the German high command didn't bother to equip them with vehicles, or even with horses. These divisions, which were known as *Bodenständige* (static defense) outfits, were virtually immobile. The high command even neglected to issue them their share of German weapons; they used instead a hodgepodge of captured Polish, French, Yugoslav, Czech, and Soviet guns.

Had the 29th Division stormed Omaha Beach five months before it actually did, it would have brushed aside German resistance with little difficulty. In January 1944, Gen. Erich Marcks, the one-legged commander of the German LXXXIV Corps, remarked that the Normandy coastal sector, for which he was responsible, could not be adequately defended even if his men were doubled in number.

But Hitler knew that the deterioration of the army in France had gone too far. In the fall of 1943, he learned of the massive American build-up in Great Britain. Two or three US divisions, it was reported, would arrive in England each month. On November 3, Hitler overhauled German military strategy in France with his Führer Directive Number 51. "I can no longer justify the further weakening of the West in favor of the other theaters of war," Hitler declared.

A remarkable transformation was about to take place. Hitler immediately transferred Field Marshal Erwin Rommel, the famous "Desert Fox," from Italy to France to lead a new army group. Rommel's arrival lifted the spirits of the troops in the western theater. The mere presence of the Desert Fox indicated that OKW would surely take the troops' needs more seriously. In addition, Hitler's Directive 51 ordered several fresh divisions to be raised, trained in France, and equipped with high-quality weapons. Activated on November 5 in the Hanover region of northern Germany, the 352nd Infantry Division was one of these new outfits. The 29ers would come to know this division intimately.

The new division, still under-strength, arrived at St. Lô in Normandy on December 5. According to German army orders, the 352nd Division was supposed to be fully trained and ready for combat by May 15, 1944, but in the event of an earlier Allied invasion of Normandy, the division was to be prepared to deploy to the coast, twenty miles distant, at a moment's notice.

It proved extraordinarily difficult to properly organize and train the 352nd Division. Everything was in short supply: men, ammunition, equipment. "I had the impression that it was only of importance to the High Command to announce as soon as possible that another division had been reformed and was at its disposal," recalled Lt. Col. Fritz Ziegelmann, the 352nd's chief staff officer. "Whether the Division was sufficiently trained to accomplish its missions was not of interest."

But the divisional cadre was slowly built up to full strength by the addition of thousands of fresh Hanoverian recruits. Despite Ziegelmann's complaints, the 352nd eventually turned into a first-rate division. In the spring of 1944, it was rated in the German army's highest *Gefechtswert* (combat value) category, indicating full readiness for attack missions—a rare distinction for a German infantry division in the west.

The 352nd had two strengths that the 29th Division lacked: *Friedensheer* (Regular Army) soldiers and combat veterans. In fact, it was standard practice in the German army to raise new divisions by combining large numbers of new recruits with a small core of men who had already been in battle. Forming the nucleus of the 352nd Division was a *Rahmen* (cadre) of depleted combat units from the 321st Infantry Division, smashed by a Soviet offensive in the Ukraine in the summer of 1943. Some of the 321st's ancestral units were comprised of pre-war Regular Army troops, and the surviving professional soldiers became members of the 352nd when it moved to Normandy. Remarkably, in spite of their defeat by the Russians, the veterans of the 321st were still imbued with *Osthärte*, the "spirit of the Eastern Front."

At the height of World War II, Germany was probably one of the most militarized countries in the history of the world. One out of every five Germans performed military service during the war; in the United States, the number was about one out of nine. Many of the Hanoverians who came to Normandy to flesh out the 352nd Division were not first-rate physical specimens and would have been rejected for service in the US Army. "Almost all these people, being physically of limited capacity as a result of the shortage of food in Germany, were fit only for limited military duties," declared Lieutenant Colonel Ziegelmann. "Marches over 15 kilometers led to high casualties. A division proposal to grant these people a milk allowance was ignored."

Yet, somehow, the green eighteen-year-olds made excellent soldiers. Their remarkable transformation can be traced in part to the German army's policy of distributing young recruits to outfits sprinkled with combat veterans. In training, the veterans imparted a little *Osthärte* along with their knowledge of tactics. Furthermore, the new men in the 352nd doubtless felt right at home among their mostly Hanoverian fellow soldiers. The Germans had learned in World War I that mixing different Germanic groups, such as Prussians and Hanoverians, was bad for morale.

Probably the most important factor that turned Fritz Müller into a top-notch grenadier was his training. On the surface, German military indoctrination appeared little different from the American method. German basic training consisted of sixteen weeks of elementary military instruction and up to three weeks more of advanced combat lessons. However, the methods by which the two armies taught tactics to recruits were vastly different. From the very beginning, German enlisted men were told that their own initiative could decide a battle. Surprisingly, given the German military stereotype, German troops were warned that rigid obedience to orders in action was a prescription for disaster. Declared the *Truppenführung* (Troop Leadership) field manual, "Orders should be binding only insofar as circumstances can be foreseen."

Maj. Gen. Dietrich Kraiss, the commander of the 352nd Division, had the classic upbringing of a German general. He was educated at a *Kadettenanstalt*, a kind of military high school. In 1909, when his American counterpart, Charles Gerhardt, was a thirteen-year-old Army brat, Kraiss was commissioned as a nineteen-year-old lieutenant in Kaiser Wilhelm's army.

Thirty-four years later, when Kraiss took over the 352nd Division, he was a distinguished general with two-and-a-half years of experience as a division commander. On July 8, 1941, only two weeks after the German invasion of the Soviet Union, Kraiss took command of the 168th Infantry Division in southern Russia and led it in twenty months of hard fighting, for which he was decorated with the *Ritterkreuz* (Knight's Cross of the Iron Cross). On April 15, 1943, he took over the 355th Infantry Division. Five months later, the 355th was so badly mauled by the Soviets in the fighting along the Dnieper River that it was broken up to provide a cadre for a new division. Kraiss assumed command of the 352nd in the fall of 1943 with orders to move his outfit to France rather than to the Eastern Front. He thought he was going to a quiet theater.

2. ROMMEL

Field Marshal Rommel was unhappy with what he saw in the west. The Desert Fox, inspecting German coastal defenses from Denmark to Brittany in November 1943, was shocked by the condition of beach fortifications. Furthermore, he disagreed with other generals concerning the appropriate deployment of German combat troops to meet the expected Anglo-American invasion. For years, Hitler had been boasting about his *Festung Europa* (Fortress Europe): "A belt of strongpoints and gigantic fortifications runs from Kirkenes [in Norway] to the Pyrenees. . . . It is my unshakable decision to make this front impregnable against every enemy." But Rommel quickly realized that *Festung Europa* was a sham, and he set out to overhaul German strategy in the west. He had to work fast, for the Allied invasion was expected in only a few months—sometime in the spring or summer of 1944.

Rommel was in a delicate position. He was, nominally, the chief inspector of all German coastal defenses in the west and had a free hand to make such improvements in beach fortifications as he saw fit. He was also expected to take charge of the battle once the Allies invaded. So on January 15, 1944, his special headquarters, designated Army Group B, took over operational control of the 7th and 15th Armies, which guarded the English Channel and North Sea coast from Brittany to Holland. Army Group B, however, was not a supreme headquarters. It was directly answerable to Field Marshal Gerd von Rundstedt's *Oberbefehlshaber West* ("OB West," or Western High Command), which controlled all German armies in France and the Low Countries.

Rommel was a realist. He knew that the Allies would control the sea and the air in the upcoming battle, and he was convinced—especially after his experiences in North Africa—that given these handicaps, German ground troops would not be able to maneuver freely. The Desert Fox was also painfully aware of Allied technological and numerical superiority. He realized that if the Allies established a secure beachhead and rushed troops and supplies ashore, the Germans would lose all hope of ever gaining the strategic initiative. He reasoned that the Germans would be forced to fight a purely defensive battle, which they would inevitably lose because of the almost limitless resources of their enemies.

According to Rommel, only one strategy could defeat the western Allies, and that was crushing the Anglo-American invasion as it came ashore. Rommel asserted that coastal fortifications could offset the German inferiority in numbers. Furthermore, there was a good chance that a counterattack by German mobile reinforcements deployed a short distance inland, directed against enemy troops who would be vulnerable and disorganized in their constrictive beachheads, would be successful.

"We must stop him in the water, not only delaying him, but destroying all his equipment while it is still afloat," wrote Rommel.

Many German generals disagreed completely with Rommel's defensive philosophy. Gen. Georg von Sodenstern of the 19th Army, who was responsible for the defense of the 250-mile Riviera coast with only a few second-rate divisions at his disposal, argued that it was impossible to be strong everywhere at once. Any effort to strengthen *Festung Europa* was therefore pure waste. Gen. Leo Freiherr Geyr von Schweppenburg, who in November 1943 assumed command of a special armored reserve force called Panzer Group West, asserted that the key to the defense of France was the mobile panzer divisions. Deployed far inland, these units could react immediately to an invasion anywhere along the coast. Both von Sodenstern and Geyr von Schweppenburg were convinced that the beaches should be defended only with meager delaying forces and that the decisive battle should be fought where the German army could best concentrate its strongest forces: somewhere in the interior of France. If German divisions were dispersed to defend every inch of the shoreline, they said, concentration would be impossible.

The Desert Fox was firmly convinced that there should be more to coastal defense than pillboxes and obstacles on the beach. It was also necessary, he insisted, to maintain powerful divisions capable of offensive missions near enough to the coast to enable them to counterattack the enemy beachhead within hours of the initial landing. "It is more important to have one panzer division in the assaulted sector on D-Day than to have three there by D-plus 3," Rommel noted.

Field Marshal von Rundstedt was not fully convinced by the arguments of either side, so the elderly commander of OB West steered a compromise strategy. Rommel would retain the right to develop the coastal fortifications as he saw fit, but he was not permitted to control the deployment of most of the key panzer divisions. Rommel thereby faced the difficult task of preparing to defeat the invasion without being allowed to command several units that could decide the battle.

In May, Rommel asked for permission to transfer the powerful 12th SS Panzer Division from its encampment at Evreux, over thirty miles from the sea, to the area around Isigny, directly on the coast at the mouth of the Vire River, only nine miles from Omaha Beach. But Hitler, with von Rundstedt's approval, denied the request.

"The job has been very frustrating," wrote Rommel. "Time and again one comes up against bureaucratic and ossified individuals who resist everything new and progressive. But we'll manage it all the same."

Rommel set out eagerly to concentrate all available manpower—including combat troops—on labor and construction duties on the beaches. The troops were ordered to work feverishly, particularly in the Pas de Calais region, where the invasion was expected, as well as in Normandy. They built thousands of beach obstacles and laid countless mines to wreck Allied landing craft. They also flooded coastal rivers to block the enemy from moving inland.

The Desert Fox tramped along the beaches day after day, evaluating field positions and forcefully explaining to the troops his ideas on how the invasion could be repelled. Every unit on the coast down to the smallest squad, he said, must concentrate its fire on the water, since the enemy troops would be most vulnerable when they were debarking from their landing craft. Rommel asserted that the beach fortifications must be strong enough to allow the defenders to survive the inevitable enemy air and naval barrage prior to the invasion. Admiral Friedrich Ruge, a naval advisor to Army Group B, accompanied Rommel on his coastal inspections and noted that the troops "enthusiastically supported" the field marshal's views.

Rommel was working against time. If the Allies did not invade Europe until late summer or early fall of 1944, the fantasy of *Festung Europa* could easily become reality. If the invasion came in the spring, however, Rommel's grand scheme would be only half-realized. During a beach inspection tour, Rommel turned to a Nazi propaganda team filming him and said, "You may do with me what you like if only it leads to the postponement of the invasion for a week."

Rommel had firm plans for the 352nd Division. He visited the division in February 1944, when it was still far from combat-ready, and communicated his theories of coastal defense to Kraiss. Kraiss, who knew Rommel well, was not surprised when the Desert Fox forcefully argued his case for moving the 352nd Division northward to the Normandy coast from its training area around St. Lô.

Official orders reached Kraiss on March 15. The 352nd was directed to take over a thirty-mile coastal sector, stretching eastward from the mouth of the Vire River to the village of Arromanches-les-Bains. Most of the shoreline for which Kraiss would now be responsible was uneven and rocky. In fact, Admiral Theodor Krancke, the head German naval officer in the west, had once told von Rundstedt that it was virtually impossible for the Allies to make a major amphibious landing in that sector. According to the prevailing German view, the only place in Kraiss's sector that could be seriously considered as a potential Allied landing site was a five-mile stretch of beach between two resort villages called Colleville-sur-Mer and Vierville-sur-Mer. The Germans doubted, however, that the Allies would invade this stretch since the beach was lined with steep bluffs and cliffs which would make it extraordinarily difficult for invading troops—and especially their vehicles—to move inland.

It was this stretch of beach that Allied planners had code-named "Omaha."

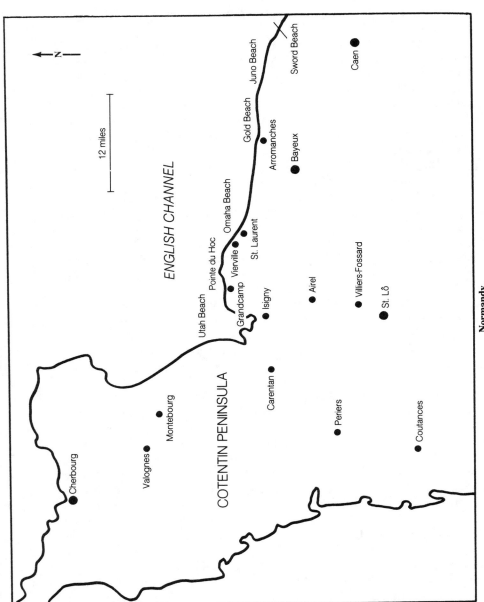

Normandy.

The rest of the 352nd Division's sector was virtually unassailable from the sea due to coastal rocks and 120-foot cliffs. Overall, Kraiss had a defensible sector.

When Rommel ordered the 352nd Division forward from St. Lô to the coast, troop deployment was left to Kraiss. Rommel, however, was perturbed when he discovered that Kraiss had views fundamentally different from his own as to how the 352nd could best perform its new coastal defense role.

The 352nd's coastal sector was formerly the responsibility of the 716th Division, a *Bodenständige* (static defense) outfit with over-aged troops and second-rate equipment. When the 352nd moved up to the coast, Kraiss assumed control of the 726th Infantry Regiment, a 716th Division unit. The absorption of these troops swelled the 352nd from its normal strength of seven infantry and four artillery battalions to ten infantry and five artillery battalions, an increase of 25 percent. But Kraiss was not sure he could trust the unenthusiastic troops of the 726th. One of its three infantry battalions, in fact, was an *Ostbataillon* of ex-Soviet POWs.

Kraiss was a frequent visitor to the LXXXIV headquarters of General Marcks in St. Lô, where German generals engaged in *Kriegspiel* (wargames) simulating an Allied invasion of Normandy. The lessons of the games, as well as Marcks's advice, shaped Kraiss's views on how the 352nd Division could best be deployed. Kraiss decided to divide his coastal sector into three areas— east, west, and central. He then assigned each area to a regiment. Kraiss also established a large division reserve, deployed twelve miles inland. The reserve consisted of the entire 915th Infantry Regiment, the divisional *Füsilier* battalion (nominally a reconnaissance unit, actually a standard infantry battalion), and most of the 352nd Division's support units.

Strangely, Kraiss was most concerned about his western zone, even though the entire zone, which stretched from the mouth of the Vire River to the town of Grandcamp-les-Bains, could not be invaded from the sea. "In the 352nd's sector, the main goal was to reinforce the left [west] wing," wrote Ziegelmann. "The deployment of our forces was definitely determined by the possibility that the enemy would isolate the Cotentin Peninsula and come into possession of the spacious Cherbourg harbor. As reinforcements arrived in the captured bridgehead, they could undertake a push for Paris."

Kraiss's concern about his western sector made little sense. Certainly, he could not have believed that this zone was the one zone most vulnerable to an enemy amphibious assault. Furthermore, the Cotentin Peninsula, beyond the 352nd's western zone, was defended by three German divisions. Although Kraiss may have been troubled by the prospect of an enemy parachute drop on his left flank—an event which actually occurred—he should have realized that an amphibious landing against the Omaha sector could have deposited a much

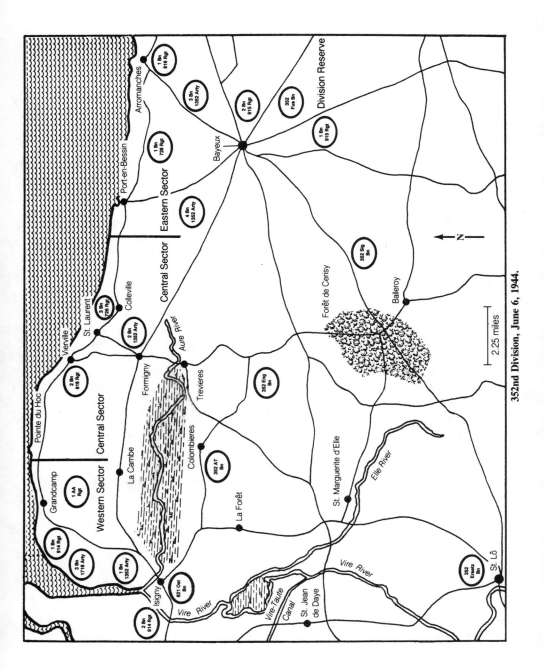

352nd Division, June 6, 1944.

larger and more potent enemy fighting force in one day than could a parachute drop.

Of course, Kraiss, like Admiral Krancke, may have been convinced that the Allies would prefer the less effective parachute drop to the seemingly more hazardous amphibious landing at Omaha. Even so, the 352nd could easily have defended against parachute landings without prior commitment of troops to the western sector. Kraiss would have had ample time to shift his troops to respond to such a threat. Furthermore, his large divisional reserve could quickly have been committed to the western sector in the event of an emergency.

The reserve amounted to about one-third of the division. The western zone, which included the entire 914th Infantry Regiment, amounted to another one-third. Consequently, the central and eastern sectors—which faced the gravest threat of invasion by sea—had only meager forces, since they had to divide the remaining one-third of the division between them.

The eastern zone, stretching from the east edge of Omaha Beach to the division's right flank at Arromanches, was the 726th Regiment's responsibility. A battalion of this regiment guarded the coast, but Kraiss was concerned that these second-rate troops would not fight with determination. He therefore assigned a battalion of the 916th Regiment, a unit he could rely upon, as a reserve.

Omaha Beach constituted part of Kraiss's central zone. The zone was guarded by the 916th Infantry Regiment, a force consisting of one artillery battalion and two infantry battalions. Thus, in the only sector in which a massed enemy amphibious assault was conceivable, Kraiss deployed only two of his ten infantry battalions and one of his five artillery battalions.

Rommel visited the 352nd Division again in May, and he did not like what he saw. During a tour of a coastal sector, he castigated Ziegelmann because there were not enough troops on the shoreline to concentrate their fire on the water. Ziegelmann countered that the division's thirty-mile frontage and its half-finished fortifications made it easy for the enemy to infiltrate the weakly defended sections of the beach. To counter this, significant reserves had to be maintained behind the coast. Rommel made no reply. It was not easy to withstand criticism from the Desert Fox, but Ziegelmann and Kraiss did not change their views and made no significant alterations in the division's deployment. Admiral Ruge, Rommel's naval advisor, later went so far as to say that Kraiss disobeyed Rommel's orders, but in the German army, tactical decisions of this kind were not the business of a field marshal.

Kraiss was clearly not one of Rommel's disciples. His deployment of the 352nd Division, like Field Marshal von Rundstedt's grand scheme for the defense of France, straddled the stances of those who thought the battle would be won on the beaches and those who believed the campaign would be decided by a German blitzkrieg once the enemy had penetrated inland.

Had one of Rommel's supporters been in command of the 352nd, its deployment would have been significantly different. First, far more men would have been committed to the division's central sector, the zone that included Omaha Beach. Furthermore, the division reserve would have been deployed much closer than twelve miles to the coast so that it could counterattack within the first hours of an invasion. Ultimately, there would have been no need for 352nd Division reserves at all if Rommel had gotten his way with the 12th SS Panzer Division, which he wanted to deploy near Isigny, only nine miles from Omaha Beach. If Rommel had been granted this wish, the entire 352nd Division could have been moved into coastal defense fortifications.

If enemy troops did come, Kraiss expected them at high tide. A low tide landing would force Allied troops to cross a tidal flat that under some conditions was as wide as 700 yards. After disembarking from their landing craft, the enemy would have no place to hide as they crossed this stretch of sand, and German machine guns sited on the bluffs behind the beach could cut them down before they reached the high water mark. An invasion at high tide, however, would minimize the time the troops would spend crossing the sands under German fire.

Assuming the Allies would come at high tide, the Germans began work on a dense belt of beach obstacles that were designed to wreck Allied boats. The simplest type of German obstacle was the "hedgehog," or "horned scully," which consisted of three steel rails welded together at crazy angles. The hedgehogs were actually old antitank barriers hauled to the beach from inland fortifications as far away as Germany proper. As an impromptu solution to the coastal defense emergency, a row of hedgehogs was placed 100 yards seaward of the high water line so that they would be completely submerged at high tide. An unwary Allied coxswain who attempted to bring his landing craft to shore during high water would thus have the bottom of his boat staved in by the hedgehogs' sharp steel rails.

A dense belt of wooden stakes and ramps extended another 100 yards seaward from the hedgehogs. This belt hardly seemed menacing to Allied intelligence officers when first examined on aerial photos, but a close look at the pictures indicated that each stake was tipped with a mine that could blow an unsuspecting coxswain and his boat to bits. As primitive as these obstacles appeared, they were not easy for the Germans to build. Wood was scarce in Normandy, the only decent source being the Forest of Cerisy, some eighteen miles from the coast. After the wood was cut—and it had to be cut by hand—it was hauled to the beaches in ox carts. Then the logs were rammed into the sand at a sharp angle so that the mine-tipped edge pointed out to sea. Severe weather in April uprooted most of the logs, so much of the work had to be redone.

At the end of May a third line of obstacles was erected 250 to 300 yards seaward from the high water mark. Labeled "Element C" by Allied intelligence officers, but more commonly known as "Belgian barn doors," these were the largest and most complex of the German obstacles. About seven feet across and ten feet high, they resembled a large wire gate. They were held in place by steel girders, and like the wooden stakes, many of them were topped by mines. Even when the tide was far below its highest point, the Germans hoped these gates would be a formidable obstacle for landing craft.

Lacking time to design and build elaborate obstacles, the 352nd Division had been forced to improvise impediments that littered the beach like grotesque flotsam. The steel rails and logs imbedded in the beaches of Normandy hardly symbolized one of the world's strongest military powers, but they were crudely effective, and they had a significant effect on Allied invasion plans.

German troops on the coast were organized into *Widerstandsnest* (resistance nests), which ranged in size from about nine to thirty men. Each nest had at least one machine gun and often boasted three or four. Twenty-one *Widerstandsnest* (abbreviated "WN" by the Germans) dotted the bluffs overlooking Omaha Beach, consecutively numbered WN56 through WN76 from east to west.

On Omaha, four critical draws, or gullies, led inland from the high water mark. Since the intervening bluffs were so steep, these draws were the only paths by which vehicles could go inland. Each draw was guarded by a *Stützpunkt* (strongpoint), consisting of a group of mutually supportive resistance nests. The typical *Stützpunkt* was about seventy men strong. In addition to its infantry, the strongpoint was provided with mortars, infantry howitzers, and a few antitank guns. An extremely powerful *Stützpunkt* manned by troops of the 3rd Battalion, 726th Infantry Regiment was located in the Vierville draw, directly in front of the spot where Company A of the 116th Infantry was scheduled to land on D-Day.

Since cement was scarce in Normandy in 1944, only a few *Widerstandsnest* could boast a concrete pillbox. As a result, according to Ziegelmann, only 15 percent of the division's resistance nests could be considered bombproof. (The *Stützpunkt* at Vierville, however, had half a dozen pillboxes.) The typical *Widerstandsnest* consisted of simple zig-zag trenches with several dugouts and tunnels connecting it to adjacent nests. Each nest was surrounded by minefields and coils of barbed wire.

A few nests were sited inside draws and behind folds in the ground so as to be almost invisible to observers on offshore ships. Although these nests were virtually invulnerable to naval gunfire, they were also incapable of firing straight out to sea. Instead, their weapons were sited to fire directly along the length of the beach. Thus, a burst from a machine gun that missed one file of Americans would be likely to hit another group further down the beach. The gentle curve of Omaha Beach worked to the Germans' advantage, since an observer on the bluffs at either end of the beach could see what was happening all along the shoreline and could direct his fire along the beach out to the limit of his weapon's range.

French resistance members attempted to alert the Allies to the presence of the new beach obstacles, and as a result the spring of 1944 was bird-hunting season for the 352nd. Every time a pigeon flew out to sea, German sharp-shooters squeezed off a few shots. This, however, was not sport; it was war, for the carrier pigeon was a basic means of communication between the French resistance and Allied intelligence.

Sometimes the Germans got lucky. In fact, troops of the 352nd Division shot twenty-seven carrier pigeons in the two months before D-Day. In late May, a German soldier recovered the carcass of a pigeon he had shot and discovered a message from a French resistance agent in Grandcamp-les-Bains. The note described the Germans' new beach obstacles and listed the deployment areas of several 716th Division units. Significantly, there was no mention of the 352nd Division.

Allied intelligence remained ignorant of the 352nd's whereabouts until D-Day. The 29ers were told that Omaha Beach would be defended by only second-rate troops of the 716th Division. Even so, the Yanks were warned that the invasion would not be easy. "These static division soldiers have been sitting along the coast for two years," declared *Army Talks*. "They can be counted on to fight hard, if for no other reason than they are behind the eight-ball. They've had the pants scared off them continuously by false alerts, by long hours of 'stand-by,' . . . by commando raids by British, French, and Polish groups, and by air attacks of Allied planes. In addition, they have done considerable manual of arms with the shovel, and the local inhabitants are most inhospitable."

At the end of May 1944, the German high command had grown some-what complacent. They had been expecting the invasion since the beginning of good weather in April. Since the coastal defenses were at their most vulnerable in the early spring, the Germans were convinced the Allies would land at that time. But when no assault came in April or May, German intelligence speculated that D-Day would occur after the Soviet army had commenced its expected summer offensive in July.

Several German generals, however, were not so sanguine. They pored over daily weather reports and tide tables, trying to predict the most likely periods of an enemy invasion. "I guess they'll land on my birthday," General Marcks concluded in a letter to his wife on May 12. His birthday was June 6.

In early June, the Allied air forces paid a great deal of attention to targets in Normandy, and the Germans did not fail to notice. German intelligence also knew that French resistance groups were suddenly receiving unusual transmissions over the BBC—another sign that an invasion was imminent.

But the German high command was not yet ready to put its troops on full alert. Even Rommel was complacent. On June 4, the Channel was rough, winds were high, and visibility was poor. Inappropriate conditions for a high tide landing and a forecast of continued poor weather had been enough to convince the Desert Fox that an enemy assault before June 9 was unlikely. So, on the morning of June 5, Rommel set out for Germany to see Hitler and ask for control of several powerful panzer divisions in the upcoming battle. The Desert Fox hoped he would be the last to see the Führer before the invasion. "The last one out of his door is always right," Rommel had mused. The invasion began before Rommel reached Hitler's headquarters.

FIVE

MEN AND GUNS
The Emptiness of the Battlefield
1944

1. SOLDIERS

The World War II battlefield was an unusually lonely place, and a soldier—whether G.I. Joe or Grenadier Fritz Müller—could experience little worse than to be separated from his comrades. The World War II battlefield, of course, was also an extraordinarily deadly place, and if a man in the front lines stuck his head out of his foxhole for more than an instant, he was likely to be shot. Herein lay the dilemma of World War II infantry tactics: men fought best when in the close company of friends, but weapons had become so lethal that soldiers were forced to disperse just to survive.

Before the invention of machine guns, soldiers had marched into battle shoulder-to-shoulder, led by a colonel who shouted his orders over the din of battle. As men were forced to disperse due to the increasing lethality of weapons, however, colonels could no longer control their troops at the front by shouting or by bugle or drum calls. Most World War II infantrymen, in fact, had little idea who their colonel was. Instead, the man to whom World War II soldiers looked for support and guidance on the battlefield was the squad leader, a sergeant, who led a team of no more than a dozen men. Declared *Army Talks*, "This is a sergeant's war."

If a 29th Division squad leader could have conversed with a 352nd Division *Gruppenführer* (squad leader), both men would have been surprised at how differently the two armies trained for war. The first thing the 29er would have noticed was that his squad of twelve men outnumbered the German *Grenadiergruppe* (squad) of nine. The American squad leader was a staff sergeant; his subordinates consisted of one "buck" sergeant, who was the assistant squad leader, and ten privates. Seven of the privates were designated riflemen, one was an automatic rifleman, another was an assistant automatic rifleman, and the last was an ammunition bearer. The German squad leader was an *Unteroffizier* (sergeant) or *Obergefreiter* (corporal). Of the eight *Grenadiere* (privates) and *Gefreiten* (privates first class) under his command, one was labeled *Schütze 1* (Soldier 1) and carried the squad machine gun. Another man was designated an assistant squad leader. A third was the assistant machine gunner. The rest were riflemen.

The medals on the chest of the German squad leader would have attracted the attention of the 29er, for the chances were that the *Gruppenführer* was a veteran of the Russian Front. The German might have had a black Tank Destruction badge on his sleeve, a silver Infantry Assault badge, the East Front Winter Campaign ribbon (nicknamed the "Frozen Meat medal" by German troops), and the bright red ribbon of the Iron Cross, 1st or 2nd Class. If the German had been wounded on the Eastern Front, he would also have had a gold *Verwundetenabzeichen* (Wound badge).

The 29th Division squad leader, on the other hand, had never seen combat and knew hardly anyone who had. He was, nevertheless, a good soldier, probably a pre-war Maryland or Virginia National Guardsman who had risen from private to sergeant since the 29th Division's activation in February 1941. He had been in training for over three years and knew his job well.

Aside from the *Gruppenführer*, few members of a 352nd Division squad were likely to be combat veterans. Five or six of the *Grenadiere* were probably eighteen- or nineteen-year-old Hanoverians. The rest were "old" soldiers in their mid-thirties—usually nicknamed "Pop" or "Daddy" by the youngsters—who had been snatched from a rear-echelon supply outfit and hastily pressed into front line service. Thus, the majority of a 352nd Division rifle squad would be as new to combat as were the 29ers.

Grenadier Fritz Müller was more inspired by patriotism than was G.I. Joe. He knew that the war had not been going well since 1942, and he figured that the 1944 campaign was Germany's last chance for victory. He particularly feared the consequences of Soviet occupation of Germany. Furthermore, unlike the typical 29er, he was deeply concerned for the safety of his family at home because the Americans and the British were regularly pummeling German cities with bombs. He also knew that the Allies had demanded Germany's unconditional surrender, which to him was unthinkable. He saw little choice except to fight on.

The élan of the 29ers was not patriotism. Jingoistic talk by generals, in fact, was scorned by the men. Nor was the divisional *esprit de corps* entirely inspired by Gerhardt, although he had turned a US Army infantry division— supposedly identical to and interchangeable with other divisions—into a highly individualistic outfit. Above all, the troops were high spirited because they knew they would fight side-by-side with their friends. The squad had been together for months, if not years. Several squad members, in fact, were probably Marylanders or Virginians who fondly remembered the "old days" at Fort Meade. The rest were draftees from all over the United States. The strong bonds between the men in each squad had been nurtured by years of training together. No one wanted to let his buddies down.

The 352nd was an ordinary German infantry division manned by ordinary soldiers. It had few ardent Nazis, since young Germans with fascist inclinations were likely to volunteer for the SS (*Schutzstaffel*, the military arm of the Nazi party). Furthermore, glory-seekers were unlikely to end up in the 352nd. Those young men who enthusiastically hungered for action opted for the prestigious *Panzertruppen* (tank forces) or the *Fallschirmtruppen* (parachute forces). Nevertheless, the men of the 352nd Division performed their duties dependably—and somewhat stubbornly—befitting the reputation of Hanoverians in the German Army. Unlike their 29th Division counterparts, the troops of the 352nd had above all a deep-rooted respect for military authority.

2. TACTICS

No soldier in any army was more fond of his rifle than an American infantryman was of his Garand M1. General Patton called the M1 "the greatest battle implement ever devised," and the 29ers would have agreed with him. The M1 was highly regarded because it was the only well-built, mass-produced semi-automatic rifle in the world. To work the weapon, a rifleman had only to pull back a small handle on the right side of the breech, shove a clip into the chamber from the top, and start shooting. As each round was fired, the gun automatically ejected the empty shell case and positioned another bullet in the chamber. A G.I. could fire the M1 as fast as he could pull the trigger. When the clip's eight rounds were expended, inserting a new clip in the rifle took only a few seconds. The men had to be very careful, however, when reloading. A properly positioned clip automatically released a heavy metal bolt that slammed forward. A G.I. who inserted the clip in an incorrect fashion stood a good chance of getting his thumb smashed by the flying bolt. Almost every rifleman had an "M1 Thumb" at one time or another during training. The thumb swelled up and turned purple, and the nail sometimes dropped off. It was incentive enough to learn the proper loading method.

The M1 was revolutionary for its day. A soldier armed with an M1 had more firepower than any rifleman in the history of warfare. US Army tacticians had boundless confidence in the weapon. According to army manuals,

An American infantryman fires his Garand M1 rifle through a hole in a Norman hedgerow, July 1944. *Courtesy Military History Institute.*

the rifle squad—in which eleven of the twelve members were armed with the M1—was deemed capable of firing so many bullets that enemy troops would not be able to keep their heads out of their foxholes for more than an instant.

The US Army had always emphasized individual rifle marksmanship. In the 29th Division, General Gerhardt had a couple of "SOPs"—Standard Operating Procedures—for shooting a rifle. One of these was the "correct sight picture," the term used in the field manuals for the proper technique of aiming and firing a weapon. "You couldn't just know it [the sight picture]," a 29er wrote. "You had to know it word for word exactly as he wrote it: 'Top of the front sight in the center of the peep sight, bull's eye resting on top of the front sight.' Leave out one word and you were wrong and not a very good soldier." Uncle Charlie himself was a crack shot with an M1. In experienced hands, the M1 was deadly out to about 600 yards.

The infantrymen usually kept their rifles cleaner than they kept themselves. The 29ers even liked to paint slogans on their rifle stocks, like "On to Berlin," "No Gum, Chum," and, of course, "29 Let's Go."

The M1 could also be used as a grenade launcher. The assistant squad leader was officially designated the squad's "grenadier," but actually all squad members could employ their M1s in this mode. Rifle grenades, however, were difficult to use. The grenade had to be attached carefully to a special holder on the muzzle and fired with the butt of the rifle firmly held on the ground. Although they were cumbersome and inaccurate, the grenades gave confidence to the infantrymen when they were not able to call upon mortars or artillery.

Organizational tables also called for a rifle platoon leader to designate one man in his outfit as a sniper. The sniper was supposed to carry an M1903 Springfield, a forty-year-old bolt-action rifle that had been the standard American infantry weapon until the adoption of the Garand. One platoon leader in Company A, 175th Infantry, recalled that his outfit's Springfield arrived only three days before D-Day, and there was no time to train the sniper in the proper use of the weapon. Even when the sniper had been trained, however, he usually discarded the Springfield in favor of the more enticing Garand at the first opportunity.

American infantrymen cherished the Browning Automatic Rifle, known simply as the "BAR," almost as much as they did the M1. The BAR was a hybrid, as it was designed to have the portability of a rifle but the firepower of a machine gun. Every twelve-man rifle squad had a single BAR. Army field manuals insisted that successful squad tactics depended on a carefully positioned and skillfully operated BAR. Accordingly, the squad leader tended to assign the BAR to one of his most reliable privates. The BAR man had to be sturdy, for the weapon weighed almost twenty pounds. Like the M1, it had an effective range of 600 yards. In action the men were told to keep the BAR functional at all costs. If the original BAR man was hit or could not handle his responsibilities adequately, another squad member—officially designated as "Rifleman, automatic, assistant"—would drop his M1 and pick up the BAR.

After D-Day, the 29ers had an amazing knack for acquiring extra, unofficial weapons. The infantrymen especially liked to get their hands on extra BARs, and it was not uncommon to find two BARs in each rifle squad. No one—not even officers—bothered to inquire as to where the men had come up with these excess weapons. The acquisition of extra BARs, in fact, was so widespread that a second BAR eventually became an official part of the rifle squad.

The biggest problem with the BAR was providing it with ammunition. Like all automatic weapons, the BAR rapidly expended its ammunition supply. With a simple turn of a lever, the gun could be set to fire either 550 or 350 rounds per minute; it could also be set to fire single rounds semi-automatically like an M1. Unlike machine guns, which fired bullets strung together in belts, the BAR used a twenty-round magazine clip that was shoved into the rifle in front of the trigger. If a BAR man kept his finger pressed on the trigger, he would expend all twenty rounds in only three or four seconds. To conserve ammunition, BAR men were trained to fire their weapons in two- or three-round bursts, using only a quick, light touch on the trigger. Even so, it was easy to use up the squad's supply of BAR magazines quickly. The BAR man, who was weighed down by the weapon itself, could carry only a few maga-

US AND GERMAN WEAPONS

Rifles

CTY NAME	WEIGHT	RANGE	RATE
USA M1 Rifle (Garand)	9	600	32
USA M1 Carbine (Winchester)	5.8	300	40
USA M1903 Rifle (Springfield)	9.7	600	15
GER K 98k (Mauser)	9	600	15

Submachine guns/Automatic rifles

CTY NAME	WEIGHT	RANGE	RATE
USA Automatic Rifle (Browning)	20	600	550
USA M2 .45 Cal (Thompson)	11	100	100
GER MP 40	10.5	200	200

Machine guns

CTY NAME	WEIGHT	RANGE	RATE
USA M1917 (Browning)	91.7	1,800	525
USA M1919 (Browning)	42.2	600	500
USA M2 .50 Cal (Browning)	129	1,800	500
GER MG 42 with bipod	26	600	1,200
GER MG 42 with tripod	55	2,000	1,200

Mortars

CTY NAME	WEIGHT	RANGE	RATE
USA M2 60mm	42	1,985	35
USA M1 81mm	136	3,200	35
GER 81mm	124	2,400	35
GER 120mm	600	5,700	20

Howitzers

CTY NAME	WEIGHT	RANGE	RATE	SHELL
USA M3 105mm*	3,800	6,150	4	35
USA M2 105mm*	4,900	10,300	4	35
USA M1 155mm	12,000	13,900	2	95
GER 105mm	3,700	10,300	4	33
GER 155mm	13,800	13,500	2	96

*M3 used by cannon companies of infantry regiments; M2 used by field artillery battalions.

Notes

RANGE: Effective range in yards; maximum range may be much further.
RATE: Rate of fire in rounds per minute. This is a maximum rate.
SHELL: Weight of shell in pounds.
WEIGHT: Weight of weapon in pounds.

zines, for if he stuffed extra ones into his pockets, his mobility suffered. In theory, the squad ammunition bearer and the assistant BAR man were supposed to help him out, but transferring ammunition when the squad was pinned by fire was not always possible. An experienced BAR man chose his targets carefully and used his trigger finger with restraint.

It was best to fire the BAR while lying down. Using this method, the BAR's bipod, fastened near the muzzle, could provide stability by supporting the weapon on the ground. The BAR could also be fired from the shoulder or the hip, but this method was not as accurate. The BAR was probably the only infantry weapon in the world that left-handers found easy to use, since the bolt handle, which had to be pulled back manually after the insertion of a magazine, was fixed on the left side of the weapon.

Some Germans were not impressed with the M1 and the BAR. World War I had clearly demonstrated to them that the only infantry weapon that mattered was the machine gun. They thereupon set about arming their infantry outfits with more machine guns than any other army in the world. By 1944, German troops were as proud of their *Maschinegewehr 42* ("MG 42" for short) as the Yanks were of their M1s. Every German squad, in fact, had a single MG 42, placed in the capable hands of *Schütze 1*. The man behind the machine gun, according to German doctrine, would do most of the fighting for the squad, so the *Gruppenführer* made sure that *Schütze 1* was his steadiest man.

The MG 42 was a remarkable weapon. It would have been difficult, in fact, to design a more deadly machine gun. The most noticeable feature of the MG 42 was its distinctive noise. It spewed out bullets at 1,200 rounds per minute, and the Yanks noted that the "rrrrrp" of the MG 42 sounded like a bedsheet being torn. In fact, they used to refer to all German automatic weapons as "burp" guns. The MG 42's rate of fire was three times as fast as comparable American machine guns, whose chugging "dat-dat-dat" sounded ponderous when compared with the MG 42s.

For all the firepower the MG 42 gave the German squad, it was surprisingly light; at twenty-six pounds it could easily be carried by one man. American machine guns, on the other hand, had to be broken down and carried by two or more G.I.'s. The MG 42 was only six pounds heavier than the BAR, but it was far more lethal. The MG 42 was also famous for its durability. *Schütze 1* usually needed only a can of lubricating oil to keep the gun working. He could drop his weapon in mud or water and, remarkably, it would still function.

Schütze 1 had to be careful not to use up his ammunition allotment in a matter of minutes, so he usually fired his MG 42 only in short bursts. But *Schütze 1* could expend ammunition more freely than an American BAR man, since the rest of the German squad was devoted almost entirely to feeding the ravenous MG 42. One of the primary duties of German riflemen, in fact, was to carry ammunition forward to the machine gun crew. An MG 42 in battle would typically expend 3,000 rounds per day—the equivalent of 150 BAR magazines.

The German squad leader and his assistant were both armed with *Maschinepistolen 40* (MP 40), a submachine gun with a fearsome reputation. It was not particularly liked by German troops, however, for it tended to jam if fired in bursts of more than a second or two. Like all submachine guns, moreover, it was inaccurate. The 29ers used to joke that a submachine gun was only worthwhile if they happened to encounter a Kraut in a closet. Although the MP 40 was ineffective at ranges over 100 yards, in the close fighting in Normandy's hedgerows it proved deadly. The MP 40 was also a valuable command tool, for a well-trained *Gruppenführer* indicated the spot at which he wished his men to fire by shooting toward the target with several bursts of tracers.

Unlike American soldiers, German grenadiers did not hold their rifles in high esteem. The German troops joked that the Mauser *Karabiner 98k*, the standard German army rifle, was designed from the lessons learned in the Franco-Prussian War of 1870–71. This humor was half-serious, for the Mauser had hardly changed since its introduction in 1898. The Mauser, or the ''K 98k'' as it was known to the Germans, resembled the American Springfield. After firing a round, a grenadier pulled back on the bolt to eject the spent cartridge, then pushed the bolt forward again to position the next bullet in the chamber. The Mauser was an inefficient weapon in comparison with the M1, but the Germans hardly cared. The only weapon that mattered to them was the MG 42.

No matter how repetitive or realistic the 29th Division's tactical exercises were, the 29ers knew that they would have to learn the subtleties of real combat the hard way, on the battlefield. In combat, however, it took a few weeks for the squad leaders to grasp the significant differences between real war and war ''by the book,'' and by then many of them were dead. Effective rifle squad leadership in the 29th Division during its first weeks in combat was hazardous, for the men discovered that the infantry tactics they had been taught were in urgent need of modification. Unfortunately for the G.I.'s, German tactics, having been refined over five years of war, needed little revision.

The man with an M1 was the theoretical key to American infantry tactics. According to US Army manuals, riflemen had to advance to close quarters with the enemy to defeat him. ''In the final stage of the assault, the hostile position is overrun in a single rush with the bayonet,'' said the US Army rifle company manual. Getting the troops to close quarters, however, was easier said than done. The major problem was to avoid getting shot by the deadly MG 42s.

The US Army's solution was "fire superiority." The manual stated that "Fire superiority is gained by subjecting the enemy to fire of such accuracy and intensity that his fire becomes so inaccurate or so reduced in volume as to be ineffective." Then the troops could rush forward to dispatch the enemy with grenades and bayonets. "Fire and maneuver" was what the tacticians called this procedure.

An American squad operating independently was trained to overcome an enemy position by breaking into separate parts. According to the manuals, two riflemen designated as scouts, and known as "Team Able," would locate the enemy position. Then the squad leader would direct his BAR man and three other riflemen, together designated "Team Baker," to lay down fire on the target. The five remaining riflemen and the squad leader himself—"Team Charlie"—assaulted the enemy position. The concentrated, rapid fire of the BAR and M1s was deemed sufficient to maintain fire superiority. If a squad ran into a strong enemy position, it could maintain fire superiority by calling upon neighboring squads for help.

The Germans also believed firmly in fire superiority, but they had a fundamentally different way of maintaining it. In the German Army the riflemen's main job was to support the squad machine gun. When the MG 42 crew moved, the riflemen covered them; when the MG 42 set up, the riflemen dug *Schützenlöcher* (foxholes) for the crew while watching for the approach of enemy troops; when the MG 42 started firing, several riflemen were delegated to carry ammunition to the MG 42 crew. The MG 42 was light enough to be used almost like a BAR. On the offensive, its bearer could keep pace with the advancing riflemen. Furthermore, the MG 42 could be set up in a matter of seconds.

On the defensive, the MG 42 was shifted back and forth between different positions to confuse the enemy. The Germans called this tactic *Stellungswechsel* (change of positions), and it was an extremely important part of their doctrine. Three firing pits for the machine gun were commonly dug at various places along the front: one to cover the expected avenue of enemy approach; another on the left or right flank to support a neighboring squad; and a third—called the *Schweige-MG*, or ambush position—about fifty yards or so behind the front lines. On June 20, only two weeks after D-Day, a major in the 116th Infantry noted that the Germans "were masters at making one man appear to be a whole squad by moving rapidly from one concealed position to another."

The German squad leader chose his machine gun positions carefully. Even company and battalion COs could be expected to visit the squad to check the MG 42's field of fire. Field Marshal Rommel himself was known to offer advice to a *Gruppenführer* in the positioning of his MG 42.

US Army field manuals emphasized the importance of fire superiority, but in truth, the Yanks found it difficult to achieve without supporting artil-

Part of a US Army infantry squad attacking along a Norman hedgerow, July 1944. *Courtesy Military History Institute.*

lery. American infantrymen simply were not provided with enough firepower to establish battlefield dominance. Each 29th Division rifle company of 193 men had only two machine guns, both of which were in an independent weapons platoon. On the other hand, a German infantry company of only 142 men had fifteen machine guns. The German company's firepower was further enhanced by its twenty-eight submachine guns. The 29ers had no weapons of this type. The American rifle company was dependent on its nine BARs for rapid fire, but these weapons could not stand up to the MG 42s. Instead of forcing the Germans to keep their heads down with a large volume of M1 and BAR fire, as the American manuals demanded, it was usually the Yanks who got pinned.

Even a depleted German rifle company, consisting of no more than fifty men, commonly covered a 1,000-yard front. Such a sector would have been considered lengthy for an American company at full strength. As long as the German company's fifteen MG 42s were functional—which required a total of only thirty men (two men per weapon)—the *Kompanieführer* (company CO) was content, for the machine guns were the linchpins of German tactics. The remaining twenty men would act as ammunition bearers and lookouts for the MG 42 crews. Thus, on the defensive, even a skeletal German company proved a tough opponent.

The 29ers had been taught to maintain tight fire discipline. According to a

1942 manual, the squad leader was to make sure "that firing [was] limited to observed or known targets." In combat, however, this system would not work since the Germans rarely let themselves become "known targets." German positions were well camouflaged, and the enemy troops were constantly shifting position. Concerned American infantry leaders urged their men to expend ammunition more freely. According to a July 1944 note in *Battle Experiences*, a classified newsletter providing tactical hints to the G.I.'s, "Riflemen must be encouraged during an advance to keep up steady fire on a suspected target instead of waiting for the appearance of a definite target. Well-distributed fire will keep the Germans down, but too often all men fire at a single spot when a target does appear instead of keeping fire distributed over all the suspected target area."

Some G.I.'s were reluctant to fire because American gunpowder was neither smokeless nor flashless. When an M1, BAR, machine gun, or howitzer opened fire, the gun emitted a puff of light blue smoke and a tiny flash that promptly betrayed the firer's position. This shortcoming seemed insignificant in training, when no one fired back. But in combat, especially in the constrictive terrain of Normandy, the problem was serious. Alert German machine gunners found it easy to zero in on the position of a heretofore hidden American squad, and once an MG 42 found them, the Yanks had little chance to raise their heads. "You really couldn't blame the men for holding their fire under these conditions," recalled Lieutenant Colonel Cooper.

Meanwhile, because the enemy used smokeless and flashless powder, American infantrymen found it difficult to pinpoint German firing positions. The Yanks tended to locate the Germans by the telltale "rrrrrrrp" of the MG 42, but this method was inexact.

The battlefield was, above all, confusing. The deadly firepower of infantry weapons forced units on both sides to disperse over such a large area that even company COs and platoon leaders had difficulty exerting control over their men. Both German and American squad leaders were therefore expected to think for themselves. "The emptiness of the battlefield demands fighters who think and act independently, who exploit each situation in a considered, determined, and bold way," said the German *Truppenführung* (Troop Leadership) manual. The American rifle company manual was even more specific: "In the absence of instructions from the platoon leader, particularly during the last stages of the fire fight, the squad leader may often have to attack important targets without orders."

3. COMBAT ORGANIZATION

German and American infantry units in World War II were triangular: three squads per platoon; three rifle platoons per company; three rifle companies per battalion; three battalions per regiment; three regiments per division. "Three sounds like a magic number, doesn't it?" *Army Talks* asked. "Well, it is. It's a fast, streamlined number. It's not so big that it gets in its own way, but big enough to fight in all directions. One unit can feel out the enemy while two move up; two can hold while one strikes; one can hold while two strike from either or both sides; one can hold while two rest. The combinations are good." Gerhardt thought so too. He had a simple "SOP" for his infantry leaders: "Two up, one back," he declared.

A man in charge of a rifle platoon had the exceptionally difficult and dangerous task of leading and fighting at the same time. During training in England, 29th Division platoon leaders had heard gloomy rumors from the fighting in North Africa and Italy that their life expectancy in combat would be short. Reality proved worse than the rumors, for 29th Division platoon leaders, on the average, survived about three weeks of combat before they became casualties.

Most platoon leaders in the 29th Division were first or second lieutenants ("shavetails") in their early twenties, fresh out of Officer Candidate School in the States. In the 352nd Division, the *Zugführer* (platoon leader) of the first platoon of a rifle company was a *Leutnant* (second lieutenant), a veteran of the Eastern Front and probably an ex-NCO. Each of the other two rifle platoons was led by a *Feldwebel* (staff sergeant) or *Unteroffizier* (sergeant), who was also likely to have had Russian front experience.

The 29th Division rifle platoon and the 352nd Division *Grenadierzug* (rifle platoon) had almost identical organizations. Both consisted of three rifle squads and a platoon headquarters. In the US Army, the headquarters comprised five men: the platoon leader, a platoon sergeant (the second in command), a platoon guide (a staff sergeant), and two messengers. A medic from the regimental medical detachment usually accompanied the headquarters group. The platoon leader and his entourage were supposed to concentrate on command and control of the platoon. Though in practice the headquarters group, including the lieutenant, often fought out of necessity as riflemen, they carried only M1s and were thus unable to enhance significantly the platoon's firepower. The platoon leader was actually supposed to carry a lightweight Winchester M1 carbine, but he frequently traded it at the earliest opportunity for a Garand.

German platoon headquarters, on the other hand, was more than just the outfit's nerve center. It was also organized as a fighting and a supply unit. In addition to the *Zugführer*, the headquarters had a *Krankenträger* (medic), two *Melder* (runners), and two men—usually ex-Soviet prisoners of war who had volunteered for German military service to avoid the horrors of a Nazi POW camp—to care for the platoon's three horses. The Germans called the Soviets *Hilfswillige* (helpers), or "Hiwi" for short. The headquarters section had one

MG 42, and the platoon leader carried an MP 40 submachine gun. Thus, in an emergency, the headquarters had enough firepower to fight as a fourth squad. The headquarters machine gun, however, was more likely to be held in reserve or attached to a rifle squad that the *Zugführer* had determined would bear the brunt of an impending skirmish. This squad was labeled the *Brennpunkt* (focal point), and with a second MG 42, it could muster enough firepower to hold off an American company.

According to official tables of organization, a German platoon was supposed to have three horse-drawn wagons to carry ammunition and food. Frequently, the Germans obtained these wagons by stealing them from French farmers. During the first few weeks of combat in Normandy, the amazed 29ers in the front lines could plainly hear the neighing of horses and the clink and clatter of pots and pans as food was delivered to German troops at night. The noise usually provoked a devastating American artillery barrage, so the Germans eventually learned to replenish their front line troops quietly.

In both armies the CO of a rifle company had only a slightly longer life expectancy in combat than did a platoon leader. Both company and platoon COs were front line soldiers, the only difference being that a company commander did more leading and less fighting than his platoon counterpart. Despite his loftier status, a company CO knew almost nothing of his division's "big picture," since he was far too busy trying to keep his men alive.

Prior to D-Day, the typical 29th Division company CO was a captain who had served with the division since the mid-1930s as a member of the Maryland or Virginia National Guard. If he had joined the guard as an officer, the CO was probably in his mid-twenties; if he had enlisted as a private and risen to commissioned rank (a "Mustang"), he would be older, probably in his late twenties or early thirties.

The German *Grenadierkompanie* (rifle company) was commanded by an *Oberleutnant* (first lieutenant). Unlike his 29th Division counterpart, a company CO in the 352nd Division had reached his position due to combat experience. Many 352nd company commanders were ex-NCOs in their early thirties, several of whom were professional soldiers whose careers dated back to before the war.

A US Army company CO was responsible for more than just his three rifle platoons. He also commanded a weapons platoon of thirty-five men who were armed with three 60mm mortars and two light machine guns. The mortar section, which usually stayed one hedgerow behind the front line, provided the CO with his own source of mini-artillery. The mortars were not very accurate and had a range of only a mile, but they were simple to use and easy to carry.

The two light machine guns were the only such weapons in the entire company. They were Browning M1919 air-cooled models, each of which weighed forty-two pounds, some sixteen pounds more than an MG 42. The Browning fired 450 rounds per minute, but at this rate the barrel overheated after a minute or two, and the gun malfunctioned. The more practical rate—150 rounds per minute—required intermittent bursts of about ten rounds. Unlike the MG 42, which could be carried by one man, the Browning had to be broken down and carried by two men: one for the tripod and another for the gun itself.

The company CO decided where his two machine guns would be placed, allocating them to a platoon or squad that needed extra firepower. The Brownings were support weapons rather than linchpins of American infantry tactics. In an attack they would set up at the front and cover the advance of the riflemen by keeping up steady fire on the enemy lines.

The German *Kompanieführer* (company CO), unlike his American counterpart, had no mortars at company level. He had, however, a special *MG Staffel* (machine gun section), which consisted of eighteen men and two MG 42s. Both machine guns were of the "heavy" variety, indicating that a telescopic aiming device and a bulky tripod, instead of the MG 42's normal bipod, had been added to each weapon to enhance its stability and range. With these additions the MG 42 could fire accurately at targets a mile away.

In both armies, the company was the largest military unit in which a soldier could come to know every man in the outfit by sight, if not by name. In garrison life, the company was a family that lived, ate, trained, and played together. The 352nd Division, however, which had been raised only a few months before D-Day, probably did not have the unit loyalty within its rifle companies that the 29th Division had developed over three-and-a-half years. Most of the young Hanoverian recruits were probably still getting to know their *Kompanieführer* when the Allies landed in Normandy. Nevertheless, their leader's East Front medals inspired immediate respect.

Company headquarters existed primarily to take care of the soldier. The American company headquarters, staffed by about a dozen men, was divided into a command and an administrative group. The command group consisted of the CO, the executive officer, the first sergeant, two wiremen, and several runners and radio operators. It remained close to the front. The administrative group, composed of mess and supply personnel, the company clerk, and an armorer-artificer (a gun repairer), remained behind the lines.

The Germans also organized their company support troops into two groups, but their administrative section was far smaller than was that of the US company. The forward detachment, consisting of twelve men, was called the *Kompanietrupp* (company headquarters). The rear-echelon section, labeled the *Tross* (supply trains), had only thirteen men, several of whom were Soviet "Hiwis."

In both armies the senior NCO at company headquarters was the CO's closest assistant. For the Americans, this was the first sergeant. In the old army he had a reputation as a tough, hard-drinking disciplinarian. In the 29th Division, however, first sergeants were probably veteran guardsmen, many of whom were still in their twenties. In the German army the key company NCO was the *Hauptfeldwebel,* who was most likely to be an old-timer and pre-war professional soldier.

In both American and German divisions, the CO of an infantry battalion linked the front lines with the commanding general. A battalion CO was the highest-ranking officer to witness every day the harsh realities of the front. Although he rarely fired his own weapon, the CO was regularly shelled, had little chance for sleep, and got his uniform as dirty as the rifleman's. At the same time, he had to communicate frequently with his regimental CO concerning front-line developments, and he occasionally attended the commanding general's meetings at division headquarters. "The key to the whole show is good battalion commanders," an American general wrote in the US Army's *Battle Experiences* newsletter. General Gerhardt agreed. Unfortunately, attrition among 29th Division battalion COs was high. Less than two months after D-Day, seven of the division's nine rifle battalion COs had been killed, wounded, or relieved of their commands.

In June 1944, a majority of 29th Division battalion COs were lieutenant colonels or majors, ten-year veterans of the Maryland or Virginia National Guard. The rest were West Pointers who had joined the division after mobilization. In the 352nd Division, *Grenadierbataillon* (rifle battalion) COs were most likely *Hauptmann* (captains), several of whom were ex-NCOs.

Although a battalion CO in each army was the lowest ranking officer to understand his division's "big picture," most of his time was devoted to tactics and not to strategy. In addition to the rifle companies, the battalion CO also had several powerful support units at his disposal. Both German and American rifle battalions included a heavy weapons company (*schwere Grenadierkompanie* in German), consisting of heavy machine guns and mortars. These weapons were labeled "heavy" for good reason, since they were too unwieldy to keep pace with attacking infantry. An American heavy weapons company boasted eight Browning M1917 machine guns, each of which weighed almost 100 pounds with all its accessories. The M1917 was water-cooled, which enabled it to fire longer than an air-cooled model before overheating. The water, of course, added considerably to its weight. The Browning had a fifty-one-pound tripod, which provided enough stability for the gun to fire effectively at ranges over a mile. The German heavy weapons company had six heavy MG 42s and three standard MG 42s.

Actually, the 29ers feared German mortars more than MG 42s. The worst thing about the mortars, the Yanks said, was that the shells were virtually inaudible in flight, so there was no warning of their arrival. An artillery shell, on the other hand, roared like a freight train, and a man had a few precious seconds to find cover. Sometimes the men got lucky and could actually see an enemy mortar shell arch into the sky. It would descend from its peak, slowly at first, picking up speed as it fell, until it crashed to the ground and exploded. By then, of course, the men who were the targets would have long since leaped into foxholes. Alert troops might even have heard the distinctive metallic cough of an enemy mortar being fired, allowing them a few extra seconds to dash for safety.

Sometimes the 29ers could predict what was in store by listening to the pattern of enemy mortar shell explosions. "When you heard that first one you pulled the bottom of your foxhole right up into your belly and prayed," wrote Maj. Glover Johns, a battalion CO in the 115th Infantry. "When you heard the second one you knew whether or not they were coming your way. If they were coming toward you . . . [each] round was a little closer, and [the Germans] were so damned deliberate about it that the waiting was worse than the crash of the shell itself. You lay there and counted the seconds between the shells until you knew that the next one was yours."

German mortarmen, like MG 42 gunners, changed their positions frequently. If they fired from the same place for too long, an American artillery barrage would surely descend upon them. But shifting a mortar was more difficult than moving a machine gun: the German 81mm mortar weighed 124 pounds; the 120mm mortar, 616 pounds.

The German heavy weapons company usually had four 120mm and six 81mm mortars; the 120s were sometimes replaced by another six 81s. The 120mm was particularly deadly. It could be fired in rapid salvos up to a range of four miles, and each shell was almost as powerful as a light artillery round. The American weapons company had six 81mm mortars.

In both armies a company's designation indicated the battalion to which it belonged. In the US Army, a regiment's 1st Battalion consisted of A, B, C, and D Companies; the 2nd Battalion, E, F, G, and H Companies; and the 3rd of I, K, L, and M Companies. (There was never a J Company in an American regiment; no one could ever satisfactorily explain why.) Companies D, H, and M were the regiment's heavy weapons companies; the rest were rifle companies. The Germans used numbers instead of letters: the 1st, 2nd, 3rd, and 4th Companies comprised the 1st Battalion; the 5th, 6th, 7th, and 8th Companies, the 2nd Battalion. The 4th and 8th Companies were the *schwere Grenadierkompanie*. Due to manpower shortages in the German army, "Type 1944" infantry divisions—of which the 352nd was an example—had only two battalions per regiment.

Because of the manpower shortage, the German high command demanded military units that were as lean as possible. Many German soldiers in rear-echelon roles were replaced by Soviet "Hiwis." Furthermore, German

A detachment of 81mm mortarmen from an American heavy weapons company prepares to fire in a Norman pasture. Wartime censors have blocked out two men's helmets, probably because they displayed divisional insignia. *Courtesy Military History Institute.*

infantry units were assigned many fewer officers than were comparable American outfits. A German infantry battalion had only four officers in its headquarters section. A US Army infantry battalion headquarters, in contrast, was staffed by eleven officers, most of whom had administrative duties. In theory, at least one officer in an American battalion was prepared to deal with any of combat's eventualities, even chemical warfare. In addition to the CO and his second-in-command, the most important officers were the S-1 (the Adjutant, commanding the headquarters company); the S-2 (Intelligence Officer); the S-3 (Operations Officer); the S-4 (Supply Officer); and the Surgeon.

The generous provision of officers allowed American units the luxury of back-up command teams. Both the battalion and company had "executives" (seconds-in-command)—a major in the battalion and a first lieutenant in the company—who were prepared to take command of the unit at a moment's notice if the CO became a casualty. Even the rifle platoon had a platoon sergeant whose primary function was to act as the outfit's second-in-command.

According to the German command system, leaders—even of squads and platoons—were expected to be thoroughly familiar not only with their own outfits, but also with the next highest command. In combat, the Germans knew that leaders would frequently be forced to take over a higher unit at a moment's notice. After an extended period of combat, in fact, it was common to find German sergeants commanding platoons, second lieutenants leading companies, and captains—and sometimes even first lieutenants—in charge of battalions. In contrast, the American leader concentrated his energies mostly upon his own sector and had little conception of his superior's problems. Such an orientation made sense given the American command system, in which the duties of fallen leaders were assumed by executives or new officers from a replacement depot.

The Germans, on the other hand, rejected the concept of the executive officer. Instead, they usually replaced fallen leaders with someone of lesser rank from the same unit. After several weeks of combat in Normandy, in fact, 352nd Division infantrymen fought for the most part without guidance from platoon and company officers, who had rapidly become casualties and had not been replaced by men of equal rank. This practice did not undermine unit cohesion as much as one might imagine. Unlike US Army training, which demanded initiative only from the infantry leader, the Germans demanded initiative from everyone—even the youngest riflemen.

In the inter-war years, infantry regiments in both the US and German armies came to consist of much more than just infantrymen. Looking back at the gruesome experiences of World War I, tacticians contemplated the perplexing problem of moving riflemen across no-man's land against an enemy plentifully supplied with automatic weapons. To accomplish this objective, the tacticians recommended that each infantry regiment be provided with its own artillery. American infantry regiments, therefore, formed a new outfit called a "howitzer company." When the US Army underwent "triangularization" in 1941 and 1942, the howitzer company became an antitank company and was replaced by a new support unit called a "cannon company." The German equivalent was the *Infanteriegeschützkompanie*, always designated the "13th Company," even in the 352nd Division, which lacked companies numbered nine through twelve.

It was strange for infantrymen to fight as cannoneers. German troops, in fact, referred to their howitzers as *Zigeunerartillerie*—"gypsy artillery." According to American field manuals, the cannon company was to deploy at the front and pound the enemy lines with close-range fire. In actual practice, though, the guns were too bulky to take part in a mobile battle. The US "M3" 105mm infantry howitzer weighed almost two tons. In combat, infantry cannons stayed out of the front lines and were usually attached to the nearest artillery outfit. The 29th Division artillerymen considered them a godsend. Although an M3 had a range of only four miles, its shells were just as powerful as those fired by the artillery's heavier "M2" howitzers. The artillerymen used the infantry cannon to shell any suitable target within its range, thus preserving their own precious M2 ammunition for targets at longer ranges. As soon as the war ended, the US Army replaced the cannon company with a tank company.

Infantrymen worried a great deal about tanks, particularly American infantrymen, who were fully aware of the famous German panzer blitzkriegs of the early war years. Without antitank weapons, infantrymen were helpless against the armored behemoths, so German and American infantry regiments both included an antitank company (*Infanteriepanzerjägerkompanie* in German, also known as the "14th Company"). The 29ers usually had little use for their antitank companies in combat since they rarely encountered German tanks. One member of the 116th Infantry's antitank company recalled that from June 1944 to May 1945 he never saw an enemy tank. This was fortunate for the 29ers, for tank technology had advanced so rapidly from 1939 to 1944 that the nine 57mm guns in each American antitank company were no more effective than peashooters against most German tanks in 1944.

The Germans, however, took antitank warfare seriously. Their regimental antitank companies each included three 75mm guns—or the even more effective captured Russian 76mm guns—whose high-velocity shells could easily knock out American Sherman tanks. Unlike the American 57mm antitank guns, however, the German "75s" were too big to manhandle—a critical shortcoming in a mobile battle. Nevertheless, the 75s were much more common than the dreaded "88s," and they were almost as effective.

An American regimental service company was responsible for supplying the regiment's twelve infantry companies with food and ammunition. One two-and-a-half-ton truck (known as the "deuce-and-a-half") was semi-permanently attached to each company as a kitchen truck. Ammunition and supply trucks, driven by service company personnel, were also frequent visitors at company headquarters during quiet periods. Each German rifle company, on the other hand, hauled its own supplies with a horse-drawn *Feldwagen* (supply wagon) and *Feldküche* (kitchen wagon).

Regimental COs had a large group of officers and special troops to serve them. An American regimental headquarters, for instance, had seventeen staff officers who performed missions almost identical to those of the battalion staff, particularly the S-1 through S-4 slots. Furthermore, large numbers of support troops, such as messengers, radio operators, clerks, and mechanics, were present at regimental headquarters. Several small combat outfits were also attached to the regiment, such as the American "I&R" (intelligence and reconnaissance) platoon. German regiments included special reconnaissance and engineer platoons, which were unofficially combined into a *Sturmkompanie* (assault company) for important attack missions.

Several of the 29th Division's older, highly respected National Guard officers would have been logical choices for regimental command. None of the three regimental COs—Colonels Slappey of the 115th, Canham of the 116th, and Goode of the 175th—were guardsmen, however. After the division's first five weeks of combat, during which all three original regimental COs departed the 29th, guardsmen were not permitted to assume regimental command. General Gerhardt insisted upon bringing in non-guardsmen, even in instances in which guardsmen were regimental executives. There seemed to be an unwritten rule that no guardsman could rise above battalion command. The one exception in the 29th Division was General Sands, the artillery chief.

The Guardsmen suspected that they were the victims of the "WPPA" (West Point Protective Association). The originator of this policy, the guardsmen surmised, was Lt. Gen. Lesley J. McNair, the commander of Army Ground Forces, who was widely suspected as an ardent enemy of the National Guard. Two months after D-Day, however, McNair was dead, an accidental victim of American bombers in Normandy. By that time, Gerhardt—and most other professional soldiers—had changed their minds about the guardsmen, having learned that real combat blurred the differences between amateurs and professionals.

In both the US and German armies, divisions had come a long way since the mid-19th century, when they had consisted of a few thousand infantrymen and nothing more. By 1944, American infantry divisions had grown three or fourfold, to over 14,000 troops. German "Type 1944" infantry divisions, like the 352nd, had almost 13,000 men.

Furthermore, World War II infantry divisions no longer included only infantry units. The most significant non-infantry force in both the 29th and 352nd Divisions was the artillery. Each division had three "light" artillery battalions, armed with 105mm howitzers, and one "medium" battalion, with 155mm (American) or 150mm (German) howitzers.

In theory, all divisions were capable of operating independently. Hence, they were provided with several different types of support units, manned by non-infantry specialists. If, for example, infantrymen needed to build a bridge—or to blow one up—they called on the divisional engineer battalion. If they needed new radios or telephones, they called on the divisional signal company (actually a battalion in a German division). If they needed guides at road junctions, they called on the division's military policemen. The ordnance company repaired weapons. The quartermaster company distributed supplies.

The Yanks referred to these support outfits (except the engineer battalion, which was considered a combat unit) as "Special Troops," and placed them under the command of a lieutenant colonel at division headquarters. The Germans called them *Versorgungstruppen* (service support troops). Not surprisingly, 284 of the 1,455 *Versorgungstruppen* in each German infantry division were "Hiwis."

A German engineer, signalman, or cannoneer did not take his job title seriously. If his division took heavy infantry losses, he knew his outfit would sooner or later be ordered to the front lines. In fact, German support troops were better armed than were American infantrymen. A German engineer battalion had more than twice as many machine guns as a US Army rifle battalion. For every signalman or engineer lost in battle, however, the Germans lost more than just a fighter; they lost a specialist who provided valuable infantry support.

In contrast, 29th Division support troops were rarely—if ever—forced to fight as infantrymen, though they were trained to do so. The preservation of intact support units kept the division functioning smoothly. Signalmen maintained top-notch communications; quartermaster troops kept everyone supplied; engineers built roads and performed demolition work.

Unlike the 29th Division, which could readily call for assistance from its corps or army commander, or even from the Army Air Force, the 352nd Division fought with limited outside help. The self-sufficiency of the 352nd was, in theory, enhanced by its *Feldersatzbataillon* (replacement battalion), a unit of several hundred soldiers fresh from basic training in Germany, who were supposed to replace battlefield casualties. In reality, however, the *Feldersatzbataillon* was frequently used as just another combat unit. The 29th Division, on the other hand, did not provide its own replacements. Instead, its depleted rifle units were rejuvenated by men drawn from rear-echelon "repple depples" (replacement depots).

The German army realized that its infantry divisions needed an intrinsic antitank capability if they were to fight with little outside support. The result was the *Panzerjägerabteilung* (antitank battalion), a mixed unit of twelve assault guns (*Sturmgeschütze*), fourteen antitank guns (*Panzerabwehrkanone*, sometimes self-propelled), and twelve anti-aircraft guns. The *Sturmgeschütze* looked and sounded like tanks. When no real tanks were available, which was generally the case in a German infantry division, the Germans used these assault guns as substitutes.

Shortly after D-Day, the 352nd absorbed a Luftwaffe flak (anti-aircraft) regiment stationed several miles west of Omaha Beach. This regiment supposedly included sixty 20mm "pom-poms" and forty-eight 88mm anti-aircraft guns. The 352nd was strengthened significantly by the "88s," for in addition to their anti-aircraft role, they could also serve as cannon substitutes, or as antitank weapons. They were particularly deadly in the antitank role, firing twenty-two-pound projectiles at 3,400 feet per second, faster than the velocity of a rifle bullet. The 88's sighting equipment was excellent, and American Sherman tanks were easy prey, even at a range of over a mile.

The 29ers feared the 88 more than any other German weapon. Everyone came to have an "88 story." One such tale was that when a speeding 88 shell came straight down a road between two files of startled 29ers, the rush of air turned everyone's helmet sideways; only after the shell had passed did the men hear its unnerving screech.

The 29th Division obtained tank support, antitank weapons, and anti-aircraft protection from independent, non-divisional units provided by the corps or army commander. In combat these outfits were attached to the 29th on a semi-permanent basis. The 747th Tank Battalion and the 821st Tank Destroyer Battalion, though never officially part of the division, fought with the 29ers for most of the war.

Both the 29th and the 352nd included a special reconnaissance unit. The 352nd *Fusilierbataillon*, however, was a reconnaissance unit in theory only. In actuality, it was an ordinary infantry battalion and was generally used as a division reserve. With only eight motor vehicles, the *Fusilierbataillon* could hardly undertake mobile scouting missions, and the equipping of one of its four companies with bicycles did not make much difference.

The 29th Cavalry Reconnaissance Troop, on the other hand, was truly mobile. It had forty-eight vehicles for only 155 men, and thirteen of the vehicles were speedy M8 "Greyhound" armored cars.

There was every expectation of significant casualties on both sides, and each army attempted to make preparations to care for its wounded. A 29er had complete confidence in his division's medical personnel. American medical troops moved their injured men from the battlefield to a doctor's care significantly faster than did the Germans. American medical technology and drugs were also top-notch. Not surprisingly, a wounded American had a far better chance of survival than did a wounded German.

When a 29er was hurt, he was promptly given aid by the front line medic accompanying his rifle platoon. His wounds were treated with antibacterial sulfa powder and then wrapped in field dressings. If necessary, he was given a morphine injection. To alert rear-echelon medical personnel that an injection had been administered, the used syringe was attached to the wounded man's collar.

A wounded soldier was first examined by a doctor in a battalion or regimental aid station some 500 yards or more behind the front. These somewhat spartan posts were occasionally hit by artillery fire, so a man who needed further care was quickly shipped out to a rear-area "collecting" station, one per regiment. A man whose wounds were severe enough to keep him out of action for a long time was then transported to a "clearing" station, which was essentially the divisional hospital. The clearing station was the limit of divisional medical care; from there, a seriously wounded man was shifted to non-divisional "evacuation" hospitals.

Each of the 29th Division's three regiments had an independent medical detachment to care for the wounded at front line aid stations. These detachments had seven doctors and furnished medics to each platoon as well as stretcher-bearers to pick up wounded in the front lines, where ambulances usually could not go. The division's 104th Medical Battalion, with thirty three-quarter ton ambulances, moved casualties from front line aid stations to collecting and clearing stations. There, the 104th's thirty doctors treated casualties in less hectic rear-area conditions.

The Germans, typically, had to make do with scarcer resources. Not only did they have fewer physicians to care for their wounded, they were also less able to move injured men to an aid station. German wounded were lucky if they were transported in rickety, horse-drawn wagons. Moreover, the Germans were usually short of medical equipment and drugs.

The American tendency to prepare for every conceivable contingency of war was never more apparent than in their division headquarters. Staff officers were plentiful in US Army divisions. The Yanks believed that each division should have a back-up command system, led by an assistant commander who would take over if the commanding general became incapacitated. In addition, a divisional chief of staff supervised planning. The chief of staff was in charge of four co-equal assistant chiefs of staff: the G-1 (Personnel), the G-2 (Intelligence), the G-3 (Operations), and the G-4 (Logistics). Each assistant chief of staff commanded a detachment of about a dozen men. Furthermore, division headquarters had several specialized staff officers, such as the chaplain, the provost marshal, the judge advocate, and the adjutant general.

The 29th's assistant commander, Brigadier General Cota, liked to stay near the front to keep close watch on his beloved infantry. The chief of staff, Col. Godwin Ordway, was a brilliant administrator who longed for a front line command. Prior to D-Day, the 29th Division had a few high-ranking officers with no official job title. One of these was Lt. Col. William Purnell, a highly regarded Baltimore lawyer who was allegedly passed over for regimental command because of his National Guard background. The unofficial post of "deputy chief of staff" was created just for him.

The most important staff officers were the G-2 and the G-3. At least one duty officer from both the G-2 and G-3 sections was required to be present in the 29th Division "War Room"—the division headquarters building or tent—at all times during combat operations. Lt. Col. Paul Krznarich, the G-2, kept track of enemy activities for Gerhardt. The 29ers nicknamed Krznarich "Murphy" because no one could pronounce his name. The G-3 was Lt. Col. William Witte, a distinguished Baltimore engineer. Witte was the classically brainy staff officer. "Witte here, has got it all figured out. He's my Napoleon," Gerhardt joked.

The Germans believed the American staff system wasted trained officers. The 352nd Division lacked an assistant commander because any senior infantry or artillery officer in the division was trained to assume emergency command. Furthermore, the chief of staff's role was performed by the "operations officer" (*erster Generalstabsoffizier*, known as the "1A"), a sort of all-powerful G-3 who supervised the divisional supply ("1B") and intelligence ("1C") officers. The 352nd Division "1A," Lt. Col. Fritz Ziegelmann, worked with General Kraiss to plan day-to-day activities.

A US Army infantry regiment became a "regimental combat team" (RCT) by the addition of an artillery battalion. The Germans did not follow the RCT concept as commonly as did the Americans; when they did, they called the teams *Regimentsgruppen*. In both training and combat, RCT attachments were virtually permanent. The artillerymen, in fact, thought of themselves as members of the regiment to which they were attached.

The proximity of 29th Division artillery and infantry units in the pre-war National Guard fostered friendly relations between cannoneers and riflemen. The 111th Field Artillery Battalion and the 116th Infantry, both from the Virginia guard, comprised the 116th RCT; the Maryland-based 115th Infantry and the 110th Field Artillery made up the 115th RCT; the 224th Field Artillery and the 175th Infantry, both of which were Maryland guard units from Baltimore or its suburbs, formed the 175th RCT. A 29th Division artillery battalion CO had an unusual command arrangement: In administrative matters, he was answerable to General Sands; in combat, however, he followed the orders of his RCT commander.

Each 29th Division RCT also included a company from the 121st Combat Engineer Battalion and a "collecting" company from the 104th Medical Battalion. In each battalion, Company A went to the 115th Infantry; Company B to the 116th; and Company C to the 175th.

Soon after General Gerhardt took over the 29th Division in July 1943, he

A camouflaged American artillery position in Normandy. *Courtesy Military History Institute.*

gave his division artillery a "superior" rating—an unusually encouraging word from a man quick to fault subordinates. The general was particularly impressed with General Sands, the surly old Norfolk lawyer who was divisional artillery chief. He was also satisfied with his four artillery battalion COs, all of whom were young Maryland and Virginia guardsmen. With the exception of Lt. Col. Thornton Mullins of the 111th Field Artillery, who was killed on Omaha Beach, the COs of the divisional artillery battalions remained in command of their units from D-Day to V-E (Victory in Europe) Day.

In the nineteenth century, European and American artillerymen trained in units called "batteries," which were the equivalent of infantry companies. Each of these consisted of several cannon and some 100 men. Batteries were organized into battalions or regiments for administrative purposes only. In World War II, however, American and German artillery were organized according to the opposite principle. Units trained and fought in battalions; batteries were administrative subdivisions of the battalion.

In a German or American infantry division, a field artillery battalion consisted of three firing batteries (A, B, and C in the US Army; 1, 2, and 3 in the German Army), each of which was armed with four howitzers (sometimes only three in German divisions) and about 100 men. The nerve center of the artillery battalion, in both armies, was the headquarters battery, to which support requests were directed and from which fire orders were issued. Quick-firing World War II howitzers were capable of expending enormous quantities of ammunition, so rapid replenishment of the firing batteries was vital. The Americans were far superior to the Germans in supplying their cannoneers. Each American artillery battalion had a service battery to handle logistical matters. With its thirteen deuce-and-a-half trucks and thirteen trailers, the service battery plied back and forth between supply dumps and the gun positions. The guns could thereby remain in action continually, and they frequently did.

In contrast, German supply trains were mostly horse-drawn. These columns were extremely vulnerable to artillery fire or air attack, and in combat, Allied artillery and fighter-bomber pilots saw to it that German cannoneers were almost always short of ammunition.

The Luftwaffe, in contrast, seldom bothered American artillerymen. Each 29th Division artillery battalion was usually protected by an anti-aircraft battery from the 459th Anti-Aircraft Artillery ("AAA" or "Triple A") Battalion, a non-divisional unit.

American artillerymen were able to pull up stakes and move to a new firing position, even two or three dozen miles away, with amazing rapidity. Every artillery battalion had 124 vehicles, so no one had to walk. Infantrymen, in fact, occasionally got a lift in the cannoneers' trucks.

German artillerymen were far less mobile. Howitzers in German infantry divisions were usually pulled by horses, much as they had been in the nineteenth century. A single German artillery battery was supposed to have 126 horses; a battalion, 516. Some hard-up German coastal defense divisions, like the 716th in Normandy, had no horses at all, and consequently their gun positions were essentially fixed.

American and German artillery equipment differed little. The "light" 105mm howitzers, which actually weighed almost 5,000 pounds each, fired a thirty-three-pound projectile up to seven miles. The "medium" 150mm (German) or 155mm (American) howitzers, each of which weighed some 12,000 pounds, fired a ninety-five-pound projectile about nine miles.

A soldier on the receiving end of an artillery shell could be hurt by shrapnel as far as forty yards from the impact point if he were standing in the open. If he were unlucky enough to be caught standing near an exploding shell, he would in all probability be injured or killed. Although lying down or diving into a foxhole could protect a 29er from shrapnel, no foxhole in the world could save him from a direct hit by a large shell. It was not uncommon, however, for a soldier to emerge unscathed from his foxhole after two or three enemy shells had detonated within five yards of him.

4. COMBAT COMMUNICATIONS

The mass army raised in the United States between 1941 and 1943 was trained to win its battles by mobility and enthusiasm. When it became evident after several painful combat experiences, however, that mechanization and ardor would not win the war by themselves, the US Army fell back by necessity upon tactical expedients. Signal equipment was one of the expedients that helped establish a new brand of warfare, one that used sophisticated technology to help achieve fire superiority. Other armies used radios and telephones, but no one used them with the frequency and skill of the Americans. US Army signal equipment became the cornerstone of American tactics.

The importance of the American signal system cannot be overestimated. Indeed, it can be seen as the major factor that helped overcome some of the disadvantages suffered by US units in battle. The Germans simply had too many automatic weapons for the Yanks to establish the "fire superiority" that US Army manuals had repeatedly emphasized as the key to battlefield success. The Yanks thereupon faced a tactical dilemma. American infantry had to learn to attack successfully if the United States was to win the war, but riflemen could not attack as long as the Germans maintained fire superiority.

The easiest way for an American rifle squad to gain fire superiority on the battlefield was to call upon other friendly units for help. To do this, the Yanks had to use their signal equipment as much as their guns. With only a few

A US Army soldier works a telephone switchboard in a command post dugout. *Courtesy Military History Institute.*

words into a radio or telephone, a platoon leader could get fire support in a matter of seconds from his company's 60mm mortars, heavier 81mm mortar fire from his battalion CO, and deadly 105mm howitzer fire from the artillery. Furthermore, if the requested fire support missed its target, a few more words by phone or radio corrected the aim.

As with any new technique, military communications took time to learn. In their first few months of active service at Fort Meade, the 29ers had more faith in telephones than in radios. Telephones had worked well in World War I. They were simple to operate, static-free, and almost invulnerable to enemy eavesdropping. But armies in the Great War were virtually immobile. Telephones were effective in this type of warfare because wires could be fixed securely in place over a period of months, or even years. In a war of dynamic movement, however, for which the 29ers were training in 1941, telephone wires were expected to be difficult to set up and maintain.

The radio was hardly more promising. The US Army of the pre-Pearl Harbor era was not particularly fond of radio communications. State-of-the-art radio equipment was too bulky to be carried by infantrymen in a mobile battle. Furthermore, radio science was relatively new, and few American soldiers understood radio gadgetry well enough to keep it in perfect working order. In training, radios were fickle. They hissed and screeched, garbling countless messages. But worst of all, radios would be security risks in battle, for transmissions could be picked up by foe as easily as by friend.

Radios were a classic example of warfare stimulating technology. When the United States entered World War II, no one—not even hard-core radio wizards—could foresee how dramatically radio science would advance in the next several years. Only thirty months after Pearl Harbor, American soldiers, for whom radios in civilian life had meant "Jack Benny" and "Amos 'n Andy" broadcasts, came to rely on radios for survival.

A radio, however, could aid an infantryman in a mobile battle only if it were light enough to be carried comfortably by one man. The development of such a piece of equipment was a daunting challenge for radio scientists, since the miniaturization of radio parts had not advanced significantly before the war. In spite of these difficulties, the US Army produced two radios in 1943 that eventually became indispensable to the 29ers. These were the SCR ("Signal Corps Radio")-300, which weighed only thirty-two pounds and could be carried by one man like a backpack; and the SCR-536, weighing only six pounds. The Signal Corps labeled these latter radios "walkie-talkies" because the troops could talk into them and walk at the same time. The G.I.'s sometimes referred to the SCR-536 as a "handy-talkie" because it could be held in one hand. The SCR-300 had a speaking range of five miles under perfect conditions, which was more than adequate even for a battalion CO. The SCR-536 had an optimum range of one mile; in practice, its range was much less. The Germans were deeply impressed by both radios when they first captured several sets in Sicily.

Static could render even the most sophisticated radios useless on the battlefield since urgent messages could not always be repeated. Pre-war US Army radios, all of which were of the AM (amplitude modulation) variety, were susceptible to static interference. Prior to Pearl Harbor, however, American policemen and amateur radio buffs were beginning to employ FM (frequency modulation) radios, which were static-free. But FM had one major drawback. It was a "line of sight" signal, meaning that there had to be a direct, unblocked path between the transmitter and the receiver if the speaker was to be heard by the listener. In combat, however, infantrymen usually used radios at short ranges, so the "line of sight" limitation did not pose a severe problem. FM, it appeared, was exactly what the infantrymen needed. The US Army adopted the new FM technology in its SCR-300.

Radios needed a power source to transmit. Pre-war radios generally used "wet cell" batteries for power, like those in automobiles. These batteries were heavy and filled with dangerous acid. If an infantryman was to carry a radio on his back in battle, the US Army needed an alternative to the wet cell. The answer was the "dry cell," like the batteries used in flashlights. Dry batteries were handy and lightweight, and it only took seconds for a signalman to flip open his radio and drop in several new cells. Unfortunately, dry cells quickly lost power during continuous operation. The SCR-300's batteries hardly lasted a day in periods of frequent use. Radiomen learned both to keep their radios turned off unless absolutely necessary and to carry several spare batteries.

Infantrymen in the 29th Division became most familiar with the little SCR-536s. Every rifle company had six of these handy-talkies: one for each of the three rifle platoons, two for the weapons platoon, and one for the company CO. The heavier SCR-300s were used for communication between battalions and companies.

Artillery forward observers and liaison officers used radios similar to the SCR-300, such as the SCR-610 or SCR-619, to direct the fire of their howitzers. Heavier radios, such as the 150-pound SCR-694 (eighty-six pounds in the backpack version), were used at regimental level. At division headquarters, the giant SCR-399 kept the commanding general in touch with higher headquarters as well as with the major units within the division. The SCR-399, with a range of up to 100 miles, was so big that it was mounted in a truck with an accompanying generator on a one-ton trailer.

As sophisticated as US Army radios were, the Yanks still preferred the security and reliability of the telephone. As soon as any 29th Division outfit, from rifle platoons to division headquarters, moved to a new position and dug in, wiremen with creaking reels of unraveling telephone wire arrived on the scene.

The omnipresent web of wires was the American army's signature. The wire carried thousands of encoded messages to American troops and a single unencoded one to the Germans: the Yanks have arrived. So much wire was laid that US Army tanks and trucks commonly cut their own telephone lines by accidentally driving over them. There was simply no time for the signalmen to lay their cables underground or to string them above ground on poles as they were supposed to. Knowing the importance of the telephone wires, German patrols cut every American cable they could find.

A military telephone system consisted of three parts: switchboard, telephone handset, and wire. Switchboards and telephones in both armies were similar to those in civilian use. Military wire, however, had to be portable. In terms of sturdiness and reliability, however, lightweight wire could not match the cables used by commercial telephone companies.

Both the US and German armies had light field wires that could be carried in reels by one man. American standard "assault" wire, labeled "W-130," weighed only about thirty pounds per mile of cable. In about an hour, a wireman could lay one-and-a-half miles of such wire. The Yanks also had a heavier and sturdier wire called "W-110." Weighing 130 pounds per mile, it

An American wireman laying light "W-130" telephone cable. *Courtesy Military History Institute.*

could not be carried by one man, and in fact, it was most efficiently laid by truck. The speaking range over the light W-130 wire was about seven miles; it was ten miles for the heavy W-110 wire. Both light and heavy wires were "double conductors" consisting of two separate cables twisted around one another. The purpose of the twin wire was to provide a closed circuit in a line between a telephone and a switchboard: one wire took the current away and the second wire returned it. In contrast, the Germans still used old-fashioned single-strand wires. To close a circuit between a German telephone and switchboard, the current had to return through the ground to the originator of a call. Because the enemy could eavesdrop on a "ground return" circuit, the US Army had long since rejected this method.

US Army tactics in World War II could never have succeeded unless American infantrymen and artillerymen had worked smoothly together. The very first sentence of Field Manual 6-100, *Tactics and Technique of Division Artillery*, known simply as "The Book," stated, "The reason for the existence of the Field Artillery is its ability to support the infantry on the field of battle. Artillery acts by fire alone and is not capable of independent action as a self-sustaining arm."

Artillerymen and infantrymen have always had a close relationship, of course, especially in the eighteenth and nineteenth centuries when they fought side-by-side in the battle line. Fortunately for World War II artillerymen, it was neither necessary nor possible to deploy guns in the front lines. By 1939, front line gunners would have been able to operate their pieces for only a few minutes before being shot by the enemy's powerful infantry weapons. Even the lightest World War II howitzers, however, could fire a high-trajectory shell over the heads of friendly troops at a range of several miles. The best place for the cannoneers to set up their guns, therefore, was a mile or so behind the lines, where they could fire with just as much effectiveness as at the front, and with much greater security. Ironically, American infantrymen, whose success depended on the artillery, rarely even saw a howitzer. But they could easily hear the boom of their own guns and the whines of outgoing shells passing overhead on their way to the German lines. The 29ers used to say that there was no better sound in the world.

Since the cannoneers could not see what was happening in the front lines, artillery personnel were assigned to the infantry and were ordered to radio or phone enemy and friendly activities back to the gun positions. An American light artillery battalion typically deployed almost 10 percent of its 521 men to the front, and there they were dirty, frightened infantrymen in everything but name.

The most dangerous artillery job of all, however, was that of forward observer ("FO"). A single FO was normally provided to every American rifle company that was undertaking an important mission. The FO operated in conjunction with the infantrymen or acted on his own initiative to seek out a good observation post ("OP") from which to observe the Germans. When an FO spotted a worthwhile target or an infantryman pointed one out to him, he phoned or radioed back to his battalion and requested a fire mission. The mission, however, was not always approved.

FOs always liked high ground. If none was available, church steeples and treetops would do for an OP. Frequently, FOs slipped into front line foxholes to get a close-up view of the enemy across no-man's land. The Germans, of course, had their own FOs and were well aware of the importance of good observation. The Germans, in fact, did everything in their power to thwart American FOs. They fought tenaciously for high ground, blew up steeples that were suitable OPs, and detailed snipers to look for and shoot Americans who were seen using binoculars.

If the FO planned to stay in an observation post that had already been in use for some time, such as a hilltop or a steeple, he fulfilled his mission by himself or with one assistant. An FO normally operated in a team, however, the size of which varied according to the FO's tasks. If the FO planned to move forward with attacking infantry into dangerous territory, he needed a dozen men or more: one sergeant, one radioman, six or seven wiremen to lay telephone cable, and a few men with rifles to provide protection.

Even if an FO were accompanied by a team, forward observation was extremely dangerous. A team was only lightly armed and operated in close proximity to the Germans. As a rule, if an FO could see the Germans, the Germans could see him. He had to operate discreetly.

The artillery's reliance on forward observation was indicative of the US Army's willingness to adapt tactical theory to reality. Few army field manuals talked about forward observation techniques; none discussed manpower requirements for forward observation. In fact, the role of FO was not officially recognized in any US Army table of organization.

Second Lieutenant John J. Pollarine, a forward observer from the 110th Field Artillery Battalion, who was killed in action outside St. Lô, June 21, 1944. *Courtesy Cooper Armory.*

The need for FOs at the front made life difficult for an artillery battalion CO, who had to take officers away from their normal duties to act in this capacity. To ease the burden, the CO rotated officers as FOs. In most 29th Division artillery units, everyone from the CO himself to the most junior second lieutenant served as an FO at one time or another.

There was no better OP than an airplane. An FO in the sky held the ultimate "high ground." In daytime, every move the Germans made was detectable from the air. To provide its FOs with this advantageous perspective over the battlefield, every American artillery battalion had two Piper Cub observation aircraft, which were referred to as "Air OPs."

The Piper Cubs were so tiny that they needed only a small, flat pasture for take-off and landing. On each mission, two men—pilot and observer—occupied the Cub's cramped cabin. The Cub pilots took advantage of the Allies' complete air supremacy in the Normandy campaign. Weather permitting, they flew back and forth along the front almost constantly. The observers reported back to the artillery battalion's headquarters on such sightings as enemy gun flashes, truck convoys, and troop movements. Airborne observation missions, however, were dangerous. The Germans fired on the hated Piper Cubs because whenever one of the snooping aircraft flew over the lines, an American artillery barrage was sure to follow.

The FOs and Air OPs may have been the eyes of the artillery, but they were eyes that focused only narrowly. Someone had to give the cannoneers at the gun positions the "big picture." This was the job of artillery liaison officers ("LO"). An artillery battalion deployed a liaison team, which consisted of the LO, a sergeant, and five or six enlisted men, to each of the three infantry battalions supported by that artillery outfit. A fourth team was assigned to regimental headquarters. Unlike FOs, a liaison team was supposed to remain in place. The LO, in fact, shared a command post with an infantry battalion commander.

The LO's main function was to inform the gunners of the infantrymen's whereabouts so that no one was accidentally hit by friendly fire. If an attack was planned, the LO arranged for supporting artillery fire according to the wishes of the infantry battalion CO. If riflemen encountered stubborn resistance, the LO could easily arrange for artillery support if the infantrymen requesting assistance contacted him at the infantry battalion command post. If contact was made, the LO hastily relayed the infantrymen's requests back to the guns. Unlike FOs, liaison teams were officially prescribed in artillery tables of organization. LOs stayed with the same infantry battalion for a long time, so long, in fact, that they thought of themselves as infantrymen.

Forward observers, liaison teams, and Piper Cub observers communicated with their battalion's fire direction center ("FDC"), an extraordinary communications headquarters little bigger than a closet, which was situated about a mile behind the front. The contrast between the FDC's ultra-modern

A view from a Piper Cub observation airplane. A gap through a hedgerow has just been blown. Tank tracks are visible in the pasture on the right. *Courtesy National Archives.*

communications equipment and its austere environment was startling at first. The inside of an FDC looked like a combination of a telephone exchange and a draftsman's workroom. The most striking feature was the abundance of wires, seemingly too many to manage. All wires led to a buzzing, flashing switchboard, manned by a soldier equipped with a headphone set and a portable microphone. Several other G.I.'s monitored bulky radios, powered by whirring generators. In the corner a few men hunched over two drafting tables, using compasses and protractors to plot artillery fire on maps and aerial photos. Had the FDC been knocked out, the FOs and LOs would have been useless. For this reason, the FDC was placed a few hundred yards away from the howitzers so that it would remain operational even if the Germans bombarded the gun positions.

Old-time artillerymen in the 29th Division remembered the days when battery COs gave the order to shoot simply by yelling the word "Fire!" However, since World War II guns were spread out, shouted commands were no longer easy to hear. Wire was generally laid to each howitzer so the crew could receive orders over the phone.

The rule of thumb for the deployment of an artillery battalion's twelve howitzers was dispersion. A hub-to-hub formation would have made an easy target for German counter-battery fire or a *Jabo* (fighter-bomber). Several well-placed shells or bombs could have knocked out all twelve guns. Instead, each firing battery of four guns was assigned its own position, called a "goose egg" for its shape on a map. The three firing batteries were separated from each other by several hundred yards. Similarly, within each battery the four howitzers were always placed at least twenty-five yards apart and were usually set up in a staggered or diamond formation rather than in line.

When an artillery battalion moved to a new firing position, it did so by "leapfrog" technique. One battery first limbered up its four guns and moved while the other two batteries remained in place. Then, when the first battery set up its guns at its destination, the remaining two batteries packed up and moved. Using this technique, a constant source of fire support was always available to the infantrymen, even in a mobile battle.

A hypothetical fire mission in the 110th Field Artillery would have been carried out in the following manner. An FO attached to Company A, 115th Infantry, spots three German 120mm mortars firing in a field. He cranks up his phone and rings the FDC.

FO: "This is Lavender 3. Fire mission. Three mortars firing. Concentration 96 is 600 right, 500 short. Will adjust." [Translation: "Concentration 96" is an artillery registration mark, circled and numbered on FDC maps. The FO has determined that Concentration 96 is 600 yards to the right ("deflection") and 500 yards short ("range") of the field.]

FDC: "Roger. Wait . . . Fuze delay. Concentration 97. Able, when ready." [The FDC has given the FO approval for the mission. The first round will use a delay fuze—one that detonates the shell a fraction of a second after it enters the ground. The spot where the shell lands will be penciled in on the maps as "Concentration 97." Battery A ("Able") will fire the round as soon as it is ready.]

A short delay. Then . . .

FDC: "On the way." [This is the signal that the round has been fired.]

The FO sees the shell explode some distance away from the field.

FO: "One hundred left, 200 short." [The shell has landed 100 yards left and 200 yards short of the target.]

FDC: "Roger."

Battery A fires another round with these adjustments.

FDC: "On the way."

This time the shell lands slightly to the right of the field and a little beyond it. Through his binoculars, however, the FO notices that the German troops are hastily packing up their mortars and getting ready to depart.

FO: "Fifty right, 100 over, fire for effect."

FDC: "Roger. Able firing for effect. Two volleys. Time fuze." [A time fuze is one that detonates the shell a pre-determined number of seconds after firing. The aim is to have the shell explode in the air about fifty feet above the target.]

The aim is perfect. The FO watches eight shells explode directly over the Germans, who abandon their mortars and scurry for cover.

FO: "Range correct, repeat fire for effect, quick fuze." [The FO wants more fire, this time using a quick fuze—one that detonates the shell upon impact with the ground.]

FDC: "Roger. Able firing for effect. One volley. Quick fuze."

Now the fire is so accurate that it hits a few feet from the German mortars, destroying them.

FO: "Mortars neutralized."

The 29ers were garrulous in combat. With the world's greatest military communications network, they figured, why not put it to good use? But the American penchant for talk on the battlefield was exploited by the Germans, who became adept at eavesdropping on their enemy's conversations. German intelligence of American plans, in fact, was gained primarily through radio interception. Once the Germans became accustomed to the American system of radio communication, they could easily determine what was happening across no-man's land. The Germans always knew when a new American division had entered the front lines just by listening to the radio. They were also able to make remarkably accurate assessments of their opponent's intentions, especially when the German signal units had good English-speakers on hand. Some German troops even understood American slang.

The 29ers could hardly be accused of poor security techniques. The G.I.'s were repeatedly warned that mentioning actual unit numbers or officers' names on the air was strictly taboo. To allow the men to speak securely over the radio, the army established a simple code. Every major unit from division to army was assigned a letter: the 29th Division was "L;" the V Corps, "V," the 1st Army, "M." Subordinate units were assigned names beginning with the code letter of their parent outfit. In the 29th Division, the 115th Infantry was "Lagoon;" the 116th, "Lemon;" the 175th, "Limestone;" the 110th Field Artillery, "Larkspur;" and the 459th Anti-Aircraft Artillery Battalion, attached to the 29th Division from V Corps, "Vascular." The first battalion of an infantry regiment was "Red;" the second, "White;" the third, "Blue." Company A was "Able;" B, "Baker;" C, "Charlie;" D, "Dog;" and so on. A CO was always number "6;" his executive was "5;" his S-1 through S-4 staff officers (or the 1st, 2nd, 3rd, and weapons platoon leaders in a rifle company) were "1," "2," "3," and "4," respectively.

These code names were used so commonly that the Germans eventually figured them out. When they heard a conversation between "Lemon Red 6" and "Able 6," they knew they were listening to the CO of the 1st Battalion,

116th Infantry and the CO of Company A. The 29ers tried to fool the Germans by using double talk and slang, but the speaker had to be sure that the American listener was not as confused as the German eavesdropper.

In front line foxholes, 29th Division riflemen eventually became wary of using their radios because they feared that the Germans could pinpoint the source of transmissions by triangulation. "Men and many officers, particularly men, were very, very reluctant to turn their radios on," an observer noted of the 29ers in Normandy. "Just using my walkie-talkie in the area of the platoon that I relieved scared the hell out of them." The US Army's *Battle Experiences* newsletter attempted to reassure the worried G.I.'s. "Inexperienced troops," it said, "are often led to believe that use of low-powered infantry radio sets will draw fire as a result of being located by German direction-finding equipment. Carelessness in providing necessary camouflage and radio security is the real reason these radio sets are subjected to enemy fire. . . . Direction-finding equipment of a sufficient accuracy to provide information for artillery fire is relatively immobile and must be set up some miles in rear of the enemy lines. The low-powered infantry radio sets do not furnish sufficient signal for this direction-finding equipment to obtain accurate information."

According to General Gerhardt, too much secrecy would hurt the 29ers' morale. Uncle Charlie was always reminding his men that they were members of a division with a distinctive character and élan. It was difficult to keep up these high spirits, the general believed, if the men had to keep quiet about who they were and what they were doing. Gerhardt figured that there was no great loss if the Germans figured out who they were dealing with. It was more important for the outside world to learn of the things the 29th Division had accomplished in the war. Once, a newspaper correspondent in Normandy came across a signpost on the side of a road. "YOU ARE NOW ENTERING 29th DIVISION TERRITORY," the sign declared in large block letters. The surprised reporter realized that this was the only uncoded sign he had ever seen at the front. He approached a 29th Division MP and inquired about the obvious breach of security. "Ah, the Krauts know we're here," replied the MP. "We want some of these other jokers around here to know who's winning the damn war."

SIX

D-DAY
"We've Got to Be Infantrymen Now"
June 6, 1944

1. INVASION PLAN

Omaha Beach was nothing like the Virginia or Maryland shore. The first thing a 29er noticed about Omaha was the steep, dark green bluffs, 120 feet high, directly behind the beach. An observer standing atop the bluffs had a panoramic view of the sea, and it didn't take a military genius to figure out that a defender could hold off a force many times his size from such a position. A single MG 42 machine gun commanded about 300 yards of waterfront.

On the 29th Division half of Omaha, the western sector, the bluffs were particularly abrupt. Even a casual tourist, unencumbered by sixty pounds of military equipment, would have found it difficult to ascend the precipitous, slippery slopes. Vehicles, of course, could not even attempt the climb. The easiest way off the beach, for men and vehicles, was through four separate draws, or ravines, which cut through the bluffs and gradually descended to the shore, almost as if Mother Nature herself were providing trails between the inland countryside and the beach. The draws were actually the products of thousands of years of erosion from rain water.

The success of the Omaha invasion depended on quick seizure of these draws. The Yanks expected to be able to drive their trucks and tanks off the beach through these gaps only three hours after the first wave. The Germans, of course, also recognized the importance of the draws and were prepared to

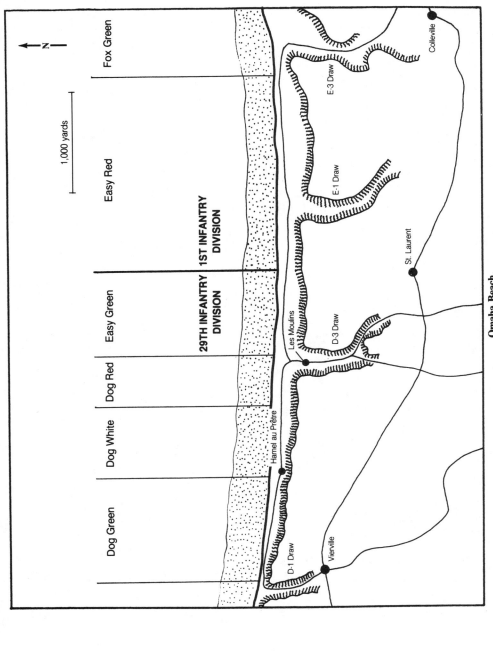

Omaha Beach.

defend them resolutely. In England, the 29ers had studied their maps and rubber terrain models of Omaha, focusing their attention on two of the four draws, one on each flank of the division's two-mile beach sector. The one on the right flank was designated "D-1" draw by the planners, but the 29ers called it "Vierville draw" because a tiny road ascended from the beach to the little village of Vierville-sur-Mer, 600 yards inland. Vierville's tall church steeple was the most prominent landmark in the 29th Division sector. The Vierville draw was the narrowest and steepest of the four draws on Omaha, and it was expected to be the most heavily defended.

The other draw in the 29th Division sector was labeled "D-3" draw, but the 29ers called it the "Les Moulins draw" after a seaside hamlet tucked between the bluffs. At the head of the draw, 1,000 yards inland, was the village of St. Laurent-sur-Mer.

Halfway between the Vierville and Les Moulins draws was another resort hamlet named Hamel au Prêtre. This village, consisting of about a dozen quaint and colorful beach villas, lay at the base of the bluffs less than 100 yards from the water's edge. The Germans built a strongpoint at the top of the bluffs behind the villas.

Another surprising feature of Omaha was the tide. During a "spring tide," when the sun, moon, and earth were aligned, as much as 700 yards separated high and low water. During less extreme tidal conditions, however, low tide exposed only some 300 yards of sand.

The Yanks were also not accustomed to rocks on their beaches. At the high tide line on Omaha, however, the waves had piled up a ten-yard belt of "shingle"—small white and tan stones polished to a gloss by the pounding sea. These rocks were deposited in steep embankments, taller than a man.

American invasion planners had a formidable task. Close to 40,000 troops and 3,500 vehicles were to land on Omaha and pass through the draws to inland assembly areas by nightfall on D-Day. Guarding the beach were hundreds of obstacles, barbed wire entanglements, pillboxes, strongpoints, and about 2,000 German troops.

Although the Germans benefitted from defensible terrain, the Allies had the advantage of dictating the precise day ("D-Day") and time ("H-Hour") of the invasion. Contrary to German expectations, the overriding planning consideration was to land the first wave during low tide so that landing craft could approach the beach unhindered by German obstacles. During low water in a spring tide, the obstacles lay fully exposed on the tidal flat, 200 yards inland from the water's edge. If the boats had attempted to land at high tide, they would have smashed into the submerged obstacles, most of which were mined. A low-tide landing also gave American engineers several hours to blast gaps through the obstacles so that later waves of troops could land safely at high water.

A pre-war postcard of Omaha Beach, looking east from the Vierville draw. The shingle, the promenade road, the bluffs, and the tops of the beach villas of Hamel au Prêtre (*upper right*) are visible. The tide is high. Companies G and F of the 116th Infantry landed in the first wave in this sector. *Courtesy Fifth Regiment Armory.*

Allied planners decided that a full moon, or close to it, would be most appropriate for D-Day. During a full moon, tidal ranges were extreme, and a low-tide invasion would enable landing craft to deposit troops ashore far short of the dangerous German obstacles. Furthermore, bright moonlight permitted ships and airplanes to navigate with relative safety at night.

The planners were convinced that the first wave must land as the tide was rising. This would allow landing craft to beach, disgorge their troops and vehicles, back off, and return to their transports. If the boats landed during a receding tide, they were likely to get stuck in the sand before they could be unloaded, and thus would be useless until freed several hours later by the next high tide.

Those who drew up the Overlord plans considered it vitally important to land in daylight so that the navy and air force could bombard the beach accurately. Furthermore, they believed that H-Hour should be set as close as possible to dawn, thereby allowing sixteen hours of daylight to accomplish D-Day's ambitious goals.

In June 1944, only June 5, 6, and 7 satisfied the requirements of the Overlord plan. The invasion was originally scheduled for June 5, but poor weather caused a one-day postponement. H-Hour on Omaha was therefore set for 6:30 A.M. on June 6, an hour after low tide and a half-hour after sunrise.

An unusual command structure existed between the 1st and the 29th Divisions to assure unity of command on the beach once the first wave landed. On June 6, the 29th's 115th and 116th Regiments would temporarily be under the

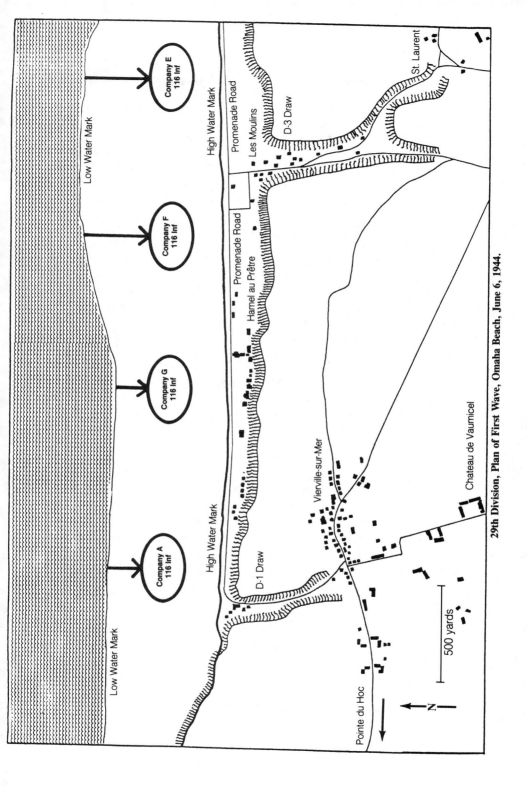

29th Division, Plan of First Wave, Omaha Beach, June 6, 1944.

command of Maj. Gen. Clarence Huebner, the commander of the 1st Division. The 29ers would remain under his control until Major General Gerow, the V Corps commander, officially activated the 29th Division, an event planned for the morning of June 7. General Gerhardt would then take over the division. General Cota, Gerhardt's assistant commander, would be the de facto leader of troops on the 29th Division's half of the beach throughout June 6. Cota, who was supposed to land about an hour behind the first wave, was to supervise the 116th's and 115th's passage off the beach to their inland assembly areas. Officially, the planners called Cota and his staff "29th Division Advance Headquarters," and the 116th and 115th were a "provisional brigade." Unofficially, Cota's command was labeled the "Bastard Brigade."

Most of the 116th Infantry was scheduled to be ashore within sixty minutes of H-Hour. In the first wave, Company A would land opposite the deadly Vierville draw on a sector known as "Dog Green"; Company G would come ashore in a zone code-named "Dog White," halfway between the Vierville and Les Moulins draws; Companies F and E would land astride the Les Moulins draw on sectors labeled "Dog Red" and "Easy Green."

Three companies of the 743rd Tank Battalion, fifty-six Sherman tanks in all, were to precede the Stonewallers ashore by several minutes, providing fire support and protection for the infantrymen. Thirty-two of these tanks (Companies B and C) were "DD" (Duplex Drive) Shermans, which were specially fitted to "swim" with a bizarre canvas flotation screen. When the screen was raised, the tanks appeared comical, seemingly trying to hide from the Germans behind a drawn curtain. The DDs were to drive off the bow ramps of their LCTs 6,000 yards offshore and head for the beach by means of a double propeller fitted at the back of each tank. The 743rd's remaining twenty-four Shermans—all in Company A—were to make a "dry" landing, driving off their beached LCTs directly onto the sand.

Two minutes after the infantrymen would come the engineers. These troops, who were not 29ers, belonged to a special outfit, the 146th Combat Engineer Battalion. This unit was specially trained to demolish German obstacles, thereby enabling later waves of troops to land unimpeded during high tide. The engineers had thirty minutes to blow gaps and mark safe lanes to the beach before the rising tide covered up the obstacles and made demolition work impossible. Eight Shermans of Company A, 743rd Tank Battalion were fitted with bulldozer blades to assist the engineers in this task.

The remaining eight rifle companies of the 116th would come ashore between 7:00 A.M. and 7:30 A.M., after the engineers had completed their demolition work. Then, from 7:30 A.M. to 8:30 A.M., the rest of the 116th, along with artillery, anti-aircraft, engineer, and medical detachments, would land.

"Dutch" Cota did not like the Omaha invasion plan. Before he came to

LANDING DIAGRAM, OMAHA BEACH
(SECTOR OF 116th RCT)

	EASY GREEN	DOG RED	DOG WHITE	DOG GREEN
H-5			Co C (DD) 743 Tk Bn	Co B (DD) 743 Tk Bn
H HOUR	Co A 743 Tk Bn	Co A 743 Tk Bn		
H+01	Co E 116 Inf	Co F 116 Inf	Co G 116 Inf	Co A 116 Inf
H+03	146 Engr CT	146 Engr CT / Demolitions Control Boat	146 Engr CT	146 Engr CT / Co C 2d Ranger Bn
H+30	AAAW Btry / Co H, HQ Co E Co H 116 Inf / AAAW Btry	HQ 2d Bn / Co H Co F Co H 2d Bn 116 Inf / AAAW Btry / 112 Engr	AAAW Btry / Co H HQ Co G Co H 116 Inf / AAAW Btry	Co B HQ Co A Co B 116 Inf / AAAW Btry
H+40	112 Engr Bn	Co D 81 Cml Wpns Bn / 149 Engr Beach Bn	149 Engr / 121 Engr Bn	HQ 1st Bn 116 / Co D 116 Inf 149 Beach Bn 121 Engr Bn
H+50	Co L 116 Inf	Co I 116 Inf	Co K 116 Inf	121 Engr Bn / Co C 116 Inf
H+57		HQ Co 3d Bn — Co M 116 Inf		Co B 81 Cml Wpns Bn
H+60		112 Engr Bn	HQ & HQ Co 116 Inf	121 Engr Bn / Co A & B 2d Ranger Bn
H+65				5th Ranger Bn
H+70	149 Engr Beach Bn	112 Engr Bn	Alt HQ & HQ Co 116 Inf	121 Engr Bn / 5th Ranger Bn
H+90			58 FA Bn Armd	
H+100			6th Engr Sp Brig	
H+110	111 FA Bn (3 Btry's in DUKWS)	AT Plat 2d Bn AT Plat 3d Bn / 29 Sig Bn		AT Plat 1st Bn / Cn Co 116 Inf
H+120	AT Co 116 Inf 467 AAAW Bn	467 AAAW Bn 149 Engr AT Co 116 Inf Beach Bn	467 AAAW Bn	467 AAAW Bn
H+150			HQ Co 116 Inf 104 Med Bn	
H+180 to H+215		DD Tanks 461 Amphibious Truck Co	Navy Salvage	
H+225	461 Amph Trk Co			

LCI | LCM | LCA | DD Tank
LCT | LCVP | DUKW

Note: Plan as of 11 May

Landing Plan, 116th Infantry, June 6, 1944. *Courtesy Center of Military History and* **Infantry** *magazine.*

the 29th Division, Cota had prepared a study on the most effective methods by which a heavily defended beach could be assaulted from the sea. Cota believed that the first wave should land during darkness. He suspected that the

Allied air and naval bombardment of the beach, even in broad daylight, would have little effect on the enemy's strong beach fortifications. As long as even a handful of German resistance nests survived, Cota reasoned, American troops would be mown down as they disembarked from their landing craft. If, on the other hand, the Allies invaded at night, Cota was convinced that the enemy could not see well enough to shoot effectively, and therefore the assault troops could safely cross the tidal flat, where they would be most vulnerable. The Germans could then be engaged at close range on terms favorable to the Americans. Since the Yanks were mobile and the enemy troops in the strongpoints were not, the G.I.'s would inevitably predominate.

Cota also believed that one of the cardinal objectives of all military operations—surprise—was best achieved by a nighttime assault. "The beach is going to be fouled-up in any case," said Cota. "Darkness will not substantially alter the percentage of accuracy in beaching—not enough to offset the handicaps of a daylight assault."

Only a few American officers in Britain in June 1944 could claim expertise in amphibious warfare. One of the few was Maj. Gen. Charles "Pete" Corlett, the former commander of the 7th Infantry Division. In February 1944, the 7th had successfully stormed Kwajalein atoll, part of the Marshall Island chain in the southwest Pacific, routing 9,000 Japanese defenders in a campaign lasting only one week. It had been the most successful American amphibious operation to date.

Corlett was transferred to England in April to assume command of XIX Corps, a headquarters to which the 29th Division would be attached only one week after D-Day. Several weeks after his arrival in England, Corlett gave a talk to senior British officers and their staffs on the techniques used in the Kwajalein invasion. Much to Corlett's amusement, one British general blurted out at the end of the presentation, "By jove! If we have an island to take, you ought to do it!"

Corlett was shocked by the Omaha invasion plan, but it was too late to change anything. He complained that Overlord did not take advantage of hard lessons learned in the Pacific. At Kwajalein, the first waves of the 7th Division had employed a newfangled assault boat called the "Landing Vehicle, Tracked" (LVT), nicknamed the "alligator" by the troops. The alligator could make five knots on the water, glide up onto the beach, and riding on its tracks, do eighteen miles per hour on land. The alligators were enormously successful at Kwajalein, and Corlett pointedly asked Eisenhower and Bradley why the first waves at Omaha were using LCVPs and LCAs instead of fresher technology. "I was pretty well squelched for my question," wrote Corlett. "I soon got the feeling that American generals in England considered anything that had happened in the Pacific strictly 'Bush League stuff,' which didn't merit any consideration. I felt like an expert according to the Naval definition, 'A son-of-a-bitch from out of town.' "

2. THE BEACH

The boys in Company A, 116th Infantry, were not in good spirits. They had lost two of their six landing craft on the run-in. As the four remaining boats slid onto the beach and ground to a halt, their bow ramps dropped with a splash. The company was right where it was supposed to be, just east of the Vierville draw on the beach known as Dog Green. But the Germans were waiting for them.

Company A didn't stand a chance. As soon as the first Stonewallers started down the ramps, they were riddled with bullets and collapsed face-first into the water as if smacked hard from behind.

Feeling like cattle in a slaughter pen, the men, who were crowded into the rear of the landing craft waiting to disembark, watched in horror. Disembarking from the boats was suicide, but so was remaining aboard. Losing all semblance of order, they scrambled to get out, leaping into frigid water over their heads. As they floundered and splashed, trying to free themselves of their heavy equipment, they could hear the "rrrrrrp" of German MG 42s atop the bluffs, 500 yards away.

There was no place to hide and no way to fight back. Those who were lucky enough to make it off the boats sought refuge in neck-deep water, bobbing up and down with the waves, moving forward imperceptibly with the rising tide. Several men dared to advance out of the water, but they were promptly killed. The only shelter—enemy obstacles—offered little protection, since the Germans fired from the flanks as well as the front.

Officers tried to get the men moving. Lt. Edward Tidrick, who had been hit in the neck as he left his boat, dropped on the sands, gasping for breath, bleeding profusely. Tidrick rose up on one elbow, looked at his fellow Stonewallers lying on the sand near him, and shouted, "Advance with the wire cutters!" Seconds later he was hit by a burst of German fire and killed instantly.

Would anyone survive this debacle? Amazingly, in one Company A boat, numbered LCA 1015, all thirty-two Stonewallers were killed, including Capt. Taylor Fellers, the company CO. In other boat sections, wounded men crawled up on the sand and gave themselves shots of morphine; then they lay still to avoid attracting German attention. Some became so weak that they could no longer move and drowned in the fast-rising tide, unless they were lucky enough to be dragged ahead of the surging water by a friend. But anyone who moved risked being cut down by a German machine gun.

Company G's six boats, which were supposed to land directly on Company A's left, strayed far to the east. This error proved fortuitous since the beach where the LCVPs eventually set down, just east of the Les Moulins draw, was hidden from the Germans by billowing smoke rising from grass fires on the bluffs. When the ramps dropped, the Stonewallers descended into knee-deep water and lumbered onto the sand.

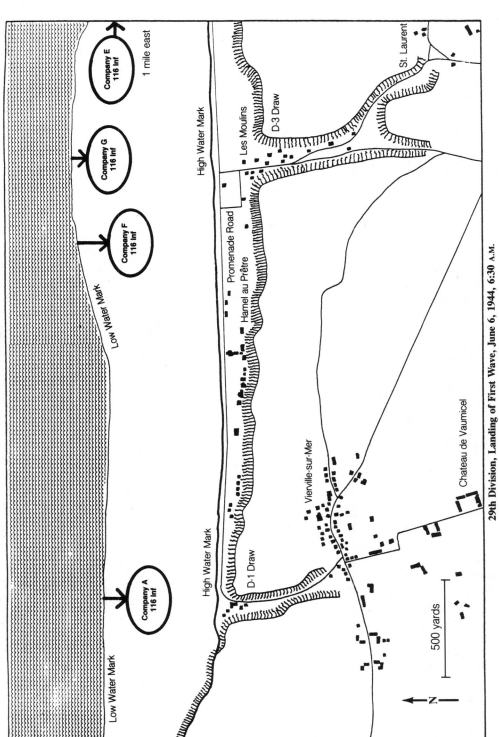

29th Division, Landing of First Wave, June 6, 1944, 6:30 A.M.

There was desultory German fire. "We didn't expect any trouble on the beach and had been told not to run," Pvt. August Bruno recalled. Within five minutes of beaching, the men of Company G had successfully crossed 350 yards of tidal flat, passed through the German obstacles in good order, and flopped down at the base of the seawall marking the high water line.

A command passed down the line: "Move to the right 1,000 yards. You are to the left of your target." Unfortunately, the order threw Company G into disarray. Filing to their right, the men bent over double so their heads would not be exposed to German fire above the seawall. The move brought the company into an area that was not covered by the brush fire smoke, and the men came under heavy German fire. It took almost two hours for Company G to move 1,000 yards westward. When the Stonewallers finally reached their intended landing zone, dozens of men had already dropped out. Some of these had been hit, others had sought a safe hiding place. A few had even moved inland on their own initiative.

Company F landed exactly where it was supposed to, directly opposite the Les Moulins draw. When the ramps went down, machine gun bullets splashed in the water and pinged off the sides of the boats. Several Stonewallers were hit as they disembarked. But a disaster like the one that befell Company A was averted because Company F landed downwind from the brushfires and was intermittently obscured by drifting black smoke.

American troops landing in the first wave at Omaha Beach. The G.I.'s are taking cover behind the German hedgehogs and wooden stakes. An LCVP is barely visible in the background. *Courtesy Military History Institute.*

Several Company F boat sections made it across the tidal flat in good order, and the Stonewallers dropped down, exhausted, behind the shingle embankment directly in front of the draw. Other sections, however, attracted heavy fire as the men waded through the surf. These unlucky 29ers dropped down behind German hedgehogs and inched their way forward with the rising tide.

A terrified Company F private named John Robertson, lying at the water's edge, glanced backwards and saw a huge Sherman tank headed straight for him. "Crossing the beach looked like suicide, but better than getting run over," Robertson recalled. He got up and dashed all the way to the seawall.

The most confused soldiers on Omaha must have been the members of Company E, the easternmost of the 29th Division's four first-wave companies. Not one Company E boat landed within a mile of its assigned sector. In fact, several boats, pushed eastward into the 1st Division sector by the inexorable flood current, beached two miles off-target. A disconcerting gap of three-quarters of a mile divided Company E from the nearest Stonewallers. Even worse, the six Company E boats scattered over 1,200 yards of beach, and the company CO, Capt. Lawrence Madill, found it impossible to control his men.

Two lucky Company E LCVPs landed in a lightly defended area. At a cost of only two wounded men, both boat sections rushed across the 300-yard tidal flat to the seawall. One of these boats was piloted by an experienced coxswain who carefully maneuvered the LCVP around hidden runnels and eddies, finally dropping the ramp on dry sand. The Stonewallers in this boat didn't even get their feet wet, probably the only 29th Division "dry" landing in the first wave.

The other four Company E boats encountered heavy German fire as soon as their ramps dropped. One unfortunate LCVP took a direct hit from a German artillery shell. Many Company E men in these four sections were shot as they raced from the water to the bluffs. Others dropped on the sand and waited for the fire to abate. "One of the episodes I remember the most was debarking from the landing craft and trying to take shelter from the enemy fire behind one of their obstacles," recalled Walter A. Smith of Company E. "Captain Madill came up behind me and others, ordering all that could move to get off the beach. I looked up at him and his left arm appeared to be almost blown off."

Despite his wound, Madill made it to the seawall but discovered that one of his company mortars, which was being set up nearby, had no ammunition. He ran back to the water's edge to pick up some shells. As he was returning, he was hit by a machine gun burst. Before he died, Madill gasped, "Senior non-com, take the men off the beach."

The Shermans of the 743rd Tank Battalion were easy prey for German antitank gunners on the bluffs, but the tankers were doing what little they could to help the desperate Stonewallers. Most of the 743rd's tanks had landed successfully, thanks to a Navy lieutenant who had decided not to launch the thirty-two "DD" swimming tanks of Companies B and C in rough seas 6,000 yards offshore. Instead, the lieutenant beached his eight LCTs. In the 1st Division sector, another tank battalion, the 741st, adhered to the original plan and attempted to swim in thirty-two DD tanks. Only five made it.

A Company B LCT was hit by a shell and sank as it neared the beach, and four tanks were lost. The rest of the 743rd's Shermans roared off the ramps of their landing craft, fanned out into a ragged line with a seventy-five-yard interval between tanks, and commenced firing. Several tanks were promptly hit and set afire. The 29ers who were pinned at the water's edge sought refuge from machine gun fire by clustering behind the Shermans, only to find themselves in graver danger: the tanks were attracting accurate German artillery fire.

The 146th Engineers, whose mission was to blow gaps through the German obstacles, probably had the most difficult time of all in the first wave. Landing a few minutes after H-Hour, the engineers fell victim to the flood current. Most of the 146th's boats were swept to the east; only a few engineers arrived where they were supposed to.

Several boxes of the engineers' explosives were hit and blew up in giant red fireballs. Still, the engineers, in full view of the Germans, raced against the rising tide to complete their demolition work before the sea covered up the obstacles. Engineers who managed to place charges under obstacles were frequently prevented from detonating them because friendly troops were pinned nearby. By the time the tide rose high enough to curtail further work, the 146th had blown only two tiny gaps in the 29th's sector. There should have been eight fifty-yard gaps.

The invasion had begun badly for the 29ers. None of the four first-wave companies had come close to accomplishing its mission. Indeed, several boat sections, including all those in Company A, had been decimated at the water's edge. Furthermore, with only two gaps through which landing craft could pass at high tide, the prospect of reinforcement was not good.

The Stonewallers lying behind the seawall were safe from enemy machine gun fire, but they were cold, exhausted, and leaderless. Some men still vomited from seasickness—or from fear. When the men looked back at the appalling carnage on the beach, they knew immediately that the invasion had gone awry. It had been a one-sided battle so far; hardly a Stonewaller had had a chance to fire his rifle. In truth, even if he had that chance, his rifle was likely to have been fouled with sand and sea water. Several level-headed Stonewallers, figuring they would need their M1s later on, decided to strip and clean them right there.

The first wave, however, was just the leading edge of a hurricane. Only one-quarter of the 116th, in fact, had landed in the first half-hour of the invasion. Eight more companies were due to land in the following half-hour. An hour after that, the entire regiment was supposed to be ashore.

The coxswains piloting the second wave boats probably had an even more difficult task than their comrades in the first wave. By the time the second wave neared the beach, the rising tide had covered many German obstacles, and the coxswains had to steer very carefully to avoid them. Even a light bump against an obstacle could be catastrophic, since most of them were mined.

Behind the unfortunate Company A, the three remaining companies of the 1st Battalion—B, D, and C—were to land near the Vierville draw at ten-minute intervals starting at 7:00 A.M. Company C landed at 7:10 A.M., ten minutes early. Luckily, the company boats had drifted eastward, and the men were deposited several hundred yards away from their intended landing sector, thereby avoiding the disaster that befell their Company A brethren. Company C made it across the beach with almost no losses.

Companies B and D, however, landed approximately where they were supposed to, and as a result, they were decimated as soon as the ramps dropped. Company B's CO, Capt. Ettore Zappacosta, was gunned down only ten yards from his boat as he splashed through the surf. As he fell, he spun around yelling "I'm hit!" A horrified medic, still on the ramp, shouted, "Try to make it in!" But Zappacosta had already disappeared beneath the waves. The medic jumped in after him and was promptly shot dead, as were several other Stonewallers who followed. In fact, every man save one on this boat was either killed or wounded in the water. The one man who escaped injury survived by hiding behind a large log he had latched onto in the surf, which he rolled forward on the sand in front of the rising tide. As German bullets cracked over the G.I.'s head, the dead bodies of his comrades tossed and tumbled in the waves and washed up next to him on the sand.

Company D's CO, Capt. Walter Schilling, was killed when his boat detonated a mine 400 yards offshore. Schilling was at that point the fourth company CO to be killed; three were from the 1st Battalion.

As the other Company D boats hit the beach, they were raked by German fire. In one boat, a British coxswain stopped the engines 400 yards offshore and announced that this was as far as he would go since there were too many obstacles ahead. Sgt. William Norfleet, however, was convinced that the water was too deep for the men to make it ashore, and he furiously turned on the coxswain, ordering him to bring the boat in closer. The coxswain, more frightened of Norfleet than of the obstacles, maneuvered the boat 200 yards further in. It hit an obstacle and promptly sank, but the men were able to wade ashore in waist-deep water.

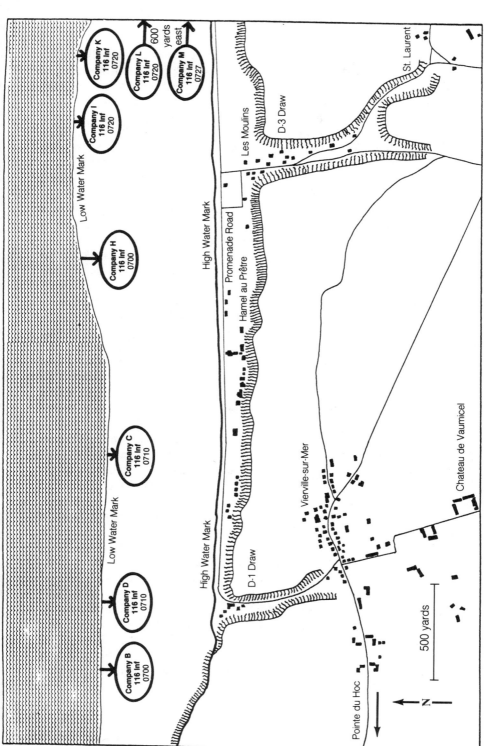

29th Division, Landing of Second Wave, June 6, 1944.

As one private struggled through the surf, a spent German bullet hit him in the helmet. Although the bullet clanged harmlessly off his helmet, he was knocked unconscious by the blow. One of his friends dragged him ashore. According to Maj. Tom Dallas, executive officer of the 1st Battalion, those who reached the seawall "made it because the man ahead caught the bullet that might have felled them."

In front of the Les Moulins draw, the last company in the 116th's 2nd Battalion, Company H, as well as the entire 3rd Battalion, Companies I, K, L, and M, were scheduled to land between 7:00 A.M. and 7:27 A.M. All the boats drifted eastward, and some of them went far into the 1st Division zone.

Company H had the bad fortune of landing directly opposite a German strongpoint. "Two of the men from my section got down behind a tetrahedron [hedgehog] to escape bullets," one private in Company H recalled. "An artillery shell hit the tetrahedron and drove the steel back into their bodies. I tried to pry the steel loose from the men, but couldn't do it. Then I figured they were dead, anyway."

Some Company H men noticed that one of their wounded comrades, Pvt. Raymond Pryor, was lying almost on top of a German mine that had washed ashore. Pryor's friends shouted for him to crawl away, but he paid no heed. Pryor survived because the mine never went off.

Maj. Sidney Bingham, the 2nd Battalion CO, landed to the east of Company H. "For some reason I thought all was well until, after struggling ashore through shoulder-deep water, I paused for a breather behind a steel tetrahedron anti-boat obstacle and noticed the sand kicking up at my feet," Bingham recalled. "It then occurred to me all of a sudden that I was getting shot at and that machine gun bullets were kicking up that sand. From then on, there was no doubt in my mind. I was scared, exhausted. . . . I finally crossed the beach and got to the shingle along the beach road where about 100 men from Company F were seeking what little shelter the road afforded."

An artillery captain accompanying Bingham described these infantrymen as "beat up and shocked. Many of them had forgotten that they had firearms to use. Others who had lost their [guns] didn't seem to see that there were weapons lying all around and that it was their duty to pick them up."

In contrast to the 2nd Battalion, the 3rd landed relatively intact. The only known casualty in Company K before the men reached the seawall was a lieutenant who was accidentally poked by a bayonet in his crowded LCVP. The ghastly sight of dead and wounded lying all over the beach, however, deadened the spirits of even the most enthusiastic Stonewallers. "All of the men seemed shakier and weaker than usual," one Company M sergeant remembered. "Seasickness was getting some but fear was getting most of us. The burdens that we could ordinarily carry, we had to drag. But we *dragged* them. Not one thing was left on the beach," even though, as another Company M sergeant recalled, "the enemy was simply throwing lead. . . . The company learned with surprise how much small arms fire a man can run through without getting hit."

General Cota was offshore in one of the 116th's transports, but he wanted to see the beach for himself. He therefore set out for Omaha in LCVP 71 with Colonel Canham and his 116th staff. As the LCVP neared the beach, it struck a half-submerged German obstacle topped with a menacing mine. Jarred loose by the collision, the mine fell harmlessly into the sea.

About fifty yards from shore, the LCVP dropped its ramp in waist-deep water. As Cota and his party splashed through the surf, the man standing next to the general, Maj. John Sours, the 116th's S-4, was killed by a machine gun burst. Everyone else made it to the beach and took refuge behind a Sherman. The tank, however, provided little protection, so the group made a break for the seawall, about 150 yards distant.

In this sector, the seawall consisted of sturdy wooden stakes, about four feet high. To prevent beach erosion, a dozen jetties projected perpendicularly from the wall toward the sea. The jetties were separated from each other by fifty feet.

Cota was shocked when he neared the wall. In the pockets between the jetties, several hundred 29ers were lying face-down, jumbled up against the low seawall, and no one dared even to stand up. Before Cota's arrival, no officer had taken charge of this disordered mass, since each pocket contained a hodgepodge of men from several different units. Several G.I.'s in the pockets were not even 29ers, but belonged to the 5th Ranger Battalion, a special commando unit that had been temporarily attached to the 116th for the invasion. The rangers were supposed to have landed near the Vierville draw, but like everyone else, their boats had drifted eastward, and the men found themselves on an unfamiliar beach, among strangers.

Even Cota had little hope of exerting firm control. Although only a few feet separated the men in each pocket from their neighbors on either side, the intervening jetties prevented communication.

German shells occasionally exploded on or between the jetties, inflicting terrible casualties. As Cota arrived, one jagged piece of shrapnel hit a 29er in the back and almost cut him in two. Cota and Canham knew that the shelling would get much worse as German artillery zeroed in on this inviting target. They set out in opposite directions to find a way for the men to get off the beach and start fighting.

German fire was growing in intensity by the minute. "So many shells were ranging along over the crest of the hill that a man standing there felt as if he could reach out and pick them out of the air," recalled Capt. Maurice McGrath of the 116th Service Company.

A German *Gefreiter* (private first class) manning an MG 42 on top of the bluffs recalled in broken English, "It was the first time I shoot at living men. I don't remember exactly how it was; the only thing I know is that I went to my machine gun and I shoot, I shoot, I shoot."

The tide had risen almost to the high water mark; scarcely fifty yards separated the pounding surf from the men cowering behind the seawall. At the water's edge, the waves deposited dozens of corpses in a neat line, as if the dead were being laid out for burial. One Stonewaller remembered, "They looked like Madame Tussaud's. Like wax. None of it seemed real."

Two or three American machine guns were set up on the shingle and fired into the bluffs, but their chugging "rat-tat-tat" fire was lost in the cacophony of the enemy's whining rockets, bursting shells, and cracking bullets. The Yanks could hardly see the enemy pillboxes and slit trenches on the bluffs. The Germans, on the other hand, could see everything.

Several US Navy destroyers boldly sailed close to shore, trying to use their five-inch guns to blast German strongpoints. If the Americans on the beaches could see little, the sailors could see even less. To make matters worse, the Stonewallers could not communicate with the ships: almost no radios on the beach were working. About 1,000 yards west of the Vierville draw, a destroyer mistook a group of Stonewallers from Company B for Germans and started shooting. This was an understandable error, since a stubborn German strongpoint stood atop the cliffs at that end of the beach. The frantic Stonewallers tried to stop the firing by signaling the ship with ad hoc signal flags. "We are Americans. Cease firing." A message came back on the destroyer's blinker: "Surrender to the Americans."

For a time, the jubilant Germans thought they had repulsed the invasion. After the first wave, the commander of *Widerstandsnest* 76, a resistance nest atop the cliffs on the beach's western flank, reported to 352nd Division headquarters by phone, "At the water's edge at low tide near St. Laurent and Vierville the enemy is in search of cover behind the coastal obstacles. A great many vehicles—among these ten tanks—stand burning at the beach. The obstacle demolition squads have given up their activity. Debarkation from the landing boats has ceased, the boats keep farther seawards. The fire of our strongpoints and artillery was well-placed and has inflicted considerable casualties among the enemy. A great many wounded and dead lie on the beach."

The plan by which the 29ers were to fight their way off the beach had long since gone awry. Most 29ers had no idea what to do. Those who had successfully crossed the beach cowered behind the seawall, leaderless, paralyzed by the gruesome sights surrounding them. All the while, they were taking German mortar and artillery fire.

A few extraordinarily brave 29ers took initiative. In exhorting the men behind the seawall to move, the leaders did not appeal to the troops' sense of duty or to patriotism. Instead, they argued matter-of-factly: the safest thing to do was advance. On the eastern half of the beach, a 1st Division colonel came to the same conclusion. "Two kinds of people are staying on this beach," he said, "the dead and those who are going to die. Now let's get the hell out of here!"

That kind of argument was persuasive. Several 29ers got up and started to move towards the base of the bluffs. Paying scant attention to textbook tactics, they advanced in separate, uncoordinated groups, varying in size from over 100 men to scarcely a dozen.

Between the jetties, where hundreds of 29ers huddled for safety, Cota cajoled a motley collection of infantrymen to get up and move. The general crawled over the seawall to a tiny rise in the ground five yards away that offered protection from German fire. He directed a BAR man to this spot and ordered him to fire on any Germans he saw on the bluffs. A paved promenade road ran parallel to and only a few yards away from the seawall, roughly where a boardwalk would be situated in an American beach resort. The Germans had deployed a belt of coiled barbed wire along the road. Even if the men were willing to follow Cota, no one could get off the beach until someone blew a gap in the wire.

While the BAR man fired, a 29er detonated a bangalore torpedo under the wire, creating a narrow break in the coil. The first soldier to run through the gap, however, was hit by a machine gun burst. "Medico, I'm hit! Help me!" he cried. As his voice faded, he sobbed "Mama" and died in full view of the men at the seawall.

Cota realized he had to do something equally dramatic or the men would never move. He leaped up, dashing across the road and through the gap. Luckily he made it, and he turned around and shouted for the men to follow. Several Stonewallers did so, and miraculously no one was hit. Their success convinced dozens more to try it.

Cota led his group forward into a field 100 yards wide, between the road and the bluffs. Tall reeds and marsh grass hid the men from German gunners. They discovered an abandoned German trench, followed it to the foot of the bluff, and began ascending in single file.

The men climbed in separate groups, sticking close to their friends, if they could find any among the many strangers. Whenever they felt like it, they stopped and rested. They paid little attention to orders from unknown sergeants and officers, but when Cota paced back and forth along the scraggly column, urging the men on, they kept moving. Little German fire was directed at Cota's party since most of the enemy strongpoints were sited to fire at the beach proper rather than the bluff slopes. The G.I.'s repeatedly came across German signposts sticking out of the ground at crazy angles. "Achtung! Minen," the signs warned, and the men didn't need to know German to understand the meaning. "There were so many of these, that a man had to disregard them if he was to proceed at all,'' one 29er recollected. But the signs were not fakes. Several men in Cota's group stepped on mines and were badly wounded.

Once, when several members of Cota's party were taking a rest during their ascent of the bluffs, their attention was momentarily drawn back to the promenade. Five German prisoners—the first enemy troops the observers had ever seen—had their hands on their heads and were hurrying along under the watchful eye of a 29th Division guard. Suddenly, the first two prisoners fell, hit by a burst of machine gun fire from their own troops. "Their captor dove towards the protecting cover of the seawall, while two of the remaining three sank to their knees," remembered Lt. Jack Shea, Cota's aide. "They seemed to be pleading with the operator of the machine gun, situated on the bluffs to the east, not to shoot them. The next burst caught the first kneeling German full in the chest, and as he crumpled the remaining two took to the cover of the seawall with their captor."

Cota's men finally reached the top of the bluffs behind Hamel au Prêtre, whose once-pretty beach villas now smoldered, wrecked by Allied naval fire. It was around 9:00 A.M. A short distance beyond the crest, a German machine gun on the outskirts of Vierville greeted the 29ers with a few desultory bursts, and the Yanks flung themselves to the ground.

Cota came up to the head of the column and arranged the men into ad hoc "fire and maneuver" teams. He directed several teams to lay down a steady stream of fire against nearby hedgerows and houses and led the rest in a series of short rushes across the open fields. The German gunners promptly retreated. It was one of the first instances of an effective American infantry attack in the campaign.

The men came upon a dirt track leading into Vierville from the east. Cota sent a few scouts ahead and deployed the rest of his men in two files, one on each side of the trail. They marched a quarter-mile into Vierville, and hardly a shot was fired in response. As the men approached the village, one G.I. found a discarded MG 42 in a hedgerow, and he and his friends examined it curiously.

About a dozen Vierville natives met the 29ers at the edge of town, the first encounter between 29ers and French civilians on D-Day. Both parties regarded each other warily; few words were exchanged. The battle was still raging and there was little time for pleasantries.

Cota directed the men to enter the town, secure it, and then move out the other side. As this mission was being accomplished, more and more 29ers who had made their way off the beach and up the bluffs appeared outside Vierville. Most of these men were from Company C, an outfit raised in the Shenandoah Valley town of Harrisonburg. This outfit was one of the few companies in the 116th to fight intact on D-Day. When the Company C men

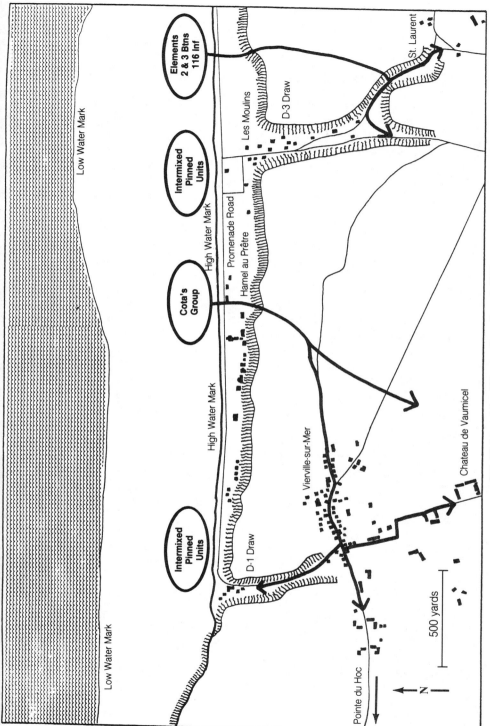

Low Water Mark

Low Water Mark

High Water Mark

High Water Mark

Elements
2 & 3 Btns
116 Inf

Intermixed
Pinned
Units

Cota's
Group

Intermixed
Pinned
Units

St. Laurent

D-3 Draw

Les Moulins

Promenade Road

Hamel au Prêtre

Vierville-sur-Mer

D-1 Draw

Chateau de Vaumicel

Pointe du Hoc

500 yards

N

29th Division, Inland Penetrations, June 6, 1944.

trod cautiously into Vierville, they met Cota walking down the narrow main street, twirling a pistol on his index finger like an Old West gunfighter. "Where the hell have you been, boys?" he asked.

Colonel Canham, CO of the 116th, also made it up the bluffs, leading a mixed group of 2nd Battalion men and Rangers. When they entered Vierville, Canham, who had been wounded on the beach but refused evacuation, fanned his men out south and west of town. After locating and conferring with Cota, Canham agreed to head east to help the Stonewallers ascend the bluffs near Les Moulins. Cota started back to the beach down the Vierville draw, still held by Germans, to open up a route by which tanks and other vehicles could move inland.

The German defenses at the mouth of the draw were now being pounded unmercifully by US Navy ships, including the battleship *Texas*, which fired six 14-inch shells into the draw at pointblank range. "The concussion from the bursts of these guns seemed to make the pavement of the street in Vierville actually rise beneath our feet in a 'bucking' sensation," recalled Shea. At the height of the barrage, Cota set out gamely down the draw with Shea and four other men. "I hope to hell they cut out that firing," remarked one member of the group. " 'That firing' probably made them duck back into their holes," retorted Cota.

But before Cota's tiny group had reached the head of the draw, the shelling suddenly stopped. Sporadic rifle fire was directed at the group from a cave on the east face of the draw. Cota's men responded with a fusillade of carbine and pistol fire. The Germans, dazed from the naval shelling, were in no mood for a fight, and five of them emerged with their hands up. As the Yanks continued down the draw with their five prisoners, they came to a minefield. The 29ers ordered one of the prisoners through first and then followed, taking care to step in the German's footprints. Shortly thereafter, the group reached the beach. By firing only a few rounds, Cota's little army of six men had seized the Vierville draw. Ironically enough, the draw was taken from the rear rather than the front.

The scene on the beach was appalling. Shea estimated that in every 100-yard section of beach, thirty-five to fifty corpses lay sprawled on the sand. Most of the men were Stonewallers; Shea could see their blue and gray shoulder patches.

Cota strode fearlessly back and forth at the mouth of the draw, rasping out orders to everyone he met. Several 29ers taking cover behind a burnt-out beach villa shouted warnings to the general to get down because there was a German sniper on the bluffs who had their range. Cota walked over and calmly reassured them that their buddies had already taken the heights, but if there was still a German lurking about, they should find him and kill him.

A tall, concrete wall in front of the draw blocked the movement of vehicles inland. "Can you blow up that antitank wall at the exit?" Cota asked an engineer colonel.

"We can, sir, just as soon as the infantry clean out those pillboxes around there," the colonel replied.

"We just came down through there," declared Cota. "There's nothing to speak of there. Get to it!"

Someone reported that there was not enough TNT. Cota spotted a bulldozer down the beach piled high with explosives. The general stalked over and demanded of a group of G.I.'s standing nearby, "Who drives this thing?" No one replied. "Well, can anyone drive the damn thing?" Still no response. "They need TNT down at the exit," Cota continued. "I just came through there from the rear. Nothing but a few riflemen on the cliff, and they're being cleaned up. Hasn't anyone got guts enough to drive it down?" A soldier finally stepped forward. "That's the stuff!" said Cota, slapping the man on the back. Cota would later regret not getting the soldier's name.

The TNT shortage at the Vierville draw remedied, Cota set out eastward along the beach. He encountered several 116th officers who told him that another group of Stonewallers had penetrated the German defenses 500 yards east of the Les Moulins draw. Like Cota's men at Vierville, these G.I.'s, mostly from the 3rd Battalion of the 116th, had advanced up the bluffs in small groups, following the orders of anyone who seemed to know what he was doing. Each group of 29ers fought independently, using few of the textbook "fire and maneuver" tactics they had mastered in years of training.

One such group consisted of thirty men from Company L, led by Lt. Donald Anderson. After crossing the beach, Anderson's team had come upon a large group of leaderless Stonewallers lying prone on the shingle. "Who in hell are you?" Anderson demanded.

"Company G, 2nd Battalion," someone replied.

Anderson turned to his sergeant. "Get the team on its way," he said. "We sure as hell aren't staying here. This beach has too many people."

Under fire, the sergeant cut a hole through the wire, and Anderson led his detachment through the gap, straight up the bluffs, and into the fields beyond the crest. They advanced a few hundred yards before being pinned by a German machine gun. Anderson raised his head over a hedgerow to see where the enemy fire was coming from and was promptly shot through the jaw. A sergeant took over, and the team eventually knocked out the offending machine gun. Anderson survived and was later awarded the Silver Star.

Company K got up the bluffs relatively intact. One group advanced across a field near St. Laurent and came to a dirt path. Suddenly, the men spotted a lone German soldier attempting to flee down the track. The Company K men fired and the German fell dead. The Stonewallers cautiously approached the body and prodded it with their feet. It was their first close-up view of a German corpse.

Shortly after noon, the 3rd Battalion, along with a party of the 2nd Battalion led by Major Bingham, reached the outskirts of St. Laurent at the head of the Les Moulins draw. The Germans, however, were well entrenched in the town and thwarted all attempts to take it. Company L, in fact, lost more men in its attempt to capture St. Laurent than it lost on the beach.

But the important thing was that the Stonewall Brigade had, at last, broken through the enemy's beach defenses in two separate places. The 29th Division beachhead, however, was only a few hundred yards deep by midafternoon. Furthermore, the 116th's casualties had been staggering. Close to one-third of the regiment—about 1,000 men—had been killed or wounded, but the percentage of loss among the rifle companies, particularly those in the 1st and 2nd Battalions, had been much higher. In fact, some companies in the first and second waves had almost ceased to exist.

Little had gone according to plan, but somehow the German defenses had been broken. "Everything that was done was done in small groups, led by the real heroes of any war," Major Bingham recalled. "Most of them were killed. . . . The minefields behind the beach were strewn with these guys; they were lying around the hedgerows on top of the bluffs and, of course, they were piled—literally—on the beach proper. . . . Very, very few were decorated, chiefly because no one was left to tell about what they did."

3. SECOND WAVE

The cannoneers of the 111th Field Artillery Battalion were unhappy with their D-Day mission. They were supposed to bring their twelve 105mm howitzers ashore two hours after H-Hour to support the 116th, whose infantrymen were expected to have already fought their way off the beach. About an hour before the guns were to land, the 111th was to send several liaison teams ashore to search for prospective gun positions. The liaison teams would be led by Lt. Col. Thornton Mullins, the 111th's CO.

What bothered Mullins and his artillerymen most was that they were to bring their guns ashore on amphibious trucks called DUKWs, pronounced "Ducks." During invasion exercises, the DUKWs had proven unseaworthy under heavy loads. Yet each DUKW was supposed to carry a single howitzer, fourteen artillerymen, fifty shells, heavy sandbags, and other military paraphernalia. With such a load, the men of the 111th knew that the DUKWs would have only a few inches of freeboard. In a heavy sea, they could easily be swamped. Some, including Mullins, pointed out that the loads could be significantly lightened with little detriment to the guns' performance on the beach. But no one listened.

The liaison teams preceding the guns ashore knew at once that it would be suicide for the DUKWs to attempt a landing. Even if the DUKWs managed to pass through the deadly German obstacles, enemy machine gun fire was still too intense to allow the cannoneers to set up their howitzers on the beach. Unfortunately, the liaison teams' radios had gotten soaked during the shoreward journey and were not functioning. The 111th's liaison team frantically searched for a working radio to warn the DUKWs to stay off the beach. But every radio on Omaha, it seemed, was out of order.

Mullins surveyed the chaos on the beach and came to a hasty conclusion. "To hell with our artillery mission," he shouted to a fellow officer. "We've got to be infantrymen now!" Mullins crept along the seawall, urging the Stonewallers to start shooting. Within minutes, he was wounded by a sniper's bullet. He died a few hours later.

When Mullins was hit, he had no idea that most of the 111th's DUKWs had already been lost. In total darkness, the DUKWs had driven off the ramp of their LST (Landing Ship, Tank) at 2:00 A.M., flopping ungracefully into the turbulent sea like first-time swimmers. The DUKWs were not scheduled to land until 8:20 A.M., so the coxswains had the nearly impossible task of keeping the unsteady DUKWs afloat for almost six-and-a-half hours.

Disaster struck almost immediately. One of Battery B's DUKWs descended the ramp, was smashed by a wave, and promptly sank. The other DUKWs made it off the LST, but while circling and waiting for word to head for shore, six more swamped and went down. During the passage to the beach, another DUKW was lost. Only four remained. "I figured that if we got those four guns ashore, at least, they'd make one battery and that might help some," recalled Capt. Jack Wilson, of Battery A.

But three DUKWs were hit by gunfire and sank as they approached the beach. The surviving DUKW was commanded by Capt. Louis Shuford of Battery C, nicknamed "Boobytrap" by his men due to his penchant for fooling with explosives. One fellow officer said of Shuford, "You could throw almost any mechanical problem at him and, somehow or other, he would figure out a way of solving it."

But Shuford had not yet solved the current dilemma. "You gotta hurry, Captain," implored the coxswain. "This thing isn't going to hold together much longer." Shuford tried to land on the 29th Division sector, but was shooed away by someone in a control boat, who yelled over that the German obstacles had not yet been cleared; the 1st Division sector, he said, was the best place to land. Shuford sailed over to the 1st Division zone, but someone else warned him not to come ashore there either.

This was too much. It was 11:00 A.M., and his team had been bobbing up and down in the ungainly DUKW for nine hours. Everyone was seasick, freezing, and frightened. The only thing left to do was save the men and the howitzer, nicknamed "The Chief" by the cannoneers. Shuford brought his DUKW alongside a huge Navy "Rhino" barge lying far offshore. The artillerymen climbed onto the barge and collapsed on deck, exhausted. Since the barge was not equipped with a crane to lift "The Chief" out of the DUKW, Shuford and the coxswain jumped back in and sailed over to another Rhino with the requisite crane. Later, the second Rhino came ashore, and its crew presented "The Chief" to a 1st Division artillery outfit.

Aboard the V Corps command ship *Ancon*, General Gerow could see nothing of Omaha except smoke and dust. But it was easy to determine that the first wave had encountered trouble on the beach. Fresh infantrymen were quickly needed ashore. The 1st Division's 18th Infantry had begun to land in support of the beleaguered first wave troops on the eastern half of the beach three hours after H-Hour, and shortly thereafter Gerow ordered Col. Eugene Slappey, CO of the 29th Division's 115th Infantry, to bring his regiment ashore.

In England, the 115th had been loaded into a dozen 246-ton LCIs ("Landing Craft, Infantry"). The LCI was a simple ship that resembled a large bathtub. It had a chimney-like tower aft and two landing ramps forward. An LCI weighed twenty-seven times as much as an LCVP and could carry 230 troops. Each of the 115th's twelve LCIs would transport one infantry company and an artillery liaison or forward observer team. Even though the LCIs were big, they could deposit their passengers directly on the beach. However, the LCIs were extremely difficult to navigate in obstructed waters, and without a clearly defined path through the German obstacles, they were likely to hit a mine at high tide. Furthermore, the LCIs were slow, making them easy targets for German guns.

Slappey planned to land opposite the Les Moulins draw. At 10:00 A.M., as the 115th neared shore in this sector, the LCI captains could see German obstacles protruding menacingly out of the sea. They searched in vain for the buoys and flags the demolition engineers were to have deployed to indicate gaps through the obstructions.

A landing here was clearly impossible. The navy captains requested instructions and were ordered to head for the 1st Division zone, a mile to the east. The 18th Infantry was in the process of landing there, and it appeared a safe place for the LCIs to beach. When the LCIs arrived there, however, the beach and the offshore waters were jammed with landing craft. LCVPs and DUKWs, many of them wrecked, were strewn all over the shingle.

This sector would have to do. The captains gamely navigated their LCIs through the narrow gaps in the obstacles, looking for a landing spot. As they approached shore, the shocked members of the 115th could plainly see the carnage on the sand. It appeared that the regiment would have to fight its way off the beach, rather than simply march unopposed through a draw to an inland assembly area as the original plan had envisioned.

The 115th did not have an easy landing. When one LCI broke its rudder, its passengers had to be transferred to another landing craft. Another LCI smashed into an obstacle. As the captain maneuvered away, the boat lost its two landing ramps in a collision with another LCI.

The Germans were firing, primarily artillery, at this landing sector. One LCI, in fact, was badly hit, but the infantrymen had already disembarked. Company B was one of the few outfits in the 115th to encounter German machine gun fire as it landed. When its LCI beached, half the company was to disembark down the left landing ramp; the other half was to use the right ramp. Lieutenant Colonel Cooper, who was accompanying Company B with four other artillerymen from a liaison team, led the first files down the right-hand side. As the men reached the foot of the ramp, a machine gun burst came from somewhere to the right and smacked into the side of the LCI, only a foot over the men's heads. Everyone froze for a moment and then streamed back up the ramp. After reboarding, they fell in behind the file of G.I.'s waiting to go down the less-exposed left-hand ramp.

According to Brig. Gen. Willard Wyman, Cota's counterpart in the 1st Division, the little village of St. Laurent was the key to Omaha Beach. The Germans had stopped a haphazard attempt at penetration of the bluffs by the 116th there, and now it was the 115th's turn to take the village, which was rumored to be defended by an entire company of the 352nd Division. Wyman located Colonel Slappey and issued attack orders. The plan was for the 1st Battalion to move around St. Laurent, cutting off the village from sources of German reinforcement. Meanwhile, the 2nd and 3rd Battalions would attack the village frontally.

The 115th got off the beach with little difficulty, thanks to several gaps that had been blown in the German wire by 1st Division troops. The 115th's problems began when it moved through the tall marsh grass between the beach and the bluffs. Minefields were everywhere, and although a few paths through the mined areas were indicated by strips of white tape, the men were convinced these lanes were not safe; they had heard a rumor that American mine detectors could not locate German anti-personnel mines. The 29ers went through the lanes carefully; with each step, the men scoured the ground for signs of enemy mines.

German snipers, well-hidden within the tall grass on the bluffs, were active. "We moved cautiously and hesitantly, partly because of fear and partly because of the strangeness of the situation," recalled Sgt. Charles Zarfass of Company A. St. Laurent was less than a mile from the beach, but the

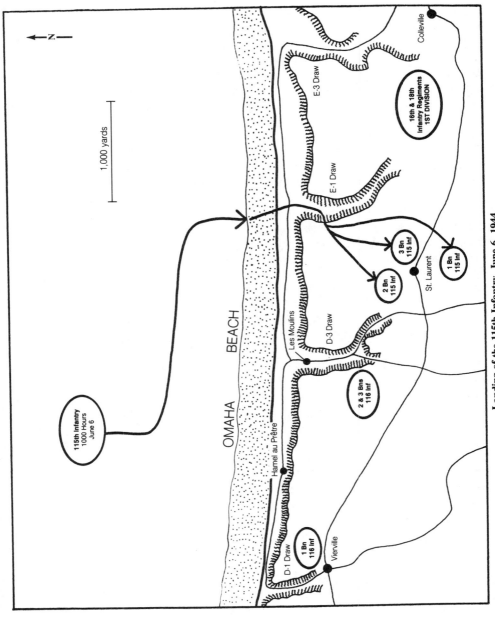

Landing of the 115th Infantry, June 6, 1944.

mines and snipers—and, later on, artillery—slowed the infantrymen's progress to a crawl. The 2nd Battalion, which landed at 10:30 A.M., did not start its attack against the village until late afternoon; the 1st Battalion did not reach its objective south of St. Laurent until 6:00 P.M.

The Germans defended St. Laurent resolutely, and all attempts to clear the village failed. St. Laurent's old stone buildings made perfect defensive positions, and the 29ers found it difficult to force the Germans out. Company K commandeered a Sherman tank and followed it into the center of town, but everyone retreated hastily when the tank came under fire from a hidden anti-tank gun. Later, Allied naval shells landed in the midst of the 2nd Battalion, throwing the men into disarray. The regiment had almost no functional radios, so it proved impossible to call off the fire.

Lieutenant Colonel Cooper tried to arrange artillery support for the 115th's attack on St. Laurent. None of the guns of Cooper's 110th Field Artillery were ashore yet, but for the moment any guns would do. On the outskirts of the village, Cooper met General Cota, who informed him that the 111th's howitzers had all been lost in the landing. The only surviving guns in the 29th Division sector, he said, were a few self-propelled howitzers of the 58th Armored Field Artillery Battalion, a V Corps outfit. One of Cooper's liaison officers, Capt. Thomas Cadwalader, had located these guns and had convinced their leaderless crews to join the battle for St. Laurent.

The crews maneuvered their guns into position as wiremen laid telephone lines to the infantrymen. For the moment, however, the artillery dared not fire, for the fighting in St. Laurent was so confused that any firing would have posed as much danger to the 29ers as it did to the Germans.

In early evening, an infantry captain asked for Cooper's help in driving a group of stubborn Germans out of several stone houses just outside St. Laurent. Cooper complied. The self-propelled guns, which looked almost like tanks, rumbled forward to a position only a few hundred yards from the buildings—point-blank range. After the first several rounds almost destroyed the houses, the Germans fled.

Meanwhile, the fighting in St. Laurent itself reached a crescendo. As the men of the 115th crept along the village streets and alleys looking for snipers, several amazed riflemen caught a glimpse of Lt. Col. William Warfield, the 2nd Battalion CO, placidly sitting on a curb with his feet extended into the street as if the war didn't concern him. He was tossing pebbles at a scruffy dog who had taken a fancy to him.

General Gerhardt came ashore in the late afternoon. A division command post was hastily set up in an old quarry in the Vierville draw, and the general sat on an empty C ration crate examining maps and questioning liaison officers. The whereabouts of the 115th and 116th were unclear until Cota reported to the quarry and briefed Gerhardt, who could then formulate his plans for the next day.

From the quarry, Uncle Charlie had a close-range view of the long files of 29ers trudging up the Vierville draw. Once Gerhardt observed a soldier eating an orange. The General sprang from his C ration box, stomped over to the startled man, and gave him a furious tongue-lashing for throwing the orange peel on the ground.

When darkness settled over Omaha, the flames of burning landing craft shed an eerie, dancing light, silhouetting the living and the dead on the beach. Those who walked along the sand that night had to be careful to avoid stepping on corpses. One V Corps staff officer made a particularly gruesome discovery. "I found this officer who was an infantry captain, who had been part of the 29th Division," he recalled. "His body was still in a crouched position behind the low part of the seawall. He was on his knees. His head was on his arms and his body was supported by the seawall, and his head was looking directly ahead. His steel hat was tilted back somewhat, and there was a bullet hole in the middle of his forehead. I had been with him the night before the invasion, on the attack transport, and he and I had discussed our own backgrounds. . . . I looked at his crossed rifles and at his captain's bars and I thought, 'Boy, he's there and I'm here.'"

Fusillades occasionally erupted beyond the bluffs. The 29ers were convinced that German snipers were everywhere, but General Cota believed that the Yanks were trigger-happy and were shooting at specters. As if the Germans were not troublesome enough, an angry dog attacked Cota's staff as it walked along the beach promenade. Someone joked that it must be a German dog. A 29er frightened it away with a few rifle shots.

Those who got the chance to do so, lay down, took a few deep breaths, and absorbed the events of the day. Cooper and Lt. Col. Lou Smith, the 115th's executive, occupied a shallow slit trench and tried to get some sleep. "We lay in the trench, head-to-head, talking," Cooper remembered. "As long as I talked, I felt all right. The instant we stopped talking, I trembled and shook like a leaf."

No one could get a peaceful rest that night because of the noise, most of which was produced by the Yanks. The G.I.'s were blowing up tiny half-pound blocks of TNT to create instant foxholes. The best way to use the TNT, the troops were told, was to place the charge in a hole about twelve inches deep and then detonate it. The resulting crater was supposed to be deep enough to get the occupants safely through the night. But according to Pvt. Robert Milbier, "They were more of a hindrance than an aid. I scooped a shallow trench in the shelter of a hedge and settled down when somebody yelled 'Fire in the hole!' quite nearby, sending me and several of my neighbors scurrying for cover. Throughout the night, as each new arrival decided to settle down near that particular hedge, cries of 'Fire in the hole!' echoed through the night, and routed us out of our rolls to take cover."

Maj. Stanley Bach, a 29th Division liaison officer, wrote down his personal observations of the invasion while lying in a foxhole near the Vierville draw on the night of June 6. When he finished his notes, Bach added a postscript. "I've seen movies, assault training demonstrations, and actual battle," Bach wrote. "But nothing can approach the scenes on the beach from 1130 to 1400 hours: men being killed like flies from unseen gun positions; Navy can't hit 'em; air cover can't see 'em; so infantry had to dig 'em out."

Gerhardt, optimistic as usual, believed the situation was under control. That night, the general tolerated no pessimism. Tragic tales of near-catastrophe on the beach were brusquely dismissed. In this spirit, Gerhardt prepared a "Battle Lessons and Conclusions" report after the invasion. Always succinct, the general summarized the lessons of D-Day in two sentences: "No reports of disaster should be allowed," he said. "THEY ARE NEVER TRUE."

SEVEN

THE BEACHHEAD
"Boche Kaput"
June 7–9, 1944

1. INTO THE BOCAGE

Fritz Ziegelmann knew the battle was lost as soon as he saw the Allied invasion armada. Ziegelmann, the "1A" of the German 352nd Division, had arrived at the front on the morning of June 7 to ascertain the condition of the German coastal defenses. Normally, the journey from Ziegelmann's headquarters to *Widerstandsnest* 76—one of the only surviving resistance nests in the 352nd zone—took only a half-hour. But Allied fighter-bombers had been so active during the trip that Ziegelmann had taken five hours to reach the coast. WN 76, situated atop a cliff at the western end of Omaha, a mile west of the Vierville draw, provided an excellent vantage point from which to observe the battle.

"The view from WN 76 will remain in my memory forever," wrote Ziegelmann. "The sea was like a picture of the 'Kiel review of the fleet.' Ships of all sorts stood close together on the beach and in the water, broadly echeloned in depth. And the entire conglomeration remained there intact without any real interference from the German side! I clearly understood the mood of the German soldier, who missed the Luftwaffe. It is a wonder that German soldiers fought hard and stubbornly here."

When the first batches of German prisoners were brought in for interrogation on Omaha, American intelligence officers reached a disconcerting conclusion. Most of the prisoners were claiming membership in the 352nd Division, an outfit that was supposed to be deployed at St. Lô, twenty miles south of the coast. The Yanks did not expect to encounter the 352nd until June 7 or 8, but these POWs were incontrovertible evidence that 352nd troops had fought on Omaha on the morning of D-Day. Allied intelligence officers deduced that the 352nd must have been conducting an anti-invasion exercise when the actual invasion began. The presence of the division on Omaha, the intelligence officers believed, explained why German resistance on the beach was so fierce.

Their deduction, of course, was wrong. The 352nd had assumed responsibility for this sector on March 15, almost three months before D-Day. Allied intelligence had simply failed to detect the transfer of the division from St. Lô to the coast. But the 352nd had not enhanced the German beach defenses on Omaha as much as the Americans thought. Actually, when the 1st and 29th Divisions stormed ashore at H-Hour, Omaha was defended only by a single second-rate battalion of the 726th Regiment, an outfit on loan to the 352nd from its eastern neighbor, the 716th Division. Another infantry battalion from the 352nd's 916th Regiment was deployed in reserve directly behind the beach and was committed to the coast as the first wave landed. Aside from a light artillery battalion stationed about two miles behind the beach, no other German combat units were in position to influence the Omaha battle during the critical morning hours.

The primary cause of the German defeat on Omaha was the faulty deployment of the 352nd Division. Had General Kraiss concentrated more than two of his infantry battalions in the Omaha sector, it would have been far more difficult—perhaps impossible—for the Americans to crack the German defenses.

Furthermore, Kraiss had completely misinterpreted Allied intentions on the morning of June 6. At 2:00 A.M., when he first heard alarming reports of American parachute landings on the 352nd's left flank, Kraiss worried that the enemy was attempting to separate his division from its western neighbor, the 709th Division. At 3:10 A.M., he ordered his precious division reserve, labeled *Kampfgruppe Meyer* after the commander of the 915th Regiment, to move westward by truck from its encampment south of Bayeux all the way to the Vire estuary where the enemy paratroopers had been reported. *Kampfgruppe Meyer* was a powerful force that consisted of the entire 915th and the 352nd *Füsilierbataillon*, more than one-third of Kraiss's infantry strength.

Kraiss overreacted. The paratroopers that so troubled Kraiss turned out to be Americans from the 101st Airborne Division who had missed their drop zone and strayed into the 352nd's sector. The Yanks' meager force hardly threatened Kraiss. In fact, more than enough German troops were situated near the drop site to contain the errant paratroopers without the assistance of *Kampfgruppe Meyer.*

It did not take long for Kraiss to realize his mistake, for at 5:50 A.M. he issued orders to Meyer to halt the *Kampfgruppe* and await further instructions. At that time the first of several frantic messages from the coastal *Widerstandsnest* reached 352nd Division headquarters, reporting that enemy warships were bombarding the beach defenses.

Kraiss held *Kampfgruppe Meyer* in place for almost two more hours, even after he had received definitive reports that the Americans were landing in force on the beaches near Vierville and St. Laurent. At 7:35 A.M., sixty-five minutes after H-Hour, Kraiss decided to commit a single battalion from the *Kampfgruppe* to help contain the Americans. The battalion was expected to reach the beach by 9:30 A.M., but Allied fighter-bombers delayed its arrival until early afternoon, long after the Yanks had made their decisive penetrations of the German defenses.

The remaining two battalions of *Kampfgruppe Meyer* were committed at 8:35 A.M. against the British 50th Division, which had landed on Gold Beach an hour after the start of the Omaha invasion. Gold lay fifteen miles east of Omaha, and due to harassment by Allied aircraft, the *Kampfgruppe* took most of the day to get there. By the time it arrived at Gold, the British had already cracked the coastal defenses. During the 50th Division's breakout from the beach, the *Kampfgruppe* was almost annihilated.

Kraiss's mistakes stemmed less from faulty reasoning than from inadequate intelligence. For most of the afternoon of D-Day, Kraiss believed that the Omaha invasion was contained. In fact, he did not learn of Vierville's fall until late afternoon, though the village had been captured by Cota and his men before 11:00 A.M. Sometime after 4:00 P.M., alarming reports of American penetrations beyond the coastal bluffs reached 352nd Division headquarters. Only two hours later, reports from the coast became so gloomy that Kraiss, who had almost no reserves left, realized the Americans could burst out of their beachhead at any moment.

At 6:25 P.M., Kraiss ordered one of the last uncommitted divisional combat units, the 352nd Engineer Battalion, to move to St. Laurent and fight as infantry. By the time the engineers reached the beach, however, it was too late to do anything except dig in and wait for the next day. As a last resort, Kraiss also directed the divisional *Feldersatzbataillon* (replacement battalion) to move north to the coast. It did not arrive, however, until the next morning. Shortly before midnight on June 6, Kraiss warned his corps commander, General Marcks, that the 352nd desperately needed help. "Tomorrow the Division will be able to offer the enemy the same determined resistance it did today [but] because of heavy casualties, . . . reinforcements must be brought up by the day after tomorrow [June 8]. Losses of men and materiel in the resistance nests are total." Marcks replied, "All reserves available to me have already been moved up. Every inch of the ground must be defended to the utmost capacity until new reinforcements can be brought up.''

The reserves Marcks had "moved up" consisted only of the 30th *Schnelle* (Mobile) Brigade, a newly formed unit of three bicycle-mounted infantry battalions stationed at Coutances, thirty-five miles southwest of Omaha. The *Schnelle* troops were inexperienced and had few heavy weapons. The brigade was hardly the equivalent of the 12th SS Panzer Division, which Rommel had unsuccessfully urged Hitler to deploy close behind the coast as a mobile reserve.

The brigade did not reach the combat zone until the evening of June 7, and only one of its three battalions was then committed to Omaha. The other two were sent eastward to help contain the British 50th Division. Kraiss knew that after the arrival of the 30th *Schnelle* Brigade, his 352nd Division would receive no further support until Hitler decided to transfer units to Normandy from other areas of France. He doubted he could contain the enemy that long.

During the fighting near Vierville on June 7, German troops captured secret American orders that covered the entire Omaha invasion plan in minute detail, including organizational charts, maps, and day-by-day objectives. "I must say that in my entire military life, I have never been so impressed as in that hour when I held in my hands the operation order of the American V Corps," wrote Ziegelmann. "I thought that with this captured order, the German 7th Army and Army Group B [Rommel] would reach a decision—*the* decision. I learned later that this captured order first lay around for days at 7th Army headquarters and only reached the high command much later. Even then, it did not get the consideration it deserved. . . . As a young general staff officer, my impression was that the high command 'looked but did not leap.' "

Kraiss's American counterpart, General Gerhardt, sat on his C ration box in the Vierville draw on the morning of June 7 and pondered his next move. Shortly before dawn, Gerhardt had received his first official order from General Gerow, directing the 29th Division to move expeditiously inland and seize Isigny, a picturesque Norman fishing village near the mouth of the Vire River, nine miles west of Omaha. Gerhardt wanted to secure the division's tenuous beachhead and give the 115th, and more particularly the 116th, a chance to reorganize following the traumatic events of the previous day. So he decided to use his only remaining fresh regiment, the 175th Infantry, which was still at sea as the V Corps "floating reserve." Gerhardt made arrangements with Gerow to start landing the 175th by noon. The official order was issued to Colonel Goode, the 175th's CO, at 11:46 A.M.

It was simple enough to issue the order to Goode. It was far more difficult, however, for Goode to pass the word to his company and battalion COs on their landing craft offshore. In truth, the transport area off Omaha, with its jumble of landing craft and warships, was as confused as the beach. A different transport carried each of the 175th's nine rifle companies, and little Navy motorboats sailed among the invasion armada blaring on their loudspeakers, "All elements of the 175th Infantry urgently needed on beach!"

Even after the word was passed to all units to head for shore, several outfits had to wait for the navy to assemble sufficient LCAs and LCVPs for the trip to the beach. Still more time was consumed by the men's precarious descent into their landing craft on flimsy cargo nets hung over the sides of the transports. As a result of these delays, the 175th set out piecemeal for the beach.

Since they were nominally the V Corps reserve, the men of the 175th had been led to believe that the landing on Omaha would be routine, not much different than the Slapton Sands amphibious assault exercises. The hard part—the fighting—would come later. But as the members of the "Dandy Fifth" strained to see over the rails of their transports on the morning of June 7, the beach, according to Capt. Robert M. Miller, "looked like something out of Dante's Inferno."

When the jittery men had an even closer look at the beach from their LCAs and LCVPs, they could see that the landing would be difficult. "You had plenty of time to think about home and mother and 'medium rare' and all those things you liked," recalled Capt. John K. Slingluff of Company G. "That was the worst part of the invasion for me. I was plenty scared. We began getting in close to the shore and occasionally machine gun bullets would rattle across the ramp in front of you, and then maybe you would stick your head up a little bit. I stuck my head up once in a while to take some pictures, and pulled it down again very quickly. But you always had that thought in your mind that, 'My God, it is going to be about five minutes and that ramp isn't going to be there, and I am.' "

Even though the Yanks had been on Omaha for thirty hours, most of the German beach obstacles had not been demolished, and they still posed a threat to Allied landing craft attempting to beach at high tide. As the 175th neared the shore, one of its boats struck an obstacle and erupted into smoke and flame. "It didn't sink," recalled Slingluff. "It went straight up in the air. Pieces of it in all directions. It must have hit a big mine and parts of it sort of sprinkled down on top of us."

A few extraordinarily brave German soldiers still resisted from scattered pockets on the bluffs, but when the ramps were lowered and the 29ers waded through the surf, German fire was wild and few were hit. Nevertheless, when the men of the 175th reached the seawall, they kept their heads down.

Gerhardt was indignant when he discovered where the 175th had landed. The general had wanted the regiment to land on Omaha's western flank so

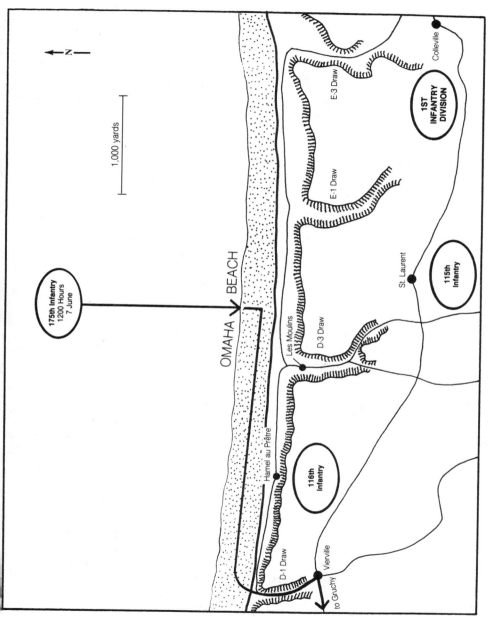

Landing of the 175th Infantry, June 7, 1944.

that it could promptly move inland through the Vierville draw toward Isigny. The navy, however, had declared that German obstacles still rendered the beach opposite Vierville too dangerous. The 175th had therefore been directed to land near the Les Moulins draw, a mile-and-a-half to the east. "The regiment was landed too far to the east, necessitating a long cross movement of the beach by the entire regiment," Gerhardt later complained. "In view of the necessity for troops ashore, this delay might well have proved costly."

After landing, the 175th was immediately ordered to move to the Vierville draw. "The 175th marched in a loose formation down the beach and was subject to sniper fire," recalled J. Milnor Roberts, Gerow's aide. "But, even worse, they were stepping over the bodies of the guys who had been killed the day before and these guys were wearing that 29th Division patch; the other fellows, brand-new, were walking over the dead bodies. By the time they got down where they were to go inland, they were really spooked."

Captain Miller led Company F, minus a mysteriously missing platoon, westward along the foot of the bluffs. Capt. Jimmy Hays, the regimental S-1, spotted Miller and warned, "Things are all screwed up. Colonel Goode was right. You can forget that invasion plan from here on. We're supposed to assemble by dusk in Gruchy. Here it is on the map," said Hays, pointing. "Tomorrow we move against Isigny, over to the west." Miller had never even heard of Isigny. According to the original scheme, Company F was to move straight south after clearing Omaha.

Company C never received word of the new plan and set out southward for its original objective only to discover later that the rest of the regiment had moved west. The company fought with the 115th Infantry for three days before returning to the 175th.

The 175th made it to the western end of the beach where it joined the throng of troops and vehicles struggling up the Vierville draw. "There was a traffic jam such as you would see at the corner of 42nd and Broadway," recalled Slingluff. "Vehicles bumper-to-bumper, tanks, men just jammed up in there, occasional 88's dropping in among them."

Trudging up the draw, the men of the 175th passed Gerhardt and his staff in the spartan 29th Division command post. "The area had been roped off so that no one could get in too close to see the operations map," recalled Lt. Sam Allsup, a platoon leader in Company A. "It seemed as if it [the command post] was just one mass of organized confusion, but the entire operations of the Division were being controlled from behind the pile of rubble."

At the top of the draw, the men of the 175th turned west at the main thoroughfare leading out of Vierville. It was sunset; as the sky darkened, the regiment marched another mile and turned south at the tiny crossroads hamlet of Gruchy. Here they took a breather before resuming the advance toward Isigny.

Just outside of Vierville, Captain Miller was approached by a Frenchwoman and her little daughter. "Les Boches! Les Boches!" sputtered the woman, gesticulating for Miller to follow her. Miller took a few members of his company and cautiously trailed the woman past a large chateau up to a small ravine. The Yanks could hear moans and German oaths coming from a well-concealed tunnel at the bottom of the ravine. Miller and two men jumped down with their weapons ready. "Achtung! Raus! Raus!" they shouted into the tunnel entrance. More moans. Miller and his men warily entered the tunnel, turned a corner and found themselves in a large underground room, face-to-face with a German medic. Yelling "Kamerad! Kamerad!" the German's arms shot up in the air. Several wounded Germans lay nearby. By the look of it, the place had once been a headquarters. As the German coastal defenses collapsed, the staff must have departed hastily, leaving behind those who were too badly injured to move.

The prompt arrival of American reinforcements and supplies on Omaha depended on an utterly secure beachhead, but the 175th's landing difficulties proved that Omaha was not yet danger-free. In fact, even as Gerhardt planned the quick seizure of Isigny, he was ordering the 115th and 116th to spend June 7 mopping up stubborn pockets of enemy resistance on the bluffs.

Germans were still fighting from houses on the western side of St. Laurent. Shortly after dawn, the 3rd Battalion of the 115th resumed its attack against the town, clearing it by 9:00 A.M. Only fifty yards from Cota's command post near St. Laurent, the 29ers captured a German in a barn who said that he had been fighting there since 8:00 A.M. on June 6. The man had been armed with a machine pistol, and seven 29ers lay dead outside the barn.

Cota was a one-man army again. He spent most of the morning with the 115th, supervising their mop-up efforts, prodding the men forward, issuing progress reports to Gerhardt. During the fighting near St. Laurent, Cota came across a group of infantrymen, pinned by a few obstinate Germans in a nearby house. Cota sought out the man in charge, an infantry captain, and asked why the men were making no attempt to take the building. "Sir, the Germans are in there, shooting at us," the captain replied.

"Well, I'll tell you what, captain," said Cota, unbuckling two grenades from his jacket. "You and your men start shooting at them. I'll take a squad of men and you and your men watch carefully. I'll show you how to take a house with Germans in it."

The astonished captain watched as Cota led his little group around the house to a nearby hedge. Suddenly, the general and his group raced forward, screaming like wild men, hurling grenades in the windows. Cota and another man kicked in the front door, tossed a few more grenades inside, waited for the explosions, and then disappeared into the house. As the rest of Cota's team followed him inside, the Germans streamed out the back and ran for their lives.

Cota returned to the captain. "You've seen how to take a house," said

Cota, still out of breath. "Do you understand? Do you know how to do it now?"

"Yes, sir," the captain replied meekly.

"Well, I won't be around to do it for you again," Cota said. "I can't do it for everybody."

Later, Lieutenant Colonel Cooper, who witnessed the scene, suggested to Cota that he stop endangering himself. "Now look, Cooper," Cota replied. "I was a poor country boy from the Pennsylvania Dutch country. I heard about West Point, and that it was free, and I went. I made a contract with the government: if they paid for my education, I would serve them. Part of my contract was to die for my country if necessary. I intend to stick to it. If I get killed, then so be it, but I don't expect to be."

After the fall of St. Laurent, the 115th moved cautiously westward and cut the main highway leading south from Vierville. This maneuver would improve beachhead security significantly, for German reinforcements coming from the south would now be blocked a mile-and-a-half short of the beach.

Despite Cota's help, the 115th was frequently held up by enemy delaying tactics. Wily German snipers and machine gun teams had carefully selected ambush positions in almost every hedgerow and farmhouse behind the beach. When the American infantrymen appeared, the Germans fired a few shots, ran to another position, fired a few more, and then disappeared.

The men of the 115th were shaken by the unpredictable enemy resistance. Whenever an MG 42 opened up, the 29ers fell to the ground and looked vainly for the source of the fire. After the shooting died down, the Yanks advanced cautiously but rarely found a trace of an enemy soldier. The Yanks came to believe that every hedgerow hid a sniper or a machine gun team, and they were usually right.

The 115th advanced less than a mile-and-a-half on June 7, hardly a lightning pace considering the Yanks' preponderance of force. But the regiment was severely handicapped by poor communications, an ammunition shortage, unfamiliarity with the terrain, and little dedicated artillery or tank support. Fortunately, the 110th Field Artillery Battalion, the 115th's supporting artillery outfit, had landed successfully during the afternoon and evening of June 7. By nightfall the sorely needed howitzers had deployed a mile south of the beach.

Gerhardt had no illusions that the battered 116th Infantry could undertake an attack, so he restricted the Stonewallers to mop-up operations on June 7. Even this task was far from easy. The 2nd and 3rd Battalions, slated to do most of the work, were critically understrength. Major Bingham, CO of the 2nd Battalion, had no more than 100 men under his command at the end of D-Day. On the morning of June 7, he collected 300 more, but his outfit was still missing more than half its men. Furthermore, he had few heavy weapons and no supporting tanks or artillery. The 3rd Battalion was in only slightly better shape.

Both the 2nd and 3rd Battalions had spent the night at the head of the Les Moulins draw, just north of St. Laurent. When they received their orders on the morning of June 7, they headed back down the draw toward the beach. The astounded Stonewallers discovered several pockets of enemy resistance still in the draw, even though the Germans there had been surrounded for an entire day.

The draw was cleared only after a hard fight. Afterward, both battalions set out westward along the beach and bluff crest toward Vierville, rousting out several more Germans on the way. At Vierville, the Stonewallers reorganized and marched southward toward the hamlet of Louvières, one of the regiment's original D-Day objectives. Plenty of Germans still blocked the way, though. The Stonewallers made only slight progress before darkness. "It was rough going. The Krauts were behind every bush," recalled Bingham.

The 1st Battalion of the 116th was in even worse condition than was the 2nd or 3rd. The 1st's survivors spent the night of June 6 in a precarious position a few hundred yards west of Vierville. The unit would have rested and reorganized on June 7 had it not been for a grave development at Pointe du Hoc, a narrow finger of land jutting into the sea four miles west of Omaha.

Two hundred men from the 2nd Ranger Battalion had landed at Pointe du Hoc on the morning of June 6 to destroy six 150mm guns, which had been labeled "the most dangerous battery in France" by Allied intelligence. The rangers climbed the 100-foot cliffs with grappling irons and ropes and drove away the German defenders, but the guns were nowhere to be found. The rangers pushed on, crossed the coastal highway leading eastward to Vierville, and dug in. Several rangers on patrol eventually found the guns, which had been abandoned, and destroyed them. By then, however, an entire German battalion had been alerted and was attacking the American enclave. Shortly before dawn on June 7, the Germans launched a ferocious assault and drove the rangers all the way back to the coast. Over half the rangers had been hit since the previous morning, and the survivors were threatened with annihilation on the afternoon of June 7.

The 1st Battalion of the 116th was ordered to collect every man at its disposal and push westward along the coastal highway with all possible speed to relieve the beleaguered rangers at Pointe du Hoc. Lt. Col. John Metcalfe, the 1st Battalion CO, could only pull together 250 Stonewallers, but his force was augmented by an equal number of rangers who had come ashore with the 29ers on Omaha and were anxiously awaiting the chance to rescue their brethren.

The relief force moved out at 8:00 A.M. on June 7. Scattered enemy resistance was brushed aside by fusillades of machine gun fire from ten Sher-

29th Division, June 7, 1944.

man tanks that accompanied the 29ers. The column made good progress, coming within a half-mile of Pointe du Hoc by 11:00 A.M. Here, however, a strong German force blocked the path, and two American attacks with tanks and infantry could not budge it. The Stonewallers and rangers dug in for the night. Although the relief force had not yet accomplished its mission, it drew German attention away from the desperate rangers, who had managed to hold out at Pointe du Hoc throughout the day.

On June 8 the Stonewall Brigade was ordered to continue the attack. The 1st Battalion was joined by the 2nd and 3rd Battalions. Thus, for the first time in the war, the 116th was to fight as an integral regiment, albeit a sadly depleted one.

The Stonewallers, accompanied by several Shermans, swept across shell-cratered fields toward Pointe du Hoc. Surprisingly, enemy resistance was only light. When the Yanks neared the coast, they heard German machine guns firing to their front. The 29ers and the tanks blazed away at the source of the fire, only to discover they were shooting at the rangers, several of whom were hit. The rangers, it turned out, were using captured enemy weapons. Later, rumors flew that someone would be court-martialed for this mix-up, but nothing came of it.

Norman terrain was not what the 29ers had expected it to be. The most astonishing feature of the countryside was the ubiquitous hedgerows. Their presence was no surprise, for they had appeared on aerial photos. Their physical structure, however, was a shock.

From the air Normandy resembled a green quilt of crazily shaped fields outlined by bushy hedgerows. The hedgerows appeared to be nothing more than thin belts of trees and shrubbery. But when the 29ers got their first close-up view of Norman terrain, they discovered that beneath the overgrown shrubs, the hedgerows were really solid earthen dikes, about four feet high and three feet thick—and sometimes much larger. The embankments were knotted with root systems, and digging into them was a back-breaking task.

The hedgerows dated back to Roman times when, according to legend, Gallic peasants marked the boundaries of fields with walls of earth. ''Bocage'' (literally, ''grove'') was the generic French word for this unique terrain, and American soldiers eventually adopted the term.

The 29ers quickly came to feel claustrophobic. Hedgerows were everywhere in Normandy, and wherever a soldier stood, his view was blocked in all directions by walls of vegetation. Even the roads felt confining. The shrubbery arched over the dirt tracks, forming leafy tunnels through which sunlight seldom penetrated.

The bocage was perfect defensive country. A hedgerow was a ready-made fortress behind which troops were invulnerable to small arms fire. If the defenders had had time to dig deep dugouts in the base of an embankment, they were almost equally safe from artillery. Troops entrenched in a hedgerow were practically invisible. In combat, it proved nearly impossible for the 29ers to tell whether a hedgerow was held by a German company or just a single sniper, or perhaps by no one at all. Unsuspecting 29ers could walk right through an enemy position without even knowing it. Furthermore, the hedgerows enabled the defenders to move quickly from position to position without showing themselves, giving the attackers the impression that the defending force was much larger than its actual size. Just a few German MG 42s could hold up an entire American company using this tactic. Tanks could offer little support in an attack since they could not penetrate the earthen dikes. In the bocage, the tanks were also easy prey for close-range antitank weapons, like the German *Panzerfaust.*

Combat in the bocage was like fighting in a maze. Between the hedgerows, dirt farm tracks that had sunk beneath the level of the surrounding fields by centuries of erosion and use formed a labyrinthine pattern that baffled the Yanks. Units commonly found themselves completely lost a few minutes after launching an attack. Just as typically, two outfits could occupy adjacent fields for hours before discovering each other's presence.

American soldiers had a difficult time getting used to the bocage. The Yanks were on the offensive for most of the Normandy campaign and regarded the hedgerows as a severe disadvantage in combat. Long before the

Troops from the 175th Infantry dig in behind a Norman hedgerow. *Courtesy National Archives.*

Americans stormed Omaha Beach, however, the Germans were fully aware of the defensive benefits provided by the hedgerows and were well-prepared to fight in this terrain.

The bocage would have been more confusing than it was for the Yanks had it not been for the US Army's remarkably detailed aerial photos and 1:25,000 maps of Normandy. The maps marked the position of every hedgerow and farm lane and displayed terrain contours with amazing accuracy. Special stereoscopic magnifying glasses were issued to American artillerymen so they could carefully scrutinize the aerial photos for prospective targets.

The Germans, on the other hand, had second-rate maps and no aerial photos at all. In truth, 352nd Division infantry officers preferred captured American maps to their own. The 352nd Division, however, had trained in Normandy for six months prior to the invasion, and its troops did not need to rely on maps as much as did the Americans.

The region directly beyond Omaha Beach through which the 29th Division would move after securing its D-Day beachhead was bordered on three sides by water: the English Channel on the north; the Vire River on the west; and the tiny Aure River on the south. Only the eastern side, shortly to become the boundary between the 1st and 29th Divisions, was devoid of a water barrier.

The 29th Division's objective in the campaign was St. Lô, a city of 12,000 inhabitants, the capital of the French department of Manche, and an important road junction. Gerhardt was in a hurry to move inland, for the region beyond Omaha Beach was a bottle waiting to be corked. To move against St. Lô, which lay twenty miles south of the coast, the division had to cross the Aure River. The Aure, less than ten feet wide for most of its course, was not itself a major obstacle. In the 29th Division sector, however, the Aure flowed through a wide valley that was up to two miles across. The entire valley, which was virtually uninhabited, was only a few feet above sea level. It was crisscrossed by deep drainage ditches and filled with wavy marsh grass and nearly impenetrable swamps.

The 29ers spoke of the Aure valley as the "flooded area." Although several narrow and little-used causeways and footpaths crossed the valley, the only Aure bridge in the 29th Division sector spanned the river at Isigny. This bridge was the major reason why Gerow had ordered the 29th Division to seize the town without delay.

The Germans, of course, had also recognized the strategic significance of the Aure valley. Prior to the invasion, the 352nd Division did everything in its power to make the valley even more untraversable. In the early spring, German engineers dammed the Aure in several places, and the mucky swamps turned even muckier. Fortunately for the Americans, the spring rainy season

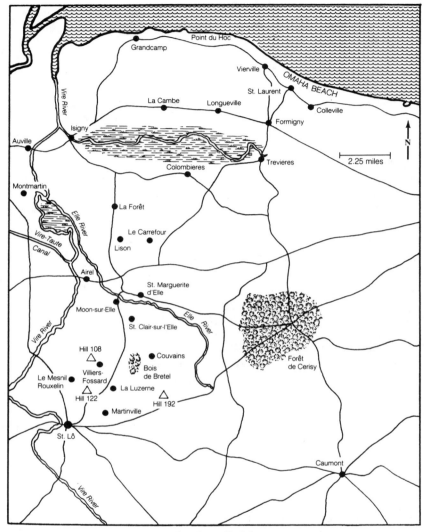

Omaha to St. Lô.

had ended long before the invasion, and the Aure valley was relatively dry in June. Nevertheless, the Germans still considered the Aure almost impassable, especially if they demolished the Isigny bridge.

Few sites between the coast and the Aure valley were of military significance. Since this region was mostly flat, only church steeples offered commanding views of the surrounding countryside. The area was dotted with dozens of tiny Norman hamlets that consisted of only a few stone houses tightly clustered around a road junction. The larger hamlets featured squat Romanesque churches with adjoining cemeteries crowded with ancient head-stones. The two largest towns in the region, Isigny and Grandcamp-les Bains, were both fishing havens.

2. BREAKOUT

Powerless to prevent an American breakout from the Omaha beachhead, General Kraiss must have been near despair on June 8. Almost half the 352nd Division was near Bayeux, fighting the British at impossible odds; several other division units were still tied down by American paratroopers near the Vire and by the rangers at Pointe du Hoc. The rest of the 352nd had been decimated on Omaha Beach. "The front line, as well as the troops' morale, was beginning to break up," recalled Ziegelmann. "The questions, 'Where is the Luftwaffe?' and 'When is the counterattack [by reinforcements] going to begin?' were often heard."

After studying his captured V Corps order, Kraiss must have realized that the odds against him were worsening every minute. Fresh troops were pour-ing ashore on Omaha by the thousands, including a new American infantry division, the 2nd. With the odds against the Germans in the Omaha sector now three divisions to one, Kraiss knew that the battle would turn into a rout unless help arrived soon. He was informed, however, that the first German reinforcements would not reach the front for two more days.

Kraiss ordered the remnants of his division to retreat south of the Aure. Despite their haste to depart the coast, the Germans would not give up Grand-camp, whose harbor was coveted by Allied logisticians, without a fight. This town, in fact, was a good place for the Germans to make a stand since it was shielded on its eastern side by a small stream with swampy banks. An Ameri-can attack against Grandcamp from the direction of Pointe du Hoc was re-stricted to the narrow coastal highway, for the ground on either side of the road was too mucky to permit the passage of troops and vehicles. Some 600 yards east of Grandcamp, the highway crossed the stream at a tiny bridge. Inexplicably, the Germans had failed to destroy the bridge, but they had sited every weapon at their disposal on the eastern edge of town to cover it.

In the early afternoon, a group of rangers was stopped at the bridge by German fire. The Yanks called for help from the navy, and the British cruiser *Glasgow* promptly shelled German strongpoints in the town for an hour. Shortly thereafter, the 3rd Battalion of the 116th, assisted by several tanks, attempted another attack. The Shermans roared across the bridge, losing one of their number to a mine, and Stonewallers from Companies K and L fol-lowed.

When the two companies got to the other side, a vicious skirmish ensued.

American BARs and light machine guns opened up and were promptly answered by buzz-saw bursts from German MG 42s. A crackling fusillade of M1s erupted and just as quickly died out. The thump of mortars from both sides could be discerned amid the racket of the small arms, but occasional blasts from a Sherman tank's big 75mm gun drowned out everything else. When the battle reached close quarters, the pop of hand grenades and wild shouts of men added to the pandemonium.

The Stonewallers won, mostly thanks to one man. In the middle of the fight, Company K had come to a standstill in front of a German strongpoint on a knoll just outside Grandcamp. Sgt. Frank Peregory, a native of Charlottesville, Virginia, crept undetected up the knoll to an abandoned German trench. He moved stealthily along the trench until he came within sight of the troublesome enemy resistance nest, which consisted of a single squad and its deadly MG 42. Peregory rushed the Germans, killing and wounding several with grenades and his M1. The rest surrendered. Like a latter-day Sergeant York, Peregory shoved his prisoners in front of him and kept going. Later, he single-handedly knocked out another machine gun nest and captured still more prisoners.

Peregory was awarded the Congressional Medal of Honor for his one-man attack. He was the only member of the 116th—and one of only two 29ers—to be awarded this medal during the war. "This action was accomplished after tank fire, rifle grenades, and bazookas had failed to dent the defenses," his citation noted. "It was directly responsible for the advance of the battalion and enabled it to take its objective, Grandcamp." Peregory, however, never knew about the award. He was killed in action six days later.

The 2nd and 3rd Battalions of the 116th cleared Grandcamp by mid-afternoon on June 8. Meanwhile, the 1st Battalion skirted the town and followed narrow dirt tracks westward toward Isigny. After their stand at Grandcamp, the Germans made few additional attempts to slow the Yanks, and by the morning of June 9, the entire coast between Omaha Beach and Isigny was under American control.

After the 116th had cleared the coast, the regiment was designated division reserve, and the Stonewallers got a chance to rest. Capt. Robert Garcia's Company E spent part of the rest period in Grandcamp. One day, the Company E men lounged on the doorsteps of Grandcamp's tightly clustered stone houses, eating K rations. Four cheerful French children skipped up to Garcia, their wooden shoes clattering on the cobblestones like Spanish castanets. "Chocolat pour le bébé?" one of them begged, sticking out his hand.

"We were perfectly willing to give them what [food] we had," Garcia recalled. "But first I had one of the French-speaking men tell them that they had to perform some little song or dance for us. This they did, all the while giggling and chattering as any children would do, apparently thrilled to find that some of the men could speak French."

But then a little girl surprised everyone by asking the Stonewallers to sing a song in return. The events of the past several days, however, did not leave the G.I.'s in the mood for singing, and at first there was an awkward silence. Garcia then thought of "Frère Jacques," a nursery rhyme he had learned as a child, and he decided to give it a try. "My singing was never anything to brag about," Garcia remembered. "And I'm certain my pronunciation of the French words was atrocious, but they immediately recognized the song and began to sing along with me with all the delighted innocence and charm of children the world over. We sang several more times, and then it was time for us to move on, and to start the war once again."

Back at the beachhead, General Gerhardt ordered the 115th Infantry to cross the flooded Aure valley. The general was by no means certain that the valley was traversable, but the only way to find out, according to Uncle Charlie, was to try. On the German side, Ziegelmann recalled, "The possibility had not been taken into consideration that the swampy Aure valley would be crossed. As a matter of fact, there were no German forces available to resist such action."

The 115th moved out of the beachhead on the morning of June 8 and discovered that the Germans had pulled out. The regiment's objective for the day was a village named Longueville, which lay astride the Isigny highway a mile north of the Aure valley. Longueville overlooked the valley, and the town was a good place from which the 115th could begin its search for paths across the flooded area.

Soon after the regiment began its trek towards Longueville, however, it was swallowed up by the bocage. Division headquarters had received no messages from Colonel Slappey, the 115th's CO, for several hours, and worried division staff officers wondered where the regiment was and whether it was headed in the right direction. Gerhardt wanted the 115th found immediately, so he dispatched his G-2, Maj. Paul Krznarich ("Murphy"), to look for it. Krznarich located part of the 115th a mile-and-a-half southwest of Vierville. He returned to division headquarters and drew in the 115th's position on Uncle Charlie's operations map.

General Cota set out in his jeep, nicknamed *Fire and Movement*, to help steer Slappey toward Longueville. Cota went to the precise spot where Krznarich said he had found the 115th, but all Cota saw there was a large, empty pasture surrounded by bushy hedgerows. "The quiet, sunny June morning seemed almost ominous in its stillness," recalled Lt. Jack Shea, Cota's aide. "The 115th was nowhere to be seen, though the terrain to the south was thoroughly searched with binoculars."

Suddenly, shouts—unmistakably American—erupted beyond a nearby hedgerow. Then a BAR opened up. Cota and Shea got out of the jeep and walked toward the source of the commotion. They crossed two or three fields and suddenly came upon the entire 2nd Battalion of the 115th. The outfit,

29th Division, June 8, 1944.

consisting of 800 men, had been no more than 200 yards from Cota's jeep, but it had been completely obscured by the hedgerows. Warfare in the bocage was indeed strange.

Cota soon found Slappey. The two men discussed the status of the 115th for a few minutes, and then Cota departed, satisfied that Slappey had the situation well in hand.

The 2nd Battalion entered Longueville about noon, and hardly a shot was fired in opposition. Dozens of discarded weapons and other pieces of military equipment hinted at the hasty departure of the enemy. Slappey set up regimental headquarters in town and ordered his three battalions to advance to the edge of the Aure valley in preparation for a crossing the next day. Meanwhile, artillerymen from the 110th Field Artillery used binoculars to peer across the flooded area from the upper story of one of Longueville's tallest houses. No sign of the enemy.

Slappey decided to send a patrol across the valley that afternoon, and Lt. Kermit Miller's 3rd Platoon of Company E was selected for the task. Miller's men set out at 5:30 P.M. Slopping through the odorous swamp, the platoon took five hours to traverse two-and-a-half miles. When the 29ers reached the far side, the men were thoroughly soaked, but they had not seen a single German.

The first village Miller's platoon came to was Colombières. Three German sentries guarded the road leading into town, but they were lax in their duties, and Miller's men ambushed and captured them in the darkness without a shot. The 29ers learned from a Frenchwoman that one of the houses in Colombières was used by the Germans as some kind of headquarters. The Yanks found the house and surrounded it, and Miller called upon the German occupants to surrender. Although completely surprised by the intrusion, the enemy troops wouldn't give up. The Yanks captured the house after a furious skirmish, during which several Germans were killed and many more captured. Only three 29ers were wounded.

At sunrise, the platoon headed back to American lines across the swamp. With the prisoners in tow and the three wounded 29ers, however, the return was more difficult than the outgoing trip. When Miller arrived on the American side, he reported to Slappey that the Aure valley could be traversed. Furthermore, few if any Germans were in position to resist an American crossing. This information delighted Gerhardt and Slappey, and Miller was later awarded the Distinguished Service Cross for fulfilling his mission.

The 29ers were beginning to feel like liberators. Early on the morning of June 8, Lieutenant Colonel Cooper and three other artillerymen drove south from the beachhead to reconnoiter a suitable position from which the 110th Field Artillery's howitzers could support the 115th's crossing of the Aure. Cooper's party met Major Krznarich, who warned them that the hamlet toward which they were headed, Asnieres, was occupied by the enemy. Cooper proceeded anyway, and enlisted the aid of two French farmers to help his team find its way in the baffling bocage. Cooper and his men left the jeep and with their carbines at the ready, crept down a narrow alley leading into Asnieres. Not a German in sight. The team cautiously moved into the center of the tiny village, keeping a sharp lookout for snipers. Cooper's party was suddenly encircled by dozens of happy civilians, who thrust forward flowers and bottles of wine and slapped the Americans on the back, shouting "Vive l'Amerique!" and "Boche kaput!" Said Cooper, "The 110th can be credited with 'capturing' Asnieres with six men, counting the two French farmers."

The seizure of Isigny, which was the 175th Infantry's task, was probably the most difficult mission assigned any 29th Division outfit on June 8. Nine miles separated the beachhead from Isigny, and according to the division's intelligence officers, the country through which the 175th would travel was overrun with Germans.

The 175th departed Gruchy, its beachhead assembly area, on the night of June 7. The men marched off in column, with one well-spaced file on either side of the road. When everyone had fallen in—1st Battalion leading, 2nd and 3rd following—the column was over two miles long. At the front of the column, the growl of Sherman tank engines drowned out the monotonous tramp of marching feet. The Shermans belonged to the 747th Tank Battalion, a newly arrived outfit assigned to support the 175th in the attack on Isigny.

The column followed the coast road out of Gruchy for a half-mile and then turned southward on a narrow gravel track. Around midnight, Germans on the left of the road opened heavy fire on the 2nd Battalion, but they were driven off. The column took a three-hour breather early on June 8, during which most of the men slept. At 4:00 A.M., the weary G.I.'s were awakened by their sergeants, and the march resumed.

The snakelike column continued to follow the track until the scouts came to a hard-surface road. Some six miles straight west down this road lay Isigny. The sun had risen, and the men at the head of the column strained to see down the highway. They suspected the Germans would defend the road every step of the way.

Company A started down the road first, accompanied by a platoon of tanks. Little white roadside signs indicated that the village of La Cambe lay straight ahead. Several French civilians standing in the fields on either side of the highway smiled and waved at the Yanks. One farmer even offered the Company A men some fresh milk.

Just outside La Cambe, the enemy was waiting. As the Yanks approached the village, the Germans suddenly opened up with MG 42s from a group of farm buildings. Several 29ers crumpled on the road, and the rest flung themselves into roadside ditches as machine gun bullets ricocheted off the pavement. A raging battle developed as the Yanks further back in the column attempted to maneuver around the buildings on either side of the highway. The tanks opened up on the farm buildings, but the Germans knocked out the lead Sherman with a well-hidden "88."

The Germans pulled out of the farm buildings and abandoned La Cambe just when the Yanks were ready to press home an attack. The enemy was seemingly satisfied simply to delay the American advance toward Isigny. Maj. John Geiglein, the S-2 (Intelligence Officer) of the 175th, examined a captured German order which confirmed this theory. The order stated that German troops must not practice rigid defensive tactics. Instead, they were ordered to fight in delaying teams, forcing the American column to deploy and thereby giving time for other German troops to form a stronger defensive line somewhere to the rear.

After the 1st Battalion entered La Cambe, it waited for the rest of the long regimental column to come up. As the 2nd and 3rd Battalions approached the village, the men of the 175th got a taste of what German soldiers in Normandy endured every day. Just outside town, nine British Typhoon fighter-bombers mistook the Yanks, strung out along the Isigny highway, for Germans. The aircraft bombed, rocketed, and strafed the column mercilessly. The 29ers scurried off the road and sought any available cover. One private in Company F ran into a house and was immediately blown back out a window by a direct bomb hit. He got up, stunned but otherwise all right. Lt. Carl Hobbs, S-2 of the 1st Battalion, was hit by a 20mm shell, which embedded in his shoulder. Fortunately for Hobbs, the shell did not explode. Even so, it was an excruciating wound. Later, a surgeon gingerly removed it.

When the Typhoons had finished their attack, six 29ers were dead and eighteen wounded. For the G.I.'s who had not yet fired their rifles in anger, this incident was a demoralizing introduction to war. The 175th's officers were furious. They had ordered their men not to fire at the aircraft in the hope that the pilots would recognize their mistake. But the attack continued for several agonizing minutes. Afterward, one tearful captain told his men that from that moment on, any plane—enemy or friendly—pointing its nose toward them as if it were about to attack should be fired upon.

Colonel Goode set up regimental headquarters in the village at 9:15 A.M. Shortly thereafter, several infantrymen brought in a batch of enemy prisoners for interrogation. Intelligence officers in the 175th were amazed. Many captives denied any knowledge of the German language and professed hatred for the Nazis and their cause. The handful of Orientals among the prisoners sparked a rumor that the Japanese had come to Normandy to teach the Germans infiltration tactics. The Orientals were actually Mongolians taken prisoner by the Germans on the Russian Front, who had chosen to serve their captors rather than to face a dubious future in a German POW camp. They had been assigned to the 621st *Ostbataillon,* along with men of dozens of other nationalities, and were attached to the 352nd Division.

The 621st occupied Isigny on D-Day. When the Americans appeared ready to break out of their beachhead on June 7, General Kraiss had ordered the battalion to move eastward and delay the American push down the Isigny highway—not an enviable assignment for even the most patriotic German troops. Surprisingly, many of the *Ost* soldiers fought stubbornly, perhaps because they were more afraid of their German officers than of their American opponents. In the next several days, the 175th captured enemy troops of so many different ethnic backgrounds that one G.I. blurted to his company CO, "Captain, just who the hell *are* we fighting, anyway?"

Colonel Goode suspected that the 175th was walking into a trap. He doubted Geiglein's report that the Germans were practicing delaying tactics only and believed that the further his regiment advanced down the Isigny highway, the more vulnerable it became to an enemy counterattack. For all Goode knew, an entire German division might suddenly appear out of the bocage and cut the 175th off from its supply source at Omaha Beach. Even worse, the 175th still lacked support from 29th Division artillery. Thus Goode decided to postpone his advance toward Isigny and wait for his direct support artillery outfit, the 224th Field Artillery Battalion, to reach the front. In the meantime, the regiment secured the La Cambe area.

General Cota, who spent most of June 8 with the 115th near Longueville, set out in his jeep for 175th headquarters late that afternoon. Only a few minutes into the journey, Gerhardt's unmistakable *Vixen Tor* came speeding down the road from the opposite direction and screeched to a halt alongside Cota's jeep. Gerhardt was agitated. "I've just seen 'Pop' Goode," Gerhardt declared. "He seems to have bogged down, and I want him to get into Isigny as quickly as possible. Go down there and see if you can push him. Light a fire under him if necessary, but get him into Isigny."

Cota found Goode in La Cambe. Goode explained his reasons for caution, but assured Cota that the 175th was almost ready to move, since the 224th Artillery had just reached the front and would shortly be in position to support the advance. Cota and Goode arranged a plan: the 3rd Battalion, accompanied by tanks, would lead the attack with one company on either side of the highway and two companies in reserve. The 1st and 2nd Battalions would follow.

Vixen Tor showed up unexpectedly at 175th headquarters at 7:00 P.M. Gerhardt leaped out of the jeep and stalked into Goode's command post, demanding to know whether the attack against Isigny had started. When Goode told him it hadn't, Uncle Charlie lost his temper. "There's nothing in your way. Get into Isigny," he growled.

Goode started to sputter something about waiting for artillery support.

Members of a German "Ost" battalion, captured in Normandy. *Courtesy Military History Institute.*

"Never mind the artillery!" Gerhardt interrupted. "Get those tanks moving and roll right in. I'll get in that jeep of mine right now and roll into Isigny. There's nothing there. Now get the hell in!" The general didn't wait for a reply. He turned on his heels, hopped into his jeep, and drove off.

Goode ordered his men to get moving, artillery or no artillery. Cota, accompanying the column, reassured Goode that the plan would work.

By the time the 175th started toward Isigny, it was almost dark. A German delaying team, with several MG 42s and an 88mm antitank gun, lay in wait in a tiny village named Arthenay, a mile west of La Cambe. The enemy opened fire on the head of the 175th's column just east of the village. Both sides' machine guns spewed red tracer bullets in the darkness, which flew back and forth like a fantastic shower of shooting stars. The American tankers spotted the dreaded "88" and knocked it out only minutes into the fight. The Germans pulled out when the farm buildings in which they were fighting caught fire.

The flames bathed the whole area in a dancing orange light. When the 175th resumed its march, the column gave the burning buildings a wide berth, for the firelight made the men easy targets for German snipers.

A half-mile beyond Arthenay, the 2nd Battalion, minus Company F, split off from the back of the column to attack a German radar station on a knoll near the village of Cardonville, 700 yards north of the highway. The outfit accomplished this mission but was heavily shelled afterward. During this bombardment, Captain Slingluff, the CO of Company G, overheard an agonized sergeant in a nearby foxhole. "How do those poor bastards in the Pacific stand it?"

By midnight the head of the 175th's main column was only a mile-and-a-half outside Isigny. Except for the distant, low rumbling of Allied bomber engines, the night was still. Isigny was burning fiercely, the result of an Allied air and naval bombardment earlier that day, and the flames cast an eerie glow on the clouds.

Gerhardt sped up to the head of the column shortly after 1:00 A.M. He jumped out of *Vixen Tor* and strutted down the highway past a file of stationary Shermans. Suddenly he stopped and banged his fist on the side of a tank. A head popped out of a hatch. Gerhardt asked what was holding everybody up. The tanker told him there were mines on the road up ahead. Continuing down the highway, the general saw a Sherman on the roadside with its right track blown off, as helpless as a bird without a wing. Further ahead, Gerhardt saw Cota's head protruding from the hatch of the lead tank. Sitting in the assistant driver's position, Cota looked ready to lead a cavalry charge into Isigny. Gerhardt laughed, "Get the hell out of that thing!"

Gerhardt, Cota, Lt. Col. Alexander George (the 175th's executive), and Lt. Col. Stuart Fries (CO of the 747th Tank Battalion) conferred next to the lead tank. This was a dangerous place for a meeting. A lucky German sniper might have killed the two highest-ranking officers in the 29th Division.

Gerhardt was angry again. "Get those damn tanks going and follow them into Isigny," he told George. "When you've got the town, send an officer-courier to report to me personally at division headquarters. Now stop fooling around and get into that town." Gerhardt then turned to Cota and asked him what he was going to do.

"Well, I was going into Isigny in that lead tank," Cota replied. "But I guess I'll just poke along and see if I can push them in."

"Fine," said Gerhardt. "Keep pushing them all the way. Get them into Isigny."

The 3rd Battalion accompanied the tanks. Gerhardt was right. There was not a German in sight, and there were no mines. The 29ers could smell the acrid smoke from the burning town. Lieutenant Shea remembered his first sight of Isigny. "Rounding a slight bend in the road," he recalled, "the burning heart of Isigny came into full view. Buildings on either side of the narrow main square were on fire. Heaped rubble had cascaded down into the streets. It was a dead town."

It would only require a handful of Germans to easily hold up the American column at the Aure River bridge, since this was the only way into Isigny from the east. Two Company K riflemen dashed over the bridge first, followed by Cota and Lt. Col. Edward Gill, CO of the 3rd Battalion. No German response. Cota turned to Gill and exclaimed, "Hell, they didn't even blow the bridge!"

It was daylight on June 9 before the entire regiment had filed into town. "Isigny looked as though somebody had picked it up and dropped it," recalled Captain Slingluff. Amid the rubble, several German snipers or, more accurately, stragglers, took a few wild shots at the Yanks before fleeing southward. Slingluff told his men to deal harshly with these snipers. "If a sniper is sticking his head out of a window and taking a quick shot at you and ducking down again, you aim a bazooka in the general direction of that man, and you take the room out from under him and you don't worry anymore about him." Slingluff later described an unusual example of Yankee fire superiority: "From our tanks we fired [75mm guns] at snipers at the tremendous range of at least fifty yards. They were unhappy when we let them have that." A

Aerial view of Isigny, looking east. The Aure River and the little Isigny bridge (*at arrow*) are visible in the top half of the photo. On June 9 and 10, 1944, the 175th Infantry approached the town from the area shown in the upper right. *Courtesy Military History Institute.*

rumor later spread among the 175th that some of the snipers had been French girlfriends of German soldiers.

Colonel Goode selected Lt. Preston Delcazal to inform Gerhardt of Isigny's capture. Division headquarters was all the way back at Vierville, so Delcazal settled into the passenger seat of a jeep for the long ride to the beach. He ordered the driver to take the coastal highway, which forked off the Isigny road a mile east of town. Shortly after turning onto this highway, a scruffy group of enemy infantrymen suddenly jumped in front of the jeep with their rifles pointed straight at Delcazal and his driver. The Yanks gave themselves up, but they could tell that their captors were unenthusiastic *Osttruppen*. The enemy troops argued among each other in several different languages—none of which was German—and took their two prisoners back to a hedgerow hideout, where a larger group waited.

Using sign language, Delcazal tried to convince them that their best course of action was surrender. For an entire day, the enemy troops resisted this proposal for fear they might be recaptured by a German unit and promptly executed. Delcazal finally persuaded the *Osttruppen* that the area had been cleared of Germans. The entire group agreed to march eastward along the highway toward Grandcamp and surrender to the first Americans they met. Shortly after the two Yanks and their captors moved out, a 116th Infantry truck column approached from the opposite direction. Delcazal and his driver waved their arms and rushed forward, shouting, "Don't shoot! They want to surrender!" Thinking it a German trick, the amazed Stonewallers raised their rifles. The enemy troops, however, had already thrown down their weapons and were waving white handkerchiefs. The Yanks took the "Germans" prisoner, and Delcazal continued toward Vierville, twenty-four hours behind schedule.

EIGHT

ON TO ST. LÔ

"It Didn't Smell Right from the First"
June 10–13, 1944

1. FALLSCHIRMJÄGER

Rommel was right. The best chance to defeat the Allies had been on the beaches. With the enemy safely ashore, the Germans could do little to stem the massive Allied build-up. After D-Day, Rommel was distraught. "It is much better to end this at once and live as a British Dominion than be ruined by continuing this hopeless war," he confided to an aide.

The 352nd Division had been smashed. According to Ziegelmann, the division's *Gefechtsstärke* ("fighting strength"), not counting "Hiwis" and other support troops, was only 2,500 men on June 9. The 352nd's normal *Gefechtsstärke* was 7,500, so the division had been reduced by two-thirds in only four days of combat. Several more days of intense fighting would reduce the 2,500 survivors to near zero.

The Germans evaluated their new American opponents. "It was noticeable that the enemy troops were enthusiastic and felt themselves to be superior," Ziegelmann wrote. "This was particularly true for the 29th Infantry Division, reinforced by one tank battalion. However, an exaggerated feeling of superiority was also apparent. For instance, the stubborn attack of tanks on highways with little support; the careless way the enemy troops rested as soon as an objective was reached instead of making full use of the success."

Even a fresh German division could not have fulfilled the 352nd's hopeless mission on June 9. Kraiss was responsible for a thirty-mile front, and his men were fighting six different Allied divisions. The 352nd, now barely equivalent to a regiment, was attempting to defend what should have been a corps sector.

After the fall of Isigny, hardly any organized German troops stood between the 29th Division and St. Lô. One of the only coherent German units in this sector was a 352nd Division artillery battalion that had destroyed its own guns before escaping over the Aure north of Isigny as the 175th entered the town. The artillerymen now fought as infantry.

The 352nd Division had no alternative but to retreat and wait for reinforcements. Kraiss issued the order on the evening of June 9. By 6:00 A.M., the 352nd's survivors were to pull back, reassemble along a placid river called the Elle, and begin entrenching. By retreating to the Elle, Kraiss would give up seven miles of ground. Furthermore, the position where he planned to make a stand was only seven miles from St. Lô—the 29th Division's major campaign objective.

The 352nd's retreat had to be undertaken in darkness to avoid detection by Allied fighter-bombers. But even with this precaution, the pullback was a hazardous operation. The German troops had to disengage from the enemy, follow crooked country roads that were baffling even in daylight, march several miles to reach the Elle, locate their new defensive sectors, and dig in. Some 352nd units fighting the British in the Gold Beach area had to march sixteen miles in only eight hours. Even if the retreat were executed flawlessly, the 352nd was not out of danger, for the Elle was not a good defensive position.

Kraiss's major concern was that his men would remain unsupported for the next several days. In the division's new position, both its flanks were completely unprotected, and Kraiss worried that the Americans would simply slide past him like an ocean wave around a rock.

Fortunately for Kraiss, American intelligence officers had no idea that the Germans were in such desperate straits. The US 1st Army G-2, in fact, was worried about a German counterattack in the St. Lô area on June 9 and 10. This faulty intelligence would hinder Gerhardt for the next several days.

To Kraiss, the battle was shaping up as a race against time. German reinforcements from Brittany were on the way, and Kraiss hoped that all holes in the 352nd's line would be plugged no later than June 11. The 275th Infantry Division, stationed in Brittany, was one of the first divisions to respond to the call for help. On the morning of June 6, one-third of the division set out for Normandy. This force was designated *Kampfgruppe Heintz* after the commander of the 984th Infantry Regiment, the *Kampfgruppe*'s primary component. Heintz planned to travel the 125 miles to St. Lô by rail and truck in two days. Because of Allied fighter-bombers, however, the trip lasted almost a week. The troops, in fact, were forced to march on foot most of the way.

An almost identical *Kampfgruppe* of the 353rd Infantry Division, named *Kampfgruppe Böhm* after the CO of the 943rd Regiment, was also ordered to Kraiss's aid. It was of no immediate help, though, for it would take a long time to reach the front from its starting point at the western tip of Brittany, 200 miles from St. Lô.

Kraiss desperately needed *Kampfgruppe Heintz* on his left flank—west of the Vire River—where hardly a German soldier stood between the Yanks and St. Lô on June 9. Later, when *Kampfgruppe Böhm* arrived, Kraiss could use it either to reinforce Heintz or to bolster the 352nd's line along the Elle.

Kraiss also had to deal with a ten-mile gap on his right flank. The 3rd *Fallschirmjägerdivision* (Parachute Division, abbreviated "FJ") was slated to fill this hole, but it had to trek 190 miles from its encampment in the mountains of western Brittany to St. Lô, and it did not set out until the evening of June 7. Kraiss, therefore, could not count on this division for several days, perhaps more than a week if Allied aircraft harassed it as much as they did *Kampfgruppe Heintz.*

According to official German tables of organization and equipment, the 3rd FJ Division had enough vehicles to move every *Fallschirmjäger* (paratrooper) to Normandy by truck. However, Maj. Gen. Richard Schimpf, the 3rd FJ Division's commander, recalled that "Only about forty percent of the required motor vehicles were available, some of which were fit for service only to a limited extent. The situation in spare parts was very poor; there was no uniformity in vehicle types. The amount of fuel was insufficient for the available vehicles."

Schimpf decided to send as many men as possible by truck. There were only enough vehicles to transport one battalion from each of the division's three regiments, along with several supporting engineer, flak, and signal troops. The rest of the division would follow on foot. The truck column, traveling mostly at night, made good progress and encountered little interference from Allied aircraft. Liaison officers were sent ahead, and they informed Kraiss that the column would join the 352nd on the Elle on the afternoon of June 10. After depositing the paratroopers at the front, the truck drivers were to return to Brittany and pick up the rest of the division.

The 29ers knew from their first encounter with the 3rd FJ Division that the paratroopers were highly motivated and extraordinarily skillful in combat. "You know, those Germans are the best soldiers I ever saw," one battalion CO in the 116th remarked to a counterpart in the 115th. "They're smart and they don't know what the word 'fear' means. They come in and they keep coming until they get their job done or you kill 'em. . . . If they had as many people as we have they could come right through us any time they made up their minds to do it." The CO from the 115th was incredulous, but the Stonewaller just shook his head and smiled. "You'll see, bud, you'll see," he said.

The *Fallschirmjäger* were actually German Air Force troops. The men were all volunteers, and mental and physical entry standards were high. The recruits were thoroughly indoctrinated in *Fallschirmjägergeist*—"the paratrooper spirit." The *Fallschirmjäger*'s rigorous training regimen emphasized initiative and improvisation. Those who survived training were thoroughly convinced of their élite status and were even more steadfastly loyal to their comrades than were typical German soldiers.

The paratroopers could easily be distinguished from German army troops by their uniforms. Their helmets looked more like American "coal scuttle" models than standard German army headgear, and their baggy gray smocks seemed more like house painters' garb than soldiers' uniforms. The men wore their prized *Fallschirmschützenabzeichen* (Parachute Badges) on their breast pockets.

By 1944, with the Allies in almost complete control of the skies and the Germans almost devoid of transport aircraft, the *Fallschirmjäger* were unlikely to parachute from airplanes again. Nevertheless, the paratroopers still trained for the airborne mission at *Fallschirmschule* (Parachute School). In fact, Schimpf noted that 87 percent of his division had completed a jump-training course.

Like the 352nd, the 3rd FJ Division was a newly raised outfit, having been established by an army order of November 5, 1943. The division was scheduled to be fully organized and ready for combat by February 1944. It first encamped 100 miles east of Paris, but in late January the division was transferred to the remote mountainous area of western Brittany where, according to Schimpf, "there were no unwholesome diversionary influences in the line of amusements, such as were usually found in France."

According to German practice, new divisions formed around a core of seasoned combat veterans. The 3rd FJ Division's cadre came from a *Fallschirmjäger* battalion that had been fighting in Italy for several months as part of the 1st FJ Division. Aside from the members of that battalion, almost no one in the 3rd FJ Division had seen combat.

German army troops must have looked upon their Luftwaffe cousins with envy, for all *Fallschirmjäger* outfits boasted more men, weapons, vehicles, and supplies than their army counterparts. "The fighting power of the 3rd FJ Division was equal to two standard German divisions," recalled Gen. Max Pemsel, the Chief of Staff of the German 7th Army. "The strength of the FJ division rested in defense, because the division was well trained for it. The *Fallschirmjäger* felt at home in the bocage and, as an individual fighter, felt himself superior to the enemy."

The 3rd FJ Division, with an official strength of 15,976, had almost 2,000 more men than the 29th Division. Furthermore, the *Fallschirmjäger* were significantly better equipped than the 29ers in virtually all weapons categories. In truth, the major reason why the 29ers considered the paratroopers such a formidable enemy was the vast superiority of their opponent's armament.

The *Fallschirmjäger* were probably the best-armed infantrymen in the world in 1944. The Luftwaffe spared no expense in providing the paratroopers with MG 42s. The 3rd FJ Division had 930 light machine guns—almost twice as many as the 352nd and over *eleven times* as many as the 29th Division. An American rifle company had two Browning air-cooled machine guns and nine BARs; a *Fallschirmjäger* company had twenty MG 42s and forty-three submachine guns. At the squad level, the only source of automatic fire for the Yanks was a single BAR; in contrast, the German parachute squad had two MG 42s and three submachine guns. Thus, in a skirmish between equal numbers of 29ers and *Fallschirmjäger,* the American quest for fire superiority was doomed to failure.

American infantrymen relied on howitzers for help; the *Fallschirmjäger* depended on mortars. German paratroopers, in fact, were so abundantly provided with mortars that it was not surprising that 29ers came to loathe the mortar as much as the Germans hated American artillery. The 3rd FJ Division was supposed to have sixty-three powerful 120mm mortars; the 29th Division had no comparable weapon. Furthermore, the paratroopers had two-and-a-half times as many 81mm mortars as the 29ers.

Artillery was the only arm in which the 3rd FJ Division was weaker than the 29th. On paper, the paratroopers were supposed to have three artillery battalions as opposed to the four in an American infantry division. However, when the 3rd FJ Division moved to Normandy in June 1944, only one of its 105mm artillery battalions had been organized. This deficiency was eventually corrected, but in the interim, the paratroopers substituted their 120mm mortars for the missing howitzers. The Germans' dependence on mortars was hardly a disadvantage, for Norman bocage was perfect mortar country. Mortars were small and easy to hide. They were also simpler to move and fire than was a howitzer. Furthermore, the mortars' high-angle fire enabled skilled German operators to shell the enemy's deep hedgerow dugouts at relatively close range.

2. AMBUSH

In the 175th Infantry, Company K seemed to get all the dangerous assignments. It had been the first of the regiment's units to enter Isigny, and now, while the rest of the regiment fanned out southward toward St. Lô on June 9, Gerhardt ordered it on a special mission. Capt. Jack Lawton, the S-3 of the 3rd Battalion, located Capt. John King, Company K's CO, in Isigny and delivered the news. "Go down that street," said Lawton, pointing westward.

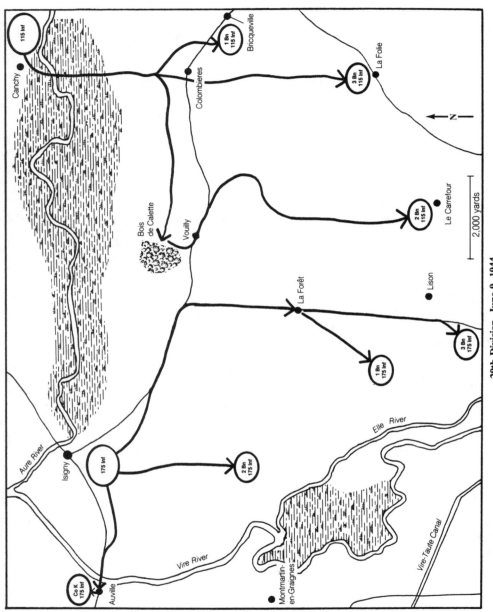

29th Division, June 9, 1944.

"It turns into a paved road. About one-and-three-fourths miles from the edge of town, you'll come to a bridge over the Vire River. As far as we know, it hasn't been blown yet. Grab it. There's a small town beyond it—Auville. Set up a perimeter defense around it and call me when you're organized. Radio silence until then. We want to keep the Jerries guessing. Any questions?"

"Why should I have any questions?" replied King. "Nobody has the faintest idea what's out there. Our intelligence reports are nil. It could be a couple of armored divisions for all you know. We don't know whether the bridge is in or out, how deep the river is, or what the Krauts have on the other side. I do know we came up short one platoon and my company headquarters section this side of La Cambe. They got lost somewhere. We do of course recognize we have been signally honored by the general. My warmest regards to Uncle Charlie."

Company K's mission was far more important than either Lawton or King realized. Thus far in the campaign, American troops who had come ashore on Utah and Omaha had fought in widely separated beachheads. However, General Bradley, the commander of the US 1st Army, was determined to link these beachheads as quickly as possible. The highway that crossed the Vire at Auville was vital to the Yanks because it was the most direct route between Utah and Omaha. The link-up promised to be difficult, however, for a four-mile stretch of German-held territory still lay between the two American forces.

As instructed, King led his men down the road, picking up a lost platoon of Company E on the way. When he reached the Vire, he discovered that the bridge had already been blown. Several coils of barbed wire lined the other side of the river, and the Yanks figured that the Germans were lying in wait somewhere beyond. King wasn't sure what to do. He deployed his men a few hundred yards east of the river and waited.

Several hours later, Gerhardt swaggered into King's command post and as usual came right to the point. "Here's what I want you to do: cross that river and capture that town over there," said Gerhardt, pointing to Auville.

"In daylight, General?" King asked.

"You've got the idea, King," Gerhardt replied. "Congratulations. In daylight. Say at 8:00 P.M. What do you need?"

"Well, aside from some way to get across that river. . . ."

"You just walk across," Gerhardt interrupted.

"Aside from that," King continued, "I'd like some more tanks for direct fire support, an artillery barrage, and a couple of ambulances."

"You'll have them," said Gerhardt. The general spun around, hopped into *Vixen Tor,* and departed.

King only had about 150 men and had no idea how many enemy troops waited on the opposite bank. To create the illusion of strength, King deployed his men in a one-rank skirmish line several hundred yards long. While the company mortars and machine guns provided covering fire against the far bank, King's men dashed into the river, which proved only a few feet deep. Several scattered German machine gun nests opened up, but they did not put up much of a fight. As the 29ers splashed across the river and onto the west bank, German resistance evaporated, and the Yanks pushed on to Auville with little difficulty. King's men captured dozens of prisoners from the 621st *Ost-bataillon*. Most were non-Germans looking for a safe opportunity to desert the German army.

Despite King's misgivings, the river crossing had been a complete success. "Maybe that's why they made Uncle Charlie a general," King mused. "About the only thing that went wrong was that I got shot through both legs by a Kraut machine gun, so *I* needed one of the ambulances."

The rest of the 175th executed an infantryman's blitzkrieg on June 9. German troops south of Isigny had mysteriously disappeared, and the 3rd Battalion, minus Company K, boldly marched eight miles southward by nightfall, following the Isigny-St. Lô highway. The 1st Battalion followed in the 3rd's footsteps. Meanwhile, the 2nd Battalion protected the main column's right, following a minor road between the highway and the Vire. Gerhardt was delighted by the 175th's progress. If the regiment kept up this pace, it would capture St. Lô within the next twenty-four hours.

The Germans offered their only significant resistance of the day at a hamlet named La Forêt, which was the site of a major 352nd Division supply dump. While a hastily organized battle group of stragglers and rear-echelon troops held off the 175th for several hours, the Germans managed to haul away many of their stores. Anything that could not be moved was blown up. When the 29ers passed the site later that day, all that remained of the supply dump was a huge crater and a mass of wreckage. "You could have put three 6x6s [trucks] in the hole side-by-side, and they would [have been] practically out of sight," recalled Lt. Sam Allsup of Company A.

General Cota visited the 175th's command post shortly before dawn on June 10. As he was talking with Colonel Goode, four bedraggled G.I.'s staggered into the headquarters enclosure. They identified themselves as members of the 2nd Battalion of the 115th. Gasping for breath, they stammered out their story. They alone, they claimed, had survived a terrible German ambush. After listening patiently, Cota remarked to an aide, "No need to start disaster rumors. Things like this just don't happen, and I don't believe it's as serious as these men think."

It was, however, almost as serious as those men thought, but it took several days to piece together the full story. It all began on the morning of June 9, when the 115th moved out to cross the flooded Aure valley. Despite Lieutenant Miller's successful patrol the previous day, which had indicated no

Two 29ers guard a captured German. The 29er in the background carries a Garand M1. The 29er in the foreground carries a Winchester M1 carbine. *Courtesy Military History Institute.*

significant German presence on the opposite side, the crossing of the flooded area was difficult. Miller's riflemen had made the tortuous journey in a few hours, but an entire regiment, with its attendant heavy weapons, supplies, and vehicles, would take much longer.

The first unit to enter the swamp was the 3rd Battalion. This outfit made little headway through the muck until 29th Division engineers arrived on the scene with strange-looking amphibious cargo carriers, nicknamed "Weasels" by the men. The indispensable Weasels enabled the engineers to bring their bulky bridging equipment and assault rafts into the marsh. Ten crude foot bridges were built for the infantrymen, but the 3rd Battalion took several hours to move only a mile-and-a-half across the valley.

The 2nd Battalion followed in the 3rd's wake shortly before noon. Several hours later, the 1st Battalion, whose crossing attempt at another site two miles east had been frustrated by German machine guns, also used the 3rd Battalion's path. Regimental support units and the 110th Field Artillery, however, could not use this route since the little foot bridges would not support the weight of vehicles and howitzers. Instead, these outfits crossed the valley on a narrow causeway two-and-a-half miles to the west. Their passage, however, was delayed almost twenty-four hours while the 254th Combat Engineer Battalion, a V Corps unit, made repairs to the damaged causeway bridges.

The 115th had accomplished only half its mission by successfully traversing the Aure. The other half was to move as rapidly as possible toward St. Lô, only thirteen miles distant. On the afternoon of June 9, all three battalions fanned out into the bocage—2nd on the right, 3rd in the center, 1st on the left.

The 1st Battalion got tied up in a fight for the village of Bricqueville, a mile-and-a-half south of the Aure, and dug in there for the night. The 2nd and 3rd Battalions plunged deeper and deeper into the bocage. Occasionally, both columns brushed into small groups of enemy stragglers, but most of the time the Germans showed little inclination to stand and fight. The further both battalions marched, the less they saw of the enemy. The Germans appeared to be on the run, and the road to St. Lô looked wide open.

The sun sank low in the west, and scraggly shrubs and shaggy apple trees cast eerie shadows across the narrow, dusty roads and the long files of marching men. The 2nd and 3rd Battalions had been on the march almost continuously for fifteen hours, and by now the men thought more about food and sleep than they thought about the enemy. Maj. Victor Gillespie, the CO of the 3rd Battalion, thought his men had done enough marching for the day; he declared they wouldn't go a step further until they got something to eat. The 2nd Battalion, on a parallel road to the west, kept going.

At 7:00 P.M., Lieutenant Colonel Cooper and his battery COs crossed the Aure in six jeeps to search for suitable firing positions for the 110th Field Artillery's guns. Much to the artillerymen's surprise, General Gerhardt greeted them on the south end of the causeway. "There are Germans somewhere around the bend of the road up ahead," Gerhardt warned. Then, with a wave of the hand, he departed.

Cooper's men continued down the road. They saw no trace of the enemy. The only troops the artillerymen encountered were a group of 100 bewildered American replacements led by a 115th Infantry captain. "They were looking for somebody to replace," recalled Cooper.

Shortly before sunset, Cooper glanced backwards and was startled to see a long column of American infantrymen plodding down the road toward him. It was the 2nd Battalion of the 115th, led by its CO, Lt. Col. William Warfield. Somehow, in the hedgerow maze, Cooper's party had gotten ahead of the infantrymen they were supposed to be supporting. Warfield's men were clearly worn out. Their heads drooped; every step was labored.

Warfield greeted Cooper. "God, my men are hungry," he said. "Our rations are almost out. Do you have any food?"

The artillerymen had thirty K Rations, and Cooper handed them all to Warfield. The food wouldn't go very far for the 600 men in the battalion, but at least it was a help. Warfield waved his thanks as the long infantry column trudged further down the road and out of sight.

Maj. Maurice Clift, the 2nd Battalion executive, had moved ahead of the column in a jeep to pick out a good bivouac area where the men could rest for the night. He chose two typical Norman enclosed pastures a few hundred yards south of a cluster of houses named Le Carrefour. (Literally, "crossroads"; US Army maps mistakenly called it "Le Carretour.") At 2:00 A.M. on June 10, battalion staff officers finally waved the weary riflemen off the road through a farm gate into the fields selected for their bivouac. The battalion had marched fifteen miles in the past twenty hours, including the difficult transit of the Aure valley. St. Lô was only nine miles away.

The Army's cardinal rule about digging a foxhole before going to sleep was ignored that night. Whole platoons slumped against hedgerow embankments, and most men were asleep within minutes. They were so tired that they didn't bother to remove their haversacks.

From somewhere in the distance sentries could hear the faint sound of vehicle engines—probably the jeeps of the 3rd Battalion, they figured. The 3rd was supposedly somewhere east of the 2nd.

Germans.

From behind every hedgerow, MG 42s and submachine guns opened fire on the slumbering Yanks. Mortar rounds fell into the pastures every few seconds, and three German *Sturmgeschütze*—tank-like assault guns—roared down the road past Le Carrefour, pointing their long-barreled guns over the hedgerows and blasting the 29ers at pointblank range. The Germans had seemingly sprung out of the ground.

The 29ers never stood a chance. With no time to set up a coherent defense, the frantic 29ers ran to and fro looking for a way to escape the death trap, but the Germans on top of the surrounding embankments could easily pick off the Yanks. The fields in which the battalion had bivouacked were bathed in the eerie light of German flares. Along one hedgerow, a platoon of dozing 29ers had only just risen when most of the men were cut down by a burst of machine gun fire. As the G.I.'s were hit, they tumbled back against the hedgerow in heaps.

Small groups of 29ers tried to fight back, but the Germans were as elusive as ghosts. The enemy popped up suddenly from behind the hedgerows, fired their guns, and disappeared. A few seconds later, they appeared someplace else. Several G.I.'s fired their M1s wildly at the hedgerows, but they were just as likely to hit their own men as Germans.

A few brave 29ers grabbed bazookas and knocked out two of the three *Sturmgeschütze,* but the battle was already lost. Most of the surviving Yanks scattered all over the countryside. "It was terrible," one of the survivors told Cota later. "We had crawled about 100 yards away from the field when we heard a lot of the guys screaming. I think that the Germans must have been making a bayonet charge."

Warfield was one of those who fought to the last. He had been meeting with his staff in a two-story stone farmhouse on the roadside when the Germans suddenly appeared out of nowhere. The officers dashed out of the house; many were promptly killed. Warfield and several other survivors tried to organize a defense, but the situation was hopeless. Some minutes later, the Germans called upon the headquarters group to give up. "Surrender! Surrender!" they yelled, in English.

"Surrender, hell!" Lieutenant Colonel Warfield roared. Armed only with a Colt .45, Warfield attempted to lead his little group down the road toward the fields where his battalion was being massacred. He and most of his party were immediately killed by enemy machine guns.

When the battle was over, about fifty members of the battalion lay dead and another 100 were wounded or captured. The rest of the unit had scattered.

Actually, the ambush of Warfield's battalion was almost accidental. The German unit that sprang the trap was a 352nd Division *Kampfgruppe* (task force) responding to Kraiss's June 9 order to pull back from the beachhead to the Elle by the following morning. The *Kampfgruppe* consisted of survivors from several battered units. By coincidence—and unknown to either side—the German column retreated in the 2nd Battalion's wake. Sometime after dark, German scouts detected Warfield's men when they moved into their bivouac near Le Carrefour. The Germans crept forward, surrounding the fields, and attacked. The battle lasted only twenty minutes.

General Gerhardt had been worried about the 115th. He had not heard a word from Warfield and the rest of the 115th Infantry since the regiment had crossed the Aure the previous morning. During the afternoon of June 9, he had sent a liaison officer, Maj. Glover Johns, across the Aure valley to determine the 115th's whereabouts. Johns's mission had proven fruitless. The major learned only that the situation south of the Aure was confused, something Gerhardt already knew. Johns's party, in fact, had had a hair-raising encounter with German troops in an area supposedly occupied by the 115th.

At dusk, Johns had managed to locate the 115th's command post near Colombières, but Colonel Slappey and most of his staff were gone. No one knew where. Johns had been alarmed to discover that the headquarters personnel had no idea where any of the 115th's three infantry battalions were.

Gerhardt turned up at the 115th command post, unexpectedly as always, at 2:00 A.M. on June 10. After excoriating Johns for failing to locate the 115th and the staff officers for not knowing the whereabouts of their regiment, the general eventually calmed down. He had decided that Slappey, still absent, was to blame.

It was not long before Gerhardt heard the story of Warfield's 2nd Battalion firsthand. Several stragglers from this outfit stumbled into the 115th command post at 4:00 A.M., sputtering that they were the sole survivors of a massacre. One agonized young lieutenant sank to his knees and pounded the ground with his fists, sobbing over and over that all his men were dead, and he had let them down. He became so disconsolate that a medic had to sedate him.

As Gerhardt listened, he became enraged. "No security!" he screamed. "They just went into the field and went to bed!"

At dawn, Gerhardt and Johns took off in a jeep to find the site of the ambush. Johns had misgivings about this mission. If the reports of the 2nd Battalion survivors were to be believed, the countryside through which he and the general would travel could be under German control. But Gerhardt didn't care. Occasionally, at confusing road junctions, he got out of the jeep, map in hand, and paraded into the intersection as if the enemy was the last thing that concerned him. "The man nearly gave me heart failure," recalled Johns. "Those two stars looked so big to me they might as well have been neon lights." Once the general made such an inviting target of himself at a major crossroads that Johns raced over like a football player and shoved him down into a roadside ditch. Uncle Charlie, already angry, got up angrier.

Gerhardt and Johns soon came upon a ragged column of two dozen exhausted and disheveled men from the 2nd Battalion. The general listened intently to their stories for about half an hour, praised them for sticking together, then sent them to the rear. He later awarded the Bronze Star to every one.

A mile down the road, Gerhardt and Johns located the site of the ambush. As the two men surveyed the carnage, they were no doubt reminded of Custer's Last Stand. American bodies littered the fields. In pidgin French, the general questioned two elderly Frenchwomen placing flowers on the bodies, but the women knew little. Gerhardt and Johns came across Warfield's corpse, lying in the road in front of several dead members of his staff. Warfield's hand still clutched his .45. "If you have to die, that's the way to do it," Gerhardt declared.

During the return trip, Gerhardt decided to make changes in the 115th. Later that day, the general assigned new COs to the 2nd and 3rd Battalions. Dissatisfied with Colonel Slappey, Gerhardt made up his mind to relieve him as soon as a suitable substitute became available.

After the ambush of the 2nd Battalion, the Germans disappeared into the bocage. Gerhardt ordered patrols to probe south of Le Carrefour to determine the enemy's whereabouts, but the 115th saw hardly a German for the rest of June 10. Unknown to Gerhardt, the 352nd Division had retreated further south and was digging in south of the Elle River.

Hundreds of stragglers from the 2nd Battalion drifted back into American lines during the afternoon of June 10, and the outfit was hastily reorganized. Gerhardt made up for the battalion's grievous casualties by assigning over 100 fresh replacements to the unit. Lt. Col. Arthur Sheppe, the 2nd Battalion's new CO, was ordered to take his unit back to the front by the same road it had traveled the day before. Prior to starting out, however, Sheppe made sure that the still-shaken members of his battalion would be spared the grisly sight of their comrades' corpses when the outfit passed the ambush site. He sent a medical detachment ahead with several ambulances to clear the bodies from the fields near Le Carrefour. When the 2nd Battalion passed through the village later that day, the solemn G.I.'s saw few signs of the desperate struggle that had raged less than twenty-four hours earlier.

The 1st and 3rd Battalions moved southward on June 10 and also encountered virtually no opposition. By the morning of June 11, most of the 115th had congregated a half-mile north of the Elle near the village St. Marguerite d'Elle, 2nd and 3rd Battalions in front, 1st in reserve. The regiment rested and reorganized for most of June 11, preparing for a big offensive across the Elle. Gerhardt had ordered that the attack be made the next morning, and this would be the 29th Division's first set-piece attack of the campaign against a prepared enemy defensive line. Uncle Charlie wanted results.

The 352nd Division was extraordinarily vulnerable on June 10 and 11, and Kraiss considered himself lucky that the Americans did not choose either day to attack. The men of the 352nd used the two-day respite to reorganize, replenish their ammunition, and dig in. The division's defensive line along the Elle was thin and overextended, but on June 11 Kraiss was permitted to shorten his front significantly when the leading elements of the 3rd FJ Division arrived. By June 12, the date Gerhardt planned to attack across the Elle, Kraiss's situation was no longer desperate.

Lieutenant Colonel Cooper's 110th Field Artillery finally caught up with the 115th on the evening of June 10. The artillerymen promptly registered their guns on suitable targets south of the Elle and began to fire harassing salvos against road junctions and suspected enemy strongpoints. Thus far in the campaign, the cannoneers had had little opportunity to use their guns. The June 12 attack promised to change that.

To support the infantrymen of the 115th with an overwhelming volume of fire, Cooper was reinforced with three independent howitzer battalions. One of these, the 230th, was on loan to the 29th from the 30th Division as a temporary replacement for the 111th Field Artillery, which had lost all its guns on Omaha Beach. Cooper had so many guns at his disposal that he decided to use a massive World War I–style barrage prior to the upcoming attack. He hoped this bombardment would overcome the enemy by sheer volume of fire.

The 116th Infantry had been out of action for several days, recuperating near La Cambe from its terrible losses on D-Day. Although hundreds of replacements had swelled the regiment's ranks, it was questionable whether the new men were fully ready for combat. Nevertheless, Gerhardt ordered the Stonewall Brigade to move to the front on June 11. The rejuvenated regiment marched across the Aure and encamped near the 115th at St. Marguerite d'Elle. The 116th was designated as division reserve, but Gerhardt warned Colonel Canham to prepare to support the 115th's attack the following day.

June 11 was the first day of rest for the members of the 115th Infantry since the men had boarded their transports for the trip across the English Channel. Since the ambush of the 2nd Battalion, the front had stabilized along the Elle, and the regiment's rear-echelon personnel used this opportunity to move from the beach to positions close behind the battle line. For the first time in the campaign, the riflemen got hot meals and even mail from home.

G.I.'s who had a few hours to kill wandered into nearby French villages and mingled with the civilians. When the 29ers had first arrived in the quaint villages, the local inhabitants had celebrated wildly and thrust flowers and bottles of wine upon their liberators. After a skirmish erupted in or around a village, solemn French civilians knelt before the corpses of 29th Division soldiers, made the sign of the cross, and laid bouquets of flowers on the bodies.

Before the invasion, however, the 29ers had been warned not to trust the French, many of whom were suspected of harboring German sympathies. After D-Day, in fact, the 29ers encountered several Frenchmen who were obviously unhappy to see the Americans. "We began to suspect every male Frenchman of being a collaborator or a German spy," recalled Maj. Donovan Yeuell, the 110th Artillery's executive. "My doubtful French came into play when invariably I was called upon to interrogate the many male suspects our little battalion picked up. I wouldn't admit it then, but I can tell you now that I hadn't the faintest idea what half of them said or what their identification cards meant, and, so far as I was concerned, practically all of those that I talked to could have been Rommel himself."

One of the unexpected delights of Normandy was calvados, a potent Norman apple brandy. Calvados was rumored to be strong enough to replace the lighter fluid in a Zippo. When the 29ers sampled the drink, they wanted more, and if they got a chance to barter with French civilians, they usually exchanged rations for calvados. Several lucky 29ers came upon caches of the drink in the basements of abandoned farm houses.

For the men of the 115th Infantry, June 12 was a frightful day. The regiment's attack across the Elle began at 3:30 A.M. with the most powerful American artillery barrage to this point in the campaign. As the nervous infantrymen moved up to the line of departure in the dark, the ground shook as if hundreds of giant hammers were smashing the earth somewhere beyond the next hedgerow.

The powerful barrage accomplished surprisingly little. For two days, the enemy had dug furiously into the hedgerows bordering the Elle, and their deep slit trenches and dugouts were nearly impervious to fire. Furthermore, the Germans, unlike their opponents, were not in the habit of deploying large bodies of troops in the front lines. In fact, the hedgerows closest to the Americans were usually only lightly defended. Most German infantrymen were dispersed behind the front, where they dug secondary lines of entrenchments. Here German reserves could form for a surprise counterattack in the event of an American breakthrough.

Military tacticians called this technique "defense in depth." It was perfectly suited to the bocage. Whenever the 29ers stormed and won a hedgerow, there always seemed to be another one 100 yards behind it resolutely defended by the enemy. Furthermore, since the German defenders were so widely dispersed, the American artillery had little effect.

Although labeled a river on US Army maps, the Elle was really nothing more than a creek. Where the 1st and 3rd Battalions of the 115th were to cross on June 12, a G.I. could practically leap over the Elle without getting wet. It was difficult to believe that the Germans had elected to make a stand there.

The Germans, however, had every inch of the Elle covered with machine guns, as the 29ers in the 1st Battalion of the 115th discovered when they launched their attack from St. Marguerite at 5:00 A.M. The Yanks were met with such withering fire on the north bank that six hours later no one had gotten within ten feet of the river. A crossing in this sector seemed impossible. It was a terrible setback for the 1st Battalion. The outfit suffered almost 100 casualties in the attack, including twenty-five dead.

The 3rd Battalion jumped off a half-mile east of the 1st Battalion, but it fared little better. Every German howitzer and mortar within range of the Elle had been carefully registered on the 115th's hedgerows over the past two days, and somehow the enemy knew when the Yanks were about to launch their attack. A furious barrage hit the 3rd Battalion when its members were crowded into the front lines preparing to jump off. The 29ers made easy targets, and German aim was perfect.

Lt. Joseph Binkoski of Company M recalled the results: "Captain Fowler [Company M CO] and I headed for a sunken road which ran parallel to the river, which was to be the LD [Line of Departure] for the attack. When we got down there we found a ghastly sight. Littered over some twenty yards of this road were the badly mangled bodies of our dead and wounded. The medics

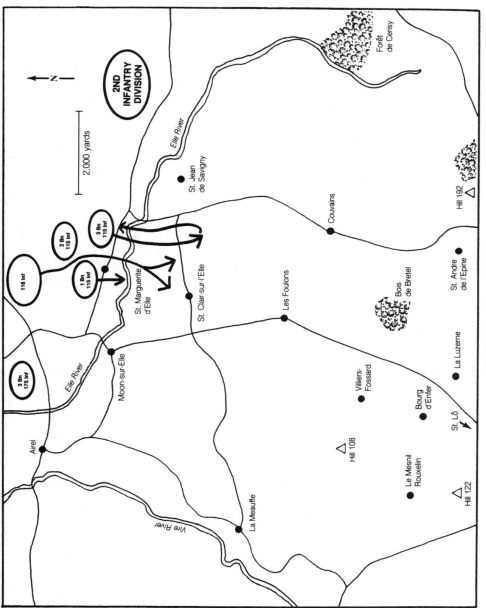

29th Division, June 12, 1944.

were on hand immediately doing what they could when the Captain and I came across the body of Captain Hille, the CO of Company K, surrounded by a pool of blood. I remember Captain Fowler saying to me, 'Today, Joe, we've lost one of the best men in the US Army.' Having seen Captain Hille in action since D-Day, I readily agreed.''

Company K was so battered by the barrage that it could take no further part in the attack. The battalion's other two rifle companies, I and L, though also disorganized, succeeded in getting a foothold across the Elle. The men mistakenly believed that the rest of the regiment was also advancing somewhere on the flanks, so the two intermixed groups from Companies I and L marched deeper into the German lines. But the bocage was playing tricks on them. After the two groups advanced a mile-and-a-half, the 29ers suddenly realized they were far out in front of the rest of the regiment.

The Germans closed in on both American groups near the village of Les Fresnes. As the Germans shelled the Yanks mercilessly, Capt. Grat Hankins, the 3rd Battalion CO, decided to retreat back across the Elle. A pullback, however, was not easy. The Germans pursued the 29ers relentlessly, and the path of retreat was littered with hundreds of discarded American haversacks, radios, and weapons. Even worse, dozens of badly wounded Yanks who could no longer walk had to be left behind, since no stretcher-bearers or ambulances were on hand. The 3rd Battalion eventually returned to its line of departure minus 130 men.

Gerhardt was furious. "Corps says we must get to objective," he radioed Capt. George Nevius, the 115th's S-3, at 3:40 P.M. "If you can't do it, we'll have to put 116th in to do it. The 115th must take objective at once. Report back at once, but get that message through to Slappey right away." Forty minutes later, when the general learned the extent of the 115th's repulse, he immediately ordered Colonel Canham to commit his 116th Infantry to the battle.

Canham conferred with his battalion COs in St. Marguerite and ordered an immediate attack across the Elle. There was no time to thoroughly brief company COs or to make a careful reconnaissance of the German lines.

Capt. Bob Garcia, the CO of Company E, recalled how he learned of the attack: "I quite vividly remember that our company was strung out in one big, long column along this road leading to the River Elle and St. Marguerite," he said, "with no particular objective in mind and not any idea at all of what was going on up ahead of us. In fact, I was down in a roadside ditch and really taking things kind of easy. All of a sudden, striding down the road towards me came Colonel Canham and his various aides and entourage. . . . 'Take your company across this field for about 200 yards, then turn to the left and go for about five hundred yards. When you come to a road, cross the road. On the other side of the road is a small stream. Cross that stream and keep going.

29th Division, June 13, 1944.

And fast. Got it?' " "Well," concluded Garcia, "there is only one reply in that situation, and the reply is 'Yes, sir.' "

Moving through the positions occupied by the shaken members of the 115th, the Stonewallers launched their attack at 7:30 P.M., only two-and-a-half hours before sunset. Although the Germans resisted stubbornly, they were caught unprepared by the commitment of a fresh regiment to the same sector where a previous attack had so recently failed. Eventually, the 116th crossed the Elle and pushed a mile through a gap in the German lines.

Gerhardt ordered Canham to press his attack at dawn on June 13. When the sun rose, a heavy mist blanketed the ground. The countryside was strangely quiet; the old-timers said that the previous day's fight had frightened the birds away. The only discernible sounds were the whispers of commands, the metallic snap of rifle bolts as clips were inserted into M1s, the clicks of bayonets being fixed to the muzzles of rifles.

The pastures were ghostly in the fog. The mist favored the 29ers since the Germans could not see well enough to take decent aim. But the bocage, confusing enough even in broad daylight, would be even more perplexing until the mist burned off.

The 2nd Battalion's objective was the village of St. Clair-sur-l'Elle. Confusion set in as soon as the attack jumped off. "The Krauts popped up where they had no business being," recalled the CO, Major Bingham. "As usual, all communications were out."

The Stonewallers could make out a church steeple through the mist as they approached St. Clair. The sharper-eyed members of the battalion could also discern several figures on bicycles pedaling furiously into the village from the north side. "Hey, Charlie, those sure look like Krauts!" Bingham yelled to his S-1, Capt. Charles Cawthon. They were. Pursuing them, the Yanks had the satisfaction, for a few glorious moments, of seeing the enemy on the run. As the bicyclists sped out the southern side of town, the Stonewallers ran in from the north. Reaching the town square, the 29ers noticed with amusement that St. Clair's World War I memorial, a statue of a 1918 French infantryman, was headless.

A mile to the east of St. Clair, the 1st Battalion attacked along the same axis the 3rd Battalion of the 115th had tried the previous day. The Stonewallers made excellent progress, pushing two miles deep into the German lines and capturing the village of Couvains, less than five miles from St. Lô.

Although initially resilient, after thirty hours of enemy artillery barrages and two massive infantry attacks, the 352nd Division had begun to disintegrate. In fact, after the Battle of the Elle, Ziegelmann estimated that the division's *Gefechtsstärke* (fighting strength) was down to only 1,900 men, about one-quarter of its normal force. These 1,900 had to cover a five-mile front.

Gerhardt was convinced that St. Lô was within the 29th Division's grasp.

Troops of the 175th Infantry on Hill 108 near Villiers-Fossard, June 1944. Note the telephone wires strung along the road. *Courtesy Military History Institute.*

A G-2 report in the division journal on the morning of June 14 stated, "Loss of enemy high, [enemy's] morale low. Much ammo and weapons are being found abandoned. . . . Civilians report enemy wearing civilian clothes in area."

But ominous intelligence reports had filtered into 29th Division headquarters. Outside Couvains, the Stonewallers had captured an unusual prisoner. He was German, all right, but he wasn't wearing the standard German army uniform. At 116th headquarters, the prisoner identified himself as a paratrooper from the 3rd *Fallschirmjäger* Division. The S-2 staff questioned the man carefully, for he was the first evidence that the 352nd Division had been reinforced.

The 29ers were also disturbed by the rumored approach of two German panzer divisions from the southeast. The 116th was warned to keep a sharp lookout for enemy tanks or any indications of a German counterattack. On the afternoon of June 13, Maj. Tom Howie, the 116th's S-3, radioed division headquarters that the Stonewallers were digging in more deeply than ever. He joked, "You got them all steamed up about the counterattack."

On the morning of June 13, Gerhardt relieved Colonel Slappey as the 115th's CO. The general had been displeased with Slappey ever since the 2nd Battalion's debacle at Le Carrefour, and after the 115th's repulse on the Elle,

Uncle Charlie was convinced that a new man would do the regiment good. Gerhardt wanted an aggressive commander for the 115th, one who could "put a fire under his men," as he liked to say. Slappey was not that kind of dynamic leader. Actually, Gerhardt liked Slappey, and his removal was an uncomfortable task. Gerhardt telephoned Gen. William Kean, Bradley's chief of staff at 1st Army. "Have you room for Slappey? He is a splendid fellow and I hope you have a spot for him. Please let me know. . . . I have placed Colonel Ordway [formerly division chief of staff] in command of the 115th in place of Slappey." Ordway, a brilliant staff officer who had been clamoring for a field command in lieu of his rear-echelon job, now got his chance.

3. RECONNAISSANCE IN FORCE

The 175th Infantry spent June 10 and 11 settling into a front line routine. The regiment held the 29th Division's right flank, but since the geography of this sector was so unusual, Colonel Goode had difficulty concentrating his troops for Gerhardt's planned offensive toward St. Lô. The regiment held a long L-shaped front, stretching almost eight miles from the mouth of the River Vire to the village of Lison, a mile west of Le Carrefour.

The 1st and 3rd Battalions, minus Company K, held the base of the L on the slope of a steep hill just south of Lison. From this height the 29ers had a commanding view of the Vire River and the surrounding countryside to the south and west. The 2nd Battalion held the stem of the L, facing west across a swampy portion of the Vire valley. Company K held the top of the L at Auville.

General Bradley was deeply concerned about the situation west of the Vire. On June 10, American paratroopers from the 101st Airborne Division had joined Company K west of Auville, finally linking the Utah and Omaha beachheads, but this connection was tenuous. An American intelligence report warned that a major enemy force was preparing to counterattack on the west side of the Vire to sever the tie between the two beachheads.

Bradley had no spare troops to block such a counterattack, so the 175th was ordered to send a force to the west side of the Vire on June 12. The mission, officially designated a "reconnaissance in force," was to discover what the Germans were up to and, more important, to seize two key bridges over a canal that the expected German counterattack would have to cross.

Cota believed that one rifle company was too small to accomplish the mission. Gerhardt, on the other hand, told Goode that "it shouldn't take the strength of a battalion to do the trick." As a compromise, two companies—C and E—were selected. Company E was to seize the westernmost bridge; Company C the easternmost. The combined force was commanded by Maj. Anthony Miller, the 1st Battalion executive.

Goode wanted the two companies to cross the Vire under cover of darkness. At 4:00 A.M. on June 12, however, only an hour before the sky lightened, Companies C and E were still far from their assigned crossing sites. Cota and Goode encountered Company C outside Lison. Capt. Alex Pouska, the CO, explained that he hadn't even heard about the mission until after midnight. He'd had to rouse his men, equip them with sufficient ammunition and rations, and brief his platoon leaders on what little he knew of their upcoming task. Then he had to march his company four-and-a-half miles in the dark over unfamiliar roads to reach the Vire.

Crossing the river in darkness was out of the question, since the sun had already risen by the time the two companies reached the Vire. As the 29ers filed down to the river, several trailers from Company C of the 121st Engineer Battalion rumbled towards the river bank on a narrow dirt track. The trailers carried sixteen rubber assault boats—eight for each company. Each boat could carry ten men. Company E was to cross the river two-and-a-half miles southwest of Isigny, just south of the St. Lô-Cherbourg railway bridge. Company C was to cross a mile upstream.

The enemy knew the Yanks were up to something. As the 29ers paddled across the river, a few machine guns opened up at long range, but they were aimed too high. The Yanks were actually safer on the river than anywhere else since both banks were lined with twelve-foot dikes. Both companies, in fact, made it over the Vire without loss, although several men were hit as they climbed over the western dike. Cota accompanied Company E across the river. "It [the plan] didn't smell right from the first, and I thought maybe I could help if they got in a jam," Cota remembered.

The sun was high in the sky as the men began their westward march. The day was hot, and several 29ers became ill-tempered. "When in hell are we going to use these things?" complained one infantryman who was carrying a heavy machine gun.

On the marshy plain west of the Vire, another G.I. spotted dozens of crayfish in a drainage ditch. "Gee! They're good to eat!" he exclaimed.

"This ain't no nature hunt," growled his squad leader. "Drag your ass towards those hills, boy."

Companies C and E were to rendezvous in a little town called Montmartin-en-Graignes, which lay on a knoll 1,000 yards west of the Vire. But the further the 29ers moved away from the river, the more German resistance stiffened. Cota realized that Montmartin was occupied by the enemy, for Company E took heavy fire as it approached the town from the northeast.

But the bridges—not the town—were the mission objectives, so Cota decided to bypass Montmartin on the north. The change of plan could not be passed on to Company C, however, since the radios had gotten soaked in the crossing and were not working. Cota had not believed that joining Company

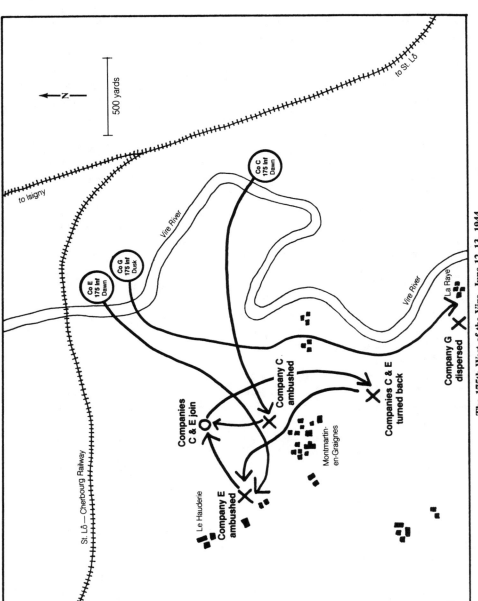

to Isigny

Vire River

to St. Lô

Co C
175 Inf
Dawn

Co G
175 Inf
Dusk

Co E
175 Inf
Dawn

Vire River

St. Lô — Cherbourg Railway

Companies
C & E join

Company C
ambushed

Companies C & E
turned back

Le Hauderie

Company E
ambushed

Montmartin-
en-Graignes

La Raye

Company G
dispersed

500 yards

N

The 175th West of the Vire, June 12–13, 1944.

C in Montmartin was necessary in the first place, since each company was supposed to seize a different bridge.

Cota and Company E marched straight into a trap. Five hundred yards northwest of Montmartin, the 29ers were filing down a narrow dirt road, bordered on both sides by hedgerows as tall as a man, when a couple of German submachine guns suddenly opened up on the head of the column at pointblank range. The Yanks promptly dropped into the roadside ditches. Muttered one prone 29er, "Christ! I never knew my dog tags was so thick!"

Lieutenant Shea, Cota's aide, recalled the chaos. "Several men were hit and the bullets sprayed along, ricocheting off the road and nipping the shrubbery near their heads. Someone yelled 'Return the fire! Shoot back at the bastards!' At intervals men would rise from the ditch and try to escape from the entrapment by either scurrying to the rear, or trying to vault over the hedges. One man attempting to cross the left hedge received a blast of burp gun fire that shoved him crashing back into the road—dead."

The Germans were on the other side of the hedgerows, pushing their submachine guns over the embankments without even looking and firing long bursts up and down the road. Several Company E men crept to the other side of the hedgerow through a large drain pipe and spotted the German culprits. A few well-aimed shots killed two of the enemy and drove off the others. But the Germans had performed their duties well. Only a handful of the enemy had scattered an entire company.

Only thirty men remained with Cota. The rest had disappeared into the bocage. "What is this? 'Cota's Last Stand'?" Cota demanded of Shea. "One minute I'm surrounded by a rifle company; those birds started to shoot, and I looked around to find myself all alone."

The Germans were not through with Company E. Like vultures circling a dying man, they surrounded Cota's party and called upon the Americans to surrender. One 29er answered by blasting an enemy-occupied hedgerow with a full clip from his BAR. "Blow it out your ass!" he shouted.

One of Cota's men peered over a hedgerow and detected an odd-looking cow in an adjacent field. "One of those dumb bastards is trying to hide behind that cow!" the 29er yelled. "Look at those boots!" A fusillade killed the German, and the cow—but a sergeant scolded the men for wasting ammunition. "You don't have to bury 'em with lead," he said.

Fortunately for Cota, the enemy force was not large. The general ordered his men to break out of their encirclement and retreat the way they had come. The breakout was executed successfully. As Cota's party headed back towards the Vire, they met Capt. Pouska and fifty men of Company C. Like Company E, Pouska's outfit had also been scattered by a German ambush just north of Montmartin.

Cota was still determined to capture the two canal bridges. After a short period of rest, during which the survivors of Companies C and E combined into a single group of eighty men, Cota decided to move toward the bridges around the east side of Montmartin between the town and the Vire.

But the Germans there were ready, and Cota's men made no progress. The general was still not ready to abandon the mission, and he turned his men around for yet another try north of Montmartin. His group retraced Company E's morning route, but they were brought to a halt by enemy fire at the exact spot where Company E had been ambushed earlier.

At 6:00 P.M., help arrived at last. As the 29ers were digging in 500 yards northwest of Montmartin, sixty members of the 101st Airborne Division stumbled into the American lines and decided to remain with Cota. The odds of seizing the bridges were still too unfavorable, even for Cota; the men's survival throughout the night had become his only goal. The general concluded that his current position on the outskirts of Montmartin was indefensible in darkness. The safest place in which to spend the night, he believed, was Montmartin itself. Cota therefore ordered an audacious attack against the village before nightfall.

It seemed unlikely that the attack would succeed, but it did. "It was the perfect example of fire and movement," Cota remembered. After a day of frustration, the Yanks had finally achieved a small success.

Now that Cota's men held the town, they settled down for the night. Said Cota, "We were all pretty tired. I just sat down under an apple tree and said, 'This is my command post.'"

Gerhardt, however, was furious. Stragglers from Companies C and E, wandering back to the east side of the Vire, were spreading stories that their outfits had been wiped out by a German ambush. The disaster that had befallen the 2nd Battalion of the 115th on June 10 seemed to be happening all over again.

On the afternoon of June 12, Gerhardt ordered Goode to send another unit, Company G, to capture the canal bridges. He also insisted that Goode gather all the stragglers he could find from Company E and send them back over the river with Company G.

Goode did not think this wise. "They won't go back unless I lead them, General," Goode declared.

"OK. Use your own judgment," Gerhardt replied. "But Company E [stragglers] must go back."

Goode issued the necessary orders and then solemnly walked among the members of Company G and the survivors of E, explaining the dangers of the upcoming mission. "I wouldn't order anybody to go into a thing like this unless I went myself, so I'm just going along for the buggy ride."

At 11:00 P.M. on June 12, Goode's force crossed the Vire at the same place where Company E had traversed the river almost twenty-four hours before. The column marched several hundred yards across the river's swampy western flood plain and then turned south. "We went through the German lines for three miles, and there was not a shot fired," recalled Captain Slingluff of Company G.

At dawn on June 13, Company G marched into a tiny hamlet named La Raye on the west bank of the Vire. The hamlet consisted only of a couple of houses clustered around the junction of two dirt tracks, and it seemed pretentious even to give the place a name. La Raye was less than a mile away from the easternmost of the two canal bridges, which had been Company C's original objective on June 12.

Company G moved due west from La Raye and occupied a hill overlooking the bridge. The 29ers had a commanding view of German supply trains. Countless trucks, wagons, and horses jammed a highway south of the canal. The Germans, however, were fully aware of the Americans' presence and were ready for a fight.

Slingluff ordered his mortars and heavy machine guns to fire on these tempting targets, but he knew his men could not stay on the hill for long. "It looked to me as though we were fighting against the whole German army down in front of us," Slingluff recalled. "We gave an awful lot of men to get there, and we gave practically all of our ammunition up when we did get there. The fire was heavy against us. When I say heavy, I will give you a couple of ideas. I had my sound power telephone strung up from my mortars to the observation post on top of the hill. I was with the mortar observer up there, and I had been talking back to the mortars. I started to hand the telephone back over to him. It was shot out of my hand. A German mortar shell landed somewhere near me and wrinkled me a bit in the left knee and in the right hip."

Slingluff's men retreated off the hill and back toward the Vire. The Germans were slipping around Company G's flanks, trying to surround it. Slingluff asked a forward observer from the 224th Field Artillery Battalion to call for supporting fire, but the FO replied that no artillery help was available.

Company G fell back to a fairly strong defensive position behind a hedgerow, but the Germans began a relentless attack. The distinctive "rrrrrp" of MG 42s sounded all over the battlefield, and atop the hedgerows defended by Slingluff's men, leaves and bits of branches, clipped off by the bullets, fell to earth as if a giant hand had shaken the shrubbery. Every few seconds enemy infantrymen burst out of nearby hedgerows, shouting, rushing forward, firing their submachine guns from the hip.

Slingluff was hit again in the right side during one of these charges and could no longer move. He realized that Company G was about to be overrun. The only escape was by way of the right flank, which was still relatively quiet. Slingluff called his executive and ordered him to take all able-bodied men to the right and fight their way back to American lines. The men who could not move without help—himself included—would have to remain behind. Slingluff yelled over to Colonel Goode, who had not been hit, and asked him to accompany the group that was about to depart. But Goode said no, he would see it through to the end.

Slingluff could do nothing more. The Germans were hurling grenades over the hedgerows and screaming for the Americans to surrender. Over the din, Goode shouted to Slingluff: "Captain, they have killed enough of your men now. I am going to surrender you."

"Yes, sir," Slingluff replied. "Wait until I tell my men to cease firing." As the shooting stopped, Goode rose, clutching a white handkerchief.

The Germans promptly leaped over the hedgerows, yelling unintelligibly. The enemy troops appeared swept up in the fury of battle, training their rifles on the prostrate Yanks, glaring over their gun sights with wild eyes, looking like they might kill everyone on the spot. One enemy soldier shoved his Mauser in the ear of Pvt. Milton Villarreal, who lay wounded in a ditch. "Surrender, you Chicago gangster!" he hissed in heavily accented English.

The Germans paid particular interest to Goode and Slingluff. "One of them said, 'Raus! Raus!' and I could not 'raus,'" recalled Slingluff. "A couple of them hoisted me up. They told me to get rid of my equipment. My left arm wouldn't move very well. I couldn't unbuckle my straps. I was very anxious to get rid of my equipment. I had a very bloody trench knife in my belt and I wasn't so anxious to have them see it. Anyway, when they saw I couldn't get rid of the equipment they came around with another knife and just cut all my straps, and I lost my worldly possessions right then and there."

Only about thirty Company G men made it back to American lines. One exhausted survivor was picked up on the east bank of the Vire by several men from Company F. The perplexed Company G soldier looked up at his rescuers. "How did I get over to this side of the river?" he asked.

"You swam," a Company F man replied.

"I never swam a stroke in my life," he said.

Meanwhile, Cota's men dug in outside Montmartin, unaware of Company G's fate. They remained there for most of June 13, too strongly entrenched for the Germans to attack, too weak to make another attempt against the canal bridges. In their present location, Cota's men could accomplish little, so at 3:00 P.M., Gerhardt decided to pull them out. "You are ordered to withdraw at once, bringing all troops with you, including airborne. Advise route and if assistance is needed," declared Gerhardt's radio message. Cota brought 110 men back across the Vire by nightfall. The next day, a V Corps staff officer asked Cota what he had learned on the mission. He said, "I learned I'm a helluva patrol leader."

The operation had been, in Cota's words, "ill-conceived, ill-planned, and ill-executed." The root of the problem was that the American intelligence prediction of an upcoming German counterattack to sever the link between Utah and Omaha beachheads, although accurate, was unduly alarming. Fewer German reinforcements were deployed west of the Vire than American intelligence had expected, and those enemy units committed there were significantly delayed by Allied air interdiction. The enemy actually managed only a modest counterattack on June 13, which was handily contained by the 101st Airborne Division with no need of assistance from Gerhardt's 29ers. The 175th was therefore drawn into battle west of the Vire unnecessarily.

The 175th Infantry was handled roughly on June 12 and 13. Three American rifle companies had been sent over the Vire to seize the canal bridges, but none had accomplished its mission. Two companies were decimated, one was almost annihilated, and the regimental CO, "Pop" Goode, was presumed dead when a patrol later discovered his bullet-riddled helmet near La Raye. Afterward, however, the 29ers learned that he had been taken prisoner.

If someone had asked Gerhardt prior to D-Day whether the 29th Division would hold St. Lô by June 14, his answer would have been an emphatic yes. But the general's unbridled confidence had taken a beating since the invasion. In only eight days of combat, the division had suffered 2,400 casualties—17 percent of its authorized strength. Furthermore, St. Lô was still five miles distant, and after the experiences of June 12 and 13, hard fighting obviously lay ahead before the city could be captured. Nevertheless, Uncle Charlie remained optimistic. Indeed, he felt that one determined attack could push all the way into St. Lô in two or three days.

The 29th Division, however, was not ready to launch another attack. The 29ers were exhausted. Furthermore, the Yanks had underestimated the enemy's tactical finesse and will to fight. No 29ers doubted that St. Lô would eventually fall, but nasty rumors were surfacing about Gerhardt's judgment, particularly after the 175th's sad affair west of the Vire. If Gerhardt knew anything of this gossip, he paid no heed.

Every day the general paid a surprise visit to at least one front line battalion. Lieutenant Colonel Cooper recalled one of Uncle Charlie's visits. "We all looked like the devil as we still had our impregnite [anti-gas] uniforms, worn since before loading in England about May 31. Orders allowed no change to other uniforms 'until further notice' for fear of gas attack. You can imagine what two weeks' sweat and digging had done to these sticky outfits. Washing, which would remove the impregnite, was strictly prohibited. The general bawled me out for some cow manure near the entrance to our command post and said, 'You and your men look like hell. Why don't you clean up?' I mentioned the order. He said: 'Get your men cleaned up right away. Put on what you can!' I immediately took action. So far as I know, this was the way the whole division got out of those stinking, filthy clothes."

Gerhardt was accompanied on his front line trips by his driver, Sgt. Bob Cuff; his aide, Lt. Bob Wallis; and a third traveling companion, who usually

Gerhardt and "D-Day." *Courtesy Fifth Regiment Armory.*

sat in *Vixen Tor's* rear jump seat next to Wallis. This companion was "D-Day," the general's new pet dog.

Like Gerhardt, D-Day was either loved or despised. The general found the two-month-old puppy on June 12 wandering around division headquarters. A scruffy black and white mongrel with droopy ears, D-Day took an instant liking to Gerhardt, and as far as Uncle Charlie was concerned, the feeling was mutual. Soon, wherever the general went, D-Day was sure to be near. The division newspaper, *29 Let's Go,* noted, "The pup rides around in the general's jeep and his behavior is such that he seems to sense that this vehicle sports a red sign with two stars and that he is something special. He has now become quite oblivious to the artillery barrages and is bucking for a Good Conduct medal."

Gerhardt made it plain that D-Day was to get first-class treatment. The dog was given the run of division headquarters. He napped on the general's cot and munched on K rations with the staff at mealtimes. When Gerhardt was in a playful mood, D-Day bounded gleefully around his master, who rewarded the dog with a special snack.

Sometimes the staff wondered whether the general treated D-Day better than he treated them. Several amazed officers received a vicious scolding from the general in front of the whole staff, only to see him turn to D-Day and murmur affectionate baby talk.

Like some of the 29ers, D-Day had a discipline problem. One of his favorite pastimes was chasing jeeps and trucks. When he spotted a truck convoy, the dog leaped out of *Vixen Tor* and, much to the general's horror, took off, barking and growling. "Sergeant, get that goddamned dog!" Gerhardt would roar. Poor Sergeant Cuff did as he was told, but he hoped that the chase would not lead him into a minefield.

Once D-Day got carried away in his pursuit of a convoy and was hit by a truck. Gerhardt rushed up to the scene of the accident and discovered that the dog was badly hurt; it appeared he would die. The general stalked up to the terrified truck driver. "If that dog dies, you're history!" he shrieked. Fortunately for Gerhardt—and the driver—D-Day was patched up by a division surgeon. After a few weeks, he was chasing truck convoys again.

Many 29ers became fond of D-Day since his approach often warned of an unexpected visit by the general. When the dog bounded happily into a front line command post, the 29ers jumped to their feet, hastily made themselves presentable—the first thing to do was to buckle the helmet chin strap—and assumed their most soldierly posture.

Gerhardt took D-Day back to the United States after the war. Some ten years later, Cuff, who had left the Army but still kept in touch with the general, received a letter. "D-Day is dead," the note began solemnly. Gerhardt thought Cuff would want to know the sad news.

NINE

STAGNATION

"Altogether It Was Hell"
June 14–July 10, 1944

1. HILL 108

One night during the Battle of the Elle, Lieutenant Colonel Cooper of the 110th Field Artillery issued orders that there must be absolutely no firing on German aircraft after dark. The order applied to everyone in the outfit, including the members of the 110th's attached flak unit, Battery B of the 459th Anti-Aircraft Artillery Battalion.

The 29ers had already learned that firing a barrage of anti-aircraft tracer bullets at night was not wise. The fiery tracers could be seen for miles, and the Germans predictably responded by shelling the originators of the fire. Even the satisfaction of downing an enemy bomber was not worth the invariable German response. Cooper was particularly sensitive about disclosing his outfit's position to the Germans since the front line had stabilized along the Elle. The 110th would probably remain in its current location for at least a week.

Only thirty minutes after Cooper issued his order, a single German bomber flew overhead. The plane flew so slowly and at such a low altitude that "he was practically insulting our gunners," recalled Capt. William Weston, the anti-aircraft battery's CO. "Didn't he know that here was Battery B of the 459th who had established world records [in training]? It was too much. They couldn't take it! Before the pilot had traversed a full 100 yards in our range, the sky was so full of tracers that it looked like the Fourth of July. It must have been visible all the way to St. Lô. Some of the boys privately claim hits on the plane but it got away, just like the big fish.''

Cooper was furious. One .50 caliber machine gunner had to pay fifty cents for each of the seventy bullets he fired—a stiff penalty for a man on private's pay. Another gunner, a corporal, was busted to private.

Gerhardt got a new boss on June 14 when the 29th Division was transferred from Gerow's V Corps to the newly created XIX Corps under the command of Maj. Gen. Charles Corlett, the former commander of the 7th Infantry Division, which had served in the Pacific. Uncle Charlie was eager to keep the pressure on the enemy by continuing the 29th Division's attack toward St. Lô, and he told Corlett that the 29ers were ready. But Corlett had direct instructions from General Bradley to curb the 29th's offensive for several days. Bradley wished to concentrate on the capture of Cherbourg, Normandy's largest harbor, situated at the northern tip of the Cotentin Peninsula forty miles northwest of Omaha Beach. Until Cherbourg was liberated, logisticians would find it increasingly difficult, if not impossible, to keep the swelling Allied armies in Normandy supplied. Bradley therefore pledged most of 1st Army's limited resources to Maj. Gen. J. Lawton Collins's VII Corps and ordered it to seize Cherbourg without delay. Other American corps, including Corlett's, would have to make do with more modest supplies for the time being.

Furthermore, Bradley was still concerned about the tenuous link between the Omaha and Utah beachheads, a worry exacerbated by the 175th's disastrous expeditions west of the Vire on June 12 and 13. Before the 29th Division pushed any further toward St. Lô, therefore, Bradley wanted to assure himself that the junction between the two beachheads was secure.

A fresh American infantry division, the 30th, came ashore on Omaha on June 14, and Bradley promptly attached it to Corlett's XIX Corps and committed it to the west side of the Vire. Gerhardt was delighted by this development. With the 29th Division's right flank secure, Gerhardt could now concentrate his forces against his real objective, St. Lô. The 30th Division, however, would take several days to deploy to its new sector. Meanwhile, the 29ers were ordered to do nothing except patrol and dig in.

Gerhardt hated waiting. He was convinced that the 29th Division could make one more determined attack against St. Lô with the supplies on hand, even after Bradley's diversion of resources to the Cherbourg offensive. Until the division got that chance, Gerhardt made sure that the 29ers did not become complacent. On June 13, Gerhardt issued an order that every front line rifle company, even in a quiet sector, was to send one patrol behind enemy lines every day. Furthermore, each battalion was to capture at least one prisoner per day. When they heard this, the 29ers cursed openly. They felt that snatching prisoners risked too many lives for too little gain.

29th Division, June 16, 1944.

The 29th Division was unexpectedly ordered to resume its attack against St. Lô on June 16, so the 29ers had little chance to become complacent. The offensive was to be launched by the 175th on the right and the 116th, supported by the 3rd Battalion of the 115th, on the left. The rest of the 115th was in reserve, but it was supposed to join the attack on June 17.

The 116th made good progress at first. The 1st Battalion, attacking southward from Couvains at 8:00 A.M., advanced a mile by noon. Meanwhile, the 3rd Battalion of the 115th moved forward rapidly against light opposition and cut the St. Lô-Isigny highway at the village of Les Foulons, a mile west of Couvains.

The 2nd Battalion of the 116th started the day in reserve in St. Clair. At 8:30 A.M., it marched behind American lines toward Couvains and then turned southwest to launch an attack against the village of La Luzerne, only two-and-a-half miles from St. Lô. Simultaneously, the 3rd Battalion of the 116th executed an almost identical maneuver on the 2nd Battalion's left (eastern) flank.

The plan was complex, but cunning. In theory, the "end runs" of the 2nd and 3rd Battalions of the 116th would hit the Germans where they least expected an attack, at a time when the enemy would probably have committed his reserves to other threatened sectors. Timing and coordination were essential.

By noon, the offensive appeared to be working perfectly. All four American infantry battalions were progressing rapidly toward St. Lô, against only minimal opposition.

But of course nothing went according to plan in the bocage. When the 2nd Battalion of the 116th moved out of St. Clair, Company E of the 115th Infantry was supposed to take over the town, but it did not arrive until after the 2nd Battalion had left. In the meantime, several dozen alert German *Fallschirmjäger* had slipped into St. Clair along an abandoned communications trench.

Company E was expecting a restful day, but when it reached St. Clair, the dismayed 29ers discovered that the enemy held the town. Eventually, the whole 2nd Battalion of the 115th had to come to Company E's support, and the village had to be retaken house-by-house.

One stubborn German paratrooper holed himself up in the church steeple and shot at any American who showed himself. He wounded Capt. Frank O'Connor, the CO of Company E, with one of his first shots. The 29ers directed a fusillade against the steeple and finally killed the sniper, although they couldn't help admiring his bravery.

One of the precepts of German tactical doctrine was that the best defense was a good offense. According to this theory, mobile reserves were to rush to the scene of an enemy breakthrough and launch an immediate counterattack.

On the afternoon of June 16, the Germans executed their doctrine perfectly. Unfortunately for the 29ers, the 352nd Division was being heavily reinforced just as the American attack started to make good progress. Fresh German units from the 3rd FJ Division and *Kampfgruppe Böhm* of the 353rd Division counterattacked all along the front and stopped the American columns cold. Gerhardt's hope of seizing St. Lô in a lightning stroke was dashed; instead, the 29ers were hard-pressed to retain their gains.

The afternoon of June 16 was a nightmare for the 3rd Battalion of the 115th. Just as the outfit was crossing the St. Lô highway at Les Foulons, the Germans ambushed it and sent it reeling to the rear. For the second time in five days, the 3rd Battalion yielded its gains and retreated a mile back to its line of departure, pursued closely by the enemy. About seventy men were lost, a particularly demoralizing statistic in light of the battalion's failure to gain any ground.

The three battalions of the 116th Infantry were also the targets of powerful German counterattcks. The Stonewallers managed to hold their ground, but the 116th was extremely vulnerable at nightfall on June 16. The regiment had made considerable gains during the day, but it had also lost many men. Furthermore, the three battalions were separated from one another by mile-wide gaps through which the Germans could easily infiltrate. The following day, the wily enemy would doubtlessly attempt to exploit these gaps and surround the entire Stonewall Brigade.

An angry Colonel Canham met with his battalion COs on the night of June 16 and told them the attack would continue the next morning. "Get around the sniper and machine gunner and wipe him out," he snapped. "If you allow your unit to bunch up behind a hedgerow and wait for hours you are only playing into Jerry's hand. He will move around where he can enfilade you or drop artillery or mortar fire on you. . . . It is time to get over the jitters and fight like hell."

Despite Canham's exhortations, the June 17 attack got nowhere, even when Gerhardt committed the 1st and 2nd Battalions of the 115th to the battle in the afternoon. Worse, casualties were high.

A few sarcastic 29th Division infantrymen wondered who was the greater enemy: the Germans or the American staff officers planning these fruitless attacks. Infantry COs had already learned that attack objectives set out by S-3s sometimes made little sense. On an operations map, the front appeared organized. Enemy and friendly positions were neatly indicated with red and blue pencils, and arrows showed the axis of American attacks. But maps were deceptive; what appeared as an inviting target on a map was usually nothing of the sort. "Give an S-3 a pencil and a map and he can win a war in nothing flat," 29th Division infantrymen used to say.

Gerhardt measured the success of an attack in miles. Anything less

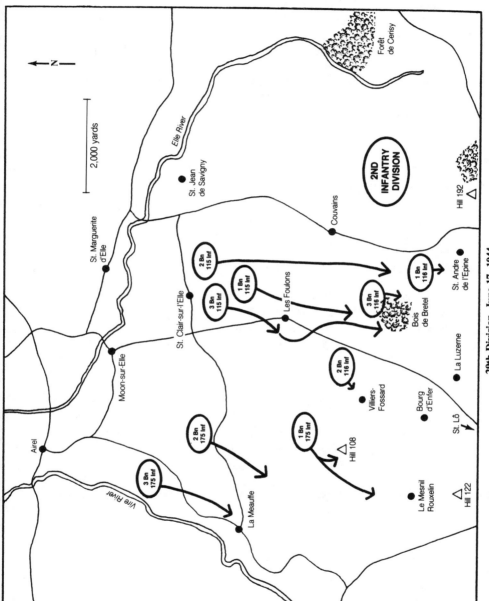

29th Division, June 17, 1944.

caused Uncle Charlie to raise his eyebrows and speculate about the problems at the front.

The biggest problem, of course, was the Germans. The enemy, nearly invisible in the bocage, contested almost every hedgerow, and the 29ers were paying a demoralizing price for every foot of ground they gained. If the division's infantry units continued to suffer casualties at the rate they had on June 16 and 17, they would run out of men long before they reached St. Lô.

"Every time they go forward, they're driven back," Gerhardt complained about the June 17 assault. The general's impatience began to show. Visiting an infantry battalion command post during the fighting, Gerhardt ordered the CO to launch an immediate attack. The CO wanted to wait until communications with his supporting artillery were restored. "What do you need artillery for?" Gerhardt growled. "You have hundreds of brave rifles." The CO launched the attack, but inwardly seethed.

Several men hypothesized about what had gone wrong. "The 116th Infantry was not the same regiment on June 16 that it was on D-Day," Maj. Tom Howie, the regimental S-3, noted a few days after the attack. "The new men are green. They need time to get to know the old men and officers and learn to work with them. This can't be accomplished simply by putting the regiment in a defensive position. They must be pulled out of the line and given a chance to effect a real reorganization." Howie reported that one of the Stonewallers' biggest problems was their frequent failure to exploit success. Whenever they penetrated deeply into German lines, they stopped, dug in, and came to believe they were cut off. "This led to defeatism and surrender," Howie declared.

Lieutenant Colonel Ziegelmann gave the German view of the American offensive: "It is noteworthy that the cautious American infantry, with very little daring, stopped when they came up against determined resistance from our side instead of bypassing these resistance nests. It was also surprising that no tanks followed the American infantry, which was otherwise well-supported by fighter-bombers and artillery reconnaissance planes. Had tanks supported the American infantry on June 16, St. Lô would not have been in German hands any longer that evening."

On the 29th Division's right flank, the 175th Infantry had much better luck on June 16 than did the division's other two regiments. In fact, when the 175th jumped off just south of the Elle River that morning, progress was so good at first that Gerhardt, as well as the enemy, believed a major breakthrough was at hand.

The 3rd Battalion, the westernmost 29th Division unit, encountered only scattered opposition and managed a southward advance of two miles along the east bank of the Vire. By nightfall, this outfit had dug in on a knoll, labeled "Hill 56" on Army maps, just beyond the hamlet of Amy. The next day, the

A 29er in a foxhole guards a French village, July 1944. *Courtesy National Archives.*

battalion advanced another mile and seized the village of La Meauffe, a stop on the St. Lô-Cherbourg railway just four miles due north of St. Lô.

General Corlett, however, was concerned about the 29th Division's right flank. The 175th's successful attack on June 16 and 17 had drawn the 29ers far ahead of the newly arrived 30th Division. The closer Gerhardt's men moved toward St. Lô, in fact, the more vulnerable they became to a German counterattack from west of the Vire River. To rectify this problem, Corlett ordered two battalions of the 30th Division's 119th Infantry to follow in the 175th's wake and drop off troops to guard the east bank of the Vire.

Meanwhile, an even more stunning success was attained by the 1st Battalion of the 175th. Penetrating the weak German line near the village of Moon-sur-Elle on June 16, the battalion set out due south for St. Lô, followed closely by the 2nd Battalion. The 1st made more than three miles that day, and for a while it appeared as if it would take St. Lô by itself.

On June 17, advance elements of the 1st Battalion pushed as far as the village of Le Mesnil-Rouxelin, only two miles north of St. Lô. The 352nd Division's headquarters was situated here, and the sudden approach of American infantrymen caught the German command post by surprise. Enemy staff officers hastily collected guards, clerks, and cooks and organized a thirty-man security detachment, which barely managed to fight off the 29ers. Meanwhile, Kraiss and his aides retreated to the northern outskirts of St. Lô and set up a new command post. There, Kraiss devised plans for the last-ditch defense of St. Lô.

Gerhardt was delighted by the 175th's progress. "I feel we'll be getting to St. Lô before long," he informed Corlett on the afternoon of June 17. Uncle Charlie was also pleased by the 1st Battalion's seizure of "Hill 108," a finger of high ground a mile northeast of Le Mesnil-Rouxelin. In the comfort of his War Room, Gerhardt had scrutinized his operations map and circled Hill 108 with a grease pencil to indicate it as an important objective. Although Hill 108 appeared to have significant military value on US Army 1:25,000 maps of the St. Lô area, it was not actually very important. The ubiquitous hedgerows blocked observation in every direction, and the 29ers on the hill could hardly even tell they were on high ground.

Even before his selection as "Pop" Goode's replacement, the 175th's new CO, Lt. Col. Alexander George, had established a reputation as the General Cota of the 175th. A few days after D-Day, George had picked up a discarded German bicycle and bounced along the rough dirt tracks near the front yelling, "Give 'em hell, boys!" as the G.I.'s watched in amazement. "He sure as hell didn't look the part of an executive officer [his former role], let alone a West Pointer," recalled one infantryman.

When the 175th opened its attack on St. Lô on June 16, George was at the front. Once he even took charge of a rifle squad, leading a successful attack against a troublesome German "88." But George's luck ran out the next day on Hill 108. "He was leading a patrol against a machine gun nest and someone lobbed a grenade, and it got him full in the face," Maj. Leslie Harness, the 175th's S-3, reported to Gerhardt over the telephone.

"He shouldn't have been up there," Gerhardt snapped.

"He was hit above the eyes and his nose is half gone and he has holes in his back," Harness replied. "He'll be a casualty for some time."

George was temporarily replaced by Lt. Col. William Purnell, a guardsman and long-standing member of the regiment. Gerhardt, however, longed for a professional soldier to take over the 175th.

By nightfall of June 17, the 1st Battalion had pushed more than a mile ahead of the closest 29th Division unit. Lt. Col. Roger Whiteford, the CO, expected to press on toward St. Lô the next day. He had little idea of the whereabouts of other 29th Division units and even less notion of what the Germans had arrayed against him.

No man in the battalion would ever forget June 18. Whiteford knew his unit would be in for a hard day when at 8:30 A.M., the Germans began hammering Hill 108 mercilessly with howitzers and mortars. The fury of the bombardment shocked the G.I.'s, for the enemy was supposed to be on the run. So far, the regiment had encountered nothing in the campaign as bad as this shelling, and the glum 29ers realized that an enemy infantry attack would soon follow.

The German counterattack was spearheaded by the *Kampfgruppe Böhm*. This two-battalion task force from the 353rd Division had reached St. Lô from Brittany on the evening of June 16. Parts of it were promptly deployed to help contain the 116th, and the rest was ordered to recapture Hill 108.

Neither side employed much tactical subtlety on Hill 108. The antagonists frequently battled one another from opposite sides of the same hedgerow, with hand grenades as the weapon of choice. The battle was fought at such close range that the enemy troops taunted the Yanks during the lulls. Whiteford replied with profanity. "Whiteford was in everybody's foxhole," a 29er recalled. Later that day, the CO was wounded and evacuated.

Soldiers in the heat of the battle did inexplicable things. One 29er in Company A, dubbed "Ali Baba" because of his swarthy complexion, had both his feet blown off by an "88" round, which killed three nearby G.I.'s. Ali Baba, in excruciating pain, surveyed the carnage, took a Colt .45 out of a holster and shot himself through the head.

By late afternoon the 1st Battalion was barely hanging on to Hill 108. Every German attack had been repulsed, but the chances of retaining the hill during darkness were slim. No help could be expected until the following morning. Even worse, communications with the 224th Field Artillery, the 175th's direct support outfit, had failed that morning, so the infantrymen would lack howitzer support.

At 6:00 P.M., however, the members of Whiteford's artillery liaison team were fiddling with a radio and announced excitedly that they had managed to contact the 224th. Supporting fire was on its way in a matter of minutes. After the 224th's howitzers pounded the German hedgerows for most of the night, the enemy attacks dissipated.

Early on June 19, the 1st Battalion, reduced to only twelve officers and 308 enlisted men, was relieved on Hill 108 by the 3rd Battalion. Shortly thereafter, the 2nd Battalion was rotated into the line. Aside from a few artillery exchanges and desultory German attacks, the battle was over; both sides were too exhausted to continue.

The 1st Battalion's stand on Hill 108 on June 18 eventually gained the

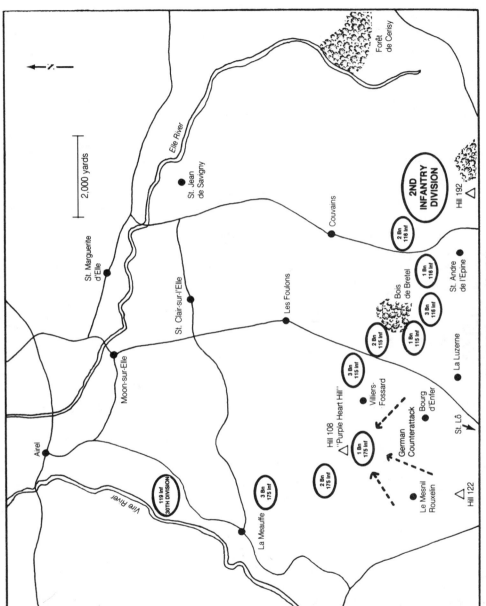

29th Division, June 18, 1944.

outfit the prestigious French Croix de Guerre and a Presidential Distinguished Unit Citation. The fight cost the 1st Battalion 250 casualties—over forty percent of its pre-battle strength. Sixty of these died. Hill 108 would always be remembered by members of the 175th as "Purple Heart Hill."

Gerhardt would wait a long time for another chance at St. Lô. When it became obvious that the 29ers could not seize the city on June 18, General Bradley ordered the offensive halted. "There has just been a big conference," the G-3 of Corlett's XIX Corps told Gerhardt over the phone as the battle for Hill 108 was raging. "The line is to be held and prepared for defense; active patrolling."

The 29th Division desperately needed a long rest. The 29ers, who had enjoyed a vast numerical superiority over the Germans only a week ago, now faced much less favorable odds as fresh enemy units such as *Kampfgruppe Böhm* reached the front. Even Gerhardt had to admit that the probability of taking St. Lô in the next several days was low.

Uncle Charlie would have been furious had he read Ziegelmann's post-war account of this battle. The 352nd Division's "1A" did not attribute the successful German defense of St. Lô to the defensive advantages of the bocage, the opportune arrival of German reinforcements, or even to the skillful tactics of German infantry. Instead, the Americans had only themselves to blame. "The reason why the American operational plan, with the objectives laid down for each day after D-Day, was not carried out could be because the enemy had the intention to preserve his forces or his men," Ziegelmann wrote. "Or else it might be found in his inability to attack with traditional soldierlike courage and bravery so as to get it over with quickly and successfully, or to exploit opportunities which came his way beyond the daily objective laid down in the plan—a thing which was never done. . . . It may not be completely correct to assert that it probably *was* the inability to attack with courage and bravery which was the cause of the enemy's failure to execute his operational plan. With the exception of operations on a fairly small scale, the enemy in principle only committed his men to an attack if he was able to make use of his superiority in materiel before and during the attack. . . . The enemy would have found himself in a predicament against an adversary equally strong in materiel."

No doubt, Gerhardt would have thought that Ziegelmann's report was nothing more than an apologia written by a man who felt the need to excuse later defeat. True, the 29th Division did not take St. Lô in the time allotted by Overlord plans. But according to Gerhardt, the division fell short of this goal because of the unexpected difficulties of the bocage, and not because of any tactical shortcomings or an unaggressive spirit among the 29ers. Furthermore, although the 29th Division outnumbered the enemy on its front, Gerhardt believed that the odds were by no means overwhelmingly in his favor. When Bradley ordered a halt to the 29th Division's St. Lô offensive on June 18, the Normandy campaign had been underway for less than two weeks, and not enough American troops had landed in Normandy to enable Gerhardt to concentrate his men on a narrow front for a powerful, coordinated assault. Time, however, would solve this problem.

2. FIGHTING FOR SURVIVAL

American generals were saying that the G.I.'s biggest problem was that he didn't hate the Germans enough. After two weeks of fighting in Normandy, however, 29th Division riflemen shook their heads. Such a harebrained theory could only have been thought up by someone who had never seen the front.

The front was, above all, a brutal place. All too easily it turned even a passive man into a killer. Most riflemen quickly learned that survival required a healthy hatred of the Germans. Animosity, in fact, was a kind of natural defense mechanism against the horrors of battle. If a terrified G.I. turned his agitated emotions inward instead of outward, he would probably break down.

Something happened to a 29er's psyche the first time he narrowly escaped a German mortar round or came across the dead body of a friend. Every infantry outfit had a collection of horror stories about the Germans that quickly taught even green G.I.'s to hate the enemy. During the battles on the Elle, a rumor spread among the 3rd Battalion of the 115th that the Germans were bayoneting American wounded. "Our motto from then on was 'no prisoners,' " one member of this outfit recalled. "And there were damn few ever taken after that."

On June 17, the men of the 2nd Battalion of the 116th were enraged when the Germans on the front lines shot at a helpless Allied pilot as he slowly descended by parachute from his burning airplane. That same day, the members of the 1st Battalion of the 115th were infuriated when Capt. Elmer "Doc" Carter, the battalion surgeon, was shot through the head by a German sniper. Carter, who was wearing his Red Cross helmet and armbands, had just jumped over a hedgerow to administer morphine to a wounded man. "They were all so mad, they wanted to go after the sniper," said a 1st Battalion officer. "Some of 'em even started over the hedgerow before Ryan [Lt. John Ryan, Company A CO] went back there himself and finally managed to get 'em back on the main job."

There was more than enough barbarity in the front lines to motivate the men to kill. The army's efforts to instill a fierce fighting spirit among the front line troops through patriotism were hardly needed and generally rejected by the riflemen. Most combat soldiers were also revolted by the propagandistic flag-waving of the home front. "Ask any dogface on the line," one G.I.

said. "You're fighting for your own skin on the line. When I enlisted I was patriotic as hell. There's no patriots on the line. A boy up there sixty days in the line is in danger every minute. He ain't fighting for patriotism."

After only two weeks of fighting in Normandy, the 29ers had been indelibly marked by combat and felt set apart from the rear echelon in some indefinable way. This attitude was particularly pronounced among the National Guardsmen who had been with the division since mobilization.

The 29ers burst into laughter at the way magazines from home depicted the war. The editor of *Le Tomahawk*, the XIX Corps daily newsletter, rebelled at one maudlin and patriotic advertisement in a May 1944 issue of the *Saturday Evening Post.* "We get pretty fed up with the sticky ads that begin, 'Dear Mom,' and end, 'And that, Mom, is what I am fighting for—the corner drugstore with its double-extra special-thick chocolate malteds,' " the editor wrote in early July. "We think it's high time the copy writers learn that this war is being fought by grown men. We are soldiers, and good ones, and we are fighting because our country is at war and for reasons which grown men understand. . . . The public seems to think that soldiers are simple asses drooling slush in the face of machine gun fire."

The same writer later noted something that would really motivate American soldiers: "As a firm believer in psychological warfare," he said, "we suggest [the US Army] prepare pamphlets addressed to our troops and drop them by air over our forward lines just before any attack: 'SOLDATS AMERIKANSHER: St. Lô, which lies ahead, is famed for its dairy produce, its textile factories, its paper mills, and its WHISKEY DISTILLERY. OK, boys, you're on your own.' We think this would do the trick."

Survival was the law of the front. Any other rules, even common military courtesy and discipline, fell by the wayside. Enlisted men rarely called their officers "sir" at the front, and saluting was almost never practiced. Most officers, particularly platoon leaders, wanted it this way. They had learned by experience that any man carrying a map or binoculars, or wearing a helmet with the officer's prescribed white stripe painted on the back, was sure to tempt a German sniper. Thus maps were quickly hidden under field jackets, binoculars discarded—they weren't of much use in the bocage anyway—and white stripes camouflaged with mud. Officers at the front were also sensitive about being addressed by their rank, just in case any Germans were within earshot. "Don't you start calling me 'lieutenant'," a platoon leader in the 116th Infantry told one of his sergeants before D-Day.

In truth, in the front lines it was hard to distinguish a 29th Division officer from a private. Gerhardt, however, routinely berated 29ers caught without their captain's bars or sergeant's chevrons. Furthermore, much to Uncle Charlie's disgust, the 29ers almost never buckled their helmet chin straps on the line. In a "Combat Battle Notes" report in July 1944, the general even tried to provide a good reason for the men to do so. "If not fastened when going over hedgerows and when hitting the ground fast," Gerhardt wrote, "the helmet must be held on with one hand or it will be lost. The practice of not wearing the chin strap arose as a result of [danger from the] blast of heavy air bombs and heavy artillery fire, which are not present in this theater." No one paid attention to Gerhardt's reasoning, unless Uncle Charlie showed up at the front.

For newly arrived G.I.'s, the sight of 29th Division combat veterans at the front was shocking. "Our rifle company moved up and relieved one of the companies of the 29th," a young lieutenant from the 35th Division recalled. "We had little idea what the 29th had been through. . . . We found all the men wearing their field jackets reversed. The field jacket had a kind of shiny, almost sailcloth kind of material. It reflected a lot of light. They had their field jackets turned inside out because on the inside was a kind of dull lining and they were trying to get the effect of camouflage. Officers . . . didn't carry anything that would mark them as officers. Their bars were all concealed. . . . They discarded a lot of their equipment. They were a pretty badly beat up outfit. . . . We hadn't expected anything like that, and our first reaction was that this is not a very good outfit." In a matter of days, however, the new troops had learned to imitate the veterans' behavior as a matter of survival.

To the 29ers, an "old" soldier was one who had survived at least three days in the line. To last that long, a G.I. always had to be alert. "You always slept with one eye open," recalled Pvt. Arnold Lindblad, a member of Company B, 104th Medical Battalion. "Unless you were on duty, you hit the hole when it got dark and stayed there till full light. There was no walking around in the dark, no talking from hole to hole. You never got used to it."

Combat was hardest on the riflemen. Although members of 29th Division rifle companies amounted to only 5,211 men—37 percent of the division's manpower—they suffered over 90 percent of the division's casualties. Most 29th Division rifle companies that landed on D-Day had a near-complete turnover in personnel by mid-July.

No 29er in his right mind went into combat without trepidation. "There was plenty of fear all around," recalled Pvt. John Robertson of Company F, 116th Infantry. "What affected us more than anything would be to look around us early in the morning and see someone sprawled across a hedgerow, lying there dead; or half in and half out of his foxhole, killed by a shell that landed during the night. Often, it was a replacement who had just come in, maybe the day before, and there he was dead. It gave you a very sickening feeling."

Every 29er had his own way of dealing with the terrors of the front line. "I always had a terrible sense of fear," said Lieutenant Colonel Cooper. "But I also had a sense of duty. The feeling which wins out determines how a soldier will act in battle. I found an antidote to fear in doing my job. Once I finished doing my job, I had time to be scared again. The human mind can really have only one emotion at a time. The secret of getting through combat is having a purpose and keeping busy. The instant you start to reflect and you hear shots whizzing past your ear, you get scared again."

Lt. Edward G. Jones, Jr., of the 29th Recon Troop, recalled his combat experiences in Normandy: "In looking back," he said, "remembering that I was not in the least scared when many who I saw were in a desperate state of nerves, I wondered why. But then there did come a change in the days ahead. You do get to a point when it finally dawns on you, that you, too, could become one of the dead or wounded. At that time you get a sort of hollow feeling in the stomach and a type of funny ache between the shoulders—a natural type of human fear. . . . It is just that each of us had a different method of expressing it."

During the heavy fighting south of Elle, a 110th Artillery forward observer team was dispatched to the front, but after an hour a liaison officer called Cooper to tell him that the team had not yet arrived. Worried that something had happened to his observers, Cooper quickly drove off in his jeep to find them. He followed the telephone cable laid by the team's wiremen as they had advanced. A half-mile away, he encountered the team sitting in a roadside ditch. The young lieutenant in charge was pale and shaking violently. "What's going on here?" Cooper demanded.

"Colonel, I just can't take it," the lieutenant replied.

"Get up here on the road," Cooper ordered. "Sergeant, you take the team up. Lieutenant, give your equipment to the sergeant and come with me."

Cooper took the lieutenant back to Battery C and told the battery CO, Capt. Arthur Flinner, to give the man a few days to calm down. In the meantime, the lieutenant could work in a relatively safe job with the cannoneers in the battery's gun positions.

It didn't work out; the lieutenant was incapable of performing his duties. "Corps had issued an order that if you had an unsatisfactory officer, you should send him up there and they would take care of it," Cooper recalled. "Well, they took care of it all right. In January 1945, I was called as a witness—the only witness—for the lieutenant's court-martial. They asked me what I thought of him. I told them that I honestly believed that his behavior was beyond his control. I didn't have any animosity towards him, and I didn't think he should be punished. I knew he could do a good job someplace else, outside of combat."

The lieutenant was acquitted of the charge of cowardice in the face of the enemy, but he was dishonorably discharged from the army.

At one time or another, combat exhaustion touched almost everyone who occupied the front lines. The symptoms, which first appeared among 29ers at the end of June, varied from soldier to soldier. Some men, dazed and deafened by the continual pounding of enemy mortars and artillery, staggered around the front aimlessly like wide-eyed drunkards. These men were usually sedated by a "Blue 88," a tranquilizer as powerful as the German 88mm gun—or so the 29ers used to joke.

Many men became jumpy and blazed away with their M1s every time something rustled in a bush. Others, including many who had performed their duties bravely in previous engagements, took off for the rear when fighting broke out. A few even shot themselves in the foot or hand to get out of the line.

During periods of heavy fighting, battalion kitchen areas, a mile or so behind the front, were sometimes crowded with men who had departed the line, with or without orders. One officer in the 116th called the kitchens "the skid row of the battle zone."

The Germans, of course, also suffered from battle fatigue. In July, a Yank found an unfinished letter in the pocket of a dead *Fallschirmjäger* outside St. Lô. A section read, "On our way back we were covered again with terrific artillery fire. We were just lying in an open area. Every moment I expected deadly shrapnel. . . . When one hears for hours the whining, whistling, and bursting of the shells and moaning and groaning of the wounded, one does not feel too well. At that moment, I almost lost my mind. I chewed up a cigarette, bit into the ground. . . . The others acted just like me. Altogether it was hell."

The Germans were more intolerant than the Americans of soldiers who tried to avoid front line duty. Mild battle fatigue was not recognized as a legitimate affliction in the German army. A German soldier generally had to exhibit physical or psychiatric signs of severe combat exhaustion, such as deafness or uncontrollable trembling, to be excused from the front. Even then, patients were usually treated in a hospital close to the front and quickly returned to their units.

Combat exhaustion affected US Army riflemen more readily than their German counterparts mainly because of the "repple depple" [replacement depot] syndrome. Replacements were the army's homeless. After a hasty separation from the units with which they had trained or fought, the lonely replacements found themselves in an unfamiliar repple depple, where they lost all sense of belonging to a cohesive military unit. Even new friendships made within the replacement depots were generally fleeting since it was unlikely that two buddies would be assigned to the same squad, or even the same platoon. Many replacements thought of themselves as nameless pieces of army equipment, like crates of ammunition, sent to the front and promptly consumed.

The US Army's replacement policy was simple. Every combat unit was supposed to have its casualties replaced as soon as possible by a roughly equal number of men drawn from a replacement depot. Each replacement was supposed to have the same "Military Occupational Specialty" (MOS) as the casualty he replaced. The most common type of replacement needed at the front was, of course, the rifleman, "MOS 745" in army parlance.

The men who drew up the army's replacement policy in World War II had a feel for history. The policy was formulated to avoid a problem that had plagued the Union Army during the Civil War. After Union regiments with an official strength of over 1,000 had been whittled down by combat and disease to less than one-quarter of that number, they were not rebuilt with new recruits. Instead, the new troops formed their own new regiments.

In the later years of the Civil War, this policy produced an army with an odd mixture of fighting units. Most regiments, comprised entirely of veterans, had only a few hundred men. Other regiments, consisting entirely of green troops, were four times as large.

In theory, the US Army's replacement policy in World War II was sound. By maintaining a giant pool of unattached replacements, battered divisions anywhere on an active front could quickly be restored to full strength by the timely infusion of fresh troops. One of the major advantages of this system, according to the army, was that a unit could remain in the front line when absorbing replacements. Furthermore, the system was flexible. If replacements were in short supply, they could be doled out only to divisions which really needed them.

The lifeblood of an infantry division was its riflemen. Theoretically, a fresh supply of "MOS 745s" could rejuvenate a depleted division overnight. In Normandy, however, the US Army discovered that combat was not a mere question of numbers. A division that remained on the front lines for weeks, whose infantry units had been filled and refilled with replacements, was likely to be quantitatively strong but qualitatively weak, since the infantrymen had no chance to get to know one another. Cohesiveness and morale were just as important to a division as its manpower strength. "Sticking together is the important thing," one infantryman noted.

When a 29th Division replacement took his place in the line, his morale was already low. As he moved up to his new unit, he witnessed the shocking sight of dead and wounded 29ers coming back from the front. The new man was also friendless. "Being a replacement is just like being an orphan," a rifleman recalled. In Normandy, this problem was acute. The 29th Division was frequently on the offensive, and the new troops got little chance to make friends. "I have seen men killed or captured when even their squad leaders didn't know their names," an infantryman said.

Replacement officers at the rank of lieutenant and captain had a particularly difficult time. The first new officers to reach the 29th Division in June 1944 had to fill the shoes of platoon leaders or company COs who had led their outfits for months or even years. For the baby-faced newcomers, working under the scrutiny of veteran enlisted men was a challenging task. Worst of all, new platoon and company COs already knew the odds against their survival.

Nothing could be more disheartening for a replacement than joining a new unit in the midst of battle. "I saw replacements headed for an infantry regiment brought in under the cover of darkness," Lieutenant Colonel Cooper recalled. "By midnight they were in a foxhole and at 5:00 A.M. they had to attack. By 5:30 A.M., some of them were coming back on stretchers—dead."

Green troops were not the only ones to suffer as a result of the army's replacement policy. Veterans, too, paid a price. The continual replenishment of depleted combat units by fresh batches of replacements meant that generals could commit divisions to the front for months without a single day of rest. Between D-Day and the fall of St. Lô, a period of forty-four days, the 29th Division was not out of the line once.

Veteran riflemen figured that the only escape from the front was on a stretcher or in a grave. "We feel the only opportunity we will have to go home is to get wounded," one demoralized rifleman said. "There isn't an old man in the company who has any hope or confidence of being able to enjoy life again." The 29th Division riflemen used to speak longingly of the legendary "million dollar wound" that could get them out of the line and back home with no disfigurement and little pain.

The German army's replacement policy was far more humane and produced better soldiers than the US Army system, but it was also less flexible. The German army was divided into two parts: the field army (*Feldheer*), which controlled all combat units on active fronts; and the replacement army (*Ersatzheer*), which handled recruitment, training, and administrative matters. The German replacement system was based on thorough cooperation between the *Feldheer* and *Ersatzheer*. Each German combat division at the front was supported by a network of *Ersatzheer* training units in Germany.

German recruits were associated with specific divisions from the moment they joined the army. New soldiers reported for duty to a kind of induction unit, called a *Grenadierersatzbataillon* ("GEB," for short). Each infantry regiment at the front had a corresponding GEB in its recruitment area in Germany; the GEB was considered the regiment's home station. Recruits stayed with their GEB only a week or two, receiving preliminary indoctrination into the division. Veterans who had recovered from wounds also awaited reassignment to their division at the GEB.

Every GEB had an associated instructional unit called a *Reserve-Grenadierbataillon* to which all its recruits were sent for basic training. Unlike American replacements, German recruits were trained by combat veterans from the regiment they would eventually join. By 1944, basic training frequently took place outside Germany so that trainees could shoulder the wearisome burden of guard duty in German-occupied countries. The three instructional units of the 352nd Division, for example, trained recruits in the Netherlands.

When the new men completed basic training, they were sent back to their GEBs, formed into a temporary "march battalion" (*Marschbataillon*) of a few hundred men, and dispatched for the front under the command of veterans headed in the same direction.

When the *Marschbataillon* reached its parent division at the front, it was disbanded and absorbed by the divisional replacement battalion (*Feldersatzbataillon*, or "FEB"). In theory, each of the three companies in the FEB provided replacements for a corresponding regiment in that division. In actual practice, however, the Germans rarely attempted to use the FEB to compensate for losses in front line infantry companies on a one-for-one basis, as the Americans did with their repple depples. Instead, the Germans tended to use the FEB to replace battlefield casualties selectively. Sometimes, for instance, the FEB's reserve leader pool (*Führerreserve*) supplied a replacement for a fallen platoon leader or a company CO. But if a machine gunner or rifleman became a casualty, a squad leader usually assigned another squad member to assume the missing soldier's role.

The major purpose of the FEB was to initiate new soldiers to the division. The FEB, however, served several other functions. It was also a divisional rest camp, a place where battle-weary infantrymen could get a hearty meal, a bath, and a few nights of decent sleep. It was also the division training center and battle school (*Divisionkampfschule*), where troops learned pragmatic tactics suited to the terrain in which they would eventually fight. The men of the 352nd Division, no doubt, found this training invaluable preparation for combat in the bocage.

An FEB, roughly equivalent in size and strength to an infantry battalion, was also trained to fight as an integral unit. In an emergency, it was the division's last-ditch reserve (*Kampfmarschbataillon*). The 352nd Division as well as many other German divisions in Normandy used their FEBs in this way.

Because of the German army's replacement system, German replacements were more content than were their American counterparts. When a German recruit departed for the front, he traveled with his closest friends. Unlike an American member of a repple depple, a German replacement belonged to a specific division even before he was shipped to the front. During the four months of his training he had developed a strong sense of unit loyalty.

A German replacement knew exactly where he was going when he set out for the front. He seldom worried about acceptance by the unit's old-timers. Indeed, since almost every infantryman in the division had gone through the same training regimen, the infusion of replacements was invariably smooth, and the new men usually made good fighters.

The US Army replacement system, however, with all its faults, was superior to the German model in many ways. German replacements may have been more highly motivated and better trained than their American counterparts, but German division commanders rarely had enough men in their *Feldersatzbataillone* to replace the casualties of even two or three days of hard fighting. When a German division's replacements were used up, or the FEB was used as a self-contained combat unit, every infantry outfit in that division was obligated to fight on with no hope of manpower replenishment.

The German system was inflexible. FEBs belonging to divisions in combat were rapidly exhausted; meanwhile, FEBs belonging to divisions on quiet fronts remained largely untapped. Furthermore, since every division in the German army had its own replacement pipeline, the allocation of fresh troops to battered divisions was not a decision made at the front by an army or corps commander, as it was in the US Army. The policy of grouping US Army replacements in a single pool close behind the front allowed American generals to allocate new men to combat divisions when and where fresh troops were needed most. In the German army, divisional training centers in faraway Germany could not respond quickly to the needs of their divisions at the front.

The German replacement system caused some of the same problems in the World War II German army as those experienced by the Union Army of the Potomac in the Civil War. After several days of hard fighting and heavy losses, typical German infantry companies had dwindled to the size of platoons and platoons to the size of squads. Because of the exigencies of battle, however, these units were invariably obligated to remain in the line with little hope of reinforcement. A division sometimes remained in combat for so long that it had almost ceased to exist by the time it was finally withdrawn.

The 352nd Division suffered this fate. Between D-Day and the Battle for St. Lô, the 352nd stayed in the line for forty-four straight days. Said Ziegelmann, "All that remained of the division was a mere fraction of its actual combat strength."

Theoretically, German divisions were pulled out of the line for rest and rehabilitation in a quiet sector after only a short period of intense combat. Battered divisions may have been relieved promptly early in the war, when the Germans had plenty of fresh units and untapped sources of manpower. But in 1944, German divisions were forced to remain in combat for much longer periods. After ten days of combat in Normandy, the 352nd Division was earmarked for withdrawal to the south of France, an inactive theater. This scheme, however, was abandoned since the Germans were critically short of men in Normandy.

Due to the urgent demands of the Normandy campaign, the distinction among infantrymen, engineers, signalmen, cannoneers, and supply personnel almost disappeared in the 352nd Division. Virtually everyone in the division eventually shouldered a rifle or an MG 42 in the front line. In the 29th Division, by contrast, the distinctions among the various branch specialties remained intact, thereby enabling 29ers to concentrate on what the army had trained them to do. Engineers built bridges and provided demolitions for the infantrymen; signalmen established and maintained top-notch communications; quartermaster troops handled supplies; artillerymen supported the infantry.

A replacement policy modeled on the German system would not have worked for the US Army if the United States were to adhere to its grand strategy in World War II. This strategy was based on the premise that applying continuous and overwhelming military force against the enemy's major ground forces was the surest and quickest path to victory. If the US Army were to maintain a continuous offensive, it had two basic choices. It could keep American divisions in the line continuously, or it could replace them with fresh divisions without interrupting the offensive. The latter alternative probably would have required as many as two divisions for every division at the front, or three times as many as the eighty-nine divisions the army ultimately raised. With eight million men under arms by 1944, the army no doubt had the manpower to raise such a force. But furnishing almost 200 new divisions with equipment would have been a monumental undertaking. Every new division would have needed hundreds of vehicles and major weapons, such as howitzers and tanks. By 1944, the US Army had procured some 190,000 vehicles and 6,000 artillery pieces to equip its eighty-nine divisions. Had the army raised 267 (three times eighty-nine) divisions instead, it would have had to obtain 570,000 vehicles and 18,000 howitzers. Furthermore, it would have needed a means of shipping the extra equipment overseas at a time when the American merchant fleet was already strained to the limit. Given these logistical difficulties, the army rejected the idea of pulling depleted divisions out of the line and replacing them with new divisions. Hence the army was obliged to keep its divisions in combat almost continuously, a decision that dictated America's World War II replacement policy.

Without a readily available source of replacements, the 29th Division would have been incapable of offensive action as early as two weeks after D-Day. In an emergency, Gerhardt could have used his support troops, such as engineers and signalmen, as infantry, as the Germans did. Since American policy dictated that US Army divisions remain in the line indefinitely, breaking up critical divisional support services and risking the lives of hard-to-replace specialists was not considered a viable alternative.

The thousands of bewildered and frightened American replacements who were thrust into the front lines in Normandy were comforted in some small degree by the fact that almost everyone in their company had, at one time or another, undergone the same travails. Within the 29th Division, in fact, replacements outnumbered the old-timers in most rifle companies only a month after D-Day, and the percentage of replacements in infantry units grew steadily thereafter.

In March 1945, when the 29th Division was momentarily in reserve, the 115th Infantry was scheduled to receive a Distinguished Unit Citation. General Gerhardt wanted each company guidon to be carried by a member of that company who had served with the outfit on D-Day. Half the regiment's companies could produce only a handful of such men. The other companies—mostly rifle companies—could find none. Every single G.I. in these units had joined the 29th Division as a replacement.

3. HEDGEROW TACTICS

It rained hard on June 19, "Weather miserable. All positions thick with mud. Worst yet encountered during campaign," read that day's entry in the unit journal of the 2nd Battalion, 116th Infantry. The 29th Division's offensive against St. Lô had been halted on June 18, and the 29ers, exhausted by three days of intense battle, were glad to have the day off.

The 29ers had little idea how much they would ultimately be affected by the bad weather. The storm, in fact, dealt a severe blow to Allied strategy in Normandy. Back at Omaha Beach, the sea churned for three days. Eight-foot waves crashed into the artificial harbor ("Mulberry") and broke it to pieces, and howling winds wrecked dozens of landing craft and stranded hundreds more on the beach.

Some meteorologists called it the worst June storm in the English Channel since the turn of the century. Virtually no troops and supplies were unloaded on the beaches for four days, and American logisticians, concerned about ammunition shortages even before the storm, now had considerably more cause for worry. For most of the next month, ammunition deficiencies, particularly artillery rounds, would plague the 29th Division.

Back at the 29th Division war room, Gerhardt was troubled by the June 19 division situation map. The 29th's offensive from June 16 to 18 had made considerable gains, but when the attack was called off, the line marking the division's front looked like a crazy stock market graph. The most irregular section of the line was in the center of the division sector near the village of Villiers-Fossard. There the Germans held a fingerlike salient pointing menacingly towards Omaha Beach.

Something about salients deeply troubles generals. When Gerhardt and Corlett examined the Villiers-Fossard bulge on the situation map, they were convinced that a limited attack should be launched to eliminate it, even though by Bradley's directive the XIX Corps was supposed to remain on the defensive. The 1st and 3rd Battalions of the 115th made an attempt against the salient on June 20 and 21 and got nowhere, suffering about forty casualties. The members of these outfits were then glad to let someone else try. During the night of June 28, Combat Command A of the 3rd Armored Division, consisting of a mechanized infantry battalion and a tank battalion, passed through the 115th's lines and prepared to attack the salient on the following morning.

Although the attack on the salient would be the tankers' first fight, they were filled with bravado. The 29ers rankled when the tankers boasted of succeeding where the infantrymen had failed. The enthusiastic CO of the tank outfit told Corlett that eliminating the salient was no problem; what he really wanted was to let his tanks go for St. Lô, only four miles away. Corlett shook his head and advised restraint. He said that he would be more than satisfied if the 3rd Armored managed to eliminate the salient.

The tankers ran into trouble as soon as the attack began. One member of the 3rd Armored recalled, "As we moved forward, soon coming to the first hedgerow beyond where the 29th Division had held, the Germans found that we were here and opened up. They had their mortars pre-laid on our position and began dropping mortar shells just behind that hedgerow. These exploding shells soon brought sudden, horrifying screams of stricken men before the dust and debris had settled. We immediately saw death and destruction in its most violent form."

The battle lasted two days, and when it ended, the tankers no longer boasted. "When the battle was in full swing, I saw dozens of them running like hell for the rear," Cooper recollected. The attack gained about a half-mile of ground, but the casualty list of some 400 tankers was an extremely high price to pay. Although the 3rd Armored was halted 1,000 yards short of its objective, Corlett was content that the Villiers-Fossard salient was adequately reduced and no longer menaced his future plans. By nightfall on June 30, the disillusioned tankers were pulled out and replaced by the 115th.

Every infantry battalion in the 29th Division got a chance to rest behind the front for several days between the end of June and the first week of July. The rest areas, located only a mile or two behind the line, offered few diversions. Most of the little villages near the camps, like St. Clair-sur-l'Elle, were off-limits and patrolled by stern-faced MPs. But plenty of movies were available, including a Spencer Tracy film called "A Guy Named Joe." Movies were shown in centuries-old stone barns and stables, long since abandoned by their owners. The film reels frequently broke or burned under the heat of projector bulbs, and the viewers let the projectionists know how they felt with good-natured catcalls and groans. Recalled a member of the Red Cross who watched a film with an outfit from the 175th Infantry, "I thoroughly enjoyed a picture while sitting for an hour and a half on a bale of horse manure."

The 29ers grumbled when they discovered that they had to do close-order

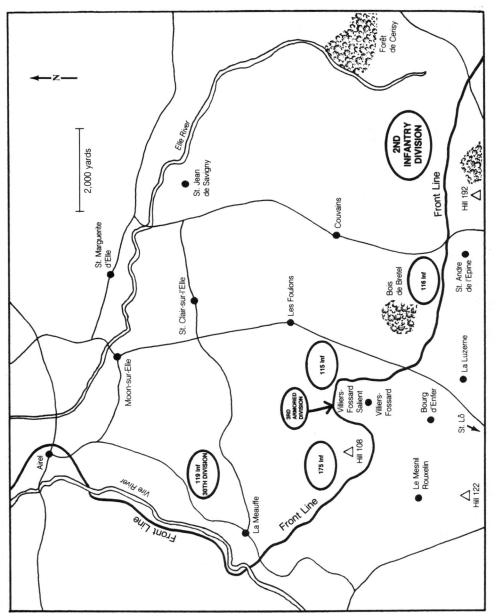

Front Line, June 29, 1944.

drill during their rest period. Sometimes Gerhardt himself came over to watch them line up in a pasture at the crack of dawn. But for the riflemen who had recently lived in foxholes, the manual of arms seemed like silly child's play compared to combat.

Nevertheless, drill turned out to be curiously intriguing. Newcomers, seeing the battalion lined up in neat ranks, felt part of a well-trained team with plenty of men and powerful weapons. The veterans, watching their company and battalion on parade for the first time in more than a month, were saddened at the sight of so many new faces and the thought of so many missing friends.

The 29ers knew that sooner or later the division would be ordered to make another assault on St. Lô. Before the attack was launched, however, Gerhardt wanted to take advantage of the division's forced inactivity by teaching his men to overcome their fear of the hedgerows.

The 29ers were still not used to the bocage. Hardly typical terrain, the hedgerows stymied standard American infantry tactics. In the division's first two weeks of combat, hastily improvised techniques for rooting the Germans out of the hedgerows were rarely successful. More often than not, the would-be attackers found themselves attacked. Tanks did not help much since they were restricted to the roads.

"One squad, one tank, one field" was Gerhardt's slogan. Under the direction of General Cota, a division training center was established near Couvains where the riflemen could watch demonstrations of the new tactics. Cota's system was simple. Enemy-held hedgerows were to be stormed by a combined force of tanks and infantry; the tanks were to protect the infantry, and the infantry was to protect the tanks. But these tactics could only work if the 29ers learned to work closely with the men of the 747th Tank Battalion, an independent unit which was currently attached to the division.

The tankers' biggest problem was to break through the hedgerows into the enclosed pastures so that they could support the infantrymen at close range. The tankers had tried to attach bulldozer blades to the front of their Shermans, but these failed to work because the dirt base of the hedgerows was reinforced by a tough tangle of roots.

The only answer was to blow a gap through the banks. A tanker figured out that the easiest way to do this in combat was to attach two sharp metal prongs to the front of the Shermans. The prongs looked like the jousting lances of medieval knights, and when they were welded to a Sherman, it seemed as if the tank was invented to impale enemy troops rather than shoot them. The tank rammed its prongs into an embankment and then backed out, leaving two holes, each about three feet deep. Into these the engineers inserted demolition charges. When detonated, the charges blasted a gap wide enough for any tank to pass through.

The tankers later discovered that if they were in a hurry, demolition

A Sherman from the 747th Tank Battalion with two "hedge-busting" prongs attached. The two tubes standing in front of the tank are explosive charges. *Courtesy Fifth Regiment Armory.*

charges were unnecessary. A tank could just smash its prongs against the middle of the embankment at high speed. The men inside the tank received a jolt, but the force of the blow was usually sufficient to knock off the top half of the hedgerow, including all its shrubbery. The bottom half could then be traversed with little difficulty.

After breaking through an embankment, each tank was to move forward and blast the enemy hedgerow with its 75mm gun and machine guns. Meanwhile, the infantry would follow close behind, keeping a sharp lookout for Germans with antitank weapons. Upon reaching the enemy line, the riflemen were to use grenades to wipe out German resistance nests in the hedgerow while the tank smashed a breach in this new embankment, thus beginning the whole process again. Whenever possible, a second tank-infantry team followed 100 yards behind the first.

The 29ers were also taught that a plentiful expenditure of ammunition was important to hedgerow tactics. Even when they saw no sign of an enemy soldier, the infantrymen and tankers learned to saturate suspicious hedgerows with fire.

The 747th had only fifty-three Shermans, not nearly enough tanks to attach one to each of the 29th Division's rifle squads. Gerhardt decided to assign most of the tanks to the 116th Infantry for the upcoming offensive. The 747th's Company A was attached to the 2nd Battalion, which was to lead the assault. The battalion planned to launch its attack with Companies E and F in front, so the seventeen tanks of Company A were almost sufficient to provide one tank for each rifle company's nine rifle squads. The 2nd Battalion was also assigned a company from the 121st Combat Engineer Battalion to clear minefields and furnish explosives for hedgerow demolition.

On July 2, Eisenhower and Bradley visited 29th Division headquarters, situated a mile southwest of St. Clair-sur-l'Elle. Gerhardt, ever the showman, welcomed his distinguished guests as the division band blared martial music probably heard by the Germans. Most of the division's regimental and battalion COs, sporting clean uniforms, lined up outside the war room. Uncle Charlie ushered his two visitors down the line, making introductions. Bradley's aide, Maj. Chester Hansen, noted in his diary that the 29th was the only division in Normandy that had greeted his boss with a formal ceremony. Bradley was surprised that Gerhardt had arranged for so many 29th Division COs to be present. Over dinner, Bradley joked to Ike, "What would have happened if a war had started on the front?"

Earlier that day, Bradley had met with Corlett to discuss plans for the XIX Corps. The XIX Corps commander enthusiastically laid out a scheme for an offensive against St. Lô using the 29th, 30th, and 3rd Armored Divisions. "You'd better hold your horses, Pete," Bradley countered. "You're not ready to go yet. We'll take that stuff by pinching it out. . . . The movements of the VIII and VII Corps should clean out opposition fronting XIX Corps and force them to move back. This is better than a frontal attack or even local maneuver." Bradley was deeply troubled by the high number of American casualties in Normandy so far, and he had no desire to expend more men and equipment on a few square miles of meaningless real estate.

By early July, Bradley had already sown the seeds of a future offensive that would become known as "Cobra." The objective of this assault, planned for the last half of July, was to break the Normandy front wide open by means of a massive VII Corps attack on a narrow front just west of the Vire, only a few miles from St. Lô. For the present, Bradley was convinced that there was little Corlett could do to support Cobra, so he ordered the XIX Corps, including the 29th Division, to remain on the defensive.

But Bradley soon changed his mind. A few days later, the general concluded that Cobra could not succeed unless St. Lô were wrested from the Germans. At first blush, St. Lô did not have much military value. The central part of the city had been pummeled by Allied bombers, and by early July, the place was a pile of rubble. The wreckage still blocked the passage of most military vehicles through the city. Still, the Germans could profit from holding St. Lô. On the map St. Lô resembled the hub of a bicycle wheel, with eight major roads radiating from its center. An important bridge crossed the Vire River at the western edge of town. Although the Vire formed a natural barrier on the VII Corps's eastern flank, the Germans could still counterattack this flank if they held St. Lô.

Although St. Lô lay in the low ground of the Vire valley, several hills to the east and west offered commanding views of the city and the surrounding countryside. Bradley wanted these heights occupied by his men before the Cobra offensive jumped off.

Now that his XIX Corps was part of 1st Army's master plan, Corlett wished to set his men in motion as soon as possible. On July 7, the 30th Division was to open the offensive by attacking southward along the west bank of the Vire. Two days later, the 29th, 35th, and 2nd Divisions would join in on the east side of the Vire. (The 2nd Division was a V Corps unit, temporarily attached to Corlett.)

The 35th Division was new to Normandy. It had arrived at Omaha Beach during the first week of July, fresh from the same training grounds in Devon and Cornwall that the 29ers had used for almost a year. Like the 29th, the 35th was a National Guard division, raised in Kansas, Nebraska, and Missouri.

On July 9, two of the 35th Division's regiments moved to the front and relieved the 175th Infantry in the sector between the Vire and Hill 108. During the relief operation, both the veterans and the green troops stared at one another in amazement. The sardonic 29ers were tired and dirty and on edge; the 35th Division riflemen, decked out in regulation uniforms, were well-scrubbed and high-spirited. For the 175th Infantry's old-timers, the realization that their regiment had recently been manned by enthusiastic young men like these of the 35th was difficult to bear.

To allow the 29th and 35th Divisions more time to plan—and the 35th a chance to adjust to its new surroundings—Corlett postponed the attack east of the Vire until July 11. Gerhardt, as always, was optimistic about the division's prospects for success. Now that the 35th was deployed on his right flank, the general's high hopes seemed for once justified. For the first time in the campaign, the 29th Division was concentrated on a narrow front. When the 175th Infantry had been relieved by the 35th Division, the length of the 29th's line was cut in half, from five miles to two-and-a-half. The men of the 175th were especially happy because their regiment held the luxurious position of division reserve on the first day of the upcoming attack.

After the division contracted its front on July 9, most 29ers could bid good riddance to the 352nd Division, which they had fought continually since D-Day. With the exception of a small sector on the 29th Division's right flank that still faced remnants of the 352nd, the 3rd *Fallschirmjäger* Division stood alone between Gerhardt's men and St. Lô.

The 29ers had first skirmished with the German paratroopers in mid-June, and although the front had been relatively quiet since that time, the Yanks had come to respect and fear the high-spirited and well-armed *Fall-*

schirmjäger. Compared with the 352nd, the 3rd FJ Division was in excellent shape. Several of its major combat units did not arrive at the front until the latter half of June. Since that time they had not been heavily engaged and were almost at full strength, which was more than could be said for the 29th Division.

Gerhardt planned to attack St. Lô from the east. To do this, the 29ers would have to smash through the 3rd FJ Division, execute a ninety-degree turn to the right (west), and advance three miles into the city. The 29th's front line, which had not changed appreciably since mid-June, was held by the 116th on the left and the 115th on the right. Although both regiments would attack simultaneously, the 116th was to make the major blow.

The Stonewall Brigade was concentrated along a front of only three-quarters of a mile, with one battalion in the line and two close behind. The plan was for Major Bingham's 2nd Battalion to punch a hole in the German line a few hundred yards wide. The other two battalions were to pass through the hole, and the entire regiment would then dash into St. Lô.

While preparing for the attack, 1st Army headquarters had ordered a July 4 salute. Americans always liked to mark the Fourth of July with lots of noise, and 1st Army figured that G.I.'s would be no exception. Besides, what better place to find explosives with which to celebrate than in a war zone?

Precisely at noon on July 4, the G.I.'s let loose with a round from every available weapon at the front, from pistols to howitzers. So much for the ammunition shortage.

TEN

TRIUMPH

The Major of St. Lô
July 11–23, 1944

1. COUNTERATTACK

A strange new batch of artillery shells arrived at the 29th Division in early July. These shells, stuffed with propaganda leaflets printed in German, were meant to demoralize enemy troops rather than to kill them. The shells were set with time fuzes so they would burst high over the German lines, where the wind would scatter the leaflets across the front.

The cannoneers doubted the leaflets would do any good, especially against tough German paratroopers. The 29th Division's big attack on July 11 was approaching fast, however, and the 29ers figured that anything that might help soften up the enemy was worth a try.

The paratroopers dove for cover when they heard the whine of approaching American artillery shells. But when the shells detonated high in the air, the intrigued *Fallschirmjäger* watched hundreds of pieces of paper fluttering gracefully down to earth. They picked up the leaflets and read (in German):

YOUR LEADERS HAVE PROMISED YOU:

That the Atlantic Wall is closed without gaps. WE HAVE BROKEN THROUGH.

That the Allied troops would not stay for even nine hours on French soil. WE'VE BEEN HERE FOUR WEEKS.

That the coastal harbors have been transformed into unbreakable fortresses. WE HAVE CONQUERED CHERBOURG.

That the German Luftwaffe is invincible. IT HAS DESERTED YOU.

That your weapons are the best in the world. YOU HAVE FELT THE SUPERIORITY OF OUR ARTILLERY.

That victory marches everywhere with the German banners. AND RUSSIA? AND AFRICA? AND ITALY? AND NOW THE WESTERN FRONT?

We, however, promise you:

That through the broken Atlantic Wall, new war materiel and fresh troops will stream into France hourly.

That Cherbourg is only the beginning of coming victories.

That your sacrifice in the sector of St. Lô is as senseless as that of your comrades on the Cotentin Peninsula.

That you can save yourselves, for yourselves and Germany, if you will see in time—WHO LIES? WHO SPEAKS THE TRUTH?

The paratroopers were too busy preparing their *Schützenlöcher* (foxholes) for the inevitable American attack to pay much attention to a dialectical argument. But the war of words was on. German propagandists hastily prepared a counterattack, and the 29th Division was hit by a retaliatory barrage of leaflets several days later.

The 29ers considered German propaganda preposterous. The enemy's leaflets were nothing more than appeals to the American soldier's sexual instincts. A typical leaflet featured a sketch of an attractive and scantily clad woman in the arms of a happy male civilian. The caption asked what the G.I.'s thought they would be doing if they were home instead of in the army. The 29ers chuckled and hoped the Germans would send more over the lines. The leaflets were a lot safer than real artillery shells, and the sketches were fairly interesting.

The war was not always bestial. On the afternoon of July 9, several members of Company B, 115th Infantry, spotted a lone German standing on a nearby hedgerow. Normally an American fusillade would have cut him down, but the German was waving a white flag. The astonished 29ers watched as he leaped off the hedgerow and strode with aplomb towards the American lines. He appeared to be a medic or a doctor, since he wore a baggy white smock over his uniform, marked prominently with a Red Cross. When he reached the wary 29ers, he came to attention, saluted, and handed the senior Yank on the scene, a sergeant, a folded piece of paper. The note contained a message in English, requesting a truce in this sector so that both sides' dead could be cleared from no-man's land.

The matter was brought to the attention of 1st Battalion headquarters, but the CO, Maj. Glover Johns, was not available. Instead, the battalion S-2, Lt. George Grimsehl, came forward to the Company B lines to meet with the German. After a short discussion, the adversaries arranged a two-hour cease-fire.

German and American stretcher-bearers promptly climbed over the hedgerows to bring in their comrades' corpses, an unenviable task since the dead had been lying in the fields under the hot sun for several days. The American medics, however, were glad to discover one Yank still alive. He was hastily treated and sent to the battalion aid station. The grisly work finished, both sides withdrew to their lines to restart the war.

At 1:30 A.M. on July 11, only four-and-a-half hours before the 29th Division's St. Lô offensive was to begin, the Germans surprised the 1st Battalion of the 115th with a full-fledged attack. Following a furious barrage, 400 German paratroopers dashed into the American lines before the 29ers came to their senses. The *Fallschirmjäger* raced along the hedgerows in the darkness, firing submachine guns and hurling grenades into the Yanks' foxholes. A platoon leader in Company B, Lt. Fletcher Harris, was lying in a hole when a German potato masher grenade suddenly landed by his side. He snatched it up to heave it back over the hedge, but it exploded and severed his right hand.

The night was too dark to see more than a few yards, and neither side could practice textbook tactics. The battle deteriorated into a wild melee at pointblank range. Most of the bewildered 29ers sensibly remained in their foxholes and shot at anything that moved.

A forward observer from the 110th Field Artillery, Lt. Robert Davis, was captured in the initial German rush. Although Davis was frisked, his captor failed to detect a hunting knife hidden in the prisoner's leggings. While being escorted back to the enemy lines, Davis whipped out the knife and killed his guard. He eventually made it back to 1st Battalion headquarters, severely shaken.

Several terrified 29ers fled to the rear, spreading stories that the Germans were close and coming fast. These tales threw the 115th's rear-echelon outfits into near-panic. In fact, one company of heavy 4.2-inch mortars, attached to the 115th from XIX Corps to support the upcoming offensive, packed up its weapons and took off without orders.

At first, nothing went right for the unlucky Major Johns at the 1st Battalion command post. His telephone lines were dead because the alert *Fallschirmjäger* had cut every wire they found. His staff reached for its radios to call for help, but they couldn't manage to contact anyone. Cut off from his company COs, Johns had little idea of what was happening on the front lines; he could only guess from the noises of battle, which unfortunately were dominated by the distinctive "brrrrp" of German machine pistols. The battle sounds grew louder and louder. The Germans were obviously nearing the 1st

Battalion command post, a few hundred yards behind the front. Johns and his staff grabbed their carbines and waited tensely for the Germans to rush the headquarters dugout. Sgt. Joe Fischhaber, a member of the 110th Field Artillery liaison team, muttered to Johns, "If you get me out of this alive, I'll dance at your wedding."

Luckily, the Germans failed to detect the command post, and the sound of enemy gunfire gradually faded as the *Fallschirmjäger* pushed deeper into American lines. (Several years after the war, Johns married, and Fischhaber kept his word.)

Back at the 110th Field Artillery, Lieutenant Colonel Cooper had ordered his gunners to start shooting as soon as he heard the eruption of small arms fire on the 1st Battalion front. With communications out, the artillerymen could not fire at targets observed by their front line forward observers, but Cooper decided to initiate the pre-planned barrage that was to have been used later that morning to support the 115th's attack on St. Lô. The targets of this barrage were in and behind the original German front.

The Americans would not have launched their attack prematurely, Cooper reasoned, so the Germans must have counterattacked. No doubt the Germans were fighting the 29ers within the American lines, but Cooper hoped that artillery shells fired at the previously targeted German front would disrupt reinforcements and mortarmen supporting the enemy attack from the rear. Cooper figured that until more specific firing instructions reached him, this pre-planned barrage would have to suffice.

Shortly after 2:00 A.M., the radios in Major Johns's command post suddenly crackled back to life. Sergeant Fischhaber promptly contacted his comrades at the 110th, passing on several requests for fire support from the forward observers. Within minutes, Cooper's gunners had adjusted their howitzers and were blasting enemy pockets within the American lines.

The German attack died out as the first rays of the sun appeared in the eastern sky. The battle had lasted more than three hours; when it ended, the Germans had pulled back to their own lines. The enemy paratroopers had made no attempt to reinforce their initial successes, nor had they made a determined effort to hold the ground they had gained. The purpose of their attack remained unclear. Possibly, the alert *Fallschirmjäger* knew of the 29th Division's impending offensive and wished to disrupt it. More likely, the raid was merely an attempt to torment an American unit new to that sector.

The *Fallschirmjäger* no doubt thought the 1st Battalion a suitable target since this outfit had recently betrayed its unfamiliarity with its new surroundings. On July 8, only a few hours after Johns's men had relieved a unit of the 116th in this sector, the nervous and trigger-happy men of Company A had fired hundreds of rifle and machine gun bullets toward a nearby hedge that rustled suspiciously. The noise, it turned out, was caused by a stray pig.

The 1st Battalion officers later speculated that the German medic's visit to the American lines the next day was no coincidence. In fact, many members of Company B came to believe that the "medic" was really a combat soldier who wanted a close-up view of the 29ers' forward hedgerows. It was clear from the enemy's July 11 assault that the precise locations of 1st Battalion outposts and the gaps through which German troops could infiltrate American lines after dark were known by the Germans in advance. The 29ers later discovered that the attack even had a code-name, *Stosstrupp-Unternehmen Kersting* ("Shocktroop Operation Kersting"), named after the CO of the 9th *Fallschirmjäger* Regiment's 5th Company, 1st Lt. Werner Kersting, who led the attack.

2. MARTINVILLE RIDGE

The 29th Division's offensive had not begun auspiciously. When Major Johns finally had a chance to analyze his situation at 5:00 A.M. on July 11, he discovered that his outfit had suffered 150 casualties—about 25 percent of its strength. His exhausted and disheartened men were supposed to join the 29th Division's attack in less than an hour.

Over the phone to regimental headquarters, the dismayed major had learned from Colonel Ordway that the 1st Battalion was expected to launch its attack on schedule. Johns had sworn it couldn't be done—and he was right. Although he worked feverishly to get the 1st Battalion in order, he was not ready by 6:00 A.M., the designated jump-off time.

Gerhardt called. "I understand you had quite a busy evening," Gerhardt said. "When do you propose to move?"

"I don't want to state a definite time, but things are looking pretty good, and it should be shortly," Johns replied.

By 9:45 A.M. Johns had still not moved. General Cota visited the 1st Battalion command post to find out why. "He said something about the urgency of the situation, then went back up the path toward the rear, leaving an irate battalion commander behind him," Johns later wrote.

Five hundred yards on Johns's left, the Stonewall Brigade attacked at 6:00 A.M., right on schedule. The 116th's well-planned assault proved to be the 29th Division's greatest success in the campaign so far. Preceded by a furious one-hour artillery barrage, the Stonewallers employed Gerhardt's "one squad, one tank, one field" tactics to perfection and broke the German front wide open.

The breakthrough had not been easy. The 2nd Battalion, with Companies E and F in front, had led the attack, only to be stopped cold at the enemy's front line hedgerow. The German defense here was particularly strong. Their line followed a sunken road—essentially a natural trench—and no-man's land

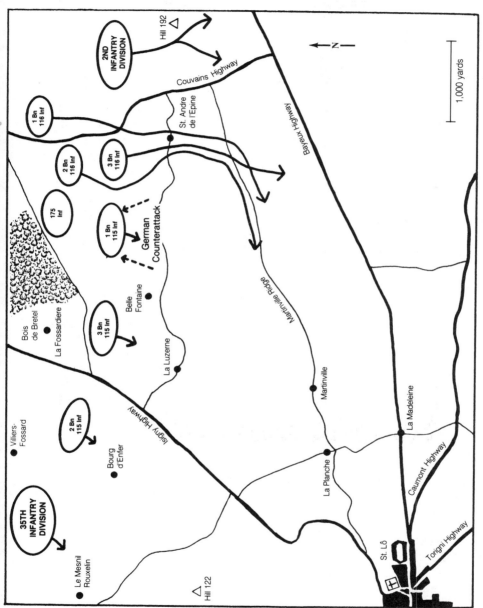

29th Division, July 11, 1944.

was strewn with mines. As the Stonewallers took their first steps toward the German hedgerows, dozens of them were felled like tenpins. Major Bingham, the battalion CO, understated the case when he recalled, "The Kraut parachute lads were determined."

Pvt. John Robertson of Company F was one of the unlucky ones. "As we were moving out behind a tank, an artillery shell landed short, right among my squad," Robertson recalled. "They told us the 155 and 105 howitzers were all firing over us, and when the tanks came in, we would fall in behind. My squad, as far as I remember, was really butchered up. Some of us were blown forward, some backward. It was a big mess. When I regained my senses, I got up and started limping back. As I was slopping along thinking about why my shoe was full of 'water,' I felt my leg and my hand went all the way to the bone. It was blood that I was slopping in. I practically passed out, but vaguely remember being patched up by a medic. I was left lying in a field that was still being shelled. I had tree limbs, shattered by the shelling, fall on me and dirt blown on me from shells exploding so close. After an eternity passed, a couple of G.I.'s bringing some prisoners back stopped and fashioned a stretcher from one of the German blankets and a few limbs. They carried me back to the battalion aid station."

Capt. Charles Cawthon, the battalion executive, later wrote that "it seemed that noise alone would destroy everything." Watching the attack from the front lines, he focused on one of the lead Shermans, churning across the deadly field with a file of Stonewallers close behind. One courageous rifleman who climbed atop the tank turret to get a better view of the German defenses was promptly hit by a hail of bullets. He fell off the back of the tank as if he had slipped on a patch of ice. "A pall of smoke was over the fields, holding in it the sweet, sickening stench of high explosives, which we had come to associate with death," Cawthon recollected. "The attacking riflemen, visibly shrunk in numbers, crouched behind the farthermost hedgerow while volumes of artillery, mortar, and tank gunfire flailed the fields beyond."

The fight continued at this intensity for five hours. By 11:00 A.M., Bingham's men had gained only 500 yards at fearful cost. "The three rifle companies were down to about sixty men apiece and these were well shaken up," Bingham remembered. "Very, very few of the NCOs and officers from England remained. We were in bad shape."

Suddenly, the pounding from the Stonewall Brigade was apparently more than the enemy paratroopers could stand, and German resistance evaporated. Furthermore, on the 29th Division's left flank, the 38th Infantry of the 2nd Division had seized an important hill, designated "Hill 192" on US Army maps. This height was an artillery observer's dream. From its summit accurate howitzer fire could be directed anywhere along the *Fallschirmjäger* front.

After the fall of Hill 192, the German line was no longer tenable. Maj.

Kurt Stephani, the CO of the 9th *Fallschirmjäger* Regiment, was ordered to pull his survivors back to establish a new defensive position a mile-and-a-half closer to St. Lô. That evening, Stephani wept when told of his losses.

When the Germans pulled out, Major Bingham wheeled his 2nd Battalion to the west and gamely ordered his men to head straight for St. Lô. Progress was good, but the Stonewallers knew that success was fleeting in the bocage. As the riflemen advanced, they carefully scrutinized every hedgerow, looking for signs of an ambush. "Advancing into territory denied you by an enemy is like setting foot on an unexplored shore; you look around, wondering at the evidence of a strange and hostile people," Captain Cawthon recalled. "German paratroopers, whole and in parts, lay about, difficult to reconcile, in their round helmets and blood-soaked camouflage smocks, with what had a short time before been among the most dangerous fighting men of the war."

Bingham had instructions to follow the crest of Martinville Ridge, a narrow finger of high ground some two miles long, projecting from Hill 192 toward St. Lô like a dagger. Bingham's first objective was Martinville, the village from which the ridge took its name. The village lay at the western end of the ridge only a mile-and-a-half from St. Lô. The next step after Martinville was St. Lô itself.

Gerhardt harbored a faint hope that the enemy on his front was smashed and would evacuate the city without a fight. He urged Bingham to "push on, [and] if possible take St. Lô."

Bingham's weary Stonewallers were hardly capable of any more "pushing" after that morning's fight. The 2nd Battalion was still 1,000 yards short of Martinville when it finally halted and dug in for the night. Gerhardt, however, was delighted with Bingham's 3,000-yard advance for the day. If the 116th could keep up that pace, the general calculated that St. Lô would be in 29th Division hands within the next twenty-four hours.

Gerhardt was concerned about Bingham's left flank, for the 2nd Battalion's right wheel towards St. Lô had left it wide open to an enemy attack from the south. To allay the general's anxiety, Colonel Canham committed the 116th's remaining two battalions to the fight at 2:00 P.M.. Both outfits followed in Bingham's wake until they reached the crest of the Martinville Ridge. Then, instead of turning west as the 2nd Battalion had done, they continued a few hundred yards down the southern face of the ridge. They met little opposition but were harassed by constant mortar fire. By nightfall, both battalions were dug in on Bingham's left, roughly perpendicular to his line, facing southwest.

Canham's two battalions had still not solved the problem of the 29th Division's southern flank. If the drive on St. Lô continued to progress on the following day, the gap between the 116th and its neighbor to the east, the 2nd Infantry Division, would be wide enough for a German panzer division to

A rare air photo of Normandy. This photo was used by the 111th Field Artillery, 29th Division, during the St. Lô battles, July 11–19, 1944. Numbered artillery concentrations are clearly visible. The outskirts of St. Lô can be seen on the left. The dense pattern of concentrations in the upper right indicates the place where the 116th Infantry broke through the German lines on July 11. *Courtesy Cooper Armory.*

pass through. Canham called Gerhardt at 9:00 P.M. and declared, ''I think we should have someone tie in with the 38th Infantry [of the 2nd Division].''

The general thought for a moment and then replied, ''We will move one battalion of Reed's outfit [Col. Ollie Reed, the new CO of the 175th Infantry] to report to you for deployment.'' Gerhardt then called Lt. Col. Purnell, the 175th's executive, and ordered him to move the 2nd Battalion immediately forward to join the 116th on Martinville Ridge. ''The other battalions [of the 175th] will move up under cover of darkness so that you will be set to go through [attack] in the morning,'' Gerhardt continued. ''Have Colonel Reed call me when he gets a plan in his head.''

The 115th's role in the July 11 offensive was secondary to that of the 116th. The original plan called for Colonel Ordway, the 115th's CO, to launch an attack in echelon, starting on his left. The 1st Battalion would jump off at 6:00 A.M., the same time as the 116th. Five hours later, the 3rd Battalion would join in, and the 2nd would follow two-and-a-half hours after that.

The German raid against Maj. Johns's 1st Battalion, however, threw these plans into disarray. By 11:00 A.M., when Bingham's men broke through the German line on Ordway's left, no one in the 115th had yet taken a step forward.

Gerhardt was unhappy. He angrily called up the frantic Ordway every half-hour to find out why the 115th hadn't started its attack yet. Poor Ordway was a nervous wreck that morning. He had just spent a sleepless night listening to alarming reports of a German breakthrough on Johns's front. When that situation finally cleared up, Ordway spent almost as much time putting off his commanding general as preparing for the attack.

When Johns's 1st Battalion finally moved out at 11:30 A.M., five-and-a-half hours late, the Germans were ready. The enemy gave up their first hedgerow without much of a fight. Every hedgerow beyond it, however, was a death trap. One platoon in Company A managed to seize a sunken road, but its success was short-lived. Having earlier registered their mortars on the road, the Germans could blast it with uncanny accuracy. The 29ers had no foxholes in which to take cover, and the platoon was virtually annihilated by the barrage.

By dusk, Johns's men had gained only a few hedgerows at a cost of some sixty men. The unit's total casualties for the day, including those inflicted in the German attack that morning, amounted to one-third of its strength. "A feeling of apathy began to descend on the whole outfit," Johns remembered. "The officers and men were not at first conscious of it, but defeat hung in the air like a palpable thing."

The 3rd Battalion joined the attack in mid-afternoon, to be joined by the 2nd Battalion in early evening. Both outfits got almost nowhere. Gerhardt continued to goad Ordway throughout the day. "Get Clift [2nd Battalion CO] going and don't worry about the 35th Division [the 115th's western neighbor] stopping for the night," Gerhardt growled. "I want some definite results out of both those battalions [1st and 3rd] tonight."

Unfortunately for Ordway, the 115th had little chance of duplicating the 116th's stunning success on July 11. Prior to the attack, the Stonewall Brigade had had a battalion of tanks and another of engineers at its disposal; the 115th had neither. The 116th held a narrow front of only three-quarters of a mile, with one battalion in line and two in reserve; the 115th held a front of two-and-a-half miles with all three battalions in line and no reserves. Finally, the 115th's right wing had to attack in full view of German observers atop Hill 122, a commanding height behind German lines a mile north of St. Lô. Unlike Hill 192, which fell to the 2nd Division on the morning of July 11, Hill 122 remained in German hands for most of the subsequent battle. In the next several days, the men of the 115th would learn why generals liked high ground.

Gerhardt believed that Hill 122 was the key to St. Lô, and he was right. The Germans knew this as well. The summit stood more than 300 feet above the level of the city. The hill was a good place to set up an easel for an artist wishing to paint a picture of St. Lô; it was an even better place for a soldier to set up an observation post from which to direct accurate artillery fire into the city and surrounding countryside. Gerhardt was convinced that the hill would be heavily defended, and he did not want to attack it head-on.

Gerhardt's plan—on paper at least—was brilliant. The general hoped to take St. Lô in a lightning stroke from the east, bypassing Hill 122 completely. By nightfall on July 11, the 116th Infantry was already well on the way to implementing this scheme. Its thrust toward St. Lô along the southern side of Martinville Ridge could not be detected by German observers atop Hill 122. If the 116th could press further down the Martinville Ridge and take St. Lô in the next forty-eight hours, all German troops north of the city, including those defending Hill 122, would be trapped. Their escape routes to the north, east, and south would be blocked by the 29th and 35th Divisions. The Vire River would bar a retreat to the west. Even if the 116th's attack along the Martinville Ridge stalled, Gerhardt believed that the threat of encirclement would oblige the Germans to abandon Hill 122. In this event, the general suspected that St. Lô could be captured handily.

Gerhardt's strategy had one major flaw. By using Martinville Ridge to bypass Hill 122 and enter St. Lô from the east, the 116th would be moving in full view of enemy observers on high ground to the south of the city. When the Germans eventually figured out Gerhardt's intentions, they would, no doubt, blast every square foot of Martinville Ridge with every mortar and howitzer within range. The longer the Stonewallers stayed on the ridge, the more they would suffer from German fire.

The 116th first felt the wrath of German artillery on the morning of July 12. Germans observers to the south could clearly see American movement on Martinville Ridge, and each time the Stonewallers attempted to advance, a cascade of enemy shells promptly crashed on their heads. Since the regiment had occupied the ridge only the previous evening, the G.I.'s had not had time to dig shrapnel-proof entrenchments. The dismayed Stonewallers also discovered that the German paratroopers defending St. Lô were hardly on the verge of disintegration, as the optimistic reports of July 11 had first indicated.

Gerhardt worked himself into a near-frenzy on July 12 trying to get the 116th, and later the 175th, to launch an aggressive assault down the Martinville Ridge into St. Lô. "Let's keep pushing now," Gerhardt told Canham at 10:30 A.M.. "Keep Dallas's outfit [1st Battalion] moving now. Get on down and get hold of Reed [175th CO] and get him set to move. We'll never get anything accomplished today unless he moves by noon. The day is short, you know."

An hour later, the general telephoned Colonel Reed and ordered him to push his 2nd and 3rd Battalions through the 116th to add fresh impetus to the attack. "What it takes is driving," Gerhardt declared. "You are the guy that has to do it. Where you are to do it from is your business, but we've got to get

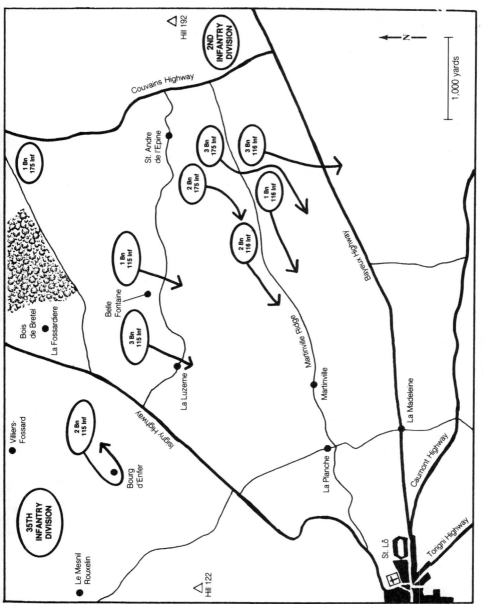

29th Division, July 12, 1944.

on those final objectives. Time is wasting, but I think your gang is in good shape, so get them rolling. When you report, get facts. There are too many uncertain reports coming in.''

The combined force of the 116th and the 175th, Gerhardt believed, would be sufficient to take St. Lô. Shortly before noon he phoned Corlett at XIX Corps headquarters and declared, ''We are going to get on that objective or else.''

Despite Gerhardt's exhortations, nothing went right on July 12. The 116th had to fight hard for every hedgerow, and by the end of the day, the regiment had advanced only 600 yards. At that pace, the 116th would take another week to capture St. Lô. But at the rate the Stonewall Brigade was suffering casualties, it would not reach the city before it ran out of men.

At dusk on July 12, the 116th held an L-shaped line. The 1st and 2nd Battalions formed the spine of the ''L'' facing west, only two miles from St. Lô; the 3rd Battalion held the base, facing south. All three outfits were under constant bombardment since they were still in full view of German forward observers.

Martinville Ridge was a shooting gallery, and the 29ers were the targets. German artillery fire was so intense on the ridge that Reed's 175th Infantry experienced terrible difficulties just moving into position to join the July 12 attack. His 2nd and 3rd Battalions, in fact, suffered almost sixty casualties in their approach march toward the front.

Gerhardt was exasperated. When he called up the 175th's headquarters at 1:20 P.M. and Reed told him the locations of the 2nd and 3rd Battalions, the general lost his temper. ''What are they doing so far back?'' he demanded.

Reed said that enemy artillery fire was heavy, but Gerhardt brushed this excuse aside. ''When are you going to jump off?'' he growled. ''Get them started. Let me know when they jump off. And make it soon.'' The general was furious when he learned later that Reed still had not been able to get the attack going by the end of the day.

Gerhardt was equally hard on Colonel Ordway. The general wanted the 115th to draw enemy attention away from Martinville Ridge on July 12 by exerting continuous pressure on the enemy. He was frequently on the phone with 115th headquarters, chiding Ordway to keep moving his men forward. ''There will be no turning back,'' Gerhardt insisted.

Ordway ordered his three battalions to attack at 8:00 A.M., but the results were just as disappointing as the previous day. The closer the 115th moved toward St. Lô, the more easily German observers atop Hill 122 could direct accurate artillery fire against it. Ordway's men were shelled almost incessantly on the afternoon of July 12, and any G.I. who stood in the open anywhere near the front risked his life. Like their fellow 29ers on Martinville Ridge, the men of the 115th were paralyzed by German artillery as much as by German machine guns. As long as Hill 122 remained in German hands, the 115th's situation would not improve.

The 2nd Battalion's attack had actually begun well. This outfit was on the right of the 115th's line, dangerously close to Hill 122. In the first hour of their attack, the 29ers gained several hedgerows against only scattered opposition and then moved cautiously over a stream, through thick apple orchards, and into a tiny hamlet named Bourg d'Enfer. They approached to within 1,000 yards of the top of Hill 122, but still the Germans were silent. Gerhardt had not expected to seize the hill by direct assault, but the 2nd Battalion's success presented an opportunity to win the battle in one stroke. "Keep pushing them, don't let them stall," the General urged Ordway.

Members of the 2nd Battalion who knew a little French thought that Bourg d'Enfer was an ominous place to fight a battle. The name, literally translated, meant "Market Town of Hell." The Yanks moved out through the southern side of the village and approached a little dirt track running through an orchard. Unknown to the 29ers, this road marked the main German line, and as the surprised infantrymen got near it, they were stopped cold by bursts of machine gun fire and a deafening deluge of mortar shells.

A German counterattack simultaneously hit the battalion's left flank, and in the confusion, a rumor spread among the Yanks that someone had ordered a retreat. No such order had been issued, but before the misunderstanding was cleared up, the whole outfit had pulled out of Bourg d'Enfer all the way back to its morning jump-off position. When the retreat was finally halted, the 2nd Battalion was badly disorganized.

Gerhardt was enraged. "I understand that you had some trouble with Clift [Maj. Maurice Clift, 2nd Battalion CO]," the general snapped to Ordway.

"His left began to break and a rumor started that they were withdrawing," Ordway replied. "Clift picked out a defensive position and is now reorganizing and preparing to attack."

Gerhardt, however, was not sure that rushing Clift's battalion into another attack on July 12 was a good idea. The 115th had no reserves. If the 2nd Battalion, already in terrible shape, encountered further trouble, no fresh units would be available to reinforce it. The general phoned Ordway in the early evening and told him to delay Clift's attack until a new plan could be worked out. But he added, "Don't let Clift get the idea he is going to back up any further."

Ordway didn't think a new plan would help. "I think everybody is enthusiastic about taking up a strong defensive position right now and I would recommend it, too," he told Gerhardt at 5:07 P.M..

Gerhardt instructed Ordway to have the 115th dig in for the night and conserve its strength for another try the following morning. "Let us know your dispositions," Gerhardt insisted. "We want aggressive patrolling tonight." The regiment's casualties for the day were twenty-one dead and eighty-seven wounded. The 1st and 3rd Battalions had managed to advance only 500 yards; the 2nd had gained no ground at all.

Uncle Charlie was extremely unhappy with Clift. "I think a change is indicated in the 2nd," Gerhardt told Ordway later that night.

Ordway pointed out that the battalion was tired. This same outfit had been ambushed at Le Carrefour four days after D-Day, and many survivors had not yet recovered from the trauma. "There are many cases of combat exhaustion among the older non-coms," Ordway informed Gerhardt.

Gerhardt was unmoved. The next morning, the general relieved Clift and placed Maj. Asbury Jackson, formerly the S-2 of the 116th Infantry, in command.

General Corlett was concerned that Gerhardt's plan for the seizure of St. Lô was not working. After the 116th Infantry's success on the first day of the offensive, the July 12 attack by all three of the division's regiments had been a costly failure. The 29ers had pushed within two miles of St. Lô, but after July 12, no one—not even Gerhardt—nurtured any illusions that the capture of the city would be easy.

"That Hill 122 in your sector is SOP," Corlett told Gerhardt on the morning of July 13.

Gerhardt, however, wanted to try to take the hill by using his original plan one more time. "I think we will have to envelop it," he replied.

Gerhardt planned a furious attack all across the 29th Division front on July 13. The intensity of this attack, he hoped, would be more than the enemy could stand. The division would again concentrate its effort on Martinville Ridge, where the 2nd and 3rd Battalions of the 175th Infantry, supported by two companies of the 747th Tank Battalion, would pass through the 116th and attack due west into St. Lô. Gerhardt also arranged to pave a path through the German lines with an air strike by Army Air Force fighter-bombers.

The July 13 attack probably would have worked if everything had gone according to plan. The first thing to go wrong was the air strike, which was cancelled due to poor weather. Next, the tankers from the 747th unexpectedly announced that they did not have enough ammunition and fuel to join the attack at 8:00 A.M., the hour at which the 175th was to jump off. Although the 3rd Battalion of the 175th attacked anyway, it immediately ran into difficulty. Lt. Col. Edward Gill, the battalion CO, tried to bypass the stubborn German strongpoints by changing the axis of his assault, but he still got nowhere.

The 2nd Battalion joined the attack on the 3rd's left, but had no better luck. Coordination between the two battalions—and even between different companies within the same battalion—was almost impossible because, as Cota reported to Gerhardt that morning, "All of the 175th's communications

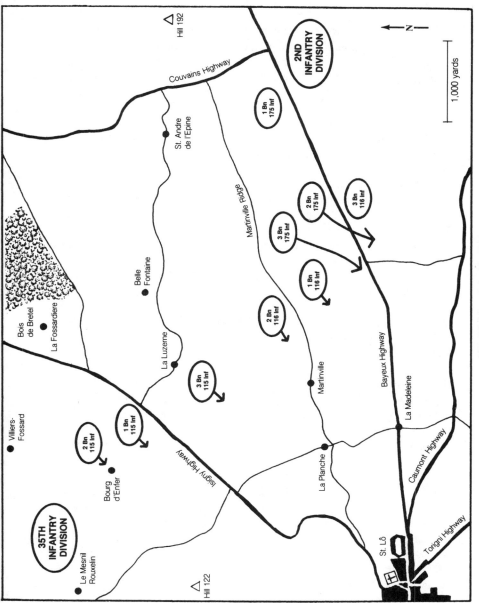

29th Division, July 13, 1944.

just got shot to hell." The final result of the attack was a gain of a few hedgerows at a cost of 152 casualties.

"I want a report in writing before midnight tonight why Colonel Gill changed direction and abandoned his mission," Gerhardt told Lt. Col. Purnell at 175th headquarters. Later, the CO of the 747th Tank Battalion, Lt. Col. Stuart Fries, was the target of the general's temper. "That ammunition and gas [shortage] was a disgrace. Swing this thing!" Uncle Charlie roared.

Signs were everywhere that the Germans were suffering as much as the Yanks. Once, Company F of the 175th Infantry warily approached the main east-west highway leading into St. Lô just south of Martinville Ridge. Capt. Bob Miller, the company CO, sent several scouts to check the road. "Captain, if you want to see a mess, come down and take a look," a scout reported upon his return.

Miller recalled the sight. "Our artillery," he said, "which we had called down to cover our movement, had apparently caught the Germans while they were moving. Supply trucks were wrecked and scattered, the road was covered with dead. I counted eleven bodies around one cart. They were probably an unloading crew and had been killed by a direct hit on the cart. The horse was still standing quietly in his harness. The road was littered with wreckage in the most indescribable confusion."

The 115th captured nothing more than a few hedgerows on July 13 and lost 108 men, the exact number of casualties suffered by the regiment the previous day. The 3rd Battalion led the attack, but it made only scant progress. Company L spent most of the day waging a bloody fight for a five-acre apple orchard, just southwest of the village of La Luzerne. The Germans were finally squeezed out of the orchard in mid-afternoon when the 1st and 2nd Battalions joined the assault on the 3rd's right and threatened the enemy with encirclement. The orchard had no military value except that it was a few hundred yards closer to St. Lô than the battalion's front line earlier that morning.

The fighting on July 12 and 13 convinced Gerhardt that his men were badly in need of a twenty-four-hour rest, and the general decided that July 14 was the day to take it. Some fortunate rifle battalions were pulled out of the line for a hot meal, a wash, and a few hours of precious sleep. Those unlucky infantrymen obligated to remain at the front stayed quiet for most of the day.

Gerhardt toured the front on July 14 and dropped in unexpectedly on several battalion COs. The general declared himself satisfied with the division's performance so far, but its mission was unfulfilled as long as the Germans retained St. Lô. The entire 1st Army, he said, was depending on the 29th to take the city.

The staffs listened solemnly to Gerhardt's inspirational talks. Everyone perked up when the general promised a long rest for the entire division after the fall of St. Lô. The 29ers had not heard such good news in a long time.

When he visited the front on July 14, Gerhardt noticed an offensive scent: the smell of decaying flesh. For the most part, the source of the odor on Norman battlefields was dead livestock, rather than the corpses of fallen soldiers, since both sides' medical personnel cleared their dead from the fields as fast as they could. Animal carcasses, however, were left to rot in the pastures. In the hot July sun, their bodies quickly bloated to grotesque proportions. Their legs turned stiff and protruded sideways or upward like toy animals that had been knocked over. On July 14, this sight was too much for Gerhardt's fastidious nature. He ordered his aide, Lt. Bob Wallis, to pass the word to all COs to get the dead animals buried.

A World War II battlefield looked like a junkyard when the fighting stopped. American soldiers, usually plentifully provided with war materiel, were particularly prone to discard unused equipment in the midst of battle. Gerhardt, however, did not tolerate waste. He called the 747th Tank Battalion's headquarters on the evening of July 14 and gave Lt. Col. Fries a lecture. "I was up in the area of Reed's outfit today and followed your tanks to their ultimate point of advance," the general declared. "They pulled out of their area and left a lot of gasoline cans, ammunition, etcetera, around. I want it out of there tonight. They left a medium [tank] sitting on the highway; get that out tonight. Give me a report in the morning."

Gerhardt, Corlett, and Maj. Gen. Paul Baade, the commander of the 35th Division, took advantage of the July 14 respite to make several changes in their plans. Although one of Baade's regiments, the 134th Infantry, was the only XIX Corps reserve, Corlett committed the regiment to the front on the evening of July 14 and ordered it to seize Hill 122 the following day. When the 134th entered the line, it took over most of the 115th's sector. Much to Gerhardt's delight, the 29th Division front was thereby shortened by 2,000 yards. Furthermore, now that Hill 122 was in Baade's area of responsibility, Gerhardt could concentrate his efforts entirely upon St. Lô.

"I have been out with the troops and just got back," Gerhardt told Corlett on the evening of July 14. "We are all set for the morning, and I think we have got a pretty good shot at doing it."

"Your men got a little rest?" Corlett asked.

"Yes," Gerhardt replied.

"Good luck to you," said Corlett.

3. ST. LÔ AT LAST

The 29ers had had ambivalent feelings towards Gerhardt from the moment he arrived to take command of the division. By the fifth day of the Battle of St. Lô, many 29th Division infantrymen were openly distrustful of their commanding general. The old-timers sarcastically referred to Gerhardt as a corps commander rather than a division commander. "He has a division in the field, a division in the hospital, and a division in the cemetery," the men used to say.

A rifleman landing on Omaha Beach with the 29th Division was extraordinarily lucky if he had not been hit by the middle of July 1944. For him, the cataclysm of the bocage fighting so far was a campaign of muddled memories. Some vivid recollections, of course, stood out above others. A 29er who witnessed the grisly sights of Omaha Beach never forgot them. The battle for St. Lô, too, would always be remembered; the 29th Division had focused on it for a month-and-a-half. Everything between these two events, however, was a blur. To the infantryman, the war seemed an interminable series of fights in a sea of endless, green hedgerows. In the line almost continuously since D-Day, he had had little time for retrospection. In the precious moments when the battle lulled, the rifleman felt only overwhelming fatigue and a numbing resignation to his fate. Looking back at recent events was the last thing on a soldier's mind when the next sunrise could be his last.

The 29ers were humble men caught up in a war of immeasurable complexity. Most 29ers had done what they were told to do, even when orders made little sense. On the deadly battlefields from Omaha Beach to St. Lô, these simple acts of obedience reflected astounding personal courage. In combat, all men fought an overwhelming desire to crawl into a hole and stay there until the fighting ended. But any soldier who could bring himself to leap over a hedgerow upon command and race, hunchbacked, across a grassy field while bullets snapped over his head like cracking whips, was a brave man indeed.

So far, the battle for St. Lô had cost Gerhardt more men than he had lost on Omaha Beach. The general's plan to seize the city from the east had failed, and now the 29ers had no more room for subtle maneuvers. The only thing left for the division to do, according to Gerhardt, was to blast its way into St. Lô. Everyone knew this would not be easy; the Germans obviously recognized the importance of the city, and by July 15 their backs were against the proverbial wall. American casualties promised to be even higher than before. But the 29ers took solace in Gerhardt's promise of a long rest after the fall of St. Lô. They fervently hoped they would live to see the day.

Gerhardt was never more of a dictator than on July 15. He spent most of the day in the war room, pacing back and forth energetically, stopping for a moment to scrutinize the situation map, grabbing the phone to rebuke his subordinates when they did not reach their goals. He was particularly hard on Maj. Elmore Swenson, the chief pilot for the division's Piper Cub reconnaissance aircraft. "Did you get word to call me?" Gerhardt demanded.

"No, sir," Swenson replied.

"Lieutenant Berry was notified to have you call me, so get on him," Gerhardt snapped. "I don't like to have people around you can't trust for veracity. You have a pilot down there who isn't stating facts. I saw this fellow do a loop and I want you to check on that. There were a couple of witnesses. If he doesn't say he made a loop, he isn't stating facts."

Shortly thereafter, Gerhardt called Swenson back. "Now look. We are giving it the full treatment today," the general declared. "If it's necessary for the planes to go over the enemy lines a little, that will be all right. We don't want to lose any of them, but if it's necessary in order to knock out some enemy gun positions, we'll have to do it."

In the midst of the July 15 attack, Gerhardt even took time to phone the division's administrative headquarters, miles behind the front, and admonish Lt. Col. Robert Archer, the 29th's adjutant general. Said Gerhardt, "Your sanitary report was lousy yesterday. It shouldn't have been . . . so get it corrected."

In the 115th Infantry's sector, the 1st Battalion had launched the July 15 assault at 6:00 A.M. and was joined by the 2nd Battalion a few hours later. Gerhardt phoned Ordway at 6:30 A.M. to see if any progress had been made. Ordway replied that the advance was slow due to enemy artillery. "The answer to that is 'keep moving,' so keep them going now," Uncle Charlie ordered.

The Germans, as usual, gave up their front line hedgerows without much of a fight. Their main line lay one or two hedgerows beyond the first, and a ferocious small arms duel erupted when the men of the 115th ran into it.

A morsel of good news reached the war room at 2:00 P.M.. Lt. Col. Lou Smith, the 115th's executive, told Gerhardt that the 2nd Battalion had captured so many German prisoners that it had lost count. The delighted Gerhardt exclaimed, "Pour it on. This may be it!"

Uncle Charlie's optimism was at fever-pitch. "We're going to keep at this now come hell or high water," he told Colonel Reed at 175th headquarters. Ten minutes later, the general phoned Corlett and declared, "We're stronger than we've ever been."

Gerhardt suspected that the Germans were on the verge of defeat. Late that afternoon, he prepared a stirring message for his regimental and battalion COs. "The division has accomplished extremely good results today," it read. "The advance should be pressed at all costs. At 1930 hours [7:30 P.M.], the full weight of all capabilities of Latitude [29th Division code-name] will be launched to achieve our objectives prior to dark. Every individual in the division should lend his utmost to this end. Fix bayonets! Twenty-Nine Let's Go!"

But the 29ers found it difficult to reconcile Gerhardt's optimism with the harsh realities of the front. As far as the infantrymen were concerned, the enemy showed few signs of panic, and no 29er had seen any "extremely good results" that day. The Germans, in fact, appeared more ready than ever to

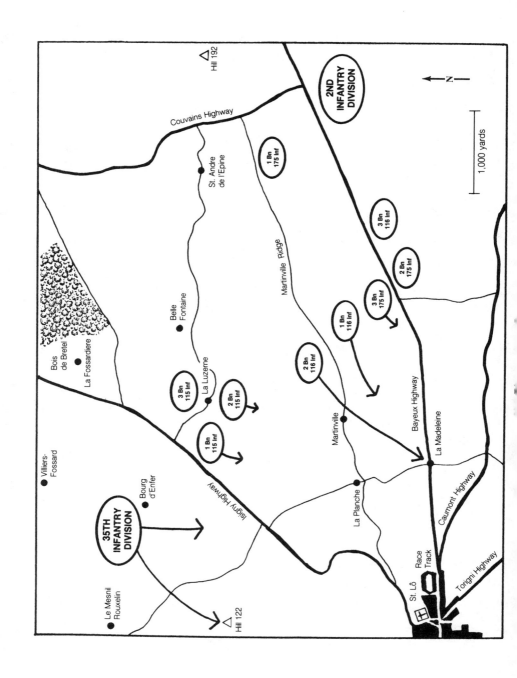

A German soldier surrenders outside St. Lô. A 29er waves him to the rear. *Courtesy Military History Institute.*

defend St. Lô to the last man, and they demonstrated their willingness by limiting the 115th to a gain of only 600 yards on July 15 and inflicting 119 casualties on the regiment, including twenty dead.

The 116th and 175th had experienced the same frustrations on Martinville Ridge. Both regiments had made several assaults during the day, but had only dented the German line. Bitterly disappointed yet again, Gerhardt decided to call off the attack at nightfall. He phoned General Robertson of the neighboring 2nd Division to exchange progress reports. Sighing, Uncle Charlie said, "We did all right today, but did not make the grade."

But then something startling happened. An hour before dusk, the German line on Martinville Ridge suddenly broke. Gerhardt was unaware of this good fortune, and his orders to dig in for the night arrived at the front at sunset, just as the 1st and 2nd Battalions of the 116th were beginning to make significant gains. Maj. Tom Dallas, the CO of the 1st Battalion, and Major Bingham of the 2nd, hastily searched for their company COs to pass the word that the attack was called off for the night. Dallas managed to rein in his outfit, but Bingham had difficulty. "I was with Company G and was actively engaged with the Krauts on the edge of Martinville," Bingham recalled. "I got Company G settled and, since wire and radio were out, I started to look for Companies E and F on the left to tell them to button up. I followed their wire and found them about a mile away astride the Bayeux-St. Lô highway near the stud farm and race track on the outskirts of St. Lô. At the time, I'm sure we could have gotten back up the hill to the rest of the battalion, but there were approximately 200 of us in the two-and-a-half companies [the force included part of Company H's heavy machine guns and mortars], and though we were completely cut off, I decided to stay put. Fortunately, the radio of the artillery liaison officer was working and we got word of our situation to regiment."

The sudden and unexpected breakthrough had brought the 29th Division close to victory. "There's no stopping this Bingham!" Gerhardt whooped when he heard the news.

The general, however, was also deeply concerned about Bingham's men. They were dug in less than a mile from St. Lô around the little crossroads village of La Madeleine, a mile in front of their fellow Stonewallers on Martinville Ridge. Everyone in the 29th Division knew the German penchant for launching powerful counterattacks against American units that had broken through the front, and it was just a question of time before the Germans realized the Yanks' predicament and hit Bingham with everything they had. Bingham's tiny force was so isolated that it would be easy for the enemy to surround and overwhelm it.

Gerhardt made some hasty decisions. "We don't want to pull him back, but we don't want him to be chewed up either," the General told Col. Philip Dwyer, the 116th's new CO. (Canham had been promoted to brigadier general and transferred to the 8th Division as assistant division commander.) "We aren't going to pull him out. He stays there. I've just been talking to Ordway, and he may push out there if necessary."

Corlett, however, wanted the 29th and 35th Divisions to take a day of rest and reorganization before resuming the St. Lô offensive. According to XIX Corps orders, "16 July 1944 will be devoted to consolidation of gains made today [July 15], particular attention to Hill 122 [which the 35th Division had just seized], reorganization of present positions, and preparation for coordinated attack on 17 July 1944." Considering the depleted condition of every infantry outfit in the 29th Division, this order was sensible, but it was drafted before the dilemma of Bingham's "lost battalion" had become evident.

Gerhardt interpreted Corlett's orders liberally. He decided to keep the 116th and 175th inactive on July 16, but he instructed Ordway to send a battalion of the 115th to Bingham's rescue as soon as possible.

Ordway was unhappy about this assignment. The 115th was a mile-and-a-half north of La Madeleine, and, although the German line on Martinville Ridge had been briefly broken by the 116th on July 15, the enemy in Ordway's sector showed no signs of collapse. The 115th, in fact, had gained less than a mile in five days of hard fighting. "I've gone over this and have selected the White [2nd] Battalion to do the job, if it's necessary," Ordway told Colonel Witte, Gerhardt's G-3. "The whole regiment wasn't able to

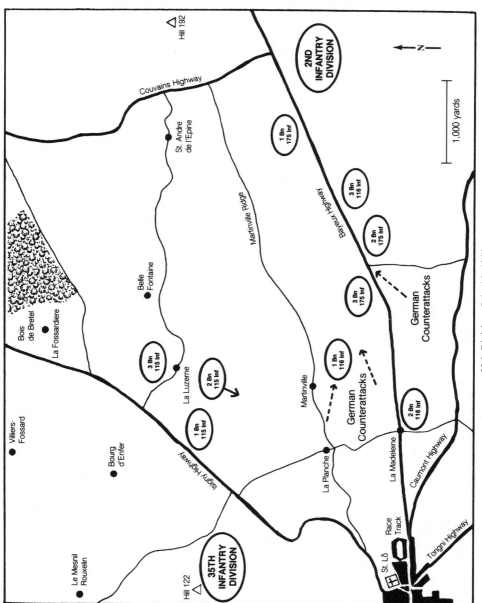

29th Division, July 16, 1944.

Hill 192

2ND INFANTRY DIVISION

Couvains Highway

St. Andre de l'Epine

1 Bn 175 Inf

Martinville Ridge

3 Bn 116 Inf

Bayeux Highway

2 Bn 175 Inf

Belle Fontaine

Bois de Bretel

La Fossardiere

3 Bn 115 Inf

3 Bn 175 Inf

La Luzerne

2 Bn 115 Inf

German Counterattacks

Villiers-Fossard

1 Bn 115 Inf

1 Bn 116 Inf

Martinville

German Counterattacks

Bourg d'Enfer

Isigny Highway

La Planche

2 Bn 116 Inf

La Madeleine

Caumont Highway

Le Mesnil Rouxelin

35TH INFANTRY DIVISION

Hill 122

St. Lô

Race Track

Torigni Highway

1,000 yards

N

[break through] during daylight [on July 15] and it doesn't seem reasonable for an outfit to get there now. If it is an emergency, we can bore in."

Gerhardt insisted that the attempt be made. At 5:25 A.M. on July 16, he told Dwyer at 116th headquarters, "The people on your right [the 115th] are either going to sail on through or they won't get anywhere. They will either go quick or they won't go at all. This means that the only solution to this thing is to have Bingham get everything he can with him, get himself set, and just hang on. The thing is, I'm trying to have ourselves in position to do something tomorrow. If we become involved today, it might spoil things tomorrow."

A few minutes later, Gerhardt called his boss, Corlett. "Ordway's outfit is moving if they can keep it going without a first-class operation to do so," he declared. "If the opposition is there, they won't get out. We are going to give Bingham artillery support. . . . I think that's the best solution."

"So do I," Corlett replied. "I'm not very much worried about him." The XIX Corps commander, in fact, was so untroubled by Bingham that he later told Gerhardt, "You are trying to do too much."

Prior to its July 16 attack, the 115th was so short of riflemen that Ordway ordered all three of his battalions to send clerks, cooks, drivers, wiremen, and other rear-echelon personnel into the front lines. These reinforcements did little good, however, for the 115th encountered strong German resistance, got nowhere, and lost sixty-six men.

Even worse, the 116th and 175th had little opportunity to rest and reorganize, since the Germans infiltrated through the wide gaps between American units on Martinville Ridge and hit the Yanks with a powerful counterattack. Enemy mortar fire, as usual, was deadly, but this time the enemy sprang a surprise by using several *Sturmgeschütze*—tank-like assault guns.

The 29ers had seen few enemy armored vehicles in Normandy and were not prepared to deal with them now. One German vehicle brazenly roared down the road that followed the crest of Martinville Ridge and sprayed machine gun fire at the passing hedgerows like a getaway car in a gangster film.

Company A of the 116th scattered when both members of its only bazooka team were killed by one of the assault guns. But Sgt. Harold Peterson, who had assumed command after all six of the company's officers had become casualties during the past week, loaded his M1 with antitank grenades and hit the leviathan with six straight shots. The vehicle was not destroyed, but the enemy driver beat a hasty retreat toward St. Lô.

The men of Company A eventually returned to their positions, but were dismayed to discover that the counterattack had cost them thirty-seven men. The experiences of several other outfits on Martinville Ridge were almost as bad. The door to St. Lô, open just a crack when Bingham's men squeezed through to La Madeleine on July 15, had slammed shut.

Officers from the 115th Regimental Combat Team. (Photo taken September 1944.) *From left:* **Lt. Col. John P. Cooper (110th Field Artillery); Capt. William Bruning; Lt. Col. Louis Smith; Maj. Glover Johns; Maj. Anthony Miller; Maj. Harold Perkins; Maj. Randolph Millholland; Maj. William Bratton.** *Courtesy Cooper Armory.*

Strangely, Bingham's beleaguered 2nd Battalion was not counterattacked. "The situation looked gloomy for us, but the Krauts weren't sure where we were or in what strength, and we had them upset and confused," Bingham recalled. "We had Companies E and F, four 81s [mortars] and four .30s [heavy machine guns] from Company H, and we made good use of them. All day on the 16th, the Krauts picked away at us from the south, east, and west. For some reason, those to the north didn't seem to give us much trouble, but we managed to upset them by shooting them up from their rear. We were taking casualties and had but one aid man. He did remarkable work. On the 17th, we picked up a Kraut medic, an Austrian, and put him to work."

The Germans were not the Stonewallers' only problem. "Sunday [July 16] all we did was dig in," recalled Sgt. Ronald Cote of Company E. "We got pretty hungry and thirsty because when we left we had only two rations apiece. Most of us had eaten both on Saturday night. By Sunday afternoon, everyone's canteen was dry. We didn't do much talking Sunday. When we did talk, we talked about food and something to drink and when they would relieve us. . . . Sunday night, some of the men sneaked halfway down the hill behind us to a couple of abandoned houses and found water."

By July 17, so few 29th Division riflemen survived that Gerhardt's infantry battalion COs wondered how Uncle Charlie could expect them to take St. Lô. The 3rd Battalion of the 115th Infantry was down to 177 men; its authorized strength was almost 900. Company E of the 175th had fifty men and one officer; it was supposed to have 187 men and six officers. One platoon in the 1st Battalion, 115th, started July 17 with eighteen men, when it was supposed to have forty-one. It ended the day with three.

Under normal circumstances these depleted units would not have been expected to keep attacking. Just holding the ground they occupied was difficult enough. If a fresh German *Kampfgruppe* showed up from Brittany and launched a major counterattack, the 29ers would not stand a chance.

But these were not normal circumstances. Gerhardt knew from intelligence reports that no massed panzers waited outside St. Lô to blitz the 29th Division. Moreover, the general took several looks at the dazed prisoners the 29ers had captured and concluded that the enemy troops were in worse condition than were the Yanks. Gerhardt brushed aside his subordinates' concerns that the division was too weak to attack. He declared, "The best defense I know of is to attack."

And attack he did. He ordered all nine of his rifle battalions to take the offensive on July 17, leaving no reserves. Said Gerhardt, "This is a critical time. We're going to throw the book at them."

Maj. Tom Howie, who had assumed command of the 3rd Battalion of the 116th on July 13, had the most important mission of the day. Howie, formerly the S-3 of the 116th, was not the type of man who thrived under Gerhardt's tutelage. The major was mild-mannered and kind. Before the war he had been a teacher of English Literature and football coach at Virginia's Staunton Military Academy. Gerhardt gruffly ordered him to attack toward La Madeleine, join Bingham's men, and press on to St. Lô. The 3rd Battalion, with only 420 men, was below half-strength, but it was probably the strongest rifle battalion in the division. "If the 116th makes this, they get a six-day rest," Gerhardt promised.

Only four days after the actual event, Colonel Dwyer described Howie's assault to an army historian. "The attack of the 3rd Battalion was not considered a means of carrying supplies to Bingham," he said. "It was intended to reinforce Bingham's battalion and then, together, the two battalions would advance west on St. Lô. Howie was given no orders to clean out the resistance between his line of departure and Bingham's battalion, as the 115th on the right and the 175th on the left were understood to be attacking that day. . . . It was felt that the pressure of these two attacks . . . would force the enemy to withdraw his troops on the nose and flanks of the Martinville Ridge. Consequently, Major Howie made it very clear to his men that their mission was above all to get to their objective. Only two men in each platoon were permit-

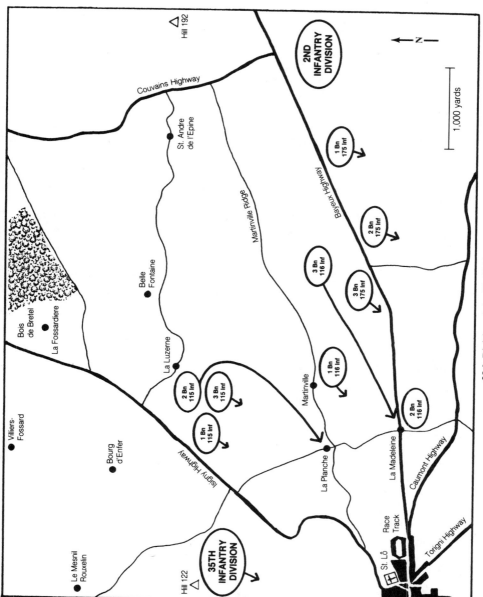

29th Division, July 17, 1944.

ted to fire, and then only in the event of an emergency. The others were to rely on their bayonets and hand grenades.''

The first part of the attack worked perfectly. The 3rd Battalion jumped off just before sunrise and penetrated the German lines silently and swiftly. Some participants recalled this as the only time in the war they ever used their bayonets. Howie's battalion reached La Madeleine just as the sun was rising. Bingham's men, dug in on either side of the highway leading into St. Lô, shouted greetings and asked for food. Howie's men gladly shared any rations they had.

Dwyer radioed Howie at 7:30 A.M. and ordered both battalions to move into St. Lô. ''Will do,'' Howie responded.

''We had just finished meeting the company COs to wind up our attack plans,'' Capt. William Puntenney, Howie's executive, recalled. ''They had been dismissed and before they could get back to their companies, the Germans began dropping a mortar barrage around our ears. Before taking cover in one of the two foxholes we were using, Major Howie turned to take a last look to be sure all his men had their heads down. Without warning, one of the shells hit a few yards away. A fragment struck the major in the back and apparently pierced his lung. 'My God, I'm hit,' he murmured, and I saw he was bleeding at the mouth. As he fell, I caught him. I called a medic, but nothing could be done. He was dead in two minutes.'' Howie had held command of the battalion for only four days.

The Germans were down but not out. Their doctrine demanded an immediate counterattack at La Madeleine, and that was precisely what they did. For the moment, Gerhardt's plan to push into St. Lô was abandoned as the G.I.'s of the 2nd and 3rd Battalions dodged enemy mortar rounds and fought off desperate *Fallschirmjäger*.

That evening, the Stonewallers radioed for help when they heard the ominous rumbling of German tanks just behind the enemy front. Division headquarters called back and ordered the riflemen to mark their positions with red panels so the front could be seen from the air. An hour later, American aircraft from the 506th Fighter-Bomber Squadron buzzed over the lines. At first, the pilots had trouble spotting the panels, but when they found them, they blasted the road between La Madeleine and St. Lô with every weapon they had.

The air attack restored the Stonewallers' spirits. The enemy counterattack was crushed before it started, and Bingham's men reported that several Germans ran into the American lines to give themselves up rather than facing the deluge of bombs. It was the first time the air force had cooperated so smoothly with the 29th Division.

The Stonewallers suspected that the last mile into St. Lô would be the hardest. At noon on July 17, however, Gerhardt suddenly had a brainstorm. The general figured that if the Germans were committing all their resources to the eastern periphery of St. Lô to hold off the 116th, the approach to the city from the northeast, in the 115th Infantry's sector, would probably be only lightly defended, especially now that Hill 122 was in American hands.

He changed his plans on the spot. Gerhardt called Ordway and directed him to send the 2nd Battalion of the 115th on an end run around the 115th's left flank. The objective was the hamlet of La Planche, 1,000 yards north of La Madeleine. This tiny village lay astride a road that led straight into St. Lô from the northeast, and Gerhardt hoped the 2nd Battalion could steal into the city using this route. "Don't let anybody take any reports seriously about enemy troops in there [La Planche]," Gerhardt told Ordway. "If you find any, run over them! Maneuver between your left flank and the 116th's right to envelop that objective."

The 2nd Battalion, however, made slow progress, and an angry Gerhardt goaded Ordway to drive his men harder. "Don't feel enthused, but Howie has some people on Objective S [La Madeleine]," Gerhardt snapped. "Now do something about it. Are you going to let the others pull you forward?"

The general got even more worked up that afternoon. "I just talked to the corps commander, and the key to this thing is your 2nd Battalion," the general told Maj. Al Warfield, Ordway's S-3. "Expend the whole battalion if necessary, but it's got to get there."

The battalion got there, but not until 2:30 A.M. on July 18. Gerhardt was miffed. "That battalion has just fooled around!" he roared. The problem was the 115th's commander. Riflemen were not the only soldiers who suffered from combat exhaustion. Ordway, a brainy staff officer who had performed brilliantly as Gerhardt's chief of staff, had shown symptoms of battle fatigue shortly after taking command of the 115th in mid-June.

Once during the current St. Lô offensive, General Cota had visited 115th headquarters, which was being shelled intermittently, to check the regiment's progress. Cota could not find Ordway. "Who's running this war?" Cota exclaimed.

"I guess we are, sir," replied Major Warfield, the S-3, indicating himself and Lieutenant Colonel Cooper of the 110th Field Artillery. The two officers were studying the regiment's situation maps, and the command post's telephones and radios were nearby.

"Where's the colonel?" Cota demanded. Warfield pointed to a nearby slit trench covered with logs, where Ordway was taking cover. Cota stalked over and yelled for Ordway to come out and get back to his job. But the colonel would not move until the shelling stopped, even when Cota issued a direct order for him to get out. Cota gave up. As he departed, he yelled over to Warfield and Cooper to remain in charge for the time being.

The failure to reach La Planche in a timely fashion was the last straw. "The corps commander is putting heat on me to get our objective, and I'm

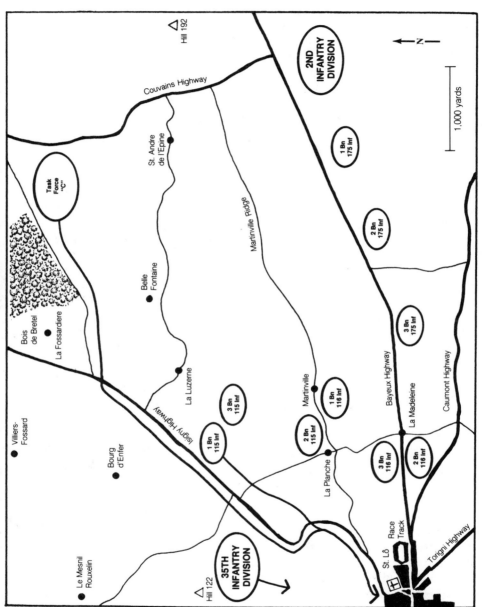

29th Division, July 18, 1944.

going to have to relieve you," Gerhardt told Ordway on the morning of July 18. "You did your best. Ednie [Col. Alfred Ednie] is coming down this morning to take over."

"I'll take the order just as I've taken the rest of your orders, sir," Ordway replied.

Gerhardt wanted to enter St. Lô with a bang, not a whimper. In preparation for the big event, the general formed a special all-motorized task force on July 17 and held it in reserve near Couvains, waiting for an opportune moment to send it smashing into the city. The task force, a strange hodgepodge of almost a dozen platoon and company-size outfits, was centered around the 29th Recon Troop, five Shermans from the 747th Tank Battalion, and twelve M10 tank destroyers from the 821st Tank Destroyer Battalion. Gerhardt named it "Task Force C," after its leader, General Cota. "This [Task Force C] may be the key to the whole business," Gerhardt declared.

Gerhardt suspected that something was afoot in the enemy camp when several unusually optimistic 29th Division progress reports filtered back to the war room on the morning of July 18. The 1st Battalion of the 115th, the westernmost unit in the Division's line, reported proudly that in the first hour of its attack it had met only light opposition and advanced 800 yards. This was more ground than the battalion had gained in the past two days. Major Johns, the battalion CO, was fearful that his men might be walking into a trap, but in the next hour they moved forward another 800 yards, and still hardly a shot had been fired.

When Colonel Ednie, the 115th's new CO, heard of the 1st Battalion's remarkable progress, he radioed Gerhardt. "I believe this is the time to alert that task force," he said. "We're continuing the advance directly into the city."

Gerhardt agreed. "I think you'd better get moving," he told Cota. Uncle Charlie ordered Task Force C to move into the city from the northeast by the St. Lô-Isigny highway. Gerhardt also directed Johns' 1st Battalion to support the task force by following in Cota's wake. The moment everyone had waited for had finally come. "Let's go to St. Lô!" Johns jubilantly told his staff.

Due to the peculiarities of the terrain in the 29th Division's sector, the 29ers could see little of St. Lô except the two massive spires of Notre-Dame Cathedral. Of course, no one expected St. Lô to be Paris, and most 29ers knew St. Lô had been heavily bombed. But the men of Task Force C and the 1st Battalion of the 115th were shocked when they came over the brow of a hill 1,000 yards outside the city. The center of the city was a lifeless pile of rubble. Few houses had been spared; roads and sidewalks could scarcely be distinguished. The 29ers shook their heads and wondered why such effort had been expended in its liberation.

Even St. Lô's pre-war population of 12,000 would hardly have qualified it as a city by the standards of the 29ers. If its population did not impress the

G.I.'s in St. Lô, near "Le Carrefour de la Bascule." *Courtesy Military History Institute.*

average American soldier, its age did. St. Lô had been founded at least 1,000 years earlier than any city in the United States. The town, originally known as Briovère, was rechristened St. Lô after its most prestigious resident—a sixth century bishop by the name of Lauto, or Lô—achieved sainthood. Over the years, St. Lô had been sacked by Vikings, Plantagenet English kings, and, during the Reformation, by reactionary French Catholics. None of those sad episodes, however, compared to the city's devastation in 1944. After the war, the French nicknamed St. Lô the "Capital of Ruins."

Led by the 29th Recon Troop's jeeps and armored cars, Task Force C roared into St. Lô. Sensing that the enemy was on the run, the 29ers advanced with all the élan of an old-fashioned cavalry charge. The first obstacle was an enemy strongpoint in a cemetery on the northern fringe of town. A skirmish erupted here, resulting in an unearthly cacophony, a mixture of the slow rat-tat-tat of the armored cars' .50 caliber machine guns, the roar of the tanks' 75mm guns, and the sharp, intermittent cracks of dozens of M1s. For once, the Yanks had overwhelming fire superiority.

"The Germans were dropping all over," recalled Lt. Edward G. Jones, Jr., the CO of the Recon Troop. "But we were still in a very, very hot spot. It seemed as if everyone in this part of the country was shooting at us."

The battle at the graveyard caused Task Force C to bunch up, and the head of the column turned into a jumble of jeeps, armored cars, and tanks. Meanwhile, the Germans had pulled out of the cemetery and had fallen back to a narrow street that led into the city. German snipers had holed up in the modest two and three-story stone buildings that lined the street and were firing from the windows.

A Sherman fired several rounds from its main gun in reply, and each booming shell produced a cascade of dust and debris. Jones sorted out the traffic jam at the cemetery and waved the Recon Troop's armored cars forward again. The 29ers knew that nothing could stop them now, and they exulted like Wild West cowboys, blazing away with their rifles and machine guns at any building that might harbor a German hide-out.

This section of town had miraculously escaped the pounding of Allied bombers. The buildings for the most part were intact, but abandoned. Fifty yards past the cemetery, the 29ers could make out a gray building with the words "Café-Restaurant" prominently displayed across the facade. Just past the café, Jones's armored cars sped into a crossroads, where five separate thoroughfares joined to form St. Lô's main street, the Rue du Neufbourg. The French called the junction *Le Carrefour de la Bascule*—"Weigh Station Crossroads." When the 29ers looked west down the Rue du Neufbourg, they could see the devastated town center and the ruins of the Notre-Dame Cathedral less than a half-mile away.

In the past the enemy had always counterattacked promptly after suffering a setback. Expecting them to do so again, Jones hastily formulated a plan to defend St. Lô and dispersed his men and vehicles to key objectives

Aerial photo of St. Lô, July 1944. *Courtesy Military History Institute.*

29th Division, Entry into St. Lô, July 18, 1944.

throughout the city. In several areas German troops attempted to make a stand, but they were flushed out by the wrathful 29ers.

That afternoon, Jones himself saw four Germans sneaking out of a house in an alley. "They looked in my direction, but for some unaccountable reason they did not see the armored car," Jones recalled. "I slowly swung my ring-mounted .50 Cal into line with them. I overlooked throwing the locking lever when I pressed the butterfly trigger and the recoil force pulled the weapon up and to the right. I shot up the entire side of the building and did not hit one German. I believe, though, that I must have scared them to death."

Cota entered St. Lô close behind the head of the column. Seeing Jones, he walked over to discuss the situation. As the two men talked, Cota was hit in the arm by a piece of shrapnel. "I can remember the blood running from his sleeve and dripping off his fingers," Jones noted. "It was not a bad wound, but he just stood there talking; it didn't bother him in the least." A medic patched up the arm, put it in a sling, and Cota went on with his work. But the wound was worse than anyone thought. Cota had to be evacuated that evening and spent more than a week in the hospital.

The infantrymen of the 1st Battalion, 115th, entered St. Lô on the heels of Task Force C. Maj. Johns had conceived a plan to clear the city, so he was incensed when his new CO, Colonel Ednie, dispersed Company C all over town with little regard to squad integrity and no capability to communicate with 1st Battalion headquarters. Expecting a German armored counterattack, Ednie wanted Johns's men to cover Task Force C's tanks.

Ednie soon departed St. Lô, much to Johns's relief, and 1st Battalion headquarters was set up in the café at the Bascule crossroads. Johns still had two intact rifle companies, A and B. He sent Company A to clear the western half of the city and Company B to clear the eastern half.

Back at division headquarters, Gerhardt assigned his chief of staff, Col. Edward McDaniel, the special mission of raising the blue and gray 29th Division flag in St. Lô. When McDaniel arrived in town, he chose to place the colors on a side wall of the café housing 1st Battalion headquarters, in full view of the Germans on the heights to the south. Sgt. Gerald Davis and PFC Francis Bein of the 115th strung up the flag while an army cameraman filmed the scene.

Capt. Robert Minor, S-2 of Task Force C, was interrogating enemy prisoners near the café when German shelling began. "I had just started to talk to a captured German when we came under 88 fire from the high ground outside the city," Minor recalled. "The rounds were bursting in the trees overhead, showering fragments. We all hit the ground, the prisoner as well as I, and fearing that he might try to run, I pulled my pistol. I'm sure the poor guy thought I was going to shoot him then and there."

The Germans barraged the city mercilessly. Enemy observers may have been provoked by the blue and gray flag hanging from the café, for the Bas-

The "Famille Blanchet" Mausoleum, near "Le Carrefour de la Bascule," the site of the headquarters of the 1st Battalion, 115th Infantry on July 18, 1944. Note the radios lying on the steps and the telephone wires leading inside to the crypt. *Courtesy National Archives.*

cule crossroads received the heaviest fire. The 29ers promptly gave the place a nickname: "Mortar Corner."

The barrage was so intense that Johns later moved his command post from the café to the "Famille Blanchet" mausoleum in the nearby cemetery. This ornate tomb had a subterranean crypt that was nearly shellproof. The crypt had a large sarcophagus which the staff used as a table for maps and a telephone switchboard.

Maj. Donovan Yeuell, the executive of the 110th Field Artillery, was visiting this headquarters when a furious German bombardment descended. "It became increasingly difficult for me to dispose of the juice from the tobacco I was chewing," Yeuell remembered. "There being only one small slit of a window in the structure, I posted myself nearby for the purpose of eliminating said juice, but within a few minutes, pieces of shell fragments started working their way in or near that slit, making my position untenable. . . . I was required to swallow the remains. . . . The ungodly effect of this indiscreet but necessary act was to inject into me a new boldness, which forced me out of the mausoleum willy-nilly, into our jeep and back like the wind to the battalion command post where my mistreated stomach could be soothed by a less violent poison."

Actually, it was the 29th Division artillery that held St. Lô. There were not nearly enough foot soldiers in the city to resist a determined German counterattack. Liaison officers and forward observers from the 110th and 227th Field Artillery Battalions had rushed into the city behind Task Force C, followed closely by teams of wiremen and their creaking reels of telephone cable. Within a few hours of St. Lô's capture, the city streets were strewn with wire, and the forward observers were able to pass the infantrymen's frequent requests for fire support back to the artillery. Several enemy counterattacks south of the city were broken up by howitzer fire.

Short of ammunition, the cannoneers were strictly limited in the number of rounds they could expend each day. But when Gen. Sands, the 29th's

A file of 29ers entering St. Lô. Two dead Germans are visible on the roadside. *Courtesy Military History Institute.*

Sgt. Peter Siekierski, wire chief of the 110th Field Artillery, inspecting damage in St. Lô, July 18. The man in the background is Cpl. Mike Jacobs, a wireman. Telephone cable is visible near Siekierski's left hand. A tower of the St. Lô Cathedral can be seen in the upper left. The 29ers used the spire as an observation post during the battle. *Courtesy Cooper Armory.*

artillery chief, visited a forward observation post south of St. Lô and witnessed several threatening enemy troop concentrations, he directed the artillerymen to fire whenever necessary. He would find a way to get more ammunition.

For a change, good observation posts were easy to find. The most inviting posts were the two 255-foot spires of Notre-Dame Cathedral. Lieutenant Colonel Cooper and Capt. Eli Gifford, a member of Sands's staff, climbed an ancient spiral stairway to the top of one of the towers to observe the view. Since the last section of stairs had been demolished by a bomb, Gifford got to the top by grabbing a rope and going hand over hand like a mountain climber. The panorama from the top was spectacular, and every German move south of St. Lô was detectable.

After descending, Cooper and Gifford located a forward observer team from the 227th Field Artillery and ordered it to set up an observation post atop the spire. Before the wiremen and radio operators could remove their equipment from a nearby jeep, however, the tower began to crack and groan, and a minute later it crashed to earth in a volcanic eruption of dust.

The artillerymen were unperturbed. They promptly set up an observation post atop the other tower and used it until relieved by the 35th Division on July 20. "Each time an enemy round whistled by and exploded a few feet from the base, the steeple trembled like a frail reed in a gust of wind," Cooper recalled.

The reason for the relative ease with which the 29th Division took St. Lô was obscured at the time. Unknown to the 29ers, the commander of the German 7th Army, Gen. Paul Hausser, had decided the night before Task Force C moved into St. Lô that the 352nd and 3rd FJ Divisions were too weak to hold the city any longer. He therefore ordered Kraiss and Schimpf to withdraw their men southward on July 18. He also directed them to leave strong delaying forces behind to hold off the Americans as long as possible, since German troops north of St. Lô would need a full day to disengage and retreat through the city. Unfortunately for Hausser, the delaying forces did not hold back the 29ers very long.

St. Lô's devastation was nearly complete. "Few towns in all of Europe suffered such destruction," wrote Lou Azrael, a reporter for the Baltimore *News-Post.* "One of the war's most touching scenes, to me, came several days later when, as we traveled through the rubble on the way to the next battleground, I saw an old woman and a child, standing amid the ruins, throwing flowers to the troops who wrecked their home and town—and liberated it from the Germans."

At division headquarters, Gerhardt was ready to tell the world of the 29th Division's triumph. At 6:30 P.M. on July 18, he sent a message to Corlett. "I have the honor to announce to the corps commander that Task Force C of the

29th Infantry Division has secured the city of St. Lô after forty-two [actually forty-three] days of continuous combat from Omaha Beach to St. Lô.''

Corlett called to congratulate Gerhardt. He joked that NBC had beaten Gerhardt to the story. A reporter had already announced the fall of St. Lô over the radio that afternoon.

Gerhardt had one more thing on his mind. Just before Task Force C assaulted St. Lô, the general approached Captain Minor in the division War Room. ''Where's Tom Howie?'' Gerhardt asked.

''Sir, he's dead,'' Minor replied.

''Damn it, I know that,'' the general snapped. ''Where's his body? I want you to take his body into St. Lô.''

At heart an emotional man, Gerhardt wanted to close the campaign by honoring a soldier who symbolized the sacrifice and ultimate triumph of the 29th Division. To Gerhardt, Tom Howie was that symbol.

Minor contacted the 104th Medical Battalion and arranged for a jeep-ambulance to take the body into St. Lô at dusk on July 18. Throughout the night, Howie's body remained on the jeep, covered only by an olive drab army blanket. The next morning, the 29ers draped the body with the Stars and Stripes and hoisted it on top of a huge pile of stones that had once been a wall of Sainte Croix Church, one block west of the cemetery.

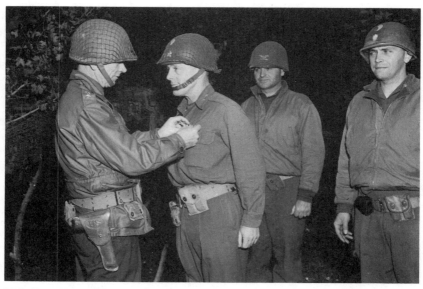

Maj. Gen. Charles "Pete" Corlett, commander of XIX Corps, decorates Major General Gerhardt shortly after the liberation of St. Lô. The officer on the right is Lt. Col. William Witte, G-3 of the 29th Division. The other officer behind Gerhardt is Col. Edward McDaniel, Chief of Staff of the 29th Division. *Courtesy National Archives.*

The first "cafey" to open in St. Lô after liberation. Wartime censors have blocked out the 29th Division patch on the left shoulders of three men. *Courtesy Military History Institute.*

The body remained on display throughout July 19, The 29ers and some of the few civilians remaining in the city adorned the site with flowers. "It was simple and direct, no fanfare or otherwise. It was a little too dangerous to do anything else," Lt. Jones of the Recon Troop recollected.

The story caught the fancy of the American public. It even inspired a poem in *Life* magazine, "Incident at St. Lô," written by Joseph Auslander. Howie's name, however, was withheld from the newspaper stories for two weeks due to censorship restrictions. During that time, the American people knew him only as "The Major of St. Lô."

"Major Howie was the finest gentleman I ever knew," Capt. Cawthon, Bingham's executive, told a reporter six days after Howie's death. "I would like to have you talk to some of his Stonewall buddies so you really can understand the fine type of man he was. But there are not many of them left."

4. THE DEAD

Uncle Charlie kept his promise. By the afternoon of July 20, the 35th Division had taken over the 29th's sector in and around St. Lô, and the exhausted 29ers trudged back to their old battlefield at St. Clair-sur-l'Elle for an eight-day rest. No rifle battalion in the division could muster more men than a full-strength company.

On July 23, the 29th Division Cemetery was dedicated at La Cambe, five miles southwest of Omaha Beach. The graveyard was already crowded with white crosses and a few Stars of David. Most of the division's 2,000 dead were buried there, and many of the graves had not yet been filled with earth. A crude rectangular signpost topped with the division's blue and gray symbol marked the entrance to the cemetery. The signpost read, "This cemetery was established on 11 June 1944 by the 29th Infantry Division, United States Army, as a final resting place for officers and men of that Division who made the supreme sacrifice on the battlefields of Normandy. . . . In command of this valiant legion of the Blue and Gray is Lt. Col. William T. Terry, Infantry, who was killed in action 17 July 1944." Terry, commanding the 1st Battalion of the 175th, was the highest-ranking 29er to lose his life since D-Day. His name had been inserted on the sign only in the past two or three days; the paint was still fresh.

Gerhardt had made certain that the cemetery site would be immaculate. The grass had been freshly cut and edged; the whitewashed wooden crosses, in perfect alignment, glistened in the sun. Several representatives from every outfit in the division formed up to the mournful music of the ninety-piece 29th Division band.

The cemetery was filled with colorful flags: the Stars and Stripes, the blue and gray divisional flag, regimental and battalion colors, and dozens of little fork-tailed company and battery guidons, blue for the infantry, red for the artillery.

The day was hot, the air was still. The battle flags hung limply from their staffs. The ceremony began with a hymn and was followed by an invocation by Maj. Harold Donovan, the division chaplain. Then Gerhardt said a few simple words: "Some of the men buried here were my personal friends. All of them, whether they believed in Christ, or Jehovah, or Allah, regardless of their creed, all of them are in the hands of a supreme being."

The roll call of the dead was moving. As each name was called, a comrade answered "Present," and the guidon belonging to the dead man's outfit was dipped. Afterward, Colonel McDaniel ordered "Present Arms," and the battle flags dropped in unison.

Gerhardt knew a lot of fighting lay ahead in this war, and he wanted to end the ceremony on a cheery and confident note. After "Taps" and "The Star Spangled Banner," Uncle Charlie stepped up to the podium. He wanted to say only one more thing, but he wanted the 29ers to join him in saying it. For a moment, thousands of voices were one: "Twenty-Nine, Let's Go!"

Then the 29ers marched away to the beat of a quickstep, the "Beer Barrel Polka."

APPENDIX

US AND GERMAN TABLES OF ORGANIZATION AND EQUIPMENT
June 1944

Organizational charts of the 29th Division, the German 352nd Division and the 3rd *Fallschirmjäger* Division—and all major subordinate units of these divisions—are included in this section. Organizationally, the 29th Division was identical to all US Army infantry divisions; the 352nd Division was typical of a German "Type 1944" infantry division, of which there were about a dozen in France and the Low Countries in June 1944. The 3rd *Fallschirmjäger* was the only fully formed German parachute division in northwest Europe at the time of the invasion. *Note:* The 352nd Division chart does not include the 726th Infantry Regiment, which was temporarily attached to the 352nd from the 716th *Bodenständige* (static defense) Division on D-Day.

The division-level organizations of the 29th, 352nd, and 3rd FJ Divisions are illustrated in the first three charts. Succeeding charts portray the organizations of most of the divisions' major subordinate units, following the chain of command downward from infantry regiments of 3,100 men, to battalions of about 900, to rifle squads of only a dozen or so troops. For the most part, only infantry organizations are provided, but the last two charts show the organization of the 29th and 352nd light (105mm) artillery battalions.

The information in the charts was drawn from the official US Army Tables of Organization and Equipment (TO&E) listed in section 2 of the Bibliography. All abbreviations used in the charts are explained at the end of the Appendix.

29th INFANTRY DIVISION (US)
Maj. Gen. Charles H. Gerhardt

UNIT	MAN	(OFF)	RIF	SMG	BAR	LMG	HMG	50C	60M	81M	BAZ	57A	105H	155H	VEH
29 Div HQ	154	(40)	125	—	—	—	—	—	—	—	—	—	—	—	—
Spec Troops HQ	9	(2)	8	—	—	—	—	—	—	—	—	—	—	—	5
29 Div HQ Co	107	(4)	94	—	—	—	—	3	—	—	6	—	—	—	35
29 MP Plt	71	(3)	70	—	—	—	—	—	—	—	—	3	—	—	18
729 Ord Co	147	(9)	133	12	—	—	—	5	—	—	5	—	—	—	42
29 QM Co	186	(10)	184	—	—	—	—	13	—	—	5	—	—	—	109
29 Sig Co	250	(9)	213	35	—	—	—	6	—	—	6	—	—	—	74
115 Inf Rgt	3119	(140)	2745	—	81	18	24	35	27	18	112	18	6	—	334
116 Inf Rgt	3119	(140)	2745	—	81	18	24	35	27	18	112	18	6	—	334
175 Inf Rgt	3119	(140)	2745	—	81	18	24	35	27	18	112	18	6	—	334
29 Div Art HQ	117	(5)	88	—	—	—	—	5	—	—	6	—	—	—	32
110 Fld Art Bn	509	(30)	428	—	—	—	—	21	—	—	40	—	12	—	124
111 Fld Art Bn	509	(30)	428	—	—	—	—	21	—	—	40	—	12	—	124
224 Fld Art Bn	509	(30)	428	—	—	—	—	21	—	—	40	—	12	—	124
227 Fld Art Bn	527	(28)	459	—	—	—	—	21	—	—	40	—	—	12	123
29 Cav Rcn Trp	155	(6)	125	30	—	13	—	3	9	—	5	—	—	—	48
121 Eng Bn	649	(27)	630	16	—	—	18	12	—	—	29	—	—	—	136
104 Med Bn	460	(34)	—	—	—	—	—	—	—	—	—	—	—	—	90
Atch Med Prsn	494	(37)	—	—	—	—	—	—	—	—	—	—	—	—	—
Chaplains	13	(13)	—	—	—	—	—	—	—	—	—	—	—	—	—
Band	58	(0)	58	—	—	—	—	—	—	—	—	—	—	—	—
TOTAL	14281	(747)	11706	93	243	67	90	236	90	54	558	57	54	12	2076

352nd INFANTRY DIVISION (GERMAN)
Generalleutnant Dietrich Kraiss

UNIT	MAN	(OFF)	RIF	SMG	LMG	HMG	AAA	81M	120M	BAZ	75A	75H	105H	150H	VEH
352 Div HQ	227	(34)	121	12	5	—	—	—	—	—	—	—	—	—	32
352 Fus Bn	708	(15)	477	127	43	12	—	6	4	—	—	—	—	—	8
352 Sig Bn	379	(16)	326	35	11	—	—	—	—	—	—	—	—	—	76
914 Inf Rgt	2008	(48)	1373	332	107	24	—	12	8	36	3	6	—	2	45
915 Inf Rgt	2008	(48)	1373	332	107	24	—	12	8	36	3	6	—	2	45
916 Inf Rgt	2008	(48)	1373	332	107	24	—	12	8	36	3	6	—	2	45
1352 Art Rgt HQ	110	(9)	81	13	1	—	—	—	—	—	—	—	—	—	5
1 Btn 1352 Art	552	(19)	460	38	17	—	—	—	—	—	—	—	11	—	7
2 Btn 1352 Art	552	(19)	460	38	17	—	—	—	—	—	—	—	11	—	7
3 Btn 1352 Art	552	(19)	460	38	17	—	—	—	—	—	—	—	11	—	7
4 Btn 1352 Art	685	(19)	604	37	17	—	—	—	—	—	—	—	—	9	4
352 AT Bn	484	(17)	318	81	29	—	12	—	—	—	26	—	—	—	113
352 Eng Bn	620	(18)	432	71	31	6	—	6	—	—	—	—	—	—	17
Div Services	1459	(58)	1181	17	57	—	—	—	—	—	—	—	—	—	204
352 Ersatz Bn	675	(18)	500	89	50	12	1	6	4	—	1	1	1	—	3
TOTAL	13027	(405)	9569	1592	616	102	13	54	32	108	36	19	34	15	618

3rd PARACHUTE DIVISION (GERMAN)
Generalleutnant Richard Schimpf

UNIT	MAN	RIF	SMG	LMG	HMG	AAA	81M	120M	BAZ	75A	75H	105H	150H	VEH
3 Para Div HQ	194	102	7	2	—	—	—	—	6	—	—	—	—	27
3 Para Rcn Co	200	89	84	8	2	—	2	—	4	—	2	—	—	10
3 Para Sig Bn	379	326	35	11	—	—	—	—	—	—	—	—	—	83
5 Para Rgt	3206	1651	751	224	24	—	39	9	54	3	6	—	—	304
8 Para Rgt	3206	1651	751	224	24	—	39	9	54	3	6	—	—	304
9 Para Rgt	3206	1651	751	224	24	—	39	9	54	3	6	—	—	304
3 Para Art Rgt	1571	1250	168	53	—	9	—	—	12	—	—	24	12	396
3 Para Flak Bn	824	729	47	22	—	30*	—	—	12	—	—	—	—	181
3 Para Mort Bn	594	290	258	42	—	—	—	36	6	—	—	—	—	123
3 Para AT Bn	484	318	81	29	—	12	—	—	36	26	—	—	—	113
3 Para Eng Bn	620	432	71	31	6	—	6	—	—	—	—	—	—	43
Div Services	1492	1200	22	60	—	—	—	—	—	—	—	—	—	253
TOTAL	15976	9689	3026	930	80	51	125	63	250	35	20	24	12	2141

*Includes 12 88mm dual-purpose flak/antitank guns.

Note: The 3rd Parachute Division was not completely organized when it was transferred to Normandy in June 1944. The numbers above are authorized strengths; in reality, the division was far short of motor vehicles and howitzers.

175th INFANTRY REGIMENT (US), 29th DIVISION
Col. Paul R. Goode

UNIT	MAN	(OFF)	RIF	BAR	LMG	HMG	50C	60M	81M	BAZ	57A	105H	VEH
Headquarters	8	(8)	4	—	—	—	—	—	—	—	—	—	—
Headquarters Co	100	(4)	100	—	—	—	2	—	—	4	—	—	29
Service Co	115	(11)	114	—	—	—	9	—	—	8	—	—	56
Cannon Co	118	(5)	118	—	—	—	3	—	—	4	—	6	20
Antitank Co	165	(7)	120	—	—	—	3	—	—	9	9	—	22
1st Battalion	871	(35)	763	27	6	8	6	9	6	29	3	—	69
2nd Battalion	871	(35)	763	27	6	8	6	9	6	29	3	—	69
3rd Battalion	871	(35)	763	27	6	8	6	9	6	29	3	—	69
TOTAL	3119	(140)	2745	81	18	24	35	27	18	112	18	6	334

916th INFANTRY REGIMENT (GERMAN), 352nd DIVISION
Oberst Goth

UNIT	MAN	(OFF)	RIF	SMG	LMG	HMG	81M	120M	BAZ	75A	75H	150H	VEH
Headquarters	24	(7)	16	2	—	—	—	—	—	—	—	—	3
Headquarters Co	198	(5)	143	32	10	—	—	—	—	—	—	—	5
1st Battalion	708	(15)	477	127	43	12	6	4	—	—	—	—	8
2nd Battalion	708	(15)	477	127	43	12	6	4	—	—	—	—	8
Howitzer Co	184	(3)	140	27	5	—	—	—	—	—	6	2	8
Antitank Co	186	(3)	120	17	6	—	—	—	36	3	—	—	13
TOTAL	2008	(48)	1373	332	107	24	12	8	36	3	6	2	45

HEADQUARTERS COMPANY, 175th INFANTRY REGIMENT (US), 29th DIVISION
Capt. Henry J. Reed

UNIT	MAN	(OFF)	RIF	50C	BAZ	VEH
Company HQ	26	(2)	26	1	4	8
Communic Plt	49	(1)	49	—	—	14
Intel and Rcn Plt	25	(1)	25	1	—	7
TOTAL	100	(4)	100	2	4	29

HEADQUARTERS COMPANY, 916th INFANTRY REGIMENT (GERMAN), 352nd DIVISION

UNIT	MAN	(OFF)	RIF	SMG	LMG	VEH
Company HQ	8	(1)	3	1	—	—
Signal Plt	32	(1)	23	9	—	—
Engineer Plt	73	(1)	53	13	6	—
Rcn Plt	31	(0)	20	7	3	—
Supply Train	54	(2)	44	2	1	5
TOTAL	198	(5)	143	32	10	5

Note: The engineer and reconnaissance platoons were usually combined into a *Sturmkompanie* (assault company).

2nd BATTALION, 175th INFANTRY (US), 29th DIVISION
Lt. Col. Millard G. Bowen

UNIT	MAN	(OFF)	RIF	BAR	LMG	HMG	50C	60M	81M	BAZ	57A	VEH
Headquarters	4	(4)	2	—	—	—	—	—	—	—	—	—
Headquarters Co	122	(5)	107	—	—	—	2	—	—	8	3	23
Company E	193	(6)	174	9	2	—	1	3	—	5	—	4
Company F	193	(6)	174	9	2	—	1	3	—	5	—	4
Company G	193	(6)	174	9	2	—	1	3	—	5	—	4
Company H	166	(8)	132	—	—	8	1	—	6	6	—	34
TOTAL	871	(35)	763	27	6	8	6	9	6	29	3	69

2nd BATTALION, 916th INFANTRY REGIMENT (GERMAN), 352nd DIVISION

UNIT	MAN	(OFF)	RIF	SMG	LMG	HMG	81M	120M	VEH
Headquarters	77	(6)	58	14	1	—	—	—	1
5th Company	142	(2)	96	28	13	2	—	—	—
6th Company	142	(2)	96	28	13	2	—	—	—
7th Company	142	(2)	96	28	13	2	—	—	—
8th Company	205	(3)	131	29	3	6	6	4	7
TOTAL	708	(15)	477	127	43	12	6	4	8

COMPANY F, 175th INFANTRY (US), 29th DIVISION
Capt. Robert M. Miller

UNIT	MAN	(OFF)	RIF	BAR	LMG	50C	60M	BAZ	VEH
Company HQ	35	(2)	35	—	—	—	—	5	—
1st Platoon	41	(1)	38	3	—	—	—	—	—
2nd Platoon	41	(1)	38	3	—	—	—	—	—
3rd Platoon	41	(1)	38	3	—	—	—	—	—
Weapons Plt HQ	6	(1)	6	—	—	1	—	—	4
Mortar Sec	17	(0)	11	—	—	—	3	—	—
Machine Gun Sec	12	(0)	8	—	2	—	—	—	—
TOTAL	193	(6)	174	9	2	1	3	5	4

Note: The weapons platoon consisted of platoon headquarters, the mortar section, and the machine gun section.

5th COMPANY, 916th INFANTRY REGIMENT (GERMAN), 352nd DIVISION

UNIT	MAN	(OFF)	RIF	SMG	LMG	HMG
Company HQ	12	(1)	8	3	—	—
1st Platoon	33	(1)	22	7	4	—
2nd Platoon	33	(0)	22	7	4	—
3rd Platoon	33	(0)	22	7	4	—
Machine Gun Sec	18	(0)	11	3	—	2
Supply Train	13	(0)	11	1	1	—
TOTAL	142	(2)	96	28	13	2

1st COMPANY, 9th PARACHUTE REGIMENT (GERMAN), 3rd FALLSCHIRMJÄGER DIVISION

UNIT	MAN	(OFF)	RIF	SMG	LMG	81M	VEH
Company HQ	36	(1)	11	14	—	3	3
1st Platoon	39	(1)	16	9	6	—	2
2nd Platoon	39	(1)	16	9	6	—	2
3rd Platoon	39	(1)	16	9	6	—	2
Supply Train	17	(0)	13	2	2	—	6
TOTAL	170	(4)	72	43	20	3	15

COMPANY H (HEAVY WEAPONS), 175th INFANTRY (US), 29th DIVISION
Capt. Edward Wolff

UNIT	MAN	(OFF)	RIF	HMG	50C	81M	BAZ	VEH
Company HQ	34	(2)	34	—	1	—	—	3
1st Mch Gun Plt	36	(1)	28	4	—	—	2	9
2nd Mch Gun Plt	36	(1)	28	4	—	—	2	9
Mortar Plt	60	(4)	42	—	—	6	2	13
TOTAL	166	(8)	132	8	1	6	6	34

8th (HEAVY WEAPONS) COMPANY, 916th INFANTRY REGIMENT (GERMAN), 352nd DIVISION

UNIT	MAN	(OFF)	RIF	SMG	LMG	HMG	81M	120M	VEH
Company HQ	20	(1)	15	4	—	—	—	—	—
Machine Gun Plt	55	(1)	31	10	—	6	—	—	—
Light Mortar Plt	66	(0)	37	6	—	—	6	—	—
Hvy Mortar Plt	47	(1)	36	7	2	—	—	4	7
Supply Train	17	(0)	12	2	1	—	—	—	—
TOTAL	205	(3)	131	29	3	6	6	4	7

3rd PLATOON, COMPANY F, 175th INFANTRY (US), 29th DIVISION
1st Lt. Frederick Gielle

UNIT	MAN	(OFF)	RIF	BAR
Platoon HQ	5	(1)	5	—
1st Squad	12	(0)	11	1
2nd Squad	12	(0)	11	1
3rd Squad	12	(0)	11	1
TOTAL	41	(1)	38	3

1st PLATOON, 5th COMPANY, 916th INFANTRY REGIMENT (GERMAN), 352nd DIVISION

UNIT	MAN	(OFF)	RIF	SMG	LMG
Platoon HQ	6	(1)	4	1	1
1st Squad	9	(0)	6	2	1
2nd Squad	9	(0)	6	2	1
3rd Squad	9	(0)	6	2	1
TOTAL	33	(1)	22	7	4

1st PLATOON, 1st COMPANY, 9th PARACHUTE REGIMENT (GERMAN), 3rd FALLSCHIRMJÄGER DIVISION

UNIT	MAN	(OFF)	RIF	SMG	LMG
Platoon HQ	3	(1)	1	—	—
1st Squad	12	(0)	5	3	2
2nd Squad	12	(0)	5	3	2
3rd Squad	12	(0)	5	3	2
TOTAL	39	(1)	16	9	6

1st SQUAD, 1st PLATOON, COMPANY F, 175th INFANTRY (US),
29th DIVISION
Staff Sgt. Lewis Weilgus

ROLE	RANK	MEN	RIF	BAR
Squad Leader	Staff Sgt	1	1	—
Asst Squad Leader	Sgt	1	1	—
Riflemen	Pvt/PFC	7	7	—
Ammo Bearer	Pvt/PFC	1	1	—
Auto Rifleman	Pvt/PFC	1	—	1
Asst Auto Rflman	Pvt/PFC	1	1	—
TOTAL		12	11	1

1st SQUAD, 1st PLATOON, 5th COMPANY, 916th INFANTRY REGIMENT
(GERMAN), 352nd DIVISION

ROLE	RANK	MEN	RIF	SMG	LMG
Squad Leader	Unteroffizier	1	—	1	—
Asst Squad Leader	Obergefreiter	1	—	1	—
Machine Gunner	Gefreiter	1	—	—	1
Asst Mach Gunner	Grenadier	1	1	—	—
Riflemen	Grenadier	5	5	—	—
TOTAL		9	6	2	1

110th FIELD ARTILLERY BATTALION (US), 29th DIVISION
Lt. Col. John P. Cooper

UNIT	MAN	(OFF)	RIF	SMG	50C	BAZ	105H	VEH
HQ, HQ Battery	132	(14)	99	—	5	6	—	36*
Battery A	100	(4)	89	1	4	8	4	19
Battery B	100	(4)	89	1	4	8	4	19
Battery C	100	(4)	89	1	4	8	4	19
Service Battery	77	(4)	62	—	4	10	—	31
TOTAL	509	(30)	428	3	21	40	12	124

*Includes two Piper Club reconnaissance aircraft.

1st BATTALION, 1352nd ARTILLERY REGIMENT (GERMAN),
352nd DIVISION

UNIT	MAN	(OFF)	RIF	SMG	LMG	105H	VEH
HQ, HQ Battery	147	(10)	118	14	2	—	7
1st Battery	135	(3)	114	8	5	3	—
2nd Battery	135	(3)	114	8	5	3	—
3rd Battery	135	(3)	114	8	5	3	—
TOTAL	552	(19)	460	38	17	9	7

Abbreviations
A: Antitank; AAA: Anti-aircraft artillery (20mm guns unless otherwise noted); ASST: Assistant; ATCH MED PRSN: Attached Medical Personnel; BAR: Browning Automatic Rifle; BAZ: Bazooka (or *Panzerschreck* for Germans); BN: Battalion; CAV RCN TRP: Cavalry Reconnaissance Troop; CO: Company; COMMUNIC: Communications; DIV: Division; ENG: Engineer; FLD ART BN: Field Artillery Battalion; H: Howitzer; HMG: Heavy Machine Gun; HQ: Headquarters; INF: Infantry; INT AND RCN PLT: Intelligence and Reconnaissance Platoon; LMG: Light Machine Gun; M (or MORT): Mortar; MAN: Total Manpower Strength (including officers); MCH GUN PLT: Machine Gun Platoon; MED: Medical; MP: Military Police; OFF: Officers; ORD: Ordnance; PARA: Parachute; PLT: Platoon; QM: Quartermaster: RCN: Reconnaissance; RFLMAN: Rifleman; RGT: Regiment; RIF: Rifles; SEC: Section; SIG: Signal; SMG: Submachine gun; SPEC TRPS: Special Troops; VEH: Motor Vehicles. *Note:* Numbers preceding weapons abbreviations stand for diameter of shell, in millimeters. (Exception: "50C" stands for .50 caliber machine gun.)

Addendum to the Second Edition

Due to space constraints, some headquarters and support units were not listed on the page 16 map showing 29th Division armory locations as of the division's February 1941 mobilization. The omitted units are provided below.

115th Infantry:
HQ Company, 1st Battalion: Easton, Maryland
HQ Company, 2nd Battalion: Laurel, Maryland
HQ Company, 3rd Battalion: Pokomoke City, Maryland
Service Company: Silver Spring, Maryland
Antitank Company: Kensington, Maryland

116th Infantry:
HQ Company, 1st Battalion, Service Company, Antitank Company: Roanoke, Virginia
HQ Company, 2nd Battalion, Alta Vista, Virginia
HQ Company, 3rd Battalion, Winchester, Virginia

176th Infantry (Transferred out of division March 1942):
176th Infantry: Richmond, Virginia, and Petersburg, Virginia, area

111th Field Artillery:
HQ Battery, Battery D: Hampton, Virginia
HQ Battery, 1st Battalion, Battery C: Portsmouth, Virginia
HQ Battery, 2nd Battalion, Battery A, Battery E: Richmond, Virginia
Battery B: Chesapeake, Virginia
Battery F: Fredericksburg, Virginia
Service Battery: Newport News, Virginia

Divisional Units:
29th Signal Company: Norfolk, Virginia
29th Reconnaissance Troop: Berryville, Virginia*

* The Virginia National Guard's Berryville company was mobilized in February 1941 as HQ Company, 88th Brigade. It was reconfigured as the 29th Recon Troop in March 1942.

REFERENCES

Most of the material in this book is based on interviews and correspondence with 29th Division veterans. Twenty-ninth Division official records and relevant unit histories were also extensively consulted. Special mention must be made of the 29th Division "War Room" Journal. This thirty-five-volume collection is a transcript of every word spoken over the radio or telephone in the divisional headquarters tent throughout the war. It was the source for most of General Gerhardt's quotations in the chapters dealing with the Normandy campaign. Contemporary newspapers, particularly the Baltimore *Sun* and the *News-Post*, were also vital sources. Both papers had full-time reporters covering the Division from mobilization to V-E Day. A complete collection of relevant articles is maintained at the Maryland National Guard Museum, Pikesville Military Reservation, in Pikesville, Maryland.

The most important source on the German Army was Lt. Col. Fritz Ziegelmann's post-war report on the 352nd Division. Col. Gerhard Elser of the West German Army was also kind enough to provide his detailed study on both the 352nd Division and the 3rd *Fallschirmjäger* Division.

Unless otherwise specified, the sources for the quotations in this book are the 29th Division veterans themselves or any of the above reference materials. Other sources are noted below.

Chapter 1.
Introduction: Twenty-nine, Let's Go
1. Go Ahead, Twenty-nine
The most important source for the description of Force O's movement from the marshalling ports to Normandy was Morison, *The Invasion of France and Germany*.

"And we all thought, isn't that nice? . . ." is quoted from J. Milnor Roberts oral history interview, US Army Military History Institute (USAMHI), Carlisle, PA.

2. Invasion

Major sources were the War Department's *Omaha Beachhead*; and 29th Infantry Division headquarters, *Group Critique Notes* (post-combat interviews conducted by Lt. Col. S. L. A. Marshall and assistants). The description of the 29ers' uniform was derived from a pencil sketch by Lt. Jack Shea, included in his D-Day recollections, held in the National Archives, Suitland Branch, 29th Division file.

Chapter 2.
Stateside: The Blue and the Gray Division
1. Mobilization

Hilton Raily's report for the *New York Times*, a copy of which is available at USAMHI, was a major reference. Kennett, *G.I.: The American Soldier in World War Two*, contained useful information concerning the US Army in the year before Pearl Harbor.

2. Heritage

Twenty-ninth Division unit histories were the major sources.

3. Wargames

The Raily Report was consulted frequently. "Gerow was not a man of the old school . . ." is quoted from J. Milnor Roberts oral history interview, USAMHI.

Chapter 3.
England: "Us and the Home Guard"
1. Transatlantic

Information on the *Queen*s is provided in Morison, *The Battle of the Atlantic, 1939–1943*.

2. Culture Shock

An excellent source describing Operation "Bolero" is Harrison, *Cross-Channel Attack*. "England's language cannot adequately portray England's weather . . ." is quoted from Weston, *History of the 459th AAA*, p. 27.

3. Gerhardt

"Full of the devil . . ." is quoted from Major Hansen's diary, USAMHI. There is an excellent chapter dealing with Gerhardt in Ewing, *29 Let's Go!*, pp. 276–89. Also, Gerhardt's unpublished memoirs, held at USAMHI, were consulted extensively. "A gutty, pushy, arrogant little bastard . . ." is quoted from Glover Johns letter, held in Gerhardt file in USAMHI.

4. Training

Details concerning the US Army Assault Training Center in Barnstaple were from Harrison, *Cross-Channel Attack*, pp. 162–64. The major source for Overlord planning was also Harrison, pp. 188–97.

5. Operation Overload

The movement to the marshalling areas and life in the "sausages" was partly derived from Baltimore *Sun* and *News-Post* columns.

Chapter 4.
The Enemy: Festung Europa
1. Grenadier Müller

Harrison's *Cross-Channel Attack* provides an excellent description of the German Army in France from 1940–1944, pp. 128–57 and 231–67. Col. Gerhard Elser of the West German army provided information concerning the training of the 352nd Division and a biographical sketch of General Kraiss. Martin van Creveld's *Fighting Power: German and US Army Performance, 1939–1945* was consulted for its excellent description of German military doctrine. "The hard-pressed Eastern Front . . ." is quoted from Harrison, p. 141.

2. Rommel

Harrison's *Cross-Channel Attack* and Wilmot's *The Struggle for Europe* were the major sources for the discussion of the German high command's coastal defense debate. *The Rommel Papers*, edited by B. H. Liddell-Hart, was the source for many of Rommel's quotes. Admiral Ruge's post-war report also provided background on Rommel's theories. A map in the German-language edition of the Ziegelmann manuscript for June 6 showed the D-Day deployment of the 352nd Division in detail. The War Department's *Omaha Beachhead*, and Morison's *The Invasion of France and Germany* both describe the German beach obstacles.

Chapter 5.
Men and Guns: The Emptiness of the Battlefield
1. Soldiers

US Army field manuals and tables of organization and equipment (TO&E) were the fundamental sources for information on American rifle squads. For the description of German squads, the War Department's *Handbook on German Military Forces* and Gerhard Elser's paper on the 352nd Division were consulted extensively.

2. Tactics

Martin van Creveld's *Fighting Power* quotes directly from the German *Truppenführung* manual, and his book was the source for this subchapter's quotations from that work. Gerhardt's "correct sight picture" SOP was obtained from Ewing's *29 Let's Go!*, p. 289. "The Germans were masters at making one man appear like a whole squad . . ." is quoted from Maj. Tom Howie's report on the 116th's June 16–18 attack (National Archives, Suitland Branch, 29th Division file).

3. Combat Organization

Martin van Creveld's *Fighting Power* and Col. Gerhard Elser's 352nd Division study provided background on the German staff system. "When you heard that first one . . ." is quoted from Johns, *Clay Pigeons of St. Lô*, p. 111. The description of 29th Division medical care was derived from Beacham's "40th Anniversary of D-Day, June 6, 1944: A Physician Remembers."

4. Combat Communications

Information on US Army signal equipment was obtained primarily from Thompson's *The Signal Corps: The Test* and *The Signal Corps: The Outcome*. "Men and many officers were very, very reluctant to turn their radios on . . ." is quoted from Francis Greenlief oral history interview, USAMHI.

Chapter 6.
D-Day: "We've Got to Be Infantrymen Now"
1. Invasion Plan

For background on the Omaha Beach landings, the best sources were the War Department's *Omaha Beachhead*, Harrison's *Cross-Channel Attack*, and Morison's *Invasion of France and Germany*. Cota's plan to land in darkness was described in Shea's account of Cota's D-Day activities. Corlett's observations on the Overlord plan were taken from his papers at USAMHI.

2. The Beach

The experiences of the 116th on the beach were derived primarily from 29th Division *Group Critique Notes*. "I shoot, I shoot, I shoot . . ." is quoted from *D-Day in Retrospect*, Group W Documentary, Westinghouse Broadcasting Company (radio broadcast, June 6, 1964).

3. Second Wave

Information on the 111th Field Artillery was derived from Bliven, "The Busy Day of Capt. Shuford." "We moved cautiously and hesitantly . . ." is quoted from Binkoski, *The 115th Infantry Regiment in World War Two*, p. 17. "I found this officer who was an infantry captain . . ." is quoted from J. Milnor Roberts oral history interview, USAMHI.

Chapter 7.
The Beachhead: "Boche Kaput"
1. Into the Bocage

Harrison's *Cross-Channel Attack*, p. 319, discusses the Allied failure to detect the movement of the 352nd Division from St. Lô to the coast prior to D-Day. The 352nd Division telephone journal for June 6 was an invaluable source for Kraiss's decision-making process on D-Day. Slingluff's quotations on the landing of the 175th were all taken from a transcript of his wartime recollections, made on November 30, 1945. "They were stepping over the bodies of guys . . ." is quoted from J. Milnor Roberts oral history interview, USAMHI. "The most dangerous battery in France . . ." is quoted from Morison, *The Invasion of France and Germany*, p. 121.

2. Breakout

The story of Sergeant Peregory was from Ewing, *29 Let's Go!* The story of the French children in Grandcamp was from Robert Garcia's unpublished three-page memoir, "A French Sing-Along." The major source for the 175th's advance on Isigny was Shea's memoirs.

Chapter 8.
On to St. Lô: "It Didn't Smell Right from the First"
1. Fallschirmjäger

Harrison's *Cross-Channel Attack*, pp. 364–66 describes Bradley's fears of a German counterattack west of the Vire. The 3rd FJ Division was described in Schimpf's post-war report, held at the National Archives. "You'll see, bud, you'll see . . ." is quoted from Johns, *Clay Pigeons of St. Lô*, pp. 80–82. "The fighting power of the 3rd FJ Division was equal to two standard German divisions . . ." is quoted from Max Pemsel's commentary on the Schimpf report.

2. Ambush

The Company K attack on Auville was described by John T. King III in an unpublished January 1975 paper entitled "The Vire Crossing." "The man nearly gave me heart failure . . ." is quoted from Johns, *Clay Pigeons*, p. 60. "Those two stars looked so big . . ." is quoted from Ewing's *29 Let's Go!*, p. 72. "We began to suspect every male Frenchman of being a collaborator . . ." is quoted from Cooper, *The History of the 110th Field Artillery*, p. 103. "I quite vividly remember that our company was strung out . . ." is quoted from an unpublished three-page memoir by Bob Garcia entitled, "The Five Paragraph Field Order."

3. Reconnaissance in Force

Shea gives a superb account of the 175th's actions west of the Vire. Slingluff's memoirs provided an excellent account of Company G's fight at La Raye. "I learned I'm a helluva patrol leader . . ." is quoted from a letter from Gen. B. B. Talley, the officer with whom Cota spoke.

Chapter 9.
Stagnation: "Altogether It Was Hell"

1. Hill 108

General Bradley's post-D-Day strategy is described in Harrison, *Cross-Channel Attack*, pp. 376–77. "Get around the sniper and machine gunner and wipe him out . . ." is quoted from Harrison, pp. 381–82. "Give a G-3 a pencil and a map . . ." is quoted from Johns, *Clay Pigeons*, p. 172.

2. Fighting for Survival

The source for many quotations in this subchapter was Stouffer, *The American Soldier*, vol. 2, pp. 90–273. "Our motto from then on was no prisoners . . ." is quoted from Binkoski, *The 115th Infantry Regiment in World War Two*, p. 45. "They were all so mad, they wanted to go after the sniper . . ." is quoted from Johns, *Clay Pigeons*, pp. 27–8. "Our rifle company moved up and relieved one of the companies of the 29th . . ." is quoted from Greenlief oral history interview, USAMHI. "The skid row of the battle zone . . ." is quoted from Cawthon, "July 1944: St. Lô," *American Heritage.* "Altogether it was hell . . ." is quoted from *Fallschirmjäger* Helmut Kasiacka letter, *V Corps Operations in the ETO*. The major sources for the American and German replacement systems were Weigley's *Eisenhower's Lieutenants*, van Creveld's *Fighting Power*, and Elser's 352nd Division study.

3. Hedgerow Tactics

The Eisenhower and Bradley visit to the 29th Division on July 2 is described in Major Hansen's diary, USAMHI.

Chapter 10.
Triumph: The Major of St. Lô

1. Counterattack

The major sources for the Battle of St. Lô were the War Department's *St. Lô*, Ewing's *29 Let's Go!*, and Blumenson's *Breakout and Pursuit*.

2. Martinville Ridge

"He said something about the urgency of the situation . . ." is quoted from

Johns, *Clay Pigeons*, p. 134. "It seemed that noise alone would destroy everything . . ." is quoted from Cawthon, "July 1944: St. Lô," *American Heritage*. (Cawthon's two other quotations in this subchapter were also from this article.) Major Stephani's tearful reaction to his losses on Martinville Ridge was described in Frühbeisser, *Opfergang deutscher Fallschirmjäger*, p. 108. "A feeling of apathy began to descend . . ." is quoted from Johns, *Clay Pigeons*, pp. 137–38.

3. St. Lô at Last

Colonel Dwyer's account of Howie's attack was obtained from 29th Division files in the National Archives, Suitland Branch. The story of General Cota's encounter with Colonel Ordway at 115th headquarters was from an oral history interview with John P. Cooper. "Let's go to St. Lô! . . ." is quoted from Johns, *Clay Pigeons*, p. 189. Information on the geography of St. Lô was obtained from Patry, *St. Lô: La Capitale des Ruines*. Task Force C's entry into the city is described in Edward G. Jones's account of his experiences with the 29th Recon Troop. "It became increasingly difficult to dispose of the juice . . ." is quoted from Cooper, *110th Field Artillery*, p. 132.

4. The Dead

The dedication of the 29th Division Cemetery at La Cambe on July 23, 1944, is described in *29 Let's Go!*, the Division newspaper.

BIBLIOGRAPHY

1. 29th Division Official Records

29th Division. *After-Action-Reports* (all units), June–July 1944.

_____. *G-3 Periodic Reports*, June–July 1944.

_____. *"War Room" Telephone-Radio Journal*, June–July 1944.

_____. *Group Critique Notes*, June 6, 1944.

Headquarters, 29th Division. *Battle Experiences of the Infantry Regiments.*

_____. *Battle Lessons and Conclusions.*

_____. *Infantry-Tank Destroyer Training.*

_____. *29 Let's Go!* (Historical Booklet).

_____. *Standing Operating Procedures for Tank-Infantry Operations.*

_____. *After Combat Battle Notes for the Month of July 1944.*

_____. *Attacks Against Villages.*

Advance Headquarters, 29th Division. *Journal, H-Hour on D-Day to 2000 Hours on D-Plus-One.*

Headquarters, 115th Infantry. *Unit History*, June–December 1944.

_____. *Record of Events, 6 June 1944.*

Headquarters, 116th Infantry. *Unit History*, June–December 1944.

_____. *Memorandum*, May 29, 1944.

Headquarters, 175th Infantry. *Unit History*, June–December 1944.

V Corps Headquarters. *V Corps Operations in the ETO*, January 6, 1942–May 9, 1945.

Twenty-Nine Let's Go. (29th Division Newspaper), June 3–July 20, 1944.

Le Tomahawk. (XIX Corps Newspaper), June–July 1944.

2. US Army Official Records

General Headquarters, US Army, *Morale of the US Army* ("The Raily Report" for the *New York Times*), October 14, 1941.

US Army. European Theater of Operations. *Army Talks*, May 31, 1944.

US Army. 12th Army Group. *Battle Experiences*, July 12–July 31, 1944.

Field Manual (FM) 23-5, *US Rifle, Caliber .30, M1.*

FM 23-15, *Browning Automatic Rifle, Caliber .30, M1918A2 with Bipod.*

FM 23-45, *Browning Machine Gun, Caliber .30, Heavy Barrel, M1919.*

FM 23-55, *Browning Machine Gun, Caliber .30, M1917.*

FM 7-10, *Rifle Company, Rifle Regiment.*

FM 7-20, *Rifle Battalion.*

FM 101-10, *Staff Officer's Field Manual.*

FM 6-100, *Tactics and Techniques of Divisional Artillery and Higher Artillery Echelons.*

FM 6-40, *Field Artillery Gunnery.*

FM 6-135, *Field Artillery Forward Observation.*

Table of Organization and Equipment (TOE), 5-15, *Engineer Combat Battalion.*

TOE 6-25, *Field Artillery Battalion, 105mm.*

TOE 6-335, *Field Artillery Battalion, 155mm.*

TOE 7, *Infantry Division.*

TOE 7-11, *Infantry Regiment.*

TOE 7-12, *HQ and HQ Company, Infantry Regiment.*

TOE 7-15, *Infantry Battalion.*

TOE 7-16, *HQ and HQ Company, Infantry Battalion.*

TOE 7-17, *Infantry Rifle Company.*

TOE 7-18, *Infantry Heavy Weapons Company.*

TM-E 30-415, *Handbook on German Military Forces.*

Operation Overlord, *Landing Schedule, Omaha Beach*, June 6, 1944.

3. 29th Division Unit Histories

Binkoski, Joseph. *The 115th Infantry Regiment in World War Two.* Washington, D.C.: Infantry Journal Press, 1948.

Brewer, James H. Fitzgerald. *History of the 175th Infantry.* Baltimore: Maryland Historical Society, 1955.

Cooper, John P. *The History of the 110th Field Artillery.* Baltimore: Maryland Historical Society, 1953.

Ewing, Joseph. *Twenty-Nine Let's Go!* Washington: Infantry Journal Press, 1948.

Weston, W. S. *History of Battery B, 459th AAA Battalion.* Unpublished (USAMHI).

4. Reports by German officers (all at National Archives)

Extract from the Telephone Diary of the 352nd Division. MS B-388.

Ruge, Friedrich. *Rommel and the Defense of the Coast.* MS A-982.

Schimpf, Richard. *The Normandy Campaign.* MS B-020a.

————. *Operations of the 3rd FJ Division During the Invasion of France, June–August 1944.* MS B-541.

Ziegelmann, Fritz. *The 352nd Division.* MS B-432 through B-439, MS B-241, MS B-490.

5. Personal Papers and Oral History Transcripts (location in parentheses)

Clift, Maurice (US Army Military History Institute [USAMHI]); Corlett, Charles (USAMHI); Gerhardt, Charles H. (USAMHI); Greenlief, Francis (USAMHI); Hansen, Chester B. (USAMHI); Jones, Edward G., Jr. (author); King, John T. III (author); McIntosh, Joseph R. (USAMHI); Mildren, Frank T. (USAMHI); Miller, Robert M. (author); Pratt, Robert H. (USAMHI); Roberts, J. Milnor (USAMHI); Russell, Carlton (USAMHI); Shea, Jack (National Archives, Suitland, Maryland); and Slingluff, John K. (author).

6. Newspapers

Baltimore *Sun* (Lee McCardell, Holbrook Bradley columns); and Baltimore *News-Post* (Lou Azrael columns).

7. Secondary Sources

Allsup, John S. *Hedgerow Hell.* Bayeux: Editions Heimdal, 1985.

Beacham, Edmund G. "The Fortieth Anniversary of D-Day, June 6, 1944: A Physician Remembers," *Maryland State Medical Journal*, June 1984.

Bliven, Bruce, Jr. "The Busy Day of Captain Shuford," *True Magazine* (no date indicated).

Blumenson, Martin. *Breakout and Pursuit.* Washington: Office of the Chief of Military History, 1961.

Carell, Paul. *Invasion: They're Coming!* New York: Bantam Books, 1964.

Cawthon, Charles R. "July 1944: St. Lô," *American Heritage*, XXV, No. 4 (June 1974).

Cochrane, Robert B. "The Story of the 29th Division," *The Baltimore Sun*, April–May 1945 (series of five articles).

Dorsey, John. "The Man Who Trained the 29th for World War Two," *Sunday Sun Magazine*, October 17, 1965.

Ferraiolo, Guy. "The Organization of the US Army, Europe, 1944–45," *Strategy and Tactics*, No. 30 (January 1972).

Frank, Stanley. "First Stop—Omaha Beach," *Saturday Evening Post*, 1946.

Fruhbeisser, Rudi. *Opfergang deutscher fallschirmjäger*, West Germany: Eigenverlag, 1966.

Fussell, Paul. *The Boy Scout Handbook and Other Observations.* New York: Oxford University Press, 1982.

Greene, Col. Joseph I., ed. *The Infantry Journal Reader.* Garden City: Doubleday, Doran, and Company, 1943.

Hamilton, Nigel. *Master of the Battlefield, Monty's War Years, 1942–1944.* New York: McGraw Hill Book Company, 1983.

Harrison, Gordon A. *Cross-Channel Attack.* Washington: Office of the Chief of Military History, 1951.

Henderson, Wm. Darryl. *Cohesion: The Human Element in Combat.* Washington: National Defense University Press, 1985.

Huston, James. *Biography of a Battalion*. Washington: Infantry Journal Press, 1950.

Johns, Glover S., Jr. *The Clay Pigeons of St. Lô*. New York: Bantam, 1985.

Kennett, Lee. *G.I.: The American Soldier in World War Two*. New York: Scribner's, 1987.

Kirk, John, and Young, Robert, Jr. *Great Weapons of World War Two*. New York: Walker and Company, 1961.

Liddell-Hart, B. H., ed. *The Rommel Papers*. New York: Harcourt, Brace, and Company, 1953.

Marshall, S. L. A. *Men Against Fire*. New York: William Morrow and Company, 1947.

Morison, Samuel Eliot. *The Battle of the Atlantic, September 1939–May 1943*. Boston: Little, Brown and Company, 1961.

_____. *The Invasion of France and Germany, 1944–1945*. Boston: Little, Brown and Company, 1962.

Patry, Robert. *Saint-Lô: La Capitale des Ruines*. St. Lô: Leclerc, 1948.

Stouffer, Samuel A., ed. *The American Soldier*, vols. 1–4. Princeton: Princeton University Press, 1949.

Thompson, G. R. *The Signal Corps: The Test*. Washington: Office of the Chief of Military History, 1957.

Thompson, G. R., and Harris, Dixie R. *The Signal Corps: The Outcome*. Washington: Office of the Chief of Military History, 1966.

Thompson, Col. Paul. "D-Day on Omaha Beach," *Infantry Journal*, June 1945.

Van Creveld, Martin. *Fighting Power: German and US Army Performance, 1939–1945*. Westport, CT: Greenwood Press, 1982.

War Department. *Omaha Beachhead*. Washington: War Department Historical Division, 1945.

_____. *St. Lô*. Washington: War Department Historical Division, 1946.

_____. *US Army Order of Battle: European Theater of Operations*. Washington: War Department Historical Division, 1945.

War Records Division. *Maryland in World War Two*. Baltimore: Maryland Historical Society, 1950.

Weigley, Russell F. *Eisenhower's Lieutenants*. Bloomington: Indiana University Press, 1981.

Wilmot, Chester. *The Struggle for Europe*. London: Collins, 1952.

ACKNOWLEDGMENTS

This book could not have been written without the help of 29th Division veterans. Since 1984, hundreds of 29ers have kindly passed on their recollections of the war to me, either orally or in writing. To all these considerate men, including those who never gave me their names, I express heartfelt gratitude.

For good reason, I have dedicated the book to John Purley Cooper, Jr., the former commanding officer of the 110th Field Artillery Battalion, 29th Division, in World War II. General Cooper graciously invited me into his home on countless occasions to discuss the history of the 29th Division. I have never met a man with a better memory or a more enthusiastic personality than General Cooper. Unfortunately, just as the manuscript for this book was completed, General Cooper died.

Another man whose help proved indispensable was Col. Robert M. Miller, the former CO of Company F, 175th Infantry. The colonel welcomed me into his home whenever a perplexing question about the 29th Division arose during research. Most of the time, Colonel Miller had the answer to that question in his files, or in his memory. No man is more interested in keeping the spirit of the 29th Division alive than is Colonel Miller, and his dedication to the division was a constant inspiration.

Brig. Gen. Bernard Feingold (Ret.), the curator of the 5th Regiment Armory Museum, gave me full access to the plentiful 29th Division records held at the Armory under the supervision of the Maryland National Guard Military Historical Society. Writing this book would have been much more difficult had General Feingold not permitted me to borrow some of the rare, highly-detailed 1:25,000 maps carried by the 29th Division in Normandy. General Gerhardt's famous jeep, *Vixen Tor*, is on permanent display at the museum, along with many other 29th Division artifacts.

Lt. Col. Arthur Flinner (Ret.), the curator of the Maryland National Guard Museum at the Pikesville Military Reservation and former CO of Battery C, 110th Field

Artillery, kindly provided the same free access to that museum's records. Also thanks to Art Flinner, the adjoining NCO Club, where 29th Division veterans gathered to discuss old times, was always open to me.

John S. Allsup, formerly a platoon leader in Company A, 175th Infantry, was deeply interested in this project and freely contributed his recollections. Rifle platoon leaders didn't expect to last long in combat, and "Sam" Allsup's perspective was vital to this book. Col. Sidney Bingham (Ret.), the former CO of the 2nd Battalion, 116th Infantry, responded enthusiastically to my request for information on the Normandy campaign. His phone calls and letters and introduction to other Stonewallers were invaluable. Brig. Gen. Edward G. Jones, Jr. (Ret.), formerly CO of the 29th Recon Troop and one of the first Yanks to enter St. Lô in July 1944, was kind enough to send me a fascinating personal account of his experiences in Normandy. This memoir was one of the most revealing portrayals of front line combat encountered during the research for this book.

Robert Cuff, General Gerhardt's trusty driver, invited me to his home in Ashton, Maryland, on several occasions and discussed with candor the general's personality. It is impossible to understand the 29th Division without understanding Gerhardt; without Bob Cuff, I could never have understood Gerhardt. Joseph Ewing, a 29er and the author of the division history, *29 Let's Go!*—one of the best unit histories to come out of World War II—kindly shared his memories of 29th Division research from forty years ago. John Robertson, a rifleman in Company F, 116th, wrote several moving letters to me concerning his memories of the St. Lô attack, during which he was badly wounded. Col. Gerhard Elser of the West German army passed on all the information he could find in the West German archives on the 29th Division's enemies. His profound knowledge of German tactics in World War II was of inestimable help; without his aid, it would have been impossible to describe Normandy from the German point of view.

The following is a list of the 29ers who graciously contributed their recollections to this book. Their former outfits are provided in parentheses.

William Akers (Battery C, 111th Field Artillery)
John S. Allsup (Company A, 175th Infantry)
Edmund G. Beacham (175th Infantry)
Sidney V. Bingham (2nd Battalion, 116th Infantry)
George Boram (Cannon Company, 175th Infantry)
Millard Bowen (2nd Battalion, 175th Infantry)
Donald S. Boyle (175th Infantry)
Clarence Burke (Company A, 115th Infantry)
Charles Cawthon (2nd Battalion, 116th Infantry)
Walter Condon (Company C, 121st Engineer Battalion)
John P. Cooper, Jr. (110th Field Artillery)
Robert Cuff (29th Division Headquarters)
Carl Curry (2nd Battalion, 115th Infantry)
Walter Eckert (3rd Battalion, 115th Infantry)
Joseph Ewing (175th Infantry)
Bernard Feingold (175th Infantry)

Joseph Fischhaber (110th Field Artillery)
Arthur Flinner (Battery C, 110th Field Artillery)
Robert K. Garcia (Company E, 116th Infantry)
Harry A. Garner (Company B, 104th Medical Battalion)
Neil Harper (227th Field Artillery)
Richard Herklotz (110th Field Artillery)
Edward G. Jones, Jr. (29th Recon Troop)
John T. King III (Company K, 175th Infantry)
Samuel R. Krauss (116th Infantry)
Arnold B. Levin (Company B, 104th Medical Battalion)
Arnold Lindblad (Company B, 104th Medical Battalion)
Robert Logan (29th Recon Troop)
Charles A. Lusby (111th Field Artillery)
Reiman McIntosh (110th Field Artillery)
Donald Miller (Company F, 175th Infantry)
Robert M. Miller (Company F, 175th Infantry)
William Miller (3rd Battalion, 116th Infantry)
Robert Minor (Assistant G-2, Division Headquarters)
Bernard Nider (Company E, 116th Infantry)
William Ogletree (Division Artillery Staff)
John Reilly (Company D, 175th Infantry)
George Richardson (Company K, 116th Infantry)
Abe Sherman (175th Infantry)
Phil Sherman (104th Medical Battalion)
Melvin Sherr (104th Medical Battalion)
John K. Slingluff (Company G, 175th Infantry)
Robert Slingluff (110th Field Artillery)
Walter Smith (Company E, 116th Infantry)
Roy Stevens (Company A, 116th Infantry)
Benjamin B. Talley (V Corps)
Milton Villareal (Company G, 175th Infantry)
Robert Wallis (Gen. Gerhardt's Aide)
Lewis Weilgus (Company F, 175th Infantry)

I would also like to thank Dr. Richard J. Sommers and David A. Keough of the US Army Military History Institute at Carlisle Barracks, Pennsylvania; John W. Listman of the Historical Society of the Militia and National Guard; Robert Rowe; Harold P. Leinbaugh; James Enos; Maj. Leonid Kondratiuk; Dr. Steven Davis; Carl Gruber; Nick Karp; Bruce Shelley; Arnold Blumberg; Peggy Senko; Toni Albert; and James T. Currie.

I must also express my gratitude to my fellow members of the Board of Directors, Maryland National Guard Military Historical Society, for their advice and support during this project. In particular, my sincere thanks goes to Dr. (and Brig. Gen., Ret.) Edmund G. Beacham, president of the society.

Last but not least, I am most grateful to Elizabeth Mizell for the long hours she spent skillfully editing this manuscript prior to its submission. Her dedicated work, which improved the book significantly, will always be appreciated.

INDEX